Laurel's Kitchen

Laurel Robertson
Carol Flinders &
Bronwen Godfrey

LAUREL'S KITCHEN

KITCHEN

A Handbook for Vegetarian Cookery & Nutrition

Nilgiri Press, Berkeley, California

Nilgiri Press, Box 477, Petaluma, California 94952,
publishers of books on how to lead the spiritual
life in the home and in the community.

©1976 by Nilgiri Press. All rights reserved
Printed in the United States of America
ISBN 0–915132–07–9

First published October, 1976
Fifth printing May, 1978

Library of Congress Cataloging in Publication Data
will be found on the last page of this book.

Foreword

I have come to know the authors of this book well since Carol Flinders stopped by my office several years ago with some questions about vegetarian nutrition. I followed the progress of their manuscript with great interest, and read the nutritional information therein to ensure its accuracy. I can recommend it wholeheartedly to anyone interested in cutting back on meat or eliminating it altogether, or for that matter to anyone who wants to experiment with whole, fresh, natural foods.

I am not a vegetarian myself. Nor do I subscribe to the philosophy of vegetarianism. As a nutritionist and educator, though, I have long been concerned that anyone interested in following a meatless diet should have access to sound nutritional knowledge. This book fills that need.

It is clear today that a vegetarian diet can be nutritionally sound as long as it is carefully balanced. *Laurel's Kitchen* provides guidelines that make this not only possible, but relatively easy. As a handbook of recipes and information it is clear, sensible, interesting, and well organized, based firmly on research that is both up-to-date and authoritative. Although it will be of interest to health professionals, the book is written primarily for people with no training in nutrition or the health sciences—people who simply want a basic reference manual of vegetarian eating for home use.

There is nothing faddish about this approach to vegetarianism—no highly concentrated "superfoods," no emphasis on vitamin or mineral supplements. The authors' Four Food Groups plan and their recipes are based on whole, fresh foods that are not difficult for most people to find or afford. Drawing on many years of personal experience, they are able to write with real practicality about the *everyday* problems of nutrition: weight control, too much fat or salt or sugar, and the special needs of children, of pregnant and lactating mothers, and of the complete vegetarian or "vegan."

Evident on every page of *Laurel's Kitchen* is the deep concern out of which it has been written. For the authors, vegetarianism is part of a way of life that involves well defined spiritual values and goals. They see their way of eating as one way to help alleviate not only some major American health problems, but also the world's shortage of food.

Warmth, concern for spiritual values in daily living, emphasis on family unity and on the invaluable role a woman can play in creating community—all these are things I have not found together in any other book of this sort. I sincerely hope that *Laurel's Kitchen* will find the widest possible audience.

GEORGE M. BRIGGS

Department of Nutritional Sciences
University of California, Berkeley

Table of Contents

Nutrition for a Meatless Diet

Acknowledgments

Many, many people have helped us with this book. In particular, beyond all the women who contributed and tested recipes and the doctors and other friends in the health sciences who contributed research and practical advice, we'd like to give special thanks to some of the people who helped us most with the nutritional basis of our presentation. Dr. George M. Briggs, Professor of Nutrition at the University of California, Berkeley, a nationally respected authority on B vitamins and an outspoken campaigner on issues of nutrition and national health, often took time out from a remarkably crowded schedule to answer all kinds of questions and read and criticize our final draft. Dr. Doris H. Calloway, also Professor of Nutrition at Berkeley and one of the world's foremost experts on protein, answered the critical questions on protein balance in all-plant vegetarian diets. Dr. Calloway's position as an FAO consultant gives her an uniquely international perspective on nutrition, and her comments greatly enhanced our understanding of vegetarian nutrition in general. Dr. Paul Benko, Associate Professor of Biology at California State College, Sonoma, gave us invaluable advice and encouragement from the very beginning, including the creation of a Four Food Groups plan to meet the needs of a vegetarian diet. Dr. Malcolm C. Bourne, Professor of Food Science and Technology at Cornell University, helped us to develop the Soy Milk recipe from his boiling water–grind method, which will add nutrition and satisfaction to the diets of all those who cannot or choose not to use milk foods. And Dr. Henry B. Bruyn, Clinical Professor of Medicine and Pediatrics at the University of California Medical School, San Francisco, and an old friend to us all, read the completed manuscript and offered some vigorous suggestions—especially on iron deficiency and allergy—out of his many years of experience as a medical practitioner.

Preface: *Laurel's Kitchen*

The test of a good poet, they say, is how well he or she can operate within the constraints of a sonnet form. Just so for cooks. It's one thing—though nothing small—to turn out a flawless soufflé; it's quite another thing to come up with an endless variety of appealing, highly nutritious vegetarian meals using only basic, inexpensive, easily available foods. This is the art our book is meant to convey. Over Laurel's protests we've named it *Laurel's Kitchen* because Bron and I and countless others learned this art from her, in a kitchen where everyone seemed at home—a kitchen that never failed to draw in Unexpected Guests when the smell of bread fresh from Laurel's oven wafted out into the Berkeley streets.

But in a way it isn't just Laurel's Kitchen, either. We might have called it Roberta's and Sally's and Ani's and Mauri's kitchen as well, and more others' than our editor will let me name. For *Laurel's Kitchen* has been a shared endeavor. Twenty-five women or more, close friends with a similar spiritual commitment, have all left their mark on it, developing and tasting and adapting recipes to make this the book *we'd* like to have had when we and our families took our first hesitant steps into the world of vegetarian cookery almost ten years ago.

But *Laurel's Kitchen* isn't just another vegetarian cookbook, no matter how complete and how well tested; we've made it a handbook for vegetarian nutrition as well. That's Bron's contribution. As a registered nurse, she has encountered over and over again the suffering that goes with America's biggest health problems, and knows how many of them are tied to unwise eating. More clearly than any of the rest of us, she can see how easily our own way of eating can alleviate these problems if we can just show people its simplicity and appeal. Her enthusiasm deepened the passion that prompted Laurel and me from the start to make this a book that anyone, everyone, can use.

But diet is just part of the total picture. "The truth is," I remember Bron telling me flatly, "that most people just don't *feel* good much of the time. They aren't really sick, and they'll find all sorts of reasons for it, like pressure at work or their baby's teething, but the truth is they just can't say they feel *well . . .*"

Over the past several years, associating with all the friends who have tried along with us to change their patterns of living, we have come to see that good health is much, much more than just the absence of disease. It is a positive, vibrant state of being which pervades the mind and emotions as well as the body, and enables us to live long, fully active, highly productive lives. The most perfectly balanced diet imaginable, all organically grown foods, cannot bring this ideal within our grasp if we live at the mercy of anger or competitiveness or greed. The medical and scientific communities are at last producing evidence of something spiritual teachers have said all along: that a calm, unified mind may be the most important key to radiant health, not merely because it makes us immune to psychosomatic ailments but also because a measure of inner security, be it ever so slight, helps us to make wise decisions in our daily life. Only when we really have our center of gravity within can we withstand the temptations that besiege us: "Drink me; eat me; smoke me." At present, as a nation, we are quite without this centeredness, and it is small wonder that a host of diseases closely linked with unwise living patterns—arterial disease, hypertension, even cancer—are sweeping over us on a truly epidemic scale.

Listen on buses, eavesdrop in corridors, watch children on playgrounds and their teachers in the coffee room. "They just don't feel good." Moving about in a welter of wrong assumptions, pressured from all sides to make wrong choices, we live in ways that are clearly destructive to ourselves and others. There are those who will tell you this is just the human condition, but there's another way to look at it. Our discomfort, our less than perfect health, can be seen as a blessing if, like the red signs on the freeway, they can warn us in time: "Go back. You're going the wrong way."

For we can still change our direction. We can, if we choose, reverse the trend away from healthful living, if we just start with ourselves and patiently begin to undo the long years of conditioning to which we have been subjected. Then changes in one's way of eating can become, most delightfully, just the beginning of a transformation of one's entire life.

What fascinates me, as I emerge blinking from my year's immersion in Food and the Body, is how this book has led all of us who worked on it to see the outlines of a much larger picture than we had ever glimpsed when we began. We see good health now not as the gift of a fortunate few, blessed by heredity and lots of protein, but as the birthright of all creatures, a birthright within our reach to the extent that we can live in harmony with our environment and with other living things. It is our deepest hope that *Laurel's Kitchen* will open at least a little of this vision to you as well.

Berkeley, 1976   CAROL FLINDERS

This book is dedicated to a glossy black calf on his way to the slaughterhouse many years ago, whose eyes met those of someone who could understand their appeal and inspire us, and thousands of others like us, to give the gift of life.

Giving the Gift of Life

Laurel's Kitchen

The Diet Revolution was big news a while back, but now it seems to have invaded just about every sphere of American life. Everyone has a slightly different idea about what should be cast out in favor of what and why, but it's at least clear that nothing is sacred now in our pattern of eating. In just a few short years, the fat, lusciously illustrated cookbooks we got for wedding presents—usually the same books our mothers and grandmothers used—have become fat, lusciously illustrated white elephants. Not just for my own generation, either—vegetarianism might be spreading fastest among young people, but for one reason or another, nutritional, economic, spiritual, or ecological, our parents and even grandparents are also beginning to experiment with new patterns of eating.

The way people eat is closely connected with the way they live. The changes in our own food habits—my family's and many of our friends'—reflect the changes that have taken place gradually, yet dramatically, in our whole life style. I'd like to tell you about these changes, in the hope that our experience might be useful to you. In particular, I'd very much like to help dispel the illusion I had myself before all this started: that is, that "giving up meat" implies some kind of grim, irreparable loss. For twenty-five years each, my husband and I lived and ate as most people do, and in all that time, I don't think we ever enjoyed food as much as we do now. One reason is quite simple—the food is good. Most of us have no idea how satisfying fruits, vegetables, grains, beans, and dairy products can be, because these foods usually play supporting roles to nonvegetarian main dishes (and heaven help the zucchini who tries to upstage a pork roast!).

To the eye, to the palate, to the entire body, the food is good. But I don't think that's the whole story of the great pleasure we find now in our meals together. The real secret, which we hope our children will cherish always, and that you, our reader, will discover if you have not already, is the simple knowledge that every meal we eat spares a fellow creature, gives the gift of life.

Let me begin by giving you a glimpse of the real heroine of this piece, the Prime Mover and Guiding Spirit of vegetarian cooking as I know it. For that, we need to go back a ways.

Tim and I first came to Berkeley in 1967. Julia was two; Chris was yet to come. Being a mother absorbed and delighted me, but still there were loose ends, wisps of energy without focus, and I found myself seeking some kind of involvement. Increasingly oppressed by the war in Vietnam, which in Berkeley as nowhere else one was never able to forget, I decided to put a timid big toe into the maelstrom of Berkeley's antiwar movement. I found a group whose program appealed to me: self-education on the one hand and helping to organize a peaceful march in San Francisco on the other. Before long I was attending weekly meetings and had long lists of people to telephone.

One Saturday, a committee meeting was scheduled at an apartment just a block west of Telegraph Avenue, the home of someone I knew only as Laurel.

Mutual friends had spoken affectionately of Laurel, but I had never met her. I knew that she had been arrested in Sproul Hall during the Free Speech Movement, had had her teaching credential withheld as a result, and now worked part-time at a low-paying library job, part-time for the American Civil Liberties Union. She was in high demand for her calligraphy, which you would often see on flyers advertising a rally, a benefit, or a demonstration. Here, I knew, was a woman of principle. I prepared myself to be intimidated, and was alarmed when I got to her apartment to see that no one else was there yet. It was a basement flat—coming in by the front door was like entering a cave. A voice issuing from the back of the apartment guided me through two dark rooms that gave way at last to a sunny kitchen opening onto a tiny patch of patio. Potted plants crowded every sill, and the walls were bright with color—poster art was in its heyday then.

Laurel was just setting out four long, fat strips of dough to rise for French bread. A light dusting of flour was especially visible on her black cat, but it covered everything in the room. Framing the whole scene was the most luxuriant sweet potato plant I had ever come across. It shot up from one corner, curled up across the ceiling, meandered along the far wall, and darted out a window. Laurel herself was right out of Vermeer—a sturdy young woman in her early twenties with wide, clear blue eyes and a thick braid, her sleeves rolled up, a vast white apron over her long skirts. I suddenly felt spindly and insubstantial. I must have looked it, too, because she pressed a handful of oatmeal cookies on me and a mug of coffee.

"These are pretty stale," she said with a wry face, "and the coffee's been on since eight. I hope it doesn't bite back."

I dropped into a wicker chair and watched her work, wondering, as I munched, what I'd been eating all those times I had thought I was eating oatmeal cookies, and remembering how my grandmother, too, always used to apologize for her cooking. Laurel's movements were sure and deft. The warmth, the bright colors, the fragrance of the room enveloped me completely, and I kept silent so as not to break the spell. In ten minutes, though, some twenty-odd people were milling about, all talking at once. The meeting went on all afternoon, and when I left at five it showed every sign of continuing on into the night, fueled by Laurel's fresh bread and a big pot of lentil soup. From this meeting and a few more, equally pleasant but utterly inconclusive, I drifted off unsatisfied. As for

Laurel, I saw her again only in passing, once or twice, as we rushed along our separate ways down the aisles of the supermarket, behind full carts. When I was finally to meet her again five years later, it was like finding something very special I thought I had lost.

During the years that intervened, Chris was born, so my free moments were fewer and farther between, but with the help of a babysitting co-op, I continued to wander in and out of political activities, tutorial projects, and encounter groups. I took up potting and dropped it; I learned to play a recorder; I thought about going back to school when the children were older. I was terribly restless. I knew that beyond the desire to be a good wife and mother, admittedly no small thing, my life had no real goal. For a long time I thought the answer lay in finding the right activity—a job, a hobby, an art form. I even enrolled in a judo class for a few weeks. I longed for something that would draw out the resources, the obscure strengths that I could feel percolating away, locked inside me.

In retrospect, I would place a high value on those years of casting about, for in time, having explored most of the avenues the external world presents (dope smuggling and sky-diving I passed up), I was ready to conclude that whatever it was I was after, it might just be somewhere else. I'm sure it's no coincidence that about then a friend persuaded us to come hear a man from India talk about meditation. I can't remember a word now of what he said that night; and I had no idea why it affected me so deeply. For a few hours, though, my driving restlessness abated. I felt as if I were coming home, after a long time away. Tim shared my response completely, and we began to practice meditation every day under the guidance of our new teacher. From that first night, our lives began to change, slowly but irreversibly.

I remember reading a story once about a woman who was a terrible housekeeper. Someone gave her a beautiful lily which she brought home and put in a vase in her parlor. The lily, though, showed up the vase for being all tarnished and dusty. She took the vase and polished it, only to see that the table it sat on now looked terrible and had to be cleaned as well. At last she stood back and contemplated the gleaming table and the white lily in satisfaction—but then the parlor itself was dim and murky by comparison. Before she knew what had happened, she was scrubbing down the whole house, washing curtains, throwing open windows, letting air and light pour into every dark corner.

That's almost the way meditation seemed to work for us. Just half an hour each morning of intense, disciplined concentration, with real clarity of purpose, made it possible to see the rest of our day in a new light. We realized for the first time how carelessly we were spending our lives. I began to understand the appeal of that old Quaker phrase "living intentionally." With the help of meditation, we were able to slow down more and more; we saw now that we didn't have to let ourselves be pushed and jostled along with the Joneses. We could take our lives into our own hands, and begin to live them meaningfully. We began to take careful stock of everything we did to see if we were doing what we really wanted to—the kind of work we did, the parties we went to, the causes we supported, the books we read. One involvement after another fell away, replaced by something better, or not replaced at all except by a little more time, a little more peace of mind.

But this is a cookbook, after all, so let me tell you what began happening to our diet. I had learned to cook the way most girls do these days: a home economics class in junior high and as much experimenting at home as your mother will tolerate. My specialties were Sloppy Joes and *profiteroles au chocolat*. I built up my repertoire somewhat when we got married, but the Standard American Diet (S.A.D. indeed) isn't all that challenging, after all, given the range of convenience food that's available. I took more and more advantage of such foods when Julia and Chris were tiny, and out of sheer habit, I continued to rely on them as the children grew older. Our diet was probably typical among people we knew. Since no one had an obvious case of rickets or beriberi, we assumed we were all pretty well nourished.

Even before we started to meditate, though, I had begun to question the way we were eating. The cost of food was providing stronger impetus each day for a radical reassessment. From 1970 on, we watched benumbed as food prices lifted off, pointed upward, and soared out of sight. We simply couldn't afford to go on eating the way we had. I couldn't buy a roast now without realizing that it jeopardized Julia's new bathrobe. Every food dollar we spent had to count. Empty calories and so-called fun-food were now beyond our budget.

Something of a subtler nature was going on as well—a growing suspicion that something was terribly wrong with our whole culture's attitude toward food. Leaf through a woman's magazine, or a standard cookbook, and notice the way they speak about food. A whole language has been worked up to convince us that a well-prepared blintz is just this side of Nirvana. In Fannie Farmer's day, you went out to the kitchen and baked a chocolate cake. Big deal. Now you're invited to "Have the Chocolate Experience." I've always liked good food—I mean, *really* liked it. But now, for the first time, helped by that little edge of detachment which meditation was providing, I just couldn't share the gravity with which friends would discuss their quest for the perfect crepe, and I found myself getting embarrassed at the prolonged intensity with which we'd all study our menus in a restaurant. I was feeling more and more like the little boy in "The Emperor's New Clothes," as it became daily more apparent that the original, all-important function of food—to nourish the body—was fast slipping into oblivion. Vegetarianism was still a ways off, but at last I was ready to become "intentional" about our diet.

We began by cutting back on the deep-fried foods and super-rich desserts. That wasn't so hard. Honey and brown sugar replaced the wicked white granules, and we started using more fresh vegetables. Still easy. From that point on, though, the going got a bit rough. I had a vague idea that we should be eating healthier food, but what that meant, I wasn't sure. I bought a natural foods cookbook, a very stern and uncompromising one that had me putting brewer's yeast into everything we ate until an unnamed party confiscated the jar. (It turned up next spring, when we spaded up the backyard to put in a garden.) Otherwise, now that I think about it, the children were awfully patient.

("Mom?"

"Uh-huh?"

"What's this stuff?"

"Broccoli-soybean loaf. Do you like it?"

"Yeah—it's okay." A long silence. "If I eat it, can I have some Spaghetti-o's?")

I began to browse about in health food stores to see if there was something I didn't know about. (Isn't it typical of our upside-down culture that we have special stores for food that's meant to nourish? Maybe someday you won't be able to buy white sugar or "balloon bread" anywhere but dark, seedy little stores in rundown parts of town.) As I bumbled about, feeling my way hesitantly into the world of health food, it began to dawn on me that a good number of people who eat for health are also vegetarians. I hadn't counted on that, and in all honesty I can't say it made me very happy. I felt strangely threatened. It's amazing how much of our security we tie to relatively superficial things like food habits.

Tim, on the other hand, was already flirting with vegetarianism. The possibility of a meatless diet had first occurred to him years before, in college, when his track coach had discovered that a vegetarian diet actually improved his boys' running time. Much more influential, though, was the fact that our spiritual teacher is a vegetarian. We knew that many Hindus are vegetarians and that in the mainstream of India's spiritual tradition, meat-eating is considered an obstacle to spiritual development. Our teacher spoke seldom about vegetarianism, though, and he never insisted that we make the change. We were grateful for this, as we wanted to be completely objective and scientific in our choice of food. After all, we reasoned, just because a vegetarian diet was best for a Hindu meditator, why should it be for us? We began to experiment with meatless days, though, and we managed, with some difficulty, to get hold of several articles about the physiological benefits of not eating meat. Few doctors at that time seemed to be aware, or even interested, but it became increasingly clear to us that outside of supplying protein, we do the body no great service by giving it meat: particularly today, when most animals raised for food are injected—and fed—with all kinds of toxic substances. Even setting aside *these* chemicals, one article pointed out that just at the moment of death, the animal's body is flooded with adrenalin. That immediately struck a chord with me, for I had read of a Hindu belief that when you eat an animal, you assimilate all the terror and agitation he feels at his death. Science and spiritual insight were converging.

I had always heard, though, that you could not get a complete protein except with meat, and I was not about to short-change my growing children. Here our friend Stuart, a biophysicist buddy of Tim's, helped by providing tables of amino acids and other information that relaxed all my fears. Eggs, it turned out, actually had more to offer by way of complete protein than beef—in fact, it appears now that the amino acid pattern of soybeans is even better than that of eggs for meeting human needs. Even more surprisingly, we learned that by combining grains, legumes (beans and peas), seeds, and milk products in specified ratios, you can have a complete protein of as high quality as meat, eggs, or milk.

"Protein complementarity" is the subject of the fascinating book *Diet for a Small Planet* by Frances Moore Lappé, published in 1971, which describes the ecological implications of relying on meat as our chief source of protein. The picture is staggering. Presently, in the U.S., we feed most of our grains and legumes to livestock, to produce meat. To produce one pound of meat protein, a cow is fed at least sixteen pounds of nonmeat protein from sources like corn and beans, most of which could be eaten (and enjoyed) just as well by human beings. The amount of protein wasted in this manner each year—this is for meat consumed entirely within the United States—is equal to *ninety percent* of the world's yearly protein deficit. In personal terms, that meant that if significant numbers of people like us would change their eating habits, adequate protein could conceivably be put within the reach of everyone in the world, for a fraction of the cost of meat. What a privilege to be able to give such a gift!

My resistance was slipping away fast. I began to remember

the wonderful weeks I'd spent as a child on my grandparents' farm—the satisfaction of feeding the animals and helping to look after them, the wrenching pain I'd felt the night the family ate my favorite rabbit (they didn't *know* he was my favorite, and they were sorry, but I really shouldn't make such a fuss about it). I began to think now about how good it would be if our little ones could be spared the "doublethink" of loving animals, with all the tenderness children do, and eating them at the same time—being told they *needed* to eat meat. The more I thought about it, the more attractive vegetarianism grew.

But habits of a lifetime change slowly. It took several factors to help us make the transition. Food prices were a strong incentive, of course. For the cost of four lamb chops (about a dollar then), yielding a hundred grams of protein, I could buy six pounds of soybeans for a total yield of more than nine hundred grams of protein. That was pretty sobering. But after all, I couldn't feed my family soybean soup every night—in fact, the one night I tried, we ended up phoning out for a pizza. I was still unconvinced that vegetarian food could be varied and interesting; when "vegetables" has never meant much more to you than frozen peas, you can be forgiven a vein of scepticism. So, vacillating between an old diet that was leaving us colder by the minute and a new one that was still unknown territory, there we sat, waiting for something—or someone—to tip the scales.

It was toward the end of this period that Laurel slipped quietly back into my life. Time, reflection, and wonderful coincidence had brought her and her husband to the same teacher we had found. I spotted her sitting near the back of the room one night, with a tall, skinny fellow whose wild mop of hair and preoccupied expression reminded me of pictures I'd seen of the young Einstein. I kept peeking at her all evening. She obviously didn't remember me. She was completely absorbed in what our teacher was saying, and afterwards, she turned with almost the same loving attentiveness to her husband (the glint of gold on her left hand had confirmed my guess). She looked radiant—one of those women, I was sure,

who doesn't come completely into her own until she has someone to take care of. She still had the same thick braid of dark brown hair, but now it was on top of her head. The whole effect was a little quaint, a little "old country," as if she belonged more to the last century than to this.

Ordinarily, we'd have gone over and visited with them afterwards. For some reason, though, I put it off. I couldn't say why, but I felt a little shy. Weeks went by and they came regularly to class, but still I didn't approach them.

Meanwhile, our days as omnivores were numbered. The scales were finally tipped—and not by financial, or nutritional, or even ecological considerations. We were spending more and more time now with our teacher, in class and during informal visits, and we were coming to see that his relationships with animals were almost as varied and personal as his relationships with people. For him every living creature revealed divinity. He was incapable of harming another being, human or animal, or of taking pleasure at their expense. For a long time, he kept silent his deepest feelings on vegetarianism. At last, though, sensing perhaps that we were all becoming gradually more receptive, he began to reveal to us how he really felt.

I'll never forget the first night he spoke openly about eating meat. He began in a very light vein, telling us about George Bernard Shaw. When Shaw first decided to become a vegetarian in his mid-twenties, physicians crowded forth to warn him that an early grave would be the result. Sixty-five years later he was asked whether he had ever gone back to Harley Street to confront his medical friends. "I would," he replied with a twinkle, "but they all passed on years ago." When he died, Shaw used to say, he wanted his pallbearers to be cows, sheep, pigs, and "a small travelling aquarium of live fish, all wearing white scarves" in his honor.

Almost imperceptibly, our teacher's tone became more and more serious. "When we come into the human context," he said, "no more precious responsibility falls upon our shoulders than that of trusteeship for the earth and all its creatures. All animal life looks to us for protection. How can we bear to be its predators?" Pindrop silence fell upon the room. That evening, though neither of us said a word, we knew our experimentation was over. We were vegetarians for life.

But a vegetarian by commitment, however determined, is still a far cry from a competent vegetarian cook. I found myself the next morning, feeling distinctly miscast, in the Organic Foods Co-op. Tubs of beans, all colors and shapes, surrounded me, and barrels of noodles—buckwheat, whole wheat, soy, and spinach. Everything was beautiful: earthen-colored and completely free of cellophane wrappers, alluringly tactile. But no packaging meant no cooking instructions—and no visible means of getting the stuff out of the store. My stomach sank. Moving about me confidently on every side were lithe, tawny young men and women in faded blue denims, peasant blouses, and skirts made from old bedspreads, their thick manes braided, rubber-banded, or falling free. I was painfully conscious of my wash-and-wear shirt-waist dress.

Suddenly there was a familiar voice at my elbow. It was Laurel, her blue eyes like deep wells of concern. She looked no more Aquarian Age than I did, but that obviously didn't faze her—she was completely at home.

"Can I help you find something?"

"Yes, I think I'm in over my head. What are the ground rules here?"

"You've never been here before? Gee, next to the Cheese Board it's my favorite place. Did you see these?" Her eyes shining, she stuck her hand into a barrel of dark brown coffee beans and let them fall in a rich, fragrant cascade.

"Aesthetically, it's the living end," I agreed stiffly. "I should have brought my watercolors—but I was sort of hoping to take a few things home with me."

Laurel kindly ignored my churlish manner and helped me

find paper bags—they hid them, apparently, to encourage you to recycle your own—and a couple of scoops.

"Now," she beamed, "what do you want?"

"I haven't the vaguest idea. What do *you* think I want?"

She put down her scoop and looked at me with new respect.

"You really *do* need help, don't you?"

I nodded sadly, mutely. Immediately, without a single wasted word, Laurel took the situation briskly in hand. Talking away about soaking times and cooking times, spices and sauces, she bagged several kinds of beans, then weighed out a few wide, flat, two-foot-long lasagna noodles made from whole wheat and soy flour. "These are fantastic. I'll give you a recipe for them. But watch out they don't crumble! They're as brittle as two-foot potato chips."

From there we moved on to the organic vegetable displays, where I met my first kohlrabi (funny, you don't *look* like a kohlrabi). At the milk cooler, she explained the difference between kefir and yogurt and why the cultured milk they're made of was such a boon. Then we worked our way through the dried fruit section, ogling the calimyrna figs and dried pineapple—"Pricey," Laurel explained, "but even a little piece goes a long way with kids." We bought a couple of "date treats" to nibble on and then paid for our booty—in cash, as it turned out; I had half expected to barter.

By this time I had gained back enough composure to invite Laurel and her husband to stop by our house for tea after class that night (herb tea, I managed to specify, not wanting her to think we were completely out of it). I still found her alarmingly competent, but something else was starting to outweigh that: warmth, and a complete lack of pretentiousness. Her enthusiasm—almost puppy-like—was hard to resist. I couldn't be sure yet, but I had a strong surmise that the help I needed was on its way.

I guess we've all had the experience of meeting someone and knowing instantly that we have something to learn from them. That's how I felt on this second meeting with Laurel. I'm not just talking about kitchen know-how. I probably couldn't even spell out what I'm really talking about, but the impression grew stronger as the four of us visited that evening.

I was sure Laurel had already solved some of the problems I was having. Finally, right in the middle of a distressingly high-level discussion of meditation, I took the plunge.

"What do you know about soybeans?"

Tim snorted. Laurel looked startled but rose to the question with real poise.

"Well . . . . They're full of proteins and vitamins—the best of all the beans, I guess—and cheap, too. But just plain they don't have much flavor and they take forever to cook soft. I add them to things—in small amounts, but often. You can grind them up and sneak them into all sorts of foods—casseroles, hot cereals, sauces, soup. I've been working out some recipes for spreads, made from soybeans and other things."

"Do you make yogurt?"

"Sure."

"I've been trying all week now, and it keeps coming out all watery and stringy with a flavor like alum."

"What's your heat source?"

"A heating pad, set on gentle."

"Do you use powdered milk?"

"Yes."

"Non-instant?"

"Yes."

Her brow furrowed, then cleared. "May I smell it?"

"The yogurt? I threw it out."

"The powdered milk."

We went to the kitchen and got out the box of milk. She looked critically at its color, sniffed it, and scrunched up her nose.

"Old."

"But I bought it a week ago."

"Smell it yourself."

I couldn't smell anything but milk.

"That's just it," she said in triumph. "If it's fresh it has no smell, and if it isn't fresh, your yogurt won't set up. See, the instant powdered milk is used so much more that sometimes the non-instant kind stays on the store shelf for ages."

Remembering the film of dust on the box, I knew she was right. I could see, too, that she was warming to the role I had thrust upon her. Within an hour I learned more about vegetarian cooking than half a dozen cookbooks had told me. Laurel had been cooking since she was a little girl, at the knee of her Pennsylvania Dutch grandma, and she had developed strong intuitive powers when it came to food. She wasn't afraid to experiment, because she usually had a rough idea what the result would be. Enthusiastic, but not in that gushy women's-magazine way, she had a sense of artistry about homemaking; you could see it in the way she talked about texture and color, the way she moved her hands, which looked like (and were, I found out later) a potter's hands. At the same time, there was a drollery about her I hadn't noticed at first—a way of undercutting herself at just the right moment, or retreating abashed when she thought she'd made too sweeping a pronouncement.

It was getting close to midnight. I realized there was far more here than I could absorb in one evening, so without further ado, I declared myself her loyal apprentice and broke out a bag of Hydrox cookies to celebrate. She took one politely, but murmured, "These will have to go, you know." I swallowed hard. No victory without sacrifice.

In the weeks that followed, I spent every free moment in Laurel's kitchen. She lived now in a classic Berkeley brown shingle house, with the requisite Tiffany glass windowpane over the front door, an avocado tree in the yard, and a pocket-handkerchief garden at the side with trellised beans, tomato bushes, and lettuce standing up in three crisp rows.

Her kitchen had evolved considerably over the years. It was as fragrant as ever, but more earthy now, and more mysterious. Several swatches of fresh herbs hung to dry on the wall and a string of pearly garlic in one corner. Glass jars let you gaze unobstructedly at contents that, for all their beauty, still didn't suggest anything edible to my uneducated eye. In time, though, I was initiated into their mysteries. I learned to make superb sandwich spreads from dried peas and beans. We experimented with all kinds of grainy casseroles and, of course, sprouted everything in sight.

Gradually, the four of us saw more and more of one another. Laurel and I were drawn together by the formidable task of turning me into a good vegetarian cook, Tim and Ed by shared obsessions with carpentry and Volvo repair. The real basis of our deepening friendship, though, was our shared commitment to meditation and the spiritual values our teacher was helping us build our lives upon.

One of the pleasantest of the disciplines we were trying to practice was walking—brisk walking, every day, for a full hour. When you begin to turn inward, concentrating intensely for even a limited period each day, it's terribly important to get the physical exercise that *any* body needs, and that our normal life style these days all but forbids. Without this exercise, it's easy to get a little indrawn, jumpy, or irritable. Laurel and I met often to walk early in the day, as soon as our families had been dispatched, while the air was still fresh. Sometimes we visited, but often we just swung along in silence.

One morning—it must have been March, because the Japanese plum trees were in full, tufty pink bloom—we had been walking along without talking for half an hour when Laurel said: "I think you're ready for bread."

I knew what was coming, and I hedged desperately. "Gee, I don't know, Laurel. We had breakfast just an hour ago."

"Silly bean. To *bake* bread."

I hemmed and hawed for several blocks. It wasn't just that I was timid, and she knew it. I was reasonably certain that if I learned to bake bread at all, even if I wasn't very good at it, she would insist that I take over the baking for my family. Up until now we'd had what I thought was an ideal arrangement: she baked our bread, and I made sprouts and soy spread for both our families. In fact, she provided bread for several other people besides us. Every Wednesday night at class a discreet brown paper bag would appear under your chair, so fragrant that if you bumped it with your foot, nostrils would flare for yards around. The tall, round loaves, baked in coffee cans and bulbing on top like a baker's cap, studded with raisins and nuts one week and the next week flecked with aromatic green herbs, had us all hooked. If I gave in now, I knew, we were on our own—or, rather, we were on *my* own.

But Laurel was in what Ed calls one of her "First Amendment moods," when nothing short of a billyclub will move her. Until I tackled breadmaking, she insisted, I was just playing at becoming a good cook: the only way I could find out how easy it was was to try it. Before I knew what was happening I found myself back in her kitchen, being tied up in one of her voluminous aprons. In seconds flat, she had kerchiefed our heads and tossed yeast, salt, honey, and warm water into a huge crockery bowl (she never baked fewer than a dozen loaves at a time). She scrubbed her hands and arms like a surgeon, dumped in a gallon or so of whole wheat flour, and started stirring mightily —at first with a spoon, then suddenly in up to her elbows and inviting me to join her.

"We'll talk about the proportions later; let's concentrate on technique today. This part is where you get the gluten going. Stir it hard—especially if you're going to add heavy flours like rye or buckwheat or cornmeal."

By this time I too was paddling about in the stuff, breaking up lumps with my fingers.

"When it gets stringy like this the gluten is awake, and you can add whatever else you like."

She pulled down a couple of gallon jars, shook them over the bowl, and plunged in again with both arms. Soon the batter was dough. It seemed to come alive in her hands. In fact, I found out later, it *was* a sort of living entity for her: Laurel thinks of herself as merely an accessory to the whole process, whose part it is to call to life the one-celled microorganisms who do all the work. She nurses a warm affection for the tiny creatures—the "yeast beasties," as she calls them—and never feels completely right about the use we put them to. I know the conflict still rankles, because just the other morning as I was about to add a small pan of leftover oatmeal to the dough we

were mixing (it keeps the bread moist and does nice things to the texture), I saw her brow contract sharply.

"Come on, Laurel, out with it. I won't be hurt."

"It's just, well, the oatmeal looks pretty hot still. I mean, for the yeasties. Do you think you could cool it off first?"

A protest was on my lips—after all, we were going to *bake* the blessed yeasties in another hour, at three hundred and seventy-five degrees—until I saw the look of mute suffering on her face, and without another word, I spread the oatmeal onto a cookie sheet to cool.

That first morning she startled me by giving the dough a hearty slap at the end of its kneading. "It should feel just about like a baby's bottom," she said with satisfaction.

My worst fears were realized. When the bread came out of the oven, she handed me one brown loaf and said, gently but firmly, "This is it. I know you don't think so, but you can do it without me."

It was only fair, I told myself. Some terribly emaciated young fellows had started coming to meditation class recently —over-zealous ascetics who were in far greater need of Laurel's bounty than my own sleek crew was. And this was what I had wanted, after all, wasn't it?

Trying hard not to feel the way I had when I first left Mother and Spokane, I threw myself heart and soul into breadmaking in the days that followed. Baking just two to four loaves seemed a light task after helping to turn out twelve at one blow. My mood picked up even faster when I discovered what a wide margin for error there actually was in the process. I began to understand Laurel's fondness for the redoubtable yeasties. They could take a lot of knocking around, and they seemed willing to extend themselves generously in deference to my ineptitude. Of course, almost anything you bake at home, with yeast, is so much better than the stuff people are used to eating, heartier and more fragrant, that all my experiments, technical failures or not, were devoured by sundown. Laurel's tender, raisin-spiked loaves loomed large, I knew, in the family's memory, but they were kind enough not to make comparisons.

I had an obscure feeling that I shouldn't go back to Laurel, in the true apprenticeship tradition, until I could demonstrate that I had not only absorbed her teaching but had added something of my own as well. My contribution, I decided, would be protein complementarity. Once I had the basic whole wheat loaf under control, I started adding other ingredients, aiming at a bread that was scrumptious but as high as it could be on the protein chart as well. Our friend Stuart, the biophysicist, came to my rescue on the mathematical side of things, and with his help I worked out several alternative formulas to test.

The day came at last when I marched to her back door with a warm, beautifully textured loaf in hand.

"Try this." I broke off a chunk in a somewhat theatrical manner, and she took it obediently. "Notice anything different?"

She munched thoughtfully.

"Well, it's very tasty." She narrowed her eyes in concentration. "Three parts whole wheat flour, maybe one of wheat germ, half that much of soy flour, milk, rice bran, and a trace of buckwheat." She took another nibble. "Gluten flour."

"Okay, Wonder Woman, do you know what that *means?*"

"Well, it's probably pretty nutritious."

"That bread has an NPU that would bring tears to the eyes of Frankie Lappé. Not an amino acid spared."

"Gee, it's good, too. Sort of nutty. Where did you get the recipe?"

It was my moment of glory. Our relationship had entered a new phase.

As Laurel came gradually into clearer focus, I found it hard to understand how I could have felt overawed at first. True, as I had anticipated, she did have strongly held principles. She had specialized in American history at Cal, and the mere mention of Thomas Jefferson would bring on a warm flush and a ten-minute disquisition. But all sorts of contradictions kept emerging. She was an odd blend of radical and conservative. Her loyalties went deep—she had used the same shampoo since she was six, and she still drove miles to get her shoes repaired at the shop she'd lived next to as a freshman. On the other hand, the wonderful energies she was possessed of used to come along sometimes and possess *her*—pick her up and carry her along willy-nilly so that she would do something completely uncharacteristic, shattering whatever image of her you had managed to construct. Half the fun of knowing her was watching her ride herd on the conflicting sides of herself. Boisterous, corny, and slapstick in the morning, she'd turn sober and introspective in the afternoon, and for all her high principles and right answers, she could now and then nearly capsize under the great waves of insecurity you would normally expect in a teenager. Indifferent, by and large, to her looks, she wore clothing that combined Traditional Berkeley (baggy, dark, somewhat ethnic, and old as the hills) with Neo–Sears and Roebuck Catalog. Every now and then, though, for an evening in San Francisco, she would haul out a full-length wool coat the color of a summer sky at twilight, and when she put it on, hair, eyes, and complexion glowing, you saw instantly what it was those Flemish painters were all trying to capture.

Her love of the solid and traditional was nowhere more evident than in the food she cooked. Laurel is the only vegetarian cook I know whose food can manage to taste just like your mother's or grandmother's without ever straying beyond what is nutritious or vegetarian. She would never serve something just because it was nutritious; it had to *taste* good—and look good, too.

The concept of protein complementarity came Laurel's way at just the right moment, for after two years of relying heavily on eggs and milk for protein, she was becoming interested in a more varied cuisine. Within two days after I had sketched out the basic idea of balancing proteins, she was conversant as a chemist with the whole mysterious business. She could call every amino acid by name and tell you where he lived and in what concentration. Little by little my cooking lessons came to be workshops, where we experimented, cautiously at first, then with a bolder hand, with all the ways you could maximize the protein in a meatless diet. Here Laurel's sure, stubborn sense of the classic rescued us—and our families— time and again. A particular dish might balance out right on the dime, but if it didn't make it on the flavor scale, nothing doing.

We didn't stop with the tired old question, "Well, but where do you get your *prot*ein?" Other challenges were presenting themselves, like coming up with a low-calorie reducing diet for vegetarians. And what about children? What are their special nutritional needs, and can a vegetarian diet really meet them all? How can we prepare vegetables so that people will want to eat lots without drenching them in caloric sauces? How can we cut expenditures to a minimum and still serve appetizing and varied meals? All these were questions of great practical importance for us. I doubt, though, that we'd have gotten quite so embroiled in answering them if we had been thinking strictly of our own needs.

For we were aware by now that we weren't the only people curious about vegetarianism, nutrition, and good eating. By this time we were spending more and more time with other meditators, people attending the same classes we were. Supporting one another, sharing our new sense of purpose and direction, we were becoming much more than just friends. Any excuse would do for an impromptu get-together: a jam session in someone's basement, a volleyball game at the beach, a work party to remodel a new meeting place for our meditation center. Whatever the occasion, food was part of the picture, and it wasn't long before we noticed that almost everyone was going through the same reorientation towards food that we were. The range of diets was remarkable—so remarkable that Laurel and I, full of our new zeal for protein balancing, began to get concerned. Finally, at a picnic, we snooped and peered shamelessly at every lunch we could get close to, asked a number of indiscreet questions, and then put our heads together afterwards.

Some people were eating just what they'd been eating all along, minus the meat: the same old white bread and sugar, processed cheese, canned vegetables, and potato chips. Steve and Debbie had dropped eggs and milk products as well as meat, but were pretty vague about where their protein was coming from now. One woman, on the other hand, was eating eggs and cheese three times daily for fear she would keel over from protein deficiency.

Sumner was convinced that vegetarianism meant you ate vegetables. Period. Raw. He proved a stubborn case. To this day, if no one is watching, he'll dine on a head of raw broccoli and a few fresh parsnips, preferably with bits of earth still clinging to the root-hairs.

One very earnest and alarmingly ethereal girl had read of a mountain yogi who subsisted on fruit that was dropped—not picked, heaven forbid—from the trees. Such food alone, she reasoned, is God's gift; all other food involves "taking." The argument was beautiful in its simplicity, but a few weeks on the regime had left her so frail she was in no danger of "taking" anything much heavier than a kiwi fruit.

Our teacher was even more distressed at our findings than we were. We decided to work on two fronts. He would start spelling out more explicitly something he'd thought we'd all realized—the absolute necessity, for the practice of meditation, of maintaining strong, healthy bodies. Laurel and I, meanwhile, would learn everything we could about intelligent vegetarian eating and share what we found with the rest of our group.

One discovery that emerged clearly from our research was

that people were making woefully inadequate use of grains and beans. Not realizing how much usable protein they could get from these sources, especially in combinations, they thought of grains as heavy or starchy—the women in particular. With charts and sample menus, we were able to show our skeptical friends that they could enjoy a very satisfying diet (including items with real body like beans and whole-grain bread) which would be no higher in calories than their present one.

Here, of course, a familiar problem arose. Most people didn't have the foggiest idea how to prepare whole grains or legumes, and much as I had, they thought of breadmaking as a highly esoteric art just this side of alchemy. At the risk of cutting into our own prestige a little, we invited people to come to our homes for demonstrations. Laurel's enthusiasm was so infectious that within a few weeks the characteristic round bread slices were showing up in the most unlikely places. The old "each one teach one" method had triumphed. People discovered all kinds of ways to fit a weekly baking into their schedules. Several of the busier women worked out a "bread pool" so that they baked only at two- or three-week intervals, while others worked out the same trade Laurel and I had, bread for soy spread and sprouts.

The practice of trading food blossomed soon into a trend. People began cooperating to minimize the time and money they were spending on food. Berkeley's famous (and successful) experiment in neighborhood cooperative buying, the "Food Conspiracy," had its origin just a block from our house, and we participated wholeheartedly. It was the first time since I was a little kid that I felt like I lived in a real neighborhood. Soon one of our number volunteered to make our own run every month to the wholesaler in San Francisco who stocked the local health food stores with dried fruits, nuts, grains, and flours. We had all become resigned to spending long Saturday mornings in supermarkets, shoving carts down glaring aisles where profiteering middlemen had placed thick (and costly) layers of cellophane between us and everything we were buying. Now we spent the same hours getting together in one another's backyards and kitchens, weighing, bagging, laughing, and visiting as we divided our spoils.

We began to exchange our *ideas* about food, too. Our group of meditators reflected something of the ethnic mix you'll find all over Berkeley—including dogs of several breeds, none of whom were eating meat now and none of whom seemed to be suffering except Frodo, whose owner was the raw-vegetable man. (We persuaded Sumner at great length that even if he wouldn't cook his own broccoli, he had better cook and blend poor Frodo's, and throw in some wheat germ and milk to boot.) Almost every national diet, we learned, had some specialty that was vegetarian, or could easily become vegetarian. Once we realized this, we rounded up a few king-sized cooking pots and a heady series of feasts ensued—Hanukkah, Greek Easter, South Indian Vishu, an American Thanksgiving, Chinese New Year, a Columbus Day spaghetti feed, a Cinco de Mayo tamale dinner. You name it, we celebrated it.

This first phase of our experimentation was wildly creative—and wildly elaborate. Casseroles fairly bristled with pine nuts, citron, chia seeds, and other exotica. After a few months, though, we began to settle down a little; our menus became simpler. I imagine meditation was bringing about the same slow transformation on our rather jaded palates as on our nervous systems. By dint of slowing down a bit and getting calmer, we were better able to appreciate the delicate pleasures of simply prepared, straightforward foods: garden vegetables, whole-grain breads, and fresh fruit. Besides, freehanded use of imported cheeses, dried fruits and nuts, or out-of-season produce can dent a food bill almost as badly as meat can. We still enjoyed our feast days—austerity has never been our style. But we had found that a varied, tasty cuisine need not depend on costly extras.

I've said very little about the children so far, and any parent probably wonders how ours reacted to the new regime. Our decision to go meatless and swing over to food that nourishes *was* something of a stopper to Julia and Chris. Of course, I vacillated for such a long time that the transition was actually quite gradual, but nonetheless, it was confusing to them to find that something we'd once eaten heartily was now looked on with distaste. Chris missed hot dogs, and Julia hankered after her old favorite, tuna fish sandwiches. We exerted very little pressure—just tried to share with them our growing sense of fellow-feeling with animals, birds, and fish. Children have this sense instinctively anyway, so it was mostly just a matter of brushing away some of the cobweb-rationalizations that had covered it over.

It *did* bother them at first to be "different" from their classmates. Now and then, in the early days, I used to find remnants of dubious sandwiches in their lunch pails, the result of playground trades. I chose not to harass them about it, though, and in time it stopped happening.

Then one Sunday afternoon, with no ulterior motive, we took the children for a walk on the Marina. It was a warm Berkeley day and both sides of the pier were lined with fishermen. Suddenly someone landed a fish right in front of us. It flopped down at our feet, gasping and writhing as it struggled to get free of the hook.

The children's eyes got very big. It was a crucial moment. At an earlier time we might have said, "Wow, what a catch! He's got himself a real dinner there!" They'd have half bought the idea, and if it were reinforced enough times, they'd have started saying it themselves, even though all the time, despite their attempts to dispel it, the image of that poor, struggling creature would have remained locked in their consciousness. Now, however, not knowing what to say, and not wanting to say the wrong thing, we said nothing—let them watch for a brief instant, then herded them gently away. It wasn't long after that before tuna sandwiches and then hot dogs faded into the past.

Now, though they bear no ill will toward their friends who eat meat, our children are quietly sure that they are right in their own decision, and their example has caused many of their playmates, even parents of playmates, to stop for a moment and question their own food habits. Their teachers have been intrigued and often helpful: Mrs. Davis, for instance, who made sure there was corn wrapped in foil for our two at the end-of-the-year barbecue. I wonder what other parents would think if they knew how many kids offered to trade their spare ribs (*whose* "spare" ribs? and what pig ever said he didn't need all of them?) for Julia's corn on the cob.

I've only touched lightly so far upon a whole other side to the developments that led to this book. Nutritional considerations aside, the last three years have changed radically some of my deeper, unconscious feelings about cooking, and about me as a cook—and (let's face it) about me as a *woman*.

It hadn't occurred to me that there could be much direct connection between kitchen work and meditation until one evening when our teacher was reading some verses from the Bhagavad Gita, in which Sri Krishna, an embodiment of the Lord, tells his disciple:

> *A leaf, a flower, a fruit, or even*
> *Water offered to Me in devotion,*
> *I will accept it as the loving gift*
> *Of a dedicated heart. Whatever*
> *You do, make it an offering to Me—*
> *The food you eat or worship you perform,*
> *The help you give, even your suffering.*
> *Thus will you be free from karma's bondage,*
> *From the results of action, good and bad.*
>
> *I am the same to all beings. My love*
> *Is the same always. Nevertheless, they*
> *Who meditate on Me with devotion,*
> *They dwell in Me, and I shine forth in them.*

He talked all evening about work, and how Gandhi had believed that work we do for a selfless goal, without thought of profit, is actually a form of prayer. Work done in this spirit unifies our fragmented energy and attention, calms the mind, and actually deepens our meditation. In Sanskrit, the path to God by way of such selfless work is called *karma yoga*. Even the smallest task can be thought of as an offering to the Lord, and when it is, it follows that it will be performed in the best possible way, with the greatest care and attention. Looked at in this light, every action becomes, potentially, an act of love— a work of art.

Our teacher closed the class with a passage from a Christian mystic, a very simple monk of the seventeenth century, Brother Lawrence:

> *The time of business does not with me differ from the*
> *time of prayer, and in the noise and clatter of my kitchen,*
> *while several persons are at the same time calling for dif-*
> *ferent things, I possess God in as great tranquility as if*
> *I were upon my knees at the blessed sacrament.*

I listened spellbound, and thought all the next day about what he had said. Then, haltingly, I began to try to put into practice what I thought I had heard him say.

It took only a few days for me to see what an enormous challenge he had placed before us. The practice of "one-pointedness" was the first big hurdle. To carry out work as something just this side of a sacrament, it's necessary to give your complete attention to whatever it is you're doing. As it turns out, this gets quite difficult at times. Say you're cutting up a cauliflower. "Idiot work," the mind sneers, and starts going great guns. Before you know it, somewhere between solving the Mideast crisis and designing the perfect day-care center, you've lacerated your thumb and have begun to think of the whole operation as a rude imposition on your time and energy.

When I asked our teacher about this problem, he knew what I was talking about instantly. His suggestion was the silent repetition of the mantram. I was skeptical at first, but I began to try it, just to see. After a while I realized how effective it was.

A mantram, very simply, is a name of the Lord, hallowed by the thousands of people who have repeated it. People have used some form of mantram in almost all the great religious traditions. "Jesus, Jesus" is a mantram; "Rama, Rama" is Gandhi's mantram. It seems paradoxical, but repeating the mantram has a way of keeping you planted firmly in the right here and right now, concentrated and calm. Not only that, but it helps you to remember all the while that you aren't just slapping together a meal; you're preparing food for the Lord in those you love.

Needless to say, becoming one-pointed didn't mesh with my Western idea of efficiency—stirring the soup with one hand, working the can opener with the other, while your mind is composing a grocery list or a limerick for your little boy. Getting myself to slow down and focus on one thing at a time went hard against the grain at first. One particular application I fought with special stubbornness. The local independent radio station used to broadcast an excellent news analysis every day at five-thirty, right in the midst of dinner preparations. (The same program would be rebroadcast the next morning, at a perfectly convenient hour; but that's *old* news, right?) For love or money, I couldn't bring myself to turn it off. After all, you can't let yourself get out of touch; and it wasn't as if it were TV—my *eyes* were still one-pointed. For months I went on working with half my mind, listening with the other.

It took a while for the evidence to mount up. Occasional injuries weren't such a big deal. Salting the soup twice or overcooking a carrot or two still wasn't serious. Missing steps in the recipe—who's to know, anyway? The real problem wasn't with the food. It was with the cook. A half hour of the Latest and I was decidedly rattled by the time I got to the dinner table—fragments of half-heard news reports skittering through my mind, veiled predictions of war, famine, and depression weighing me down, leaving a terrible taste in my mouth, distracting me from our family and their more immediate concerns. I was gradually coming to realize that it isn't just food you serve your family. I wanted to nourish them in subtler ways as well; my state of mind couldn't help but affect theirs. If I wanted our meals to take place in a congenial, relaxed atmosphere, I had no choice but to come to the table in a calm, cheerful, and relatively unified state of mind.

So little by little, news coverage gave way to music. Before long, though, that too came to be a distraction. If I were going to listen to music, I wanted to listen to *good* music, and give it my complete attention. Five-thirty was obviously not the time. At last the radio was stilled, and I was able to admit to myself how deeply satisfying it is to work in silence, the mantram bubbling away within, providing a peaceful, regular rhythm to work by.

But of course there was a more profound side to what our teacher was talking about when he urged us to make our life and all our work an offering to the Lord who lives in all. For a wife and mother to carry out her work in the spirit of karma yoga, she needs to try quite literally to see the Lord in the people she loves, clothes, and feeds. A woman who grows up in the Hindu tradition has this ideal placed before her always: her children have been named after one of the "thousand names" of the Lord or the Divine Mother, and before every meal she offers up a serving of each dish to the family deity so that what her family eats afterwards is *prasad*—"the Lord's leftovers," already dedicated to his service. To the rest of us, however, this ideal is a bit awesome. I found the concept breathtakingly attractive, but it would have remained an abstraction until, only half aware that I was doing so, I began to watch Laurel, drawn yet again by the half-unwilling suspicion that there was something I could be learning from her.

One morning, out for a walk, I stopped at Laurel's house to see if she'd join me. She was packing Ed's lunch—his dinner, rather, because he was working from twelve to nine at the time. Thinking it would take just a few minutes, I sat down and waited. She suggested a little nervously that I might want to go on without her, but I blithely told her to take her time. No lunch pail was in sight, just a big wicker basket with a lid—quite a large one, really, for just sandwiches and fruit. Then I saw the sandwiches: thick slices of dark rye around an egg salad sparked with sweet red peppers and parsley, so thick she had to cut the bread in half before assembling the finished product. But the sandwiches were the least of the story. A fragrant barley soup with translucent pieces of zucchini, celery, and mushrooms went into a wide-mouthed thermos carefully preheated with boiling water, and a tiny packet of grated cheese went in alongside to be sprinkled on top of the soup. She rinsed and dried lettuce and cherry tomatoes and put them into a plastic container with a tiny bottle of herb dressing, then got out a cantaloupe and cut it in half in perfect zigzags, scooped out the seeds, and packed one of the halves with cottage cheese and a sprinkling of toasted sunflower seeds.

I was getting more impressed by the minute. "Is that dessert?"

"Almost. These"—she held up an innocuous brown lump rolled in coconut—"are pure dynamite. I made them last night. Ed's tipping the scales at a mighty one forty-five now; I have to sneak in all the calories I can."

The breakdown was impressive, all right: peanut butter laced with milk powder, honey, wheat germ, ground sesame and sunflower seeds, soy powder, dates, and carob.

"Five grams of protein each—and *balanced* as all get-out."

"You know, Laurel"—I must have been feeling insecure—"you can *buy* those things at a health food store."

She recoiled in distaste. "Oh, I know. They're sort of expensive, though, and these are much fresher. It doesn't take fifteen minutes to make them."

I backtracked fast. The Laurels of the world have enough opposition these days without having to fend off their closest friends. After all, I didn't have to scallop Tim's honeydew or peel his grapes—he'd probably break out in hives if I did.

I watched while Laurel fixed two more thermoses (one of decaffeinated coffee, one of hot malted milk spiked with a protein supplement) and put in napkins, a spoon, a fork, and an orange, carefully scored for easy peeling. "He's fighting

a cold," she said hurriedly, without looking up. The lid was secured, just barely, and we were on our way.

That night I told Tim about the huge basket and all the little containers that fit together just so; he was as fond of Laurel's droller side as I was, and I knew he would be amused. We tried to envision the reactions of Ed's co-workers as our skinny friend sat soberly bringing out jar after box after bag after bottle of exquisitely catered food. The fantasy became more and more elaborate, and soon we were laughing so hard our sides hurt.

The next morning, though, as I was whipping lunches together in my usual assembly-line fashion, I felt a distinct drag on the operation. Something in me was balking. For the first time, I wondered whether Tim actually liked the lunches I fixed him. He'd never said he *didn't*. His lunch was always the same—an apple, an orange, and two sandwiches, one of soy spread with alfalfa sprouts, one with peanut butter and honey. Very tentatively, I put a couple of tomato slices with the soy spread, and I bagged the sprouts separately to keep them from sogging down in the mayonnaise. Banana slices and a sprinkle of leftover toasted sesame seed brightened up the peanut butter. I threw the sandwiches into the bag with the fruit, but this time I took a little more care than usual that the apple shouldn't sit directly athwart the sandwiches. I came within a hair's breadth of pulling the orange out and scoring it, but I wasn't sure he was ready for that.

Tim didn't catch on to what I was doing, or he might have called an immediate halt lest he lose face with some of our more "liberated" friends. But I couldn't help noticing that for the first time he was eating everything I gave him. I've never packed him quite the feast Ed puts down each night— Tim's home for dinner, after all—but I *have* accumulated my own modest collection of tiny containers, and now whenever I make a dessert, fruity and full of wheat germ, I make enough for bag lunches as well. Julia and Chris, too, aren't nearly as vulnerable to the allurements of the candy machine at school now that their lunches have a little more pizzazz.

The Keeper of the Keys

We began this book a couple of years ago in a pleasantly desultory manner, seeing it as a chance to share our kitchen experience and pass on a solid collection of nutritious, inexpensive vegetarian recipes. The events of the past year, though—the growing threat of world famine and the spreading awareness that all natural resources are limited—have brought a new sense of urgency to our work. For the rest of this century, the American housewife is in a uniquely important role. As never before, the "gift of life" is hers to give or withhold.

Traditionally, the world over, the woman in a house has been known as the "keeper of the keys." To hold the keys to the household, to its storerooms, attics, chests, and cupboards, was a position of great responsibility and, therefore, of great honor. In a season of impoverishment, it was the woman's wise allocation of limited supplies that would see the family through, and in times of plenty, it was her foresight that provided for future needs. Some of us have grandmothers whose linen closets and kitchen pantries, stocked with gleaming jellies and pickles, marked the last vestiges of the tradition.

In just a couple of generations, we seem to have lost sight of this beautiful custom. I don't mean in the strictly private sense; my family isn't suffering for lack of the splendid pile of embroidered linens that dowered Grandma. The *world* is suffering, though, for our having forgotten the frugal practices, the wise use of resources, that the keeper of the keys represented. Now we need to become trustees not just for our immediate families, but for the entire planet.

As of mid-1975, world famine has intensified to the point

that fifteen thousand human beings, most of them children, are dying of malnutrition each day. For the first time in its twenty-seven-year history, UNICEF has declared an emergency situation. Meanwhile, for all our own anxieties over economic recession, the major health problems in the United States continue to be those related to overconsumption. Our consumption patterns are hurting us, and they are now jeopardizing life the world over.

Our meat-based diet is perhaps the most obvious example. We now consume about twice the protein our bodies need, and beef is our hands-down favorite way of doing it. As Frances Moore Lappé has shown us, every pound of beef on our table represents sixteen pounds of grain and legumes removed from the total available to a hungry world. What we do not all realize is that this high-protein feed is administered to a steer during the last few weeks of its existence. The sole function of most of the soybeans and other feed crops we raise is to turn lean range-fed beef into the marbled-fat beef that our doctors warn us against.

The relationship between meat consumption and available grain is therefore more sensitive than we might think. If demand for meat goes down, the steer's last-minute cram session does not take place. In 1974, when the market for meat did fall, the grain that was so unexpectedly released actually *did* find its way to poorer countries.

Reducing American meat intake, therefore, by even a small, scarcely noticeable margin would help alleviate the problem and, according to Harvard's Dr. Jean Mayer, would probably improve our health as well. By the same token, our health as a nation would certainly improve if consumption of alcohol were lowered: twenty million people could live for a year on the amount of grain used by our beer and liquor industry annually.

Americans consume 3300 calories per capita each day, which helps explain why some 40 percent of us are clinically obese. Of course, that 3300 calories represents food *sold*. Some idea of how much of that we *waste* has been provided by a study of the garbage cans of Tucson, Arizona, where about 10 percent of the food that was purchased in each home ended up in the garbage. That's *edible* food, mind you: half-eaten apples, quarter heads of lettuce, etc. In a single year, a city with three hundred thousand inhabitants threw away ten million dollars worth of food. So it all adds up.

But food is just part of the picture. Because modern agriculture depends on petroleum-based fertilizers, the disappearance of cheap oil has forced a pointed choice on us all: 88 gallons of gas (one round trip from San Francisco to Las Vegas) *or* one acre of corn, not both. We *know* this, and we know that fossil fuels are limited, and yet in 1975 we are using more oil than ever before.

Though the U.S. represents just 6 percent of the world's population, we use up 40 percent of its primary resources—twice as much per person as the average Swede uses for an equally high standard of living, forty times what the average Indian or Nigerian requires. Immediately we blame the automobile, but industry itself is the bigger culprit—industry, which produces the "goods" we buy, the synthetic fabrics, the paper plates, the disposable plastic this's and that's, the elaborate packaging we grumble about but go on paying for.

We've grown up thinking of our country as possessing unlimited resources which it is our "right" to use. Actually, we go far beyond U.S. borders to support our inflated life style, importing great quantities of oil and minerals, nonrenewable resources, on the one hand, and foodstuffs on the other. The U.S., for example, is now the world's biggest *importer* of beef—and its sources include Latin American countries which are themselves critically short of protein. The entire planet, and generations to come, are imperilled by our greed.

When we first look straight on at all this, it's easy to fall into despair, overwhelmed at the picture of Yankee know-how run amok, chomping up mountains and rivers to produce Barbie Dolls and Screaming Yellow Zonkers. But before you crumple up in a heap, notice the critical link in this awesome chain of industrialism. The reason for overconsumption is overconsumers. If the consumer refuses to be manipulated and makes wise choices that are not based on advertising, he—she—*we!*—can save the planet.

For most of us, the moment of truth comes when we first

awaken to how our own lives are demeaned by overconsumption. The first glimmering can come in many forms: a week in village Mexico, say, or Greece, where needs may be few, the pace slow, and relationships much warmer than those we're used to seeing. Poverty, yes, *grinding* poverty in many cases— but a precious, ineffable something that we *don't* have, and miss sorely. The clue might be a very harsh one: a heart attack in a forty-year-old salesman, or severe asthma in his child, intensified by badly polluted air. The signals register one by one in our consciousness like those red signs on the freeway: "Turn back; you're going the wrong way."

It's somehow poignant that we pay such high prices for the hand-carved bowl, the hand-polished silver, the hand-dyed scarf from a village in Peru or Indonesia. We delight in using these very personal objects. We prize them over their mass-produced counterparts, and we cherish even their imperfections. Without denying their beauty, I wonder whether what really draws us is the way of life they suggest, where people meet their needs, and *just* their needs, by their own skilled handiwork, and by trustful cooperation with their neighbors. In painful contrast, the "high standard of living" of our own time and place has deprived us of such work, and estranged us from our neighbors. We buy our bread, we buy our clothing, we buy our transportation, our entertainment, our artistic satisfactions; and the price of it all is much higher than it appears to be. For just as serious as the cost to world resources is the threat that our life style poses to life itself. Our exploded notions of what is "enough," conditioned by long exposure to Madison Avenue, drive us mercilessly to earn more, spend more, eat, drink, and smoke more, at whatever the cost to our health and environment. The diseases most Americans die of as a result, cardiovascular disease, cancer, and emphysema, are all but unknown in some parts of the world. We watch with alarm as violent crime becomes the order of the day, and we sense dimly a connection between these crimes and a general atmosphere that encourages greed, and values things above people.

The changeover is in our hands. It can only take place if women like us will change our own habits and help family members to change theirs. I say "women" very stubbornly, because we are still the ones who decide how most of the money is spent. More important, by example and instruction, we are the ones who influence coming generations most directly. The challenge is immense, but women all over the land are finding it irresistible. Hesitantly, we are taking the first steps; then, exhilarated by the growth in health and well-being, we are taking a few steps more. Little by little, a quiet but effective revolution may be taking place. Diet is part of the change, but the larger picture takes in every aspect of our daily life.

The first step, then, is to cultivate a keen eye for the inessential—in food, clothing, transportation, appliances, entertainment, in our use of resources of every kind, direct and indirect. There is a deep satisfaction in rousting a supposed need out of its hallowed niche.

When you start thinking in this way, your life can never be quite the same. If we are concerned with wise use of resources, food, for example—this *is* a cookbook, after all—appears in a new light. One of the best arguments for serving whole, fresh, unprocessed foods, like homemade, whole-grain bread, is that this practice conserves what is most precious in food—its nutritional value. When you refine away nutrients you have to replace them somehow, and a whole industry springs up to manufacture vitamin supplements, at high cost to you, high profit to them. Processed foods are not just unhealthy; they are wasteful, even before you consider the cost in elaborate packaging and competitive advertising. In 1974 we Americans spent ten billion dollars on packaging, five times the amount that the World Food Council in Rome estimated it would take to stave off famine for nine months.

The next inevitable insight is that we women ourselves are a valuable and often misused resource. A sidelong look at my own activities, and I have been forced to ask myself—very tactfully, of course—whether part of my time could not be spent in ways that would more directly contribute to solving the world's problems, or even my own community's. Planting a garden is one way, teaching a neighbor to make bread is another, raising money for famine relief a third. Our time, talent, and energy are resources the world needs desperately.

This leads to a troubled and troubling question—in some circles, even, an explosive one: How is my time best spent? Gardening, cooking with whole, fresh foods, making our own clothes and upholstering our own couches, all require time spent at home. To "retrench" and return to less mechanized and commercialized methods of homemaking may mean I won't have time for a job, or golf lessons, or a course in silk-screening. Even if it *is* necessary for women to make this shift, how palatable would it be? Could I stand it? Could I carry it off without feeling, and expressing, resentment?

I would like to face this question squarely. Convinced as I am that women have a vital role to play in steering our small planet out of its present disaster course, I want to examine some of the attitudes and assumptions—and pressures, too—that are keeping us from doing it. Let me emphasize that everything I'll be saying is drawn from eight years of shared experience of a group of women who have undertaken these changes in their own lives.

Most women have come to see housework as tedium, a real threat to individual growth. The truly creative and challenging activities, it is generally agreed, lie outside the home. Moreover, staying home is *lonely*. The isolation is something fierce, and when you come right down to it, there isn't really all that much to do at home. Parkinson's Law can stretch the morning cleanup on into the afternoon, but how clean does a house need to be?

Housework, as it is generally practiced today, is indeed tedious. Worse, it insults the spirit, and wearies us profoundly. But need this be so? Has it always been so? Granted, there are aspects of housework that are monotonous, but this is the case in any job or, indeed, any "creative pursuit." Ask any teacher, artist, or executive. What really troubles us most about housework is that in our desire to be freed from its tedium, we have welcomed a host of time- and labor-saving devices which have not only not eliminated tedium but cut us off from the truly pleasurable, creative side of our work. If that were all they did, it would be bad enough, but in addition, they actually lower the quality of our lives by rendering everything we eat, drink, wear, and sit on quite uniform, uninteresting, and even downright harmful. What possible satisfaction can I get from preparing a bag lunch for my little boy if it means slapping together a sandwich from "balloon" bread and pre-ribboned peanut butter and jelly spread, dropping in a miniature can of fruit cocktail and a bag of potato chips, and adding a dime (milk money) which will end up in the soft drink machine? For that matter, how much satisfaction can child-rearing itself offer when our children spend six hours a day with the electronic babysitter? Worst of all, these labor-saving products and devices represent an enormous sinkhole for the world's diminishing resources. *The world cannot afford this version of homemaking.*

The less than thrilling side of homemaking will always be there. But as soon as we take into our own hands some of the tasks we'd previously consigned to machines and manufacturers, our work becomes vastly more gratifying. (I mean that literally, by the way, about the hands. Until I started making our bread, dragged out my old knitting needles, and planted our side plot in vegetables, my hands were in serious danger of atrophy.)

Obviously, when you're bored, it's hard to concentrate. Only lately have I been helped to realize that I could actually eliminate boredom no matter *what* I was doing, by simply concentrating more. In the old days, cooking dinner was just a matter of getting something onto the table that people would like. A certain listlessness pervaded the whole affair. Now, though, nutrition is as crucial as appetite appeal. I'm *interested* in what I'm doing—and boredom is quite out of the picture. Anyone who's started cooking with whole foods knows that the work itself actually is much more engrossing: the variety of texture, shape, and color calls out the artist in anyone.

I have begun to wonder, of late, about this belief that housework is *essentially* tedious. To what extent do you suppose it has been foisted upon us by those very same commercial interests who so obligingly provide us with dishwashers, dehydrated dinners, and disposable diapers—all meant very generously, of course, to relieve us of all that horrible work, obviously an evil in itself? Is it possible that somewhere on Madison Avenue a very wicked but very brilliant junior executive has built his career on the age-old principle known to Julius Caesar as *divide et impera*—divide a people among themselves and they are easy to keep in line? In this case, it's our consciousness that's being divided into more and more nagging desires so that, continually frustrated, we will obediently buy a little more "stuff" every year. Sit down one afternoon and watch an hour or so of TV commercials, or flip through the pages of any women's magazine. Two images of yourself will flash at you alternately with strobe-light rapidity: one moment you are a loving, devoted wife and mother who wants only the best (best flower-embossed paper towels, best frozen tamales) for her loved ones; the next moment, or even simultaneously, comes the subtle or blatant suggestion that you're really much too good to be stuck at home. The real thrills in life are out in the world: life at the office has a certain glamor that your little bungalow is bound to lack. The gist of the typical commercial is, "We know you love your family, but let us free you from its drudgery and give you Time to pursue a more Meaningful Existence."

The tactic is most insidious. For business and industry, the ideal situation is for us to be trying to have a family *and* a job, for when we do, we spend a lot more money on a lot more things. It's not just because we have more money to spend: a working wife and mother needs a second car (or bus fares), dressier clothing, more nylon stockings, a babysitter, and perhaps a cleaning lady. She's pressed for time in the morning and worn out in the evening, so restaurant meals regularly take the place of bag lunches and home-cooked dinners. Prepared quick-serve foods, far more expensive than basic foods, take another bite out of the budget, along with a dishwasher, a microwave oven, and ready-made clothing for the children—and, in all probability, more money spent on random gifts *for* them because she feels bad at spending so little time *with* them. All this on top of the regular operating expenses of the household. "Household" is hardly the word—at this point, when the emphasis falls increasingly on speedy refueling and immediate departure, "pit stop" might be closer to the truth. This is the pattern of life now for a vast number of American families.

It is grim indeed to realize that Big Business has everything to gain from my inner fragmentation. As I run in several directions at once, the sense of incompleteness within can only deepen. The more insecure I am, the more money I spend in the pathetic belief that I can purchase security. The spending spree would taper off abruptly if I were to discover within myself the fulfillment I lack. So it's no wonder, really, that the media's image of the home nowadays has all the charm of *Stalag 17*.

We have been hoodwinked somehow into believing that creativity is in a separate category from the simple acts of daily life. Art is something you do in a crafts studio or a writer's workshop. We dispatch our housework as swiftly as mechanization and frozen dinners will let us so that we can hustle off to the Y to get recharged with a few hours of "creativity." Meanwhile, to support this pattern of life, we Americans are consuming the lion's share of world resources, and time is ticking out for the poor people of the world—and, just a little more slowly, for ourselves. Surely our "creativity" need not have so high a price.

Why compartmentalize our lives so that art is a thing apart? There is an artistic way to carry out even the simplest task, and there is great fulfillment to be had from finding out that way and perfecting it. That is the silent message that comes to us in the village handicrafts we value so. A culture that gives priority to speed and greed and multiplicity—well, it *is* no culture, it *has* no culture. To lead lives of artistry, we have only to slow down, to simplify, to start making wise choices.

Certainly, for a great number of women, holding a job is not a matter of choice. But for hundreds of thousands of us it is. Confused desire for a "higher standard of living" or a sense of utter bewilderment at the idea of staying home thrust us willy-nilly onto the job market. I know women who would rather *not* work, who would be quite happy to simplify their family's material needs and concentrate on the subtler ones, but who are embarrassed to admit it. ("Am I a dullard? Lazy? Timid?") To counteract this absurd development, and reverse it as soon as possible, is essential if we are to help relieve the food and resource crisis. To my mind, the solution lies in our taking seriously the role of wife, mother, homemaker, in a way we are not being encouraged to do. We can talk back firmly to those who would belittle the significance of our work; better yet, we can demonstrate by quiet personal example that no other job or career involvement can be quite so effective in bringing about the world we all long to see.

Idleness is a genuine fear for many of us. A friend, eight months pregnant, mentioned her plan to return to work a month after her baby was born. At my look of dark dismay, she gave a helpless gesture: "I know myself well enough to know I would go batty if I stayed home and did nothing." With a new baby, nothing to do! When you have a job, you are spared, by and large, the anxiety of figuring out how to structure your day. More little tasks usually fall across your desk than time to do them in. That's very comfortable. We tend not to trouble ourselves over the *ultimate* importance of these tasks; it's just a job, after all. If you dig in your heels at home, though, and refuse this rather easy out, you are truly thrown back on your own inner resources. (No small matter, considering how little help we've had in *developing* those inner resources.) But if you can hold out and look around you at your home, neighborhood, and community, you will see a host of challenges, very real problems that are crying out for creative attention and hard work to solve. By foregoing the temptation to feather your own nest, you free yourself to tackle them. No paycheck comes at the end of the month, and no promotion: the incentive here is much less obvious, and much more worthy of you as a human being.

What about isolation? For many women, a job in an office or store means the relief of human contact and nothing more. They'd work for almost nothing—and do. The loneliness of the typical suburban family is profound. No simple problem, it has to do with deep-rooted inadequacies in our present life style, and especially with our astonishing mobility. A new home every seven years is the national average: make the move or lose the promotion. No wonder so little effort is made to meet our neighbors: it's much easier just to get a job. Through constant daily exposure, we can get to know our fellow workers very quickly. Of course, they aren't our neighbors, or the mothers of our children's friends, or the wives of our husbands' co-workers, but they're better than nothing. The pattern that results is well known: strangers to our neighborhood, we have to drive considerable distances to see our friends, and separately, in different directions. The idea of the whole family visiting another whole family seems to have disappeared with bronzed baby shoes.

This state of affairs is a clear threat to any kind of warmth or interdependence on the family or community level. We only prolong it when we knuckle under. The real cure for loneliness is not to "glom" on to other folks just for the sake of glomming, as we do in so many of our pursuits. Instead, suppose we were to commit ourselves to building up a *neighborhood* where we live: a kind of village, where lives overlap and intermingle in a rich and productive way? What greater challenge to our creativity? Loneliness comes whenever we dwell on ourselves, and it leaves immediately once we start working for the welfare of others, beginning with those immediately around us.

I may seem to have come a ways from that first-stated intention: to prove that American women have the key to the food and resource crisis. But look—see how it all fits together. A neighborhood that meets its needs cooperatively takes a much smaller bite out of world resources. Car pools form naturally; a communal garden springs up. Joint wholesale food purchasing comes easy; families may even find they can live under one roof. One lawnmower, one Rototiller, one sailboat does for a whole block. The barter system can flourish: fresh-baked muffins for minor car repairs, knitting lessons from the elderly lady down the block in exchange for a lift to the grocery store. (So you already know how to knit—she needs the *ride,* and your kids can use a nearby grandma!) Outgrown clothing gets passed around among the children until it's threadbare, and gradually, in the evening, people can even be seen out-of-doors, visiting with one another as they did twenty or thirty years ago before television locked us up in our separate houses like so many Sleeping Beauties.

Judging from our experience, women are the people who can best accomplish these changes, by bringing warmth, self-sufficiency, and interdependence to our homes and communities. I am *not* insisting that women should not take jobs. The nurturant impulse, the eye for the good of all, may have its most obvious place in a domestic setting, but it is a blessing to hospitals, offices, and classrooms as well. No, I would never go on record as saying "a woman's place is in the home." But to my mind, the most effective front for social change, the critical point where our efforts will count the most, is not in business or professions, which tackle life's problems from above, from outside, but in the home and community, where the problems *start*. Any woman about to take a job should think carefully about the pressures compelling her choice and decide which are legitimate and which questionable. She should consider what her home and family and neighborhood stand to lose—and she should never underestimate her own worth.

Recipes & Menus

Four Food Groups for a Meatless Diet: A Daily Guide

Grains, Legumes, Nuts, & Seeds

Six servings or more. Include several slices of yeast-raised, whole-grain bread, a serving of beans, and a few nuts or seeds.

Vegetables

Three servings or more. Include one or more servings of dark leafy greens, like romaine, spinach, or chard.

Fruit

One to four pieces. Include a raw source of vitamin C, like citrus fruits, strawberries, or cantaloupe.

Milk & Eggs

Two or more glasses of fresh milk for adults, three or more for children. (Children under nine use smaller glasses.) Other dairy products or an egg may be used to meet part of the milk requirement. Eggs are optional—up to four per week.

Recipes and Menus

Laurel's Kitchen is meant to be the book we wish *we* had had five or six years ago: good, practical recipes that hold up well over time, along with the basic information on cooking whole foods which you used to have to piece together—often from contradictory sources. We remember very well our early months as vegetarians—finding brown rice to be awfully chewy, not yet feeling quite up to a twice-a-week breadmaking, falling back periodically on cheese omelet dinners just in case our mothers were right about protein after all. Keeping those times in mind, we've tried to provide a wide variety of recipes for you to choose from. Some families can make the transition to a healthful vegetarian diet very quickly. Most of us, though, find a phased approach to be most effective, and this is where a good range of recipes helps.

Our own transition was very gradual, and it is still going on without our consciously pushing it. We take increasing pleasure in the simplest foods and feel less and less need for sauces, garnishes, and the like. Beans and grains play a larger part; eggs and cheese appear very seldom. It seems quite natural now to eat the vegetables that are really in season, even if it means eating the same ones several times a week rather than buying something imported from Mexico. All of these adjustments have taken place little by little, accompanied by no pangs of deprivation.

It isn't just our appetite that has to make a transition, either. You will look in vain in our book for a section on time-saving tips, for one of our firmest beliefs is that we Americans wouldn't be in the pickle we're in today were it not for our burning desire to *save time* at any cost. So be prepared to spend more time in the kitchen than you might be used to, but go by easy stages. Don't start making bread, yogurt, and sprouts the same week you plant a vegetable garden.

These recipes fit into a carefully planned scheme of things. Wise vegetarian eating is based on a number of simple guidelines that will be explained in detail in our nutrition section, but a brief outline now will help you see these recipes in the larger context of a well-balanced diet.

In summary, our advice goes like this: eat a good variety of whole, fresh, natural foods (vegetarian, of course) that are cooked with love and taken in temperate quantity. That just about says it, but here are a few of the hidden implications and some more specific pointers, followed by a rough sketch of what a single day's menu might be.

◅ Eliminate foods that are neither whole nor wholesome: white flour, polished rice, and refined sugar, for instance. In fact, cut *all* sugar, and honey too, down to rock bottom.

◅ Avoid all highly processed foods: frozen, canned, or dehydrated, for example. They've lost valuable nutrients, and their packaging wastes resources.

◅ Cut way back on fats of all kinds, saturated fats in particular. The American diet, measured in calories, is 40 to 45 percent fat, so most of us have a distorted idea as to what's "normal" and "okay."

◅ Decrease your salt consumption. Years of pretzels and potato chips have accustomed Americans in particular to a dangerously high intake.

◅ Use a gentle hand with all spices: an overstimulated palate is hard to control and insensitive to the subtler flavors of whole, fresh food.

Once you've cut out all the *wrong* foods, you're halfway there. Now all you have to do is get the right balance and variety of what remains. Acquaint yourself with the vegetarian Four Food Groups outlined on page 66 and it's a snap.

The diversity of these whole foods assures you of all the vitamins, minerals, and protein you need each day. You may adjust the portion sizes to your own calorie needs: lose weight safely, for example, by eating smaller quantities from each group. Because it all but eliminates eggs and includes very little butterfat, this diet is extremely low in cholesterol and therefore much healthier than a meat-based diet.

Those six servings of grains and legumes might look rather hefty if you're used to thinking of bread and beans as starch, hence high in calories. In the vegetarian diet, though, these whole foods play a crucial role in providing protein, vitamins, and minerals. Besides, once you've eliminated junk food, there is plenty of room in your diet for the "staff of life" foods.

If you take three servings of milk or other dairy products instead of two, beans are not essential. But they are such a satisfying, inexpensive, nutritionally splendid and ecologically magnificent food that we recommend them strongly. Almost every recipe section includes ideas on how to use beans.

Soybeans are the cheapest form of protein available, and we take full advantage of this fact. Cooked and puréed, they can be added to many foods. Keep a batch of ground soybeans in the refrigerator and you'll be surprised how many ways you find to use them: in soups, spreads, casseroles, patties, and breads.

Texturized soy protein is replacing meat in many homes. We're glad it's replacing meat, but we haven't been able to get very interested in it—surely if you're sincere about not wanting to eat your fellow creature, you won't want to eat something made to look and taste just like him either.

Soy grits are toasted pieces of the soybean. Add them to any grain dish, or put them in breads. They have a slight crunch, like chopped nuts. Soy cheese or tofu is an excellent source of protein: low in calories, with a very enjoyable, light texture. See our Soy Milk recipe too (p. 134) if you want a well-balanced milk substitute.

We recommend eating no more than four pieces of fruit daily. We know vegetarians who eat from six to eight pieces, but that's excessive, considering the calories involved. Fresh and dried fruit is very often the last stronghold of a sweet tooth that's overdeveloped—as whose isn't these days?

In meeting the milk requirement, skim or low-fat milk products are preferable if you're interested in keeping butter-

THE FOUR FOOD GROUPS

GRAINS, LEGUMES, NUTS, & SEEDS
6 servings or more, including several slices of yeast-raised, whole-grain bread, a serving of beans, & a few nuts or seeds

VEGETABLES
3 servings or more, including 1 or more servings of dark leafy greens

FRUIT
1 to 4 pieces, including a raw source of vitamin C like citrus fruit

MILK & EGGS
2 or more glasses of milk for adults, 3 for children. Other dairy products or an egg may substitute for part of the milk requirement. Eggs are optional—up to 4 per week.

fat consumption low. Fresh milk has a nutritional edge over dried milk and other more processed dairy products. Butter-milk is a late and happy addition to our diet: made from skim or low-fat milk, it's a most refreshing beverage and has many uses in cooking. If you can't digest milk easily please see our discussion of lactose intolerance in the Four Food Groups chapter of the nutrition section.

For a great many of us, milk-drinking got lost in the shuffle around our sixteenth year, and we balk a little at re-suming the habit. Give it a second chance, though, especially if you have children. Nothing will persuade them of its value as effectively as your example. After all, would you have stopped drinking it if *a*) someone hadn't told you it would make you fat, or *b*) you hadn't noticed that grown-ups all drank coffee instead?

Fortunately for the recalcitrant, there are a hundred and one ways besides that twice-a-day glass to incorporate milk and milk products into the diet. Cheese is probably the most eagerly received. A little of it goes a long way towards meet-ing your protein needs—one ounce contains 6.5 grams of pro-tein while a whole glass of milk only contains 8.5 grams. A lot of it, though, will pile on unwanted pounds, because it is high in fat—and saturated fat at that. Cheese is expensive, too. Furthermore, it's a separated food, meaning that vitamins and minerals are wasted when the whey is drained off. Still and all, cheese is a real help to people making the transition to a vegetarian diet, so we've included more of it in these reci-pes than we actually eat ourselves nowadays. Low-fat cottage cheese can take its place a good deal of the time. Similarly, you may like to replace sour cream with yogurt—start by mixing them half and half. In fact, give yogurt a prominent place in your diet: made at home with dried skim milk, it's inexpensive and healthful.

Vegetarian restaurant menus are typically so laden with quiches, omelets, and *frittatas* that our sparing use of eggs might puzzle some readers. Certainly, when we first became vegetarians we used them heavily. As we learned more about nutrition, though, we realized there was no real need for us to stuff ourselves with these very concentrated, rather heavy foods. We were amply nourished without them, and since the cholesterol issue has not yet been resolved, we felt it wisest to be moderate. Now we have all but eliminated eggs from our own breakfasts, preferring to reserve them for casseroles, breads, and desserts, where even a few eggs make a big difference in adding variety and taste appeal. Using the recipes in this book, you'll find it's no great challenge to enjoy a diet low in cholesterol without completely eliminating this nourishing food.

Obviously, there are any number of ways you can fulfill the Four Food Group requirements. A daily menu that looks something like the one in the margin, for example, would be quite adequate. Please see our Menu section for an entire week's worth of menus.

Readers of Frances Moore Lappé's fine book *Diet for a Small Planet* will undoubtedly wonder why we've paid no attention to the finer points of protein complementarity, particularly the idea that it is necessary to balance amino acids within a half-hour period. We have discovered that there is good reason to relax on that score and consider the whole day's menus rather than just the foods in each meal, for there is considerable evidence that the body is able to make the fine adjustments of amino acid balance if we just give it *enough* protein from a diet of balanced foods. (The chapter on protein in our nutrition section has the details.)

Nothing could be more natural and obvious than the Four Food Groups diet. Yet, so far has our culture come from the natural and obvious that the foods which make up a sensible diet are often hard to come by. Getting across this hurdle is crucial to anyone wanting to change her family's diet, so here are the foods you should be looking for and some suggestions on how to get them, based on our own experience.

Whole-grain products of all kinds are the backbone of this diet: especially wheat, in every form imaginable, from whole wheat berries through cracked wheat and bulgur wheat to whole wheat flour and pastas. You won't find these in the average supermarket. Nor will you find the several grinds of undegermed cornmeal, or millet, kasha, brown rice, and

BREAKFAST
Hot cereal with milk, fruit, and sunflower seeds
Whole-grain bread, toasted, with margarine or peanut butter

LUNCH
Bean spread sandwich on whole-grain bread with lettuce
Raw vegetables or vegetable soup
Fresh fruit
Glass of milk or buttermilk

DINNER
Green salad with dressing
Cooked vegetables
Grain, bean, or noodle dish
Yogurt or cottage cheese

whole barley ("pearl barley" is polished). If you can't get your local supermarket to stock these items, explore all of the health food and organic food outlets in your community, and be sure to compare prices carefully. Sleuth around to find out who the wholesalers are that stock the smaller stores. You may be able to purchase from them directly, especially if you go in with friends and order in bulk. If all else fails (the cost will be rather high), the El Molino company will mail order a wide range of excellent whole-grain products anywhere in the United States. To find the distributors nearest you, write to El Molino Mills, 3060 West Valley Boulevard, Alhambra, California. For advice on forming your own cooperative buying venture, get a copy of William Ronco's *Food Coops* (Beacon Press, 1974; $3.95), or the *Food Conspiracy Cookbook,* by Lois Wickstrom (101 Productions, 834 Mission Street, San Francisco, California; $4.98).

Good yeast-raised, whole-grain bread, the vegetarian's mainstay, is not easily had in most places unless you make your own. If you don't bake your own bread, at least read labels carefully: the first ingredient should be 100 percent whole wheat flour. Much of the bread sold as whole wheat bread today contains little or no whole wheat flour and is tinted brown with raisin syrup. "Enriched flour," remember, means refined and *then* enriched with only a few of the nutrients that were discarded in the refining.

Dried beans and peas are much more accessible than whole-grain products. Most markets carry them in good array, though for soybeans, black beans, azuki beans, and mung beans you may have to go further afield. Again, health food or organic food stores or distributors will supply you. These foods, too, should be bought in bulk. With the exception of whole wheat flour, all the whole-grain foods and legumes we've mentioned can be stored for long periods without spoilage.

As for seeds (sunflower, sesame, and, for that matter, caraway and poppy), never buy them at the supermarkets. Sunflower seeds are normally sold as snack food still in the shell—roasted at high temperatures, salted, and very expensive. Sesame seeds, on the other hand, have usually lost their calcium-rich and perfectly edible hulls and are sold on the spice shelf at prices that would make our heads spin if we knew any better. Buy seeds in bulk at the same stores where you buy whole-grain products. Prices are much lower, and the seeds are untoasted; the sunflower seeds have been shelled and the sesame seeds are still brown and mineral-rich.

There is little doubt that organically grown produce is more desirable than fruits and vegetables grown by typical agribusiness practices. Protection against cumulative effects of pesticides is one factor; the long-range productivity of our soils is another. Foods grown and harvested on a small and human scale can be richer in nutrients and much tastier than the usual commercial product.

For two reasons, though, we hesitate to make a blanket recommendation that people purchase only organically grown food. First, when food is advertised as "organic," it isn't always clear what that means, or that it means anything at all, so loose are the laws and regulations in this area. Second, although one should expect to pay more, since the organic farmer doesn't have the economic advantage of mass production, the price of these foods is occasionally exorbitant. So we leave it to your own discrimination.

At the very least, though, there is bound to be one produce market in your town where fresher, better fruits and vegetables can be obtained. There may even be a farmer's market, open only certain days of the week, where you can go and talk to the farmers yourself, find out what methods they use, and pick out fresh, locally grown produce.

The obvious, all-round best solution is to grow your own. Then you can be assured that it's free of pesticides and that mineral-rich waste matter has enriched the soil in which it's grown instead of polluting the environment. You will benefit physically from the exercise, and best of all, you will have the satisfaction of knowing you are helping in a small way to offset the world food crisis.

A number of good introductions to organic gardening are now available in paperback. Some of the best are published by the Rodale Press (Emmaus, Pennsylvania 18049), who also publish *Organic Gardening and Farming* magazine.

Dairy products are no problem. They are widely available at reasonable prices. Yogurt is an exception—make your own for pennies. Non-instant powdered milk, which we recommend for yogurt making and other cooking purposes, is not always on the grocery shelves. Request it, and failing that, see if you can purchase it in bulk from a dairy and divide it with friends. This way, you're assured it's fresh, too.

If you can get them, eggs from free-ranging chickens who haven't been fed chemicals are definitely better for you than the usual products. Fertile eggs are highly touted for their nutritional value, but as vegetarians, we prefer to bypass them.

THE POLITICS OF TRANSITION

It's hard to predict which member of a family is going to lead the way towards either vegetarianism or a generally better diet. The move away from meat is often initiated by younger members. Even if the first impulse comes from the older generation, children and teenagers can respond readily, for love of animals is second nature to them. But the move towards an overall healthier eating pattern is sometimes more difficult. Here, it's usually the mother who gets the ball rolling, and she may have to keep it rolling unassisted for a long while.

The critical factor in bringing about any such change is the example of the parent. On the one hand, children can sense ambivalence a mile away. If they see you dragging your heels at taking up a particular food item, you can bet they'll drag theirs even harder. So be patient with them *and* yourself. On the other hand, your enthusiastic appreciation of new foods won't be lost on them either, provided it's genuine.

Change lanes gradually, and you will help your family discover that their likes and dislikes need not be fixed for life. Much more is involved here, ultimately, than just food. We all know people who have rigid likes and dislikes, and we know what constant anxiety accompanies them. They live, very often, at the mercy of external circumstances. If we can help our children learn to tolerate and even enjoy variety in foods, we are doing them a real service, not just in terms of good nutrition, but in terms of sound, happy, secure living.

Breads

Home-baked bread is perhaps the most important part of our diet. Therefore, we've put a good deal of time into developing breads that are truly irresistible. It struck us only recently that the real solution to the terrible problem of excessive sugar consumption—the solution, at least, that has worked beautifully for us—is baking our own bread. Bread isn't a dessert at all. It abounds in vitamins, minerals, and protein, and it contains little or no sugar. Yet, for all its nutritional worth, a warm, fragrant loaf of bread is far more satisfying than any number of sugary desserts.

If you have children, try to involve them in breadmaking. It's a great way to spend time together, and once they get the hang of it, they can be a big help. Share with them the beauty of the whole process: the clever ways of the fabled yeasties, the transformation of the dough, as you knead it, into liveliness and resilience, and the very distinctive qualities that the different flours bring to a loaf. Children can start by greasing the cans, shaping the loaves, and forming cinnamon buns with extra dough. In time, they may want to be in charge of a whole baking. Hopefully, an early initiation will lead to a lifelong habit.

Before recording our bread recipes for you, let us share some kitchen lore on method, ingredients, and equipment. We thought you might enjoy knowing some of the "why's" that are normally left mysterious. What follows is a kind of running commentary on the Basic Whole-Grain Bread recipe. Please read these instructions carefully before you make any of our breads.

Freshly baked bread has a mysterious power to cause friends to drop in unexpectedly. Friends you may not have seen for months will appear at exactly the right moment. Fresh, whole-grain bread, baked with love, is such good food, such *whole* food, that it is a source of real satisfaction to share it around, hot from the oven: so our first piece of advice is just to be sure you bake twice as much as you think you'll need!

Ingredients

Before talking about technique, something needs to be said about the ingredients themselves. It is worth mentioning that for almost any bread, yeast-raised or not, the ingredients should be at room temperature when you start. Whole wheat flour, wheat germ, and a good many of the other ingredients you'll be using will have been refrigerated, so it's wise to take them out of the refrigerator at least an hour before you begin. This is most important for yeast-raised breads. If you forgot, just put the flour into a warm oven for ten minutes or so to take the chill off. To keep the dough warm throughout the mixing and rising, we like to use the big, old-fashioned crockery bowls. They hold heat beautifully.

LEAVENINGS

We buy yeast in bulk. It's much cheaper than the packets, more ecological, and fresher too. Try a bakery for compressed yeast; active dry yeast can usually be purchased from natural food stores or suppliers. One tablespoon of active dry yeast is the equivalent of one cake of compressed yeast. Packaged dry yeast, too, comes in one-tablespoon packets.

Dissolve yeast in warm water (about 100° for dry yeast, slightly cooler for the compressed kind). Throughout the mixing and rising, they work best when they are kept warm, say 80° to 90°. Much hotter and they will meet an untimely end; much cooler and they will grow too slowly. In either case, the bread will be like a brick.

As the yeasties multiply, feeding on sugars in the dough, they make carbon dioxide bubbles. These bubbles are held in place by the stretchy gluten (see flours below); hence the porous texture of good bread. Drafts can undo the yeast's work by breaking the gluten structure and causing the loaf to fall; but yeasties are actually quite intrepid and will flourish if we but respect their simple needs.

You will notice that some of our recipes tell you to dissolve the yeast; others say you should wait until it bubbles to the top. Yeast will only bubble to the top if a sweetener is present. Bubble or no bubble, it takes a couple of minutes to dissolve.

Yeast-raised breads are probably the most healthful, as you will learn in our nutrition section, and certainly, our own recipe collection is weighted accordingly. There is definitely a place in the world, though, for quick breads. Corn bread, biscuits, muffins, and cakes can get rising power, with or without the help of eggs, from the interaction of baking soda with acidic ingredients like buttermilk, vinegar, fruit juice, molasses, or honey. These interactions release tiny carbon dioxide bubbles, which are locked in place by the heat. Most quick-bread recipes nowadays use a minimum of baking soda, opting instead or in part for *baking powder* of one kind or another. Baking powder contains both baking soda and an acidic ingredient like tartaric acid. When the powder is moistened, these two interact. Some of these mixtures release most of their carbon dioxide while the batter is cold. Others, the "double-acting" variety, react again in the oven.

Baking powders are to be used at a ratio of 1 teaspoon to 1 cup flour, and no more. Often, people are tempted to strive for lighter biscuits or muffins by increasing the amount of soda or baking powder—particularly when they first start using whole wheat flour. This is a mistake, because increasing the baking powder also increases the loss of thiamin, a B vitamin susceptible to heat and air and hence almost completely lost in bread crusts by dry heat. Thiamin is also destroyed by alkalinity, which doesn't pose any threat to yeast-bread dough but is a potential problem in quick breads if the proper ratio is upset. This might seem odd, since the acid and base substances in baking powders are presumably balanced to produce an ultimately neutral environment. On the way to that neutral point, however, alkaline particles can interact with and destroy thiamin. The more particles there are, the more likely this is to happen. What a shame to switch to whole wheat flour for B vitamins and then destroy the vitamins by unwise cooking methods!

We use a single-acting baking powder and are more than pleased with the volume of our quick breads. A light hand is part of the secret: stir quick-bread batters just enough to mix, and no longer. The object in making yeast bread is to awaken the gluten: here, though, you want to do everything you can to keep it asleep, or your muffins will be tough and heavy. Whole wheat *pastry* flour is helpful, because it contains little or no gluten.

The second secret to getting light quick breads is to pre-heat your oven well and hustle the bread in as soon as possible. That's the rule, anyway: and yet, with pancake batter, the last pancakes we make are invariably a bit lighter than the first.

LIQUIDS

Yeast dissolves best in water, so for convenience we usually use water for all of the liquid. Where milk is preferred, we add it in the form of non-instant dried skim milk and sift it in with the flour. When whole milk is used, it should be scalded and cooled to lukewarm in order to destroy enzymes that can retard the yeast's growth. Broth and fruit juices are sometimes recommended but we've been unhappy with each: broth because it can give an off flavor and fruit juices because they are a bit too acidic.

Bread made with water has a coarser, chewier crumb and a tougher crust than that made with milk. These are hardly flaws: classic french bread is the perfect illustration.

Egg yolks lend richness, moistness, tenderness, and cholesterol. The whites give lift and protein. Add leftover egg whites to french bread for especially airy, crunchy loaves. Eggs can be very tasty in bread; quick breads especially gain from including one or two. Our "daily bread" contains no eggs, though. It's better for us that way, and we never tire of its simple, straightforward flavor.

Sugar, honey, and molasses: bread can be made without them (french bread has none) but most people prefer bread that contains a little sweetener. If you don't miss it, all the better, but if adding a tablespoon or two of sugar or honey to a baking of bread will quell the urge to spread honey or jam on each slice, you're coming out ahead. Besides, the yeasties do appreciate some extra sugar to grow on, though they will settle for the little bit of natural sugar in the flour if they have to.

The more sweetener, the browner the crust. Honey helps preserve freshness and gives a lovely aroma. A little blackstrap molasses goes a long way, on the palate as well as the nutrition chart. Use it in combination with quieter sweeteners except in frankly dark breads.

Oil, margarine, butter, or Better-Butter are not at all necessary, but they do add flavor and richness. Fat makes for a tender crumb and a softer crust, and adds to the keeping quality as well. In view of the need to cut back on dietary fat wherever possible, however, we've minimized the oil in our recipes. Generally speaking, we prefer to use oil except when the flavor of margarine or Better-Butter seems to make a significant difference, as in Spoon Bread (p. 253).

Terminology can be confusing when you're shopping for bread flour. *High extraction flour* includes more of the whole wheat berry than low extraction flour does and is therefore more desirable, as the parts of the berry that milling removes are primarily the bran and germ, which contain a wealth of important nutrients. *Wheat germ* contains polyunsaturated fats, vitamin E, B vitamins, iron, and the amino acid lysine, in which wheat is limited. *Wheat bran* provides the grain fiber whose protective role in the intestines is just now coming into full recognition.

Standard white flour is 70 percent extraction: it contains just 70 percent of the wheat berry. *Patent flours* are even lower, 40 percent or less. Buy *whole wheat flour,* or 100 percent extraction, and preferably *stone ground.*

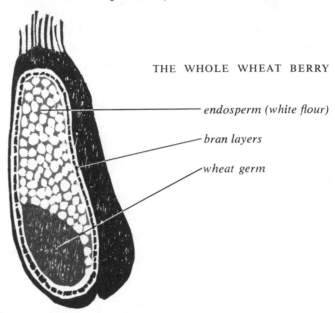

THE WHOLE WHEAT BERRY

—— *endosperm (white flour)*

—*bran layers*

wheat germ

The El Molino people say that unlike stone grinding, conventional steel-roller milling raises the temperature of the wheat so high that some B vitamins and much of the vitamin E are destroyed. In stone grinding, they tell us, the germ oil is rubbed evenly into the flour; in high speed methods, the germ becomes flaked into a small, oily mass which is prone to rancidity. Stone-ground flour is a little coarser, so it usually requires more kneading, but it makes delicious breads and is definitely slower to go rancid. Its price compares favorably with that of ordinary whole wheat flour.

Any extraction can be ground from either hard or soft wheats. Hard grain indicates high protein—the difference is partly a matter of the environment in which the grain is grown. Hard spring wheat is especially prized, for it yields a high-gluten flour for high-rising bread. *Pastry flour,* made from soft wheat, lacks gluten, and yeast breads made from it will not rise; but it's great for piecrust and as a whole wheat substitute for cake flour, when you want a more flaky or crumbly texture.

Gluten is a protein substance present in wheat flour; it is not found in significant quantities in flours prepared from other grains. Gluten's special property is its ability to become stretchy—think of it as forming rubbery balloons in the bread that are then filled with carbon dioxide by the developing yeast. When you are making yeast-raised bread with added nonwheat ingredients like rye, buckwheat, triticale, rice flour, and cornmeal, always knead the gluten-containing whole wheat flour first, and well, before adding the others. This enables the gluten to do its work uninhibited by stodgier particles whose virtues lie elsewhere.

Some of our bread recipes call for small amounts of *gluten flour.* This is meant mostly as an aid to beginning breadmakers. If your kneading arm is strong, try replacing the gluten flour with whole wheat flour. Why? Sheer economics is one factor: gluten flour costs about ten times as much as whole wheat flour. Worse, far from being a whole food, gluten flour is 45 percent patent flour, 55 percent gluten—the gluten having been *extracted* from wheat flour. Touted often for its high protein content, gluten flour's amino acid makeup is in fact severely imbalanced. Once again, the whole food is superior to any fraction thereof!

Substituting whole wheat for white flour in your favorite recipes is definitely fair play. If you're using coarse-grind flour, though, use just ⅞ cup for every cup of white flour that's called for. When a recipe says "sift," just stir lightly with a fork so as to keep the bran.

The *moisture content* of whole wheat flour seems to vary with age and storage conditions. This can account for slight variations in the water-to-flour ratio you use in bread from week to week. We find that the bread is always just a little heavier when made from the last of a bag of flour. See the storage instructions on page 83 to control this factor.

Vary whole wheat bread from time to time by substituting a cup or two of other flours—*rye, oat, rice, millet,* or *barley. Buckwheat flour* is delicious too, but use no more than half a cup per recipe, as its flavor is pretty strong. Remember to add these flours only after a vigorous kneading has brought the gluten into play. It's inevitable that the more of them you add, the heftier the loaves will be. But then, you were fed up with balloon bread anyway, right?

Rolled oats, cooked or raw, improve the flavor and texture of bread. Cooked rice, kasha, or millet give a pleasant, nubbly texture.

Cornmeal comes in several grinds, and each can be used in bread. *Stone-ground* or *water-ground cornmeal* retains its germ, which is valuable for many of the reasons wheat germ is. The flavor of water-ground cornmeal is definitely superior, too. Refined cornmeal has been shorn of the amino acids lysine and tryptophan. You may now and then see "bolted" cornmeal; that means it has undergone a crude sifting to remove hulls, lowering slightly the fiber and calcium content but not affecting other nutrients. Ordinary degermed cornmeal makes for extremely crumbly corn bread; that's why most recipes you see call for added wheat flour. Ours do not, because we assume you will be using unrefined cornmeal, which is usually labelled "undegermed."

Soy flour should never be eaten raw. Unless it has been heat-treated or, as is sometimes the case, peroxide-treated, it contains an enzyme which inhibits protein digestion. Normal cooking destroys this enzyme. *Soy powder* is more soluble and has usually been heat-treated, so it is appropriate to use, for example, in beverages; but check the label carefully. Soy flour's taste is strong, so use it with discretion. It takes very little to boost protein content enormously: maximum protein complementarity calls for 60 percent wheat *protein* to 40 percent soy protein, or about ¼ cup of soy *flour* to every cup of wheat flour; but that's still high for the ordinary palate. This is why we developed our tasty Soy Bread, which uses the whole soybean instead of straight soy flour, giving the same quality of protein but with a very pleasant flavor. The bitter taste of soy flour apparently has something to do with its processing. You will find that full-fat flour is much less bitter than the defatted kind. Let's hear it again for whole foods!

Freshness is all. White flour, degermed cornmeal, polished rice, and such products are so denuded of nutritional value that they will keep indefinitely, simply because they won't support life—not even at the microbial level. Whole grains *nourish*. Consequently, they will also spoil, and the fat they contain in the germ is the first thing to go. Eventually, it will go rancid. If you're in doubt about your own supply, taste it. Rancid flour tastes distinctly bitter—and so does the bread made from it.

When wheat is milled, polyunsaturated fats are exposed to air and will go rancid in time. The ideal solution, therefore, is to buy wheat berries (like rice, or beans, they are much hardier than flour itself) and grind your own flour. We know people who do this, and quite happily. We've always had access to good, fresh flour, though, so it's never seemed top priority.

Make sure your source is reliable. Inquire sweetly of the man behind the counter how fast his flour sells; whole wheat flour will keep for at least two weeks in a reasonably cool place, and even longer if cooler. Most other whole-grain flours are more stable still. Store whole-grain flours in a cool, dry place if they will be used up within a week or two. If not, refrigerate, but be sure to seal the container against moisture, as flour absorbs moisture from the atmosphere. Kept dry, flour will not support the growth of microorganisms. High kitchen shelves, by the way, are usually pretty hot places. Ours is 95° when the oven's been on for a while: good for drying herbs, bad for storing grains.

Methods & Tips

So much for ingredients: back to bread. The art of kneading is best communicated on the spot, from a mother, a grandmother, or a friend. Basically, it's a matter of pushing the dough with the heels of your hands, turning, folding, pushing, and turning again, rocking all the while so that your whole

KNEADING

weight is used. It's a very rhythmical, pleasing activity, and the more kneading you do, the lighter and more evenly textured your bread will be. If you are making more than two loaves, knead only as much of the dough at a time as you can handle comfortably.

Be sure not to knead in too much flour. Try not to exceed the flour called for in a recipe, especially when you're starting out. The dough may still feel sticky, particularly if it's made with rye flour, but trust the recipe your first time around. Flours do vary in moisture content, so there will be exceptions, but it's safer to err on the side of too little.

Never put flour on top of the dough you're kneading. Put it on the table or board, then knead the dough on top of it. There's no explaining the why of this: try it and see the difference. Flour your hands, or oil them lightly.

RISING

Find the best place you can for letting your bread rise: a really warm corner, quite free of drafts. The top shelf that was too warm for storing flour might be perfect. If your stove has a pilot light, tuck the bread bowl into the oven with the door ajar. On cold days, place it on a heating pad set at medium heat. A layer of towel placed between the bowl and the pad will prevent overheating.

The best insulation we've found is newspapers. Old newspapers hold the heat in well, and they don't stick to the dough the way, say, terrycloth towels do.

Most breads require two risings—one in the bowl and one in the pan—but if you like, let it have a third, in the bowl. Just punch it down and let it rise again—the bread may be a bit lighter for it.

BAKING

Never forget to preheat the oven. If you place the bread in the oven while it's heating, here's what happens: the yeasties go berserk, and within 15 minutes the dough may rise very fast, overreach itself, and collapse, leaving a giant cavern in the top of the loaf or caving in altogether. There's no harm in such cave-ins when they take place outside the oven: just take the dough out of the cans, knead it down, and let it rise again. If such catastrophes happen in the oven, though, resign yourself to a heavier bread. Just slice it thin and call it pumpernickel.

There may be days when even after 45 minutes or more, the bread is still languishing lower down than it should in the pans or cans. It may well be that it isn't going to rise any higher. The test is to administer a gentle half-inch poke. If your finger mark remains, the dough has done all the rising it's going to do. Be of good cheer—it happens to everyone. But do allow extra baking time. Heavy bread, for whatever reason it's heavy, always takes longer to cook.

For a shiny crust, brush with egg or milk *before* baking. Brushing with oil *after* baking makes a soft crust. For a tough, chewy crust, brush with water before baking and again 15 minutes before taking the bread out of the oven. For a crust you can really get your teeth into, the bread should be free of fat, egg, and milk. If you have a tiny baby, form little lumps of bread dough the size a baby can grasp easily and bake them in a low oven (250°) for an hour: teething biscuits at a song, free from packaging or additives.

The moment of truth has come. Here we are in your warm kitchen full of the tantalizing aroma of baking bread. The unexpected guests have assembled and are joyfully busying themselves finding butter and knives, and brewing a pot of tea. Open the oven and remove the first loaf. Is it done?!? This is of the utmost importance, because undercooked bread can render a whale of a tummyache to the unsuspecting unexpected guest. Overcooked bread, on the other hand, is dry and woolly.

The first test is color, and this will vary a lot depending on what kind of flour and how much sweetener you used. (A nutritional aside: the color of your loaf is a clue to the percentage of the B vitamins thiamin and folacin you've managed to retain. Assuming the loaf is done, lighter is better.) Even if it's a rich golden brown, it still may not be done. To find out, don your oven mitts, turn the pan or can upside down, and shake. If the loaf slides out easily, it's pretty surely done. If it doesn't, it may be done but stuck. Whack the pan or can respectfully with the heel of one hand. If this doesn't work and you are pretty sure it is cooked, slide a thin knife around the edges and try once more. Bread made in conventional loaves should be out by now, but if you used cans, it could conceivably still be stuck. If worse comes to worst (you forgot to grease it) you can always take a can opener to the bottom of the can and push the loaf out.

Once the bread is out of the can, tap it smartly with your fingertips. It should sound hollow. Pinch the loaf gently just below the middle. Does it spring back? If not, put it back and give it a few more minutes.

If you're still in doubt, slice off a piece. Poke the crumb. Does the dent from your finger remain? If so, put it back into the can, and back into the oven for ten minutes.

The perfect bread-slicing knife is a piece of kitchen equipment no baker can survive without—mostly because of the unexpected guests, who can seldom be cajoled into waiting until the bread is what the cookbooks term "cool enough to slice." Even the hottest bread will slice nicely if your knife has a long, thin, firm, sharp blade with a ribbed edge.

BAKING IN CANS

The reason we generally use cans instead of loaf pans is simply that they allow us to bake up to ten loaves at a time in an ordinary oven. (Start with six and work up.) Juice cans, the 46-ounce size, give slices just the right size for sandwiches. (I know, you have no cans because you don't use canned foods anymore, but you surely have a less enlightened neighbor who does.)

New, shiny cans give a softer, paler crust than old, seasoned, blackish cans. The new ones require ten minutes more baking time, though, and are more likely to stick, so grease them well. This may well be the only legitimate use for white, artificially hydrogenated shortening. Oil and better-quality margarine slip right down the sides and puddle uselessly at the bottom, and butter burns!

Two more tips, if you go in for large bakings. First, buy a dough cutter. This inexpensive piece of equipment divides dough very efficiently without damaging tabletops. There's nothing like it for scraping the table surface clean afterwards.

Second, when you're placing the cans in the oven, be sure to allow a good margin around each can to ensure even circulation of heat. After a few bakings, you may notice a hot spot in the oven—if so, try shifting the bread cans around mid-baking to avoid overdone loaves.

Suppose you've mixed your dough, and it's begun to rise, when suddenly you're called away. Just take the dough and divide it into loaf-sized lumps, flatten them into discs, wrap them loosely, and freeze them. If flattened, the dough will freeze (and thaw) quickly and evenly. Once it's thawed, allow it to rise and resume wherever you left off. You may leave the frozen dough in the refrigerator for weeks: the bread will be fine.

FREEZING DOUGH

We've tried to recall all the little ambiguities that confront the novice breadmaker, but basically, the secret is just to set aside all hesitancy and plunge in, good-humoredly and enthusiastically. Don't worry if the bread turns out a little different each time for a while. Your family will probably enjoy all the variations. For that matter, don't feel tied to the recipes we've given you. Once you have a feel for it all, invent your own!

Basic Whole-Grain Bread

2½ cups warm water
1 tablespoon brown sugar
1 tablespoon active dry
   yeast
1 tablespoon salt
6 cups whole wheat flour

Here is the blueprint for our standard miracle loaf. Every frill
has been removed, so it's perfect for beginners. Please read it
carefully before trying any of the yeast bread recipes, and for
that matter, please read the preceding section carefully before
you follow the recipe below.

Pour the warm water into a large bowl. Add the sugar
and sprinkle the yeast on top of the water. In a few minutes,
when the yeast comes bubbling to the top, stir in half of the
whole wheat flour and beat very well, until the dough ceases to
be grainy and becomes smooth and stretchy.

Add the salt and the remaining flour cup by cup, mixing well. Knead it in the bowl until it is no longer sticky, then
turn it out onto a floured board.

As the dough gets stiffer and harder to knead, sprinkle
the remaining flour a little at a time on the tabletop or board
and knead the dough on top of it.

Knead, push, and fold until the dough is soft and springy to touch, and return it to the bowl. Cover the bowl snugly, allowing room for the dough to double in bulk.

Grease two loaf pans or two 46-ounce juice cans. Divide the dough in half and flatten each half into an oblong the length of the loaf pan, or, if you are using cans, mold the dough into an egg-shaped blob, pinching the dough tightly together at the seams. Slide the formed loaves into the pans or cans, and push down all around the sides so that no air is trapped below.

Cover pans or cans to protect from drafts and let the loaves rise once more, until they have doubled in bulk.

Preheat the oven to 375° towards the end of this rising period. When the bread is rounded just above the rim, bake it for about 40 minutes. When you remove it from the pan and tap it on the sides or bottom, it should sound slightly hollow. The color should be a rich golden brown. Allow the bread to cool, then slice and serve.

Makes 2 loaves.

VARIATION

Knead in 1 cup raisins *or* a handful of chopped herbs: oregano, dill, basil, parsley, thyme.

Form round loaves, brush with beaten egg, and bake on cookie sheets. Dough should be quite stiff for this.

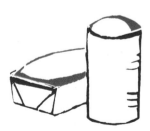

Whole Wheat French Bread

1½ *cups warm water*
1 *cup yogurt, butter-*
milk, or whey
1 *tablespoon active dry*
yeast
1 *tablespoon salt*
6 *cups whole wheat flour*
cornmeal

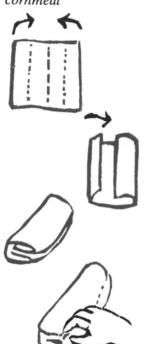

Basic Whole-Grain Bread becomes French Bread, with a real sourdough flavor. The secret is to eliminate the sugar, and for part of the water substitute very sour buttermilk or yogurt; if you have homemade yogurt, chances are that enough whey has separated out for you to drain some off and use it. The latter is ideal, as milk solids detract somewhat from the coarse, airy texture of the bread.

Combine water and yogurt. Their combined temperature should be about 100°. Add yeast, and when it has dissolved stir in half of the flour. Beat well until the dough becomes smooth. Add salt and remaining flour, cup by cup, mixing well.

Knead the dough in the bowl until it is no longer sticky, then turn it onto a floured board and knead very well. Knead in extra flour if the dough is not very stiff. The loaves are baked on a cookie sheet, without support, so the dough needs to be sturdy.

After the dough has risen once, punch it down. Divide it in half. Flour the board and rolling pin and roll out each portion of dough into a large square. Fold as illustrated. Pinch the edges together so that the seam is invisible.

Grease two cookie sheets and dust them with cornmeal. Place a loaf on each and let them rise in a warm place until doubled in bulk. Preheat oven to 400° towards the end of the rising time.

With a serrated or very sharp knife, and very gently, make diagonal slashes across each loaf, about ½ inch deep and 2 inches apart.

Brush or spray the loaves with water as they are going into the oven and repeat about halfway through the baking time: this is the secret to producing the chewy crust so characteristic of good french bread.

Bake the loaves for about 40 minutes. The time will vary depending on the thickness of the loaves.

Makes 2 loaves.

High Protein Bread

The nutritional value of our basic bread is greatly increased when you add a combination of foodstuffs so full of protein, B vitamins, and minerals that we call it Health Mix. Make Health Mix in quantity if you plan to use it frequently.

Mix wheat germ, soy flour, milk powder, and rice bran. Set aside.

Pour boiling water over oats. Allow to cool to lukewarm.

Prepare Basic Whole-Grain Bread from remaining ingredients. The only difference is that ½ cup of whole wheat flour has been replaced by gluten flour. This change is optional, but will make for a lighter loaf.

Add Health Mix and oatmeal after half of the whole wheat flour has been added and beaten well so that the dough is very elastic.

Add remaining flour, knead well, allow to rise, and proceed as in the Basic Whole-Grain Bread recipe.

Makes 2 loaves.

We think you'll be delighted with the pleasant flavor and texture of this bread. Its extra nutrients are especially desirable during the transition period from a less healthful diet.

HEALTH MIX

¼ cup wheat germ
¼ cup sifted soy flour
¼ cup non-instant dried skim milk
¼ cup rice bran or polishings

¼ cup rolled oats and
    ½ cup boiling water
OR
½ cup cooked oatmeal

2½ cups warm water
1 tablespoon brown sugar
1 tablespoon active dry yeast
1 tablespoon salt
5½ cups whole wheat flour
½ cup gluten flour

Basic Whole-Grain Bread can be different each time you bake it, as you begin replacing part of the whole wheat flour with other flours or meals. Start out by adding just one, to acquaint you with its own special qualities, and when you have developed a fairly good kneading arm, try Pumpernickel.

Pumpernickel

2 tablespoons active dry
 yeast
1 tablespoon brown sugar
5 cups warm water
6 to 7 cups whole wheat
 flour
1 cup dark rye flour
⅔ cup buckwheat flour
⅓ cup cornmeal
4 teaspoons salt
⅔ cup cooked soy meal

A hefty bread with a superb Old World flavor, our pumpernickel stays moist for several days.

Prepare dough (it will be quite wet) from first four ingredients as in Basic Whole-Grain Bread recipe, using just 6 cups of whole wheat flour.

When the dough is stretchy, add other flours and meals and mix together. Turn onto a floured surface to knead the dough well. Add the seventh cup of whole wheat flour if necessary.

Proceed as in Basic Bread. Allow extra time for both risings.

Preheat oven to 375° towards the end of the second rising and bake for almost an hour.

Makes 2 large loaves or 3 cans.

Soy Bread

2½ cups warm water
1 tablespoon brown sugar
1 tablespoon active dry
 yeast
1 tablespoon salt
6 cups whole wheat flour
2 cups cooked and
 drained soybeans
 OR
1½ cups cooked soy grits

Soybeans without tears! You can add the extraordinary benefits of soybeans to the diet of the finickiest eaters simply by kneading the beans right into your bread. One way is to use cooked and ground soybeans; the other is to cook soy grits. In either case, you are spared the distinctly bitter taste soy *flour* has. Try both methods. The flavor is excellent, and the extra moistness gives Soy Bread exceptional keeping quality. The secret to keeping it light is to knead it very well before adding the beans, so that the gluten is fully developed. We like to cook soybeans overnight in an electric slow cooker: this way they are quite soft and easy to grind in a meat grinder or even a food mill.

Grind soybeans.

Prepare Basic Whole-Grain Bread dough. After adding the first half of the flour, beat particularly well until the dough is quite elastic. Add salt and remaining flour cup by cup, turning onto a tabletop when the dough is stiff enough.

After the flour has been kneaded in, add bean pulp or

grits. They should be lukewarm. Freshly ground soybeans make for the best results.

Knead well until the dough is stretchy and supple. Let it rise and prepare for baking as described in the Basic Bread recipe.

During the final rising, preheat the oven to 375°. The dough is much moister with soybeans, so allow 45 minutes for baking. After 30 minutes, reduce heat to 350°.

Makes 2 loaves.

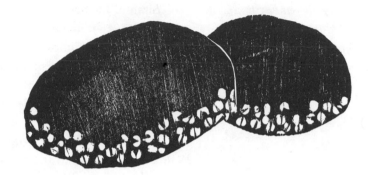

Black Bread

A sweet and chewy, nutritionally high-powered version of the bread that made Vladivostock famous.

Dissolve the yeast in warm water in a large, shallow bowl. Stir in the gluten and whole wheat flours and knead vigorously until you have a rubbery ball of dough. Spread this dough over the bottom and slightly up the sides of the bowl. Sprinkle the remaining ingredients, except the additional whole wheat flour and rolled oats, over the dough. Using a potato masher, mix the ingredients in until they are well distributed. Knead the dough until it is the same color and texture throughout. At this point knead in additional whole wheat flour until the dough is no longer sticky.

Let the dough rise in a warm place until doubled in bulk, at least an hour.

Punch down and shape into two loaves. Roll them in rolled oats, place side by side on a greased cookie sheet, and let them rise again for about 45 minutes.

Preheat oven to 350°. Bake for 45 minutes or longer.

Makes 2 loaves.

1 tablespoon active dry yeast
1 ½ cups warm water
1 cup gluten flour
2 cups whole wheat flour
1 cup wheat bran
1 cup dark rye flour
1 cup wheat germ
½ cup rolled oats
1 cup warm water
½ cup blackstrap molasses
4 teaspoons salt
½ to 1 cup additional whole wheat flour
rolled oats

Rye Bread

1 cup water
1 tablespoon caraway
  seeds
2 tablespoons oil
1 tablespoon active dry
  yeast
¼ cup brown sugar
1 cup warm water
3 cups whole wheat flour
½ to 1 cup gluten flour
2 teaspoons salt
grated peel of 2 oranges
3 to 4 cups rye flour

The flavor of rye bread depends upon the kind of rye flour you use. If it is dark and moist, the bread will be dense and aromatic; if it is the light variety, the bread will be airy and softly textured. This recipe is written for either dark or light rye flours; if you choose the dark rye flour, use the larger amount of gluten flour. The stronger your kneading arm, the less gluten you will need. Dark rye bread will take longer to rise and bake.

Simmer the caraway seeds in 1 cup of water for 10 minutes. Remove from the heat. Add the oil and enough cold water to make 1½ cups liquid.

Dissolve yeast and sugar in 1 cup warm water, in a large bowl. When the yeast bubbles to the surface, stir in gluten flour and 2 cups of the whole wheat flour and knead until the dough is springy.

Add salt and grated orange peel to the seed mixture. Pour this mixture into the dough and mix.

Add 2 cups of the rye flour and knead the dough briefly. Add the remaining 1 cup of rye flour, knead, and finally add the last cup of whole wheat flour. Knead the dough well, adding more rye or wheat flour to make a rather stiff dough.

Place the dough in a greased bowl, cover, and let rise in a warm place. When it has doubled in bulk, punch it down and shape it into two oblong loaves.

Place the loaves side by side on a greased cookie sheet and let them rise. For a shiny crust, brush with beaten egg yolk.

Preheat the oven to 350°, and when loaves have doubled in bulk, bake for about 40 minutes until quite brown. If you have used dark rye flour, baking time may increase to one hour.

Makes 2 loaves.

Sour Corn-Rye Bread

This bread is excellent for toasting. The tangy rye flavor mellows mysteriously. If you use buttermilk instead of yogurt, reduce the amount of water slightly.

Dissolve the yeast and sugar in the warm water in a large bowl, and wait until yeast bubbles to the surface.

Heat the yogurt to lukewarm and add to it the salt, oil, and 1 tablespoon of the caraway seeds. Stir this into the yeast. Stir in the whole wheat and gluten flours and continue stirring vigorously to develop the gluten. Add the rye and cornmeal cup by cup.

Turn the dough onto a floured surface and knead in the last of the cornmeal and rye. Knead the dough thoroughly.

Return the dough to the bowl, cover, and let rise until doubled in bulk. Punch it down, divide it in two, and shape loaves. Roll the sides and bottom in cornmeal before putting loaves into greased pans or cans. Sprinkle the remaining caraway seeds on top.

Preheat the oven to 325°. When the loaves have doubled in bulk, bake them for one hour. Put a pan of hot water on the oven floor to produce a chewier crust. For a crisp crust, brush the loaves with slightly salted water after pulling them out of the oven.

Makes 2 loaves.

2 tablespoons active dry yeast
1 cup warm water
2 tablespoons brown sugar
2 cups yogurt or buttermilk
1 tablespoon salt
¼ cup oil
3 cups rye flour
2½ cups whole wheat flour
½ cup gluten flour
1 cup coarse cornmeal
2 tablespoons caraway seeds

Cracked Wheat Bread

2½ cups boiling water
1½ cups cracked wheat
    OR
½ cup cracked wheat and
    ¾ cup soy grits
½ cup raisins, or dates,
    chopped fine

1 scant tablespoon salt
2 tablespoons oil
1 tablespoon active dry
    yeast
½ cup warm water
6 cups whole wheat flour

Pour boiling water over the wheat, raisins, salt, and oil. Let this mixture stand until lukewarm, at least 20 minutes.

Dissolve yeast in ½ cup warm water. Combine the yeast and cracked wheat mixtures. Add whole wheat flour cup by cup, stirring briskly after the first two cups have been mixed in.

Turn the dough out and knead thoroughly until its surface is satiny. Place dough in bowl, cover, and set in warm place until doubled in bulk. Punch down, form two loaves, and place them in two greased loaf pans, 3½″ × 7½″.

Preheat oven to 375°. When loaves are doubled in bulk, bake for half an hour (45 minutes for cans). Soften the top crust by brushing with oil.

Makes 2 loaves.

Oatmeal Bread

3 cups rolled oats
3 cups boiling water
½ cup toasted wheat
    germ
1 tablespoon salt
2 tablespoons oil
¼ cup honey
1 tablespoon active dry
    yeast
½ cup warm water
5 to 5½ cups whole
    wheat flour
⅔ cup dried skim milk

The slightly chewy texture of this traditional favorite makes it eminently toastable.

Put the rolled oats, oil, honey, salt, and toasted wheat germ in a large bowl. Pour boiling water over this mixture and let it cool to lukewarm.

Dissolve yeast in ½ cup warm water. Add to the lukewarm rolled oats mixture.

Sift the powdered milk with the flour and add it cup by cup to the liquid mixture. Knead thoroughly. When the dough begins to get stiff, turn it out onto a floured surface and work in the remaining milk and flour mixture.

Put the dough in a greased bowl and let it rise until it doubles in bulk. Punch it down, form it into two loaves, and place them seam-side down in two greased loaf pans. Let the loaves rise again until doubled in bulk.

Preheat the oven to 400° as the loaves are rising. Bake for 45 minutes.

Makes 2 loaves.

Pine Nut Pinwheels

For special dinners, these delicious pinwheels are the most attractive advertisements we know of for the humble soybean. If you have Soy Spread around anyway, what could be easier? And if you don't, why don't you? (See Lunch section, page 140.)

Prepare bread dough with first five ingredients, as in the Basic Whole-Grain Bread recipe. After the dough has doubled in bulk, punch it down and roll it out on a floured surface into an 11" × 14" rectangle.

Spread the dough with Soy Spread and sprinkle with pine nuts. Roll the dough up tightly into a long log. With a sharp knife, slice into 1-inch pieces. Place them in a greased baking dish with their sides just touching and let them rise again.

Preheat oven to 375°, and when pinwheels are doubled in bulk (about 20 minutes), bake them for 30 to 35 minutes.

Makes 16 pinwheels.

1 tablespoon active dry yeast
1½ teaspoons salt
1 teaspoon brown sugar
1¼ cups warm water
1 tablespoon oil
3 cups whole wheat flour
1½ cups Soy Spread (page 140)
½ cup toasted pine nuts
OR
½ cup toasted sunflower seeds

Breadsticks

When you're making French Bread or Basic Whole-Grain Bread, you may wish to make breadsticks with half the dough. After the first rising, divide the dough into balls the size of golf balls.

Preheat the oven to 400°.

Using a brisk back and forth motion, roll each ball into a stick about ½ inch by 12 inches. If the dough is sticky, a light dab of grease on the hands will help.

Roll the breadsticks in sesame or poppy seeds. Place them on a greased cookie sheet and let them rise 15 minutes before baking, or put them immediately into the oven for about 15 minutes, until they turn a warm golden brown. Those baked on the lowest rack will probably need to be turned after 10 minutes.

One recipe of Basic Whole-Grain Bread (two loaves' worth) makes between 24 and 30 breadsticks.

Arab Bread

2½ cups warm water
1 tablespoon active dry
*   yeast*
2 tablespoons oil
1 tablespoon salt
6 cups whole wheat flour

You'd never know it, but once again, it's Basic Whole-Grain Bread, with just a few changes. These individual bread puffs rise and then collapse to form pockets which can be stuffed to make a splendid one-dish supper or picnic lunch. Falafel, which are little balls made primarily of garbanzo beans (see page 263 for recipe), along with sliced tomatoes, cucumbers, lettuce, and yogurt, are our favorite filling, but you might also enjoy trying some of the sandwich ideas in our Lunch section (pages 137 to 143).

If you have a gas range, bake Arab Breads directly on the floor of your oven, or, if that seems too outlandish, place an ungreased cookie sheet on the oven floor and use that. If your oven is electric, remove the upper heating element (most of them snap out easily for cleaning) and bake breads on an ungreased cookie sheet placed on the lowest rack.

Dissolve yeast in warm water. Add oil and mix in 3 cups flour. Beat very well until the dough is smooth and stretchy. Add the salt and begin adding remaining flour cup by cup, mixing well. Knead it in the bowl until it is no longer sticky, then turn it onto a floured board. Stop kneading in flour when the dough is firm and smooth but not stiff. Return the dough to its bowl, brush it with oil, and let it rise until double in bulk.

Punch the dough down and divide it into 24 pieces. Shape them into perfectly smooth balls, and *allow the dough to rest for 10 minutes.*

Preheat the oven to 450°.

Take three or four dough balls and roll them on a floured board into ¼-inch-thick flat cakes with no creases. Use flour on your rolling pin too if the dough cakes are sticky.

Bake on oven floor as directed above for about 5 minutes, or until the breads puff up and start to brown. If they begin to brown on the bottom before they are done on top, finish baking them on the top rack of your oven while beginning the next batch on the bottom, lowering the temperature slightly.

To keep them soft for stuffing, cover the breads with a

warm, damp towel and tuck them away from drafts in a corner. They are at their best served warm or reheated.

One recipe, the equivalent of two loaves of bread, makes 24 Arab Breads. If you wish, simply make part of the dough into a conventional loaf and bake as usual.

Bagels

Dissolve yeast in warm water—potato water is preferable. Add sugar, oil, and salt. Beat in flour a half cup at a time until the dough is too stiff to beat. Knead in the rest of the flour, enough to make a dough that is not too stiff. Continue to knead for at least 10 minutes.

Let dough rise in a greased bowl in a warm place until doubled in bulk.

Punch down and knead again for a few minutes. Let rise once more until doubled.

Punch down and divide into 18 pieces. Roll each one into a rope 1 inch in diameter and 6 inches long. Form rings, pinching the ends together firmly.

Preheat oven to 375°.

Bring 4 quarts of water to a boil, adding 2 tablespoons of brown sugar. Drop 4 or 5 bagels at a time into the boiling water and cook them for 5 minutes after they have risen to the surface. Lift these out with a slotted spoon; let them rest on a greased cookie sheet while boiling the next 4 or 5 in the same manner.

Glaze if desired with mixture of 1 egg yolk and 1 tablespoon of water, and sprinkle if you like with the seeds or onions.

Bake for 25 to 30 minutes, until golden brown.

Makes 18 bagels.

For a tasty variation, add raisins and spices OR nuts and lemon peel to the dough.

2 cups warm water
2 tablespoons active
    dry yeast
1 teaspoon brown sugar
¼ cup oil
1 tablespoon salt
5 or more cups whole
    wheat flour
4 quarts water
2 tablespoons brown
    sugar

OPTIONAL
1 egg yolk
1 tablespoon water
poppy seeds, sesame
    seeds, or sautéed
    onions

Wheat Berry Dinner Rolls

1⅔ cups warm water
2 tablespoons dried skim
    milk
1 cup sprouted or cooked
    wheat berries
1½ tablespoons active
    dry yeast
1 tablespoon brown sugar
1 tablespoon oil
1 tablespoon salt
5 cups whole wheat flour
cornmeal

Put the warm water, wheat berries, and dried milk in a blender and turn it on briefly at a medium speed. Pour this over the yeast and sugar in a large bowl.

After the yeast bubbles up to the top of the liquid, add the oil, salt, and flour. Knead this well, until the dough is soft and elastic. Cover and let rise 10 minutes. Knead the dough again briefly.

Pinch off 24 even pieces from the dough and shape them into rolls. Place them, not quite touching, in baking pans that have been greased and lightly sprinkled with cornmeal.

Let the rolls rise in a warm corner.

Preheat oven to 375°. When rolls are doubled in bulk, bake for 15 to 20 minutes.

Makes 24 rolls.

Brown and Serve Rolls

Follow the Wheat Berry Dinner Roll recipe, baking the rolls in a preheated 275° oven for 30 minutes.

Cool rolls in pans by placing them on baking racks for 15 minutes. Turn them out of the baking pans and allow them to cool completely. They are now ready to be wrapped in freezer paper and stored, either in the refrigerator for up to two weeks or in the freezer for longer periods.

When you wish to serve them, preheat oven to 450°. Unwrap refrigerated rolls and place them on cookie sheets. Glaze with a beaten egg and sprinkle with sesame or poppy seed if you like. Bake for 20 minutes.

If you chose to freeze the rolls, thaw them (still wrapped) in a 300° oven for 30 minutes, or leave them out on the counter for several hours or overnight. When they are thawed, follow the same baking procedure that you would for refrigerated rolls.

English Muffins

Dissolve yeast in warm water.

Mix together the yogurt and boiling water in a large bowl. Stir in the yeast, then 2 cups of flour, and cover the bowl with a towel. Let this sit in a warm place until doubled in bulk, or leave it overnight. The dough is spongy and will get more sour the longer it sits. Left overnight it may rise and fall several times.

After the dough has doubled in bulk (about 40 to 60 minutes), mix in the remaining flour along with salt and soda. Knead vigorously, adding more flour as needed until you have pliable but slightly sticky dough.

Return the dough to the bowl, cover it again, and let it rise a second time. This takes 30 minutes or more. Punch the dough down and turn it onto a floured surface. Roll it into half-inch thickness with a floured rolling pin. Cut into circles with a four-inch cookie cutter, or use the end of a one-pound coffee can.

Dust both sides of the muffins with cornmeal and set on cookie sheets to rise until doubled in bulk, for 45 minutes to an hour. If this has been an overnight operation, the dough will be cold, so allow about 2 hours' rising time.

1 tablespoon active dry yeast
½ cup warm water
½ cup yogurt
½ cup boiling water
1 teaspoon salt
3 or more cups whole wheat flour
½ cup fine cornmeal
½ teaspoon baking soda

Cook on an electric griddle or skillet for 10 minutes on each side at 400°, or on a heavy iron griddle over a medium high burner.

The traditional approach to English muffins is *not* to slice them, but to insert a fork all around the sides and pull them apart gently. Toast them lightly under the broiler.

Yields 7 to 8 large muffins.

Everyone's Muffins

OATMEAL VARIETY

1½ cups warm water

1 tablespoon active dry yeast

1½ teaspoons salt

1¾ cups whole wheat flour

2 tablespoons oil

2 tablespoons brown sugar

1½ cups rolled oats

2 pinches nutmeg

BUCKWHEAT VARIETY

1½ cups warm water

1 tablespoon active dry yeast

1½ teaspoons salt

2 cups whole wheat flour

2 tablespoons oil

¾ cup buckwheat flour

½ cup raisins

¼ cup toasted sunflower seeds

Most muffin recipes call for eggs and milk, which some people's diets exclude. To right this situation we developed a muffin for everyone. Because it is yeast-rising it has a nutritional advantage over ordinary muffins. We introduce you to two delicious varieties: oatmeal and buckwheat.

For either variety, dissolve the yeast in the water in a large bowl. Add the salt, oil, sugar (for oatmeal), and whole wheat flour, and beat well.

Add the remaining ingredients and beat vigorously. Cover the batter with a towel and let the dough rise for an hour in a warm place. Stir down the batter and spoon it into greased muffin tins, filling each cup two-thirds full. Let the muffins rise again.

Preheat the oven to 400° and bake about 20 minutes.

Each recipe makes 12 large, crusty muffins.

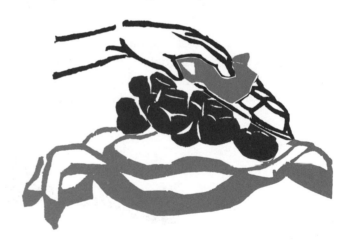

Puffs

Puffs are light, airy, yeast-rising muffins, chock-full of protein. They seem delicate, but they are sturdy and quite simple to make. Allow time for a somewhat longer rising period than most breads require. The first version is for caraway puffs, but try poppy puffs and herb puffs too.

Sauté onion in margarine until soft. Add the cottage cheese, sugar, and salt and heat the mixture to lukewarm (100°).

In a medium-sized bowl dissolve the yeast in the warm water and add the warm cottage cheese mixture. Stir in the egg, seeds, and 1¼ cups of the flour. Mix this batter very well, then add the remaining flour, mixing thoroughly, and turn onto a floured surface. Knead the dough lightly until it is plump.

Place the dough in a greased bowl and leave in a warm place to rise about 1½ hours, or until it has doubled in bulk.

Punch the dough down and divide into 12 balls. Place balls in a greased 12-cup muffin tin. Let the muffins rise another 40 minutes. Preheat oven to 400° and bake the muffins for 15 minutes.

Makes 12 puffs.

1 tablespoon active dry yeast
¼ cup warm water
1 cup cottage cheese
2 tablespoons brown sugar
1 tablespoon margarine
1 teaspoon salt
1 egg
2 teaspoons caraway seeds
2 teaspoons fresh minced onion
2¼ cups whole wheat flour

POPPY PUFFS

Substitute poppy seeds for the caraway seeds and grated lemon peel for the sautéed onion. Melt margarine and warm the cottage cheese along with it.

HERB PUFFS

Increase the onion by 1 tablespoon. Substitute for the caraway seeds a selection of your favorite herbs: dill weed, basil, parsley, and celery leaves are all pleasant.

Apple Bran Muffins

2 cups whole wheat flour
1½ cups wheat bran
½ teaspoon salt
1¼ teaspoons baking
    soda
½ teaspoon nutmeg
1 tablespoon grated
    orange rind
1 cup chopped apple
½ cup raisins
½ cup chopped nuts or
    sunflower seeds
juice of one orange
scant 2 cups buttermilk
    or sour milk
1 beaten egg
½ cup blackstrap
    molasses
2 tablespoons oil

Moist, dark, and fruity, these are unforgettable when served with small slices of jack cheese.

Preheat oven to 350°.

Toss flour, bran, salt, soda, and nutmeg together with fork.

Stir in orange rind, apples, raisins, and nuts or seeds.

Pour the juice of one orange into a 2-cup measure and add buttermilk to make two cups. Add to egg, molasses, and oil, and stir thoroughly.

Stir liquid ingredients into dry ingredients with a few swift strokes.

Pour into greased muffin tins, filling them two-thirds full, and bake for 25 minutes.

Makes 24 two-inch muffins.

Lynne's Muffins

These delicious muffins are nutlike in flavor and texture. They are simple to make, too, but you do need to start them the night before. To sour the milk, put 1 tablespoon vinegar in the required amount of milk.

1½ cups sour milk
2 cups rolled oats
1 cup whole wheat flour
1 teaspoon baking soda
1 teaspoon salt
1 or 2 beaten eggs
2 tablespoons brown
    sugar

Soak the oats in the sour milk for an hour or two or overnight, in a large bowl.

Preheat oven to 400°.

Toss together with a fork flour, salt, and baking soda. Combine dry ingredients and beaten eggs with the oats and stir lightly just until the batter is mixed. Add sugar.

Drop batter into well-greased muffin tins, filling each cup two-thirds full.

Bake for 20 minutes.

Makes 12 muffins.

Date Nut Muffins

This very simple muffin recipe can be the basis for many variations. When you aren't using a sweet addition like dates or raisins, 1 tablespoon of honey or brown sugar may be added.

Preheat oven to 400°.

Toss the flour, salt, cinnamon, and baking powder with a fork to mix. Add the dates and walnuts to the flour mixture.

In a separate bowl beat the egg and stir in milk and oil.

Add dry ingredients to wet ingredients and stir them together briefly. (A few lumps are all right.)

Fill greased muffin tins to two-thirds full. Bake for 20 to 25 minutes.

Makes 12 large muffins.

2 cups whole wheat flour
½ teaspoon salt
2 teaspoons baking powder
1 teaspoon cinnamon
½ cup chopped dates
½ cup chopped walnuts
1 egg, beaten
1 cup cold fresh milk
1½ tablespoons oil

Stratford Hall Biscuits

This recipe can be relied upon to turn out a tender, flaky biscuit on short notice. Whole wheat pastry flour yields an extra-tender product, but is not essential. Serve Stratford Hall Biscuits hot with Better-Butter, or slice them and cover with creamed vegetables or a bean stew.

Preheat oven to 425°.

Toss dry ingredients together with a fork. Cut margarine into dry ingredients with a pastry cutter or with two knives until the mixture is the consistency of coarse crumbs. Pour in milk all at once, and stir just until the dough holds together.

Turn the dough onto a lightly floured surface and knead gently for half a minute, just until the dough is no longer sticky and the ingredients are well distributed. The lighter your touch, the lighter the biscuit.

Pat and roll the dough with a floured rolling pin, quickly and lightly, to ¾-inch thickness. Cut with a floured biscuit cutter by pressing down firmly. Don't twist, or you'll pinch the sides of the biscuits so that they won't rise.

Place biscuits on an ungreased cookie sheet and bake for about 15 minutes.

Makes 12 biscuits.

2 cups whole wheat pastry flour
2 teaspoons baking powder
½ teaspoon salt
¼ teaspoon baking soda
¼ cup margarine, chilled
¾ cup buttermilk or sour milk

Boston Brown Bread

1½ cups whole wheat
  flour

½ cup rye flour

1 cup cornmeal

1½ teaspoons baking
  powder

½ teaspoon baking soda

1 teaspoon salt

2 cups buttermilk

¼ cup whole or skim
  milk

½ cup blackstrap
  molasses

½ cup raisins

½ cup chopped toasted
  sunflower seeds

So moist and tender you'd imagine it to be terribly rich, but not so! The secret is in the steaming. This bread is easy to prepare, and certainly easy to eat, but it takes as long as three hours to cook, so start early.

Grease and dust with cornmeal or flour one 2-pound coffee can, or three 20-ounce (#2) cans, or five 12-ounce cans.

Mix dry ingredients. Mix liquid ingredients separately with the seeds and raisins. Add the liquid to the dry ingredients. Stir just enough to moisten thoroughly. Fill cans to two-thirds full.

Cover the cans with greased foil or heavy greased paper and tie with rubber bands or string. Set the cans in a large pot on top of a trivet or baking rack. (Even crumpled foil will do, or an old jar lid.) Fill the pot with boiling water to halfway up on the cans. Cover the pot and let the bread steam on very low heat for 3 hours (check after 2 hours if you're using small cans).

Let the bread cool for 1 hour before removing it from the cans.

Boston Brown Bread keeps very well wrapped in foil and refrigerated. You can reheat it to serve again.

Corn Bread

The following recipe makes a delicious and nutritionally exemplary corn bread. In our numerous tests we've found that you can vary most of the ingredients and *still* have your friends tell you it's the best corn bread ever. For example, more buttermilk makes for a moister version, and another egg, if you're still within your week's quota, will enrich the flavor and produce a more tender crumb. A little more oil will extend its keeping qualities, and a cup of grated carrots adds appeal.

Preheat oven to 425°.

In a large bowl stir together the dry ingredients. In another bowl mix the wet ingredients. Combine the two just until they are well mixed. Turn into an 8″ × 8″ baking pan, well greased. Bake for 20 to 25 minutes.

2 cups cornmeal
½ cup wheat germ
1 teaspoon salt
½ teaspoon baking soda
1 teaspoon baking powder
1 tablespoon brown sugar
1 large egg, beaten
1 tablespoon oil
2 cups buttermilk

Crispy Seed Wafers

This large, paper-thin, very tasty cracker keeps for several days if stored airtight.

Preheat the oven to 400°.

Mix dry ingredients together. Add 2 tablespoons of the melted margarine, warm water, and vinegar, and mix thoroughly. Knead for a minute or two in the bowl until the mixture forms a stiff dough.

Shape the dough into a 12-inch cylinder (grease your hands lightly first). With a sharp knife slice the roll into 16 pieces.

For each piece spread ¼ teaspoon of seeds on a tabletop or counter and then press the dough into the seeds. Roll with a rolling pin into a paper-thin wafer. Spread another ¼ teaspoon of seeds and turn the wafer onto these.

When you've finished 4 or 5 wafers slide them onto an ungreased cookie sheet, using a long, wide knife with a sharp edge. Brush the wafers lightly with margarine. Bake them for 5 to 7 minutes, until golden brown. Repeat with remaining wafers.

Makes 16 wafers.

1 cup whole wheat flour
¼ cup cornmeal
¼ teaspoon baking soda
¼ teaspoon salt
1 teaspoon brown sugar
¼ cup melted margarine
¼ cup warm water
1 tablespoon apple cider vinegar
poppy or sesame seeds

Sally's Savory Crackers

1 cup whole wheat pastry
flour
½ cup toasted wheat
germ
½ cup brown rice flour
2 teaspoons salt
5 tablespoons oil
½ teaspoon basil
¼ teaspoon curry powder
1½ teaspoons active dry
yeast
¾ cup warm water or
stock
¼ teaspoon brown sugar

Mix the dry ingredients together in a large bowl. Stir in the oil, mixing until the dry ingredients form crumbly balls.

Dissolve the yeast in warm water or vegetable stock with the sugar. Let the yeast bubble, then stir liquid into dry ingredients. Knead the dough until it is thoroughly mixed.

Roll out dough on a floured surface with a floured rolling pin. The dough should be thin, about 1/16 inch to ⅛ inch thick. Cut the dough into desired shapes and use a spatula to place them on a greased cookie sheet. Alternatively, roll the dough right on the greased cookie sheet and cut it into squares with a table knife.

Set the crackers in a warm place to rise.

Preheat oven to 425° and, when the crackers have doubled in height, bake them for 6 to 8 minutes.

Makes about 36 crackers.

Whole Wheat Crackers

1½ cups whole wheat
pastry flour
2 teaspoons salt
¼ cup oil
½ cup warm water
1 tablespoon active dry
yeast
sesame seeds

Whole wheat pastry flour makes for a crisper cracker, but regular whole wheat flour will do.

Mix the flour and salt together, then pour in oil and mix well by rubbing the ingredients swiftly between both hands.

Dissolve the yeast in warm water and add it to the flour and oil, kneading gently as you pour. Knead thoroughly.

Let the dough rise in a warm place about half an hour.

Preheat the oven to 325°.

Turn the dough onto a floured surface and roll it until it is about 1/16 inch to ⅛ inch thick. Cut the dough into attractive shapes and transfer to greased cookie sheet with a spatula, or roll the dough out on a greased cookie sheet and cut it right there. Sprinkle the crackers with sesame seeds, rolling over them once more with the rolling pin to be sure they stick.

Let the cut dough rest for 10 minutes.

Bake for about 15 to 20 minutes.

Makes about 24 crackers.

Tortillas

Unsatisfied with the nutritional value of store-bought tortillas or even with "authentic" recipes for homemade ones, we experimented in our own kitchens. The result, we think, is a happy combination of good nutrition, south-of-the-border flavor, and easy home preparation.

Bring water to boil in a small saucepan. Add half the margarine. Stir in cornmeal quickly; then immediately lower heat and cover pan. Let the cornmeal cook over very low heat for 5 minutes. Stir in remaining margarine and set aside to cool.

Mix flour and salt. Stir in cooled cornmeal and knead, adding water if necessary (or more flour) until a soft dough is formed. Pinch off 12 pieces and roll into 2-inch balls.

Flatten each ball between palms or against a board, making a flat circle. Roll with a rolling pin to 6 or 7 inches. Keep turning the circle to keep it round, and sprinkle board and pin with cornmeal as needed to prevent sticking.

Cook on a hot ungreased griddle for 1½ minutes on each side, or until flecked with dark spots.

Line a basket or bowl with a large cloth. Stack the tortillas in bowl and keep covered with cloth.

They may be made long in advance, even a day or two before needed. Heating for a few seconds on each side makes them soft and pliable for handling again. You may heat them on a griddle or directly over a medium gas flame.

Makes 12 tortillas.

VARIATIONS

For crisp corn chips as an accompaniment to soup or salad, increase the amount of margarine and roll the tortillas somewhat thinner.

If you prefer a flour tortilla, the recipe for chapathis on the following page gives good results.

*1 cup stone-ground
   cornmeal
1½ cups water
3 tablespoons margarine
1¼ cups whole wheat
   flour
1 teaspoon salt*

Chapathis

3 cups whole wheat flour
1 cup water
1 scant teaspoon salt
2 tablespoons oil

These delicious unleavened breads are the traditional accompaniment to curries and other vegetable dishes all over India. See our Dinner section, pages 219 to 223, for a selection of Indian recipes.

Mix the flour and water, salt, and oil, adjusting the quantity of water to make a stiff dough. The dough is often kept for a few hours or overnight before kneading, but this is not necessary.

Knead the dough until the texture is smooth and elastic. Pinch off the dough into 15 balls. Flatten each ball between the palms of your hands and roll it out on a well-floured surface into a circle 7 inches in diameter. Roll out no more than three at a time or they may dry out.

Have an iron or other heavy griddle hot. Teflon works particularly well. Chapathis often blow up like little balloons after a minute on the hot griddle; however, this usually requires a little encouragement in the form of light pressure with a large spoon or spatula. If the large bubbles don't appear the chapathi will still be good, but the hot air inside helps to cook it nicely. When the bottom starts to brown, turn and cook the other side.

Makes 15 chapathis.

Breakfast

Food is the fuel for your day's activity, so it makes no sense at all to eat your biggest meal at night when it's all behind you. Breakfast should include protein *and* carbohydrate—at least one third of your day's requirement of each—and a stretch of brisk exercise as well. The word "diet" used to mean not just food, but exercise, too: for the Victorians, in fact, it seems to have implied a good stint of deep knee bends in front of an open window each morning.

For a great many of us, admittedly, the sight of anything beyond juice, toast, and coffee is more than we can handle when we first wake up; so when the children refuse to eat more than a bowl of sugared cold cereal, it seems hypocritical to argue with them. The key to enjoying an ample breakfast is to be up and around for at least an hour before you eat. (A light supper the night before helps.) There are hidden dividends in this practice. The early morning hours are the loveliest of the entire day. The air is fresher then, and once you've broken free of the pillow, your mind is likely to be at its clearest too. This is traditionally the time of day which is thought most auspicious for meditation. If you don't meditate, the silence of early morning is still a perfect background for studying, writing letters, taking a walk, or doing those deep knee bends.

The earlier you get up, the more leisurely your morning can be; that's all-important, because the pace you set in the morning is the pace you'll maintain all day. Keep your family's breakfast time as slow and tranquil as can be. It might take some hanky-panky with alarm clocks, but try to get everyone together at the table long enough to get a good look at one another. If eyelids are heavy, offer some incentive: a fresh camellia, or a bowl of bright purple plums.

If you've been up long enough to get breakfast well underway before your family appears, you can actually sit down and eat with them instead of flying around the kitchen bagging lunches, burning toast, and feeding the cat. Your children will be much more likely to eat a well-balanced break-

fast if you're eating with them. Beyond a few gentle queries, it doesn't seem to matter if you say much. Just being together in a peaceful, warm atmosphere will make all the difference in how they get through their day. Food eaten in this relaxed and leisurely manner will be digested much more easily than when one eye is on the plate and the other on the kitchen clock.

Our breakfast mainstay is toast made with homemade bread—any kind—spread with Better-Butter or peanut butter, almond butter, or perhaps ricotta cheese. For an occasional treat, we place a slice of jack or Swiss cheese on our toast and slide it under the broiler for a minute. Eggs we have very seldom, preferring to spend our cholesterol ration where it really counts. Spoon Bread, for instance, is a bigger favorite with us than scrambled eggs ever were. Try it for Sunday breakfast—when you don't mind eating late! Another Sunday morning favorite is toasted bagels, Better-Buttered and served with cottage cheese, Mock Sour Cream, and Tzimmes.

Our growing awareness of what makes for good nutrition has altered our breakfast habits in many ways. We've learned, for instance, that loss of thiamin and folacin, two very important B vitamins, is high in any grain or flour that is exposed to dry heat or air. (Hence the crust of bread contains very little of either.) Thiamin loss in toasting bread is normally about 15 or 20 percent, but it can go up to 30 percent when bread is thin and it is toasted dark. Similarly, 10 to 20 percent of the amino acid lysine, which is already low in wheat, gets bound up in the "browning reaction" when we toast grain products of any kind. Low, light toasting minimizes such losses. So encourage your family not to toast their bread heavily. If there are enough of you around, put sliced bread in a loaf pan, covered with a damp towel, for 20 minutes at 325°; then remove the towel and heat for another 10 minutes. Even if the bread is a few days old, it will taste as if it's freshly baked when heated this way.

Toasted dry cereals present an even bigger nutritional problem than bread, because more surface area is exposed directly to dry heat. Cooked cereals are excellent, because the B vitamins stay right there in the water, and the lysine is not destroyed. Besides, could anything be more satisfying than hot, whole-grain porridge? With sliced bananas, raisins or dates, dried apricots or nuts, hot cereal can be mouthwatering to even the pickiest little one. I always thought it had to be sweetened, but try it with Better-Butter. Milk is traditional, but buttermilk and cottage cheese both go well with hot cereal. The full, nutty flavor of the grains is much more distinct when it's not masked over by sugar or honey, and a sprinkle of sesame salt enhances it too (though if you're going to use sesame salt you shouldn't salt the cereal itself).

Don't let the time factor keep you from fixing hot whole-grain cereals for your family's breakfast. Many of us are in the habit of setting up the coffee pot as soon as we can grope our way to the kitchen—it takes no more effort to get the cereal started, and within a half hour (while you're dressing or meditating) it's cooked. Measure out the cereal and water the night before, so it's all ready to go. Even faster is the thermos method: Put ¾ cup or so of cereal into a preheated pint-size thermos, fill it up with boiling water, cap it, and let it stand overnight. By breakfast time, the cereal is cooked and piping hot. If it's thick, thin it to taste with more hot water.

Hot cereals are preferable, but there are mornings when ready-to-eat cereals are certainly helpful. Commercial granolas are expensive and usually loaded with sugar or honey. The homemade versions can contain much more nutritious ingredients (the commercial varieties lean too heavily on oats, by and large) and can be much tastier. Our method of preparation minimizes the nutrient loss which is inevitable in toasting cereals.

We learned a while back that many of the ingredients of the granolas we were making can pass right through the intestines undigested unless they are chewed very well. For children this is critical: children have been malnourished in countries where food was ample but the grains were too coarsely ground for young digestive systems. Seeds, in particular, need to be ground if they are to be assimilated well. With this in mind, we put a great deal of experimentation into developing "Hi-Pro," which we think is an exceptionally good toasted cereal, in which most of the ingredients are in a form easy for the body to assimilate. Hi-Pro is so concentrated that a few tablespoons will stave off hunger for hours. Enjoy it with milk, yogurt, or cottage cheese, or sprinkle it on hot cereal for added flavor and a bit of crunch.

You will want to keep good supplies of toasted wheat germ and toasted sunflower and sesame seeds around—they make a pleasant, vitamin-packed breakfast food when mixed together, though for the most part we recommend using the *whole*-grain cereals. Individually, wheat germ and seeds play a host of roles in everything from sandwich spreads to casseroles and desserts. So make a habit of a weekly "toast-in": bread day is a good opportunity, because you're in the kitchen for a fairly long stretch anyway and will be preheating the ovens for the bread.

Breakfast Beans might seem odd to some. It all started several years ago, during a visit to the Tassajara Zen monastery near Santa Cruz. We were startled to encounter a steaming hot bowl of azuki beans at the breakfast table, served with a pungent pickled radish and a chunk of their hefty, whole-grain bread. Maybe it was the mountain air, but we couldn't have been more pleased, and since then, beans have become a staple breakfast item. Morning is the ideal time to eat beans, a slow-to-digest super-protein if ever there was one. The newly popular electric slow-cookers make overnight bean pots a breeze to prepare. A slice of leftover corn bread toasted under the broiler is a fine companion to a thick bean soup at breakfast.

A current favorite among some of our friends is pancakes with beans. ("Huh," says a mistrustful ten-year-old, "then what do you put the syrup on?") Actually, syrup has quietly passed from our midst—it's such an easy way to take in a tremendous amount of sugar. When you have to eagle-eye children as they lavish syrup or honey over their favorite buckwheats, it takes all the pleasure out of the meal. Blackstrap molasses is a step up from syrup because its flavor is so strong we're rarely moved to excess. The happiest solution, though, is the collection of fresh fruit sauces we've improvised. Plain old applesauce, in fact, is probably our favorite. For that matter, whole wheat pancakes are so much more flavorful than those made with white flour that they stand remarkably well on their own, with a little Better-Butter or one of the cream sauce variations on page 230.

Besides breakfast recipes, this chapter includes instructions for preparing yogurt, soy milk, toasted wheat germ and seeds, and sprouts. These are some of our "basic foods," which actually get used in meals all day long; we've put them here for lack of a more logical slot.

Beverages

Herbal teas are refreshing alternatives to coffee or black tea. Try red clover blossom, lemon grass, spearmint, camomile, raspberry leaf, and rose hips tea. For a spicy flavor, combine anise seed or a whole clove with the tea leaves while they are brewing. Mint grows well in pots or in gardens where there is plenty of light and water; add a fresh sprig to boiling water for a particularly nice drink.

From Mahatma Gandhi's *Satyagraha in South Africa* we culled the instructions for a drink popular in Gandhi's South African ashram. It's quite simple, really. We've taken to calling it "Gandhi's Coffee"—not that any inveterate coffee drinker would be fooled, but it's certainly enjoyable. Toast cracked wheat in a heavy pan, stirring regularly. Grind the wheat fine in a grain grinder. To make "coffee," put 1 teaspoon in a cup and add boiling water. Stir, and you have a good, warming drink—the grounds are delicious too.

Porridge

ALL IN ONE CEREAL

2 cups cracked wheat

1 cup rolled oats

½ cup toasted wheat germ

½ cup raw wheat germ

½ cup soy grits

½ cup wheat bran

1 cup coarse cornmeal

STUART'S CHOICE

2 cups cracked wheat

1 cup coarse cornmeal

Hot cereal is a staple item on our breakfast table, not only because it's a nutritionally excellent way to serve grains (B vitamins are not exposed to dry heat), but because it's so inexpensive, simple, and satisfying. Keep a good variety of cereals on hand. Wheat is perhaps the best all-round cereal, but each has its own nutritional strengths and its own personality.

One way to ensure variety is to mix up a good supply of cereal combinations. Prepare them as indicated on the chart below. Buying in bulk minimizes cost and wasteful packaging. Kept in a dry, cool place, in airtight containers, cereal grains will keep well almost indefinitely. In the case of All in One, though, mix up just a week's worth at a time, *or* add the wheat germ when you're preparing it; wheat germ needs refrigeration.

Cereal grains cooked for breakfast call for a little more water than those served at dinner; otherwise, the cooking method is the same. Use ¼ to ½ teaspoon salt for each cup of grain. Bring salted water to a boil and pour cereal in slowly. Cook and stir for a minute or two, then cover and cook over *very* low heat (a double boiler is ideal) for 20 to 25 minutes. Milk may be used in place of water.

COOKING PROPORTIONS FOR BREAKFAST CEREALS

Cereal *(1 cup dry measure)*	Water	Yield
Cracked wheat	4 cups	4 cups
Cracked triticale	4 cups	4 cups
Rolled oats	2 cups	1¾ cups
All in One	4 cups	4 cups
Stuart's Choice	5 cups	5 cups
Coarse cornmeal *(polenta)*	4 cups	3½ cups

NOTE: *A double boiler is a carefree way to prepare hot cereals, and as the cereal is not directly over the flame, B vitamins are not destroyed.*

High Protein Granola

Our "Hi-Pro" recipe is an old favorite that has evolved gradually over the years, changing from time to time in accord with our better understanding of sound nutrition, but never losing its appeal. Hi-Pro is concentrated. A small serving stays with you all through the morning.

Preheat oven to 300°.

Toast the seeds as instructed on the following page and grind. Mix all ingredients together except for seeds and raisins or other dried fruit. Place in a shallow baking dish. Toast for 45 minutes, stirring every 15 minutes. Add toasted seeds and raisins. Cool and store in covered container in the refrigerator.

For an especially fragrant cereal, place a vanilla bean in the container.

Makes 11 cups.

3 cups raw wheat germ
2 cups rolled oats
1 cup wheat bran
1 cup sesame seeds
1 cup sunflower seeds
½ cup soy flour
¼ cup oil
¼ cup brown sugar
1 cup raisins

OPTIONAL
2 tablespoons torula yeast
1 cup wheat flakes or
    rye flakes
2 tablespoons rice bran
    or polishings
pumpkin seeds
toasted soy nuts, chopped
chopped nuts
chopped dried fruits
honey or barley malt
    extract in place of
    sugar

Toasted Wheat Germ

The advantage of buying your own wheat germ and toasting it at home is that you can have it fresh and can aim for a lighter color than the overbaked commercial varieties have.

The secret to preserving nutrients is to keep the oven temperature low, no higher than 300°. Use a wide, flat baking dish and stir the toasting wheat germ away from the sides and bottom frequently; that's where the browning reaction takes place. Allow wheat germ to cool completely before storing in an airtight container in your refrigerator.

Toasted Nut and Seed Meals

We all know how tasty and nourishing nuts are, but get acquainted with sesame and sunflower seeds too. When you have them on hand, you will find endless uses for them. Their nutritional strengths, balanced by their low cost, make them a far better buy than most nuts. Look at the charts and see.

Nuts and seeds that are ground into a meal are far easier to digest than those eaten whole. For use in cooking, you will want them raw, but for other purposes, like sprinkling on hot cereal or yogurt, their flavor is enhanced by light toasting. *Toast the whole nuts and seeds before you grind them:* remember, the less surface area exposed to dry heat, the better. Toast seeds and nuts at 300°, and stir them often.

There are several ways to grind nuts and seeds into meals. A grain grinder works best, but you can also try a meat grinder with its finest attachment. To use an electric blender, put the nuts or seeds in a dry blender jar, just ¼ cup at a time, and blend at high speed for a few seconds. Turn off the blender and stir the mixture. Repeat until the meal is uniformly ground.

NUT AND SEED BUTTERS

To make nut butter, simply mix a small amount of oil into the meal. Start with 1 tablespoon per cup of meal and add gradually until it reaches the desired consistency.

SESAME SALT (GOMASHIO)

In Japan, gomashio or sesame salt is a popular way to season one's food. Grind toasted sesame seeds coarsely and add sea salt, 1 part salt to 8 parts seeds. An excellent garnish for any grain or vegetable dish, gomashio is to be used *in place of* salt.

Old Fashioned Pancakes

When we're making these, or Sarah's Sourdough Pancakes, we like to sprinkle the griddle first with sesame, sunflower, or poppy seeds.

Stir together all the dry ingredients with a fork.

Beat the egg slightly and combine with the milk; then add to the dry ingredients and stir briefly.

Stir in oil with a few strokes.

Heat the griddle but do not grease it. It should be hot enough so that when you sprinkle water drops on the surface, they dance. Pour the batter onto griddle by large spoonfuls. Cook over medium heat, turning once when bubbles come to the surface and pop and the edges are slightly dry.

Makes 18 pancakes.

½ cup wheat germ
2 cups whole wheat flour
2 teaspoons baking powder
1 tablespoon brown sugar
1 teaspoon salt
2 large eggs
2½ to 3 cups fresh milk
2 tablespoons oil

FRESH CORN PANCAKES

Just add a cup of cooked corn and proceed as above.

BUTTERMILK PANCAKES

Simply replace baking powder with 1 teaspoon baking soda and substitute buttermilk for sweet milk.

Sarah's Sourdough Pancakes

Pancakes made with yeast need longer cooking at lower temperatures than ordinary pancakes. These very flavorful pancakes are moist inside and somewhat chewy when done. If you like them drier, warm them in the oven for a few minutes.

Dissolve yeast in warm water. Add yogurt and 2 cups of flour, beating until very smooth. Cover loosely and set aside for several hours or overnight.

Next morning, stir together remaining dry ingredients and add them with water to the batter; let it rest again for about 15 minutes. Spoon onto seasoned griddle at medium heat, spreading the batter immediately to about ¼″ thickness. Turn when the top is no longer shiny. Makes 20 four-inch pancakes.

2 cups warm water
1 tablespoon active dry yeast
1 tablespoon yogurt
2 cups whole wheat flour
1 cup water, or more for thinner pancakes
1 cup whole wheat flour
½ teaspoon baking soda
1 teaspoon salt

Oatmeal Pancakes

1⅛ cups milk
1 cup rolled oats
2 tablespoons oil
2 eggs, beaten
½ cup whole wheat flour
1 tablespoon brown sugar
1 teaspoon baking
    powder
¼ teaspoon salt

Combine the milk and rolled oats in a bowl and let them stand at least 5 minutes.

Add the oil and beaten eggs, mixing well. Then stir in the flour, sugar, salt, and baking powder. Stir just until the dry ingredients are moistened.

Bake on a hot, lightly oiled griddle, using ¼ cup of batter for each pancake. Turn them when the top is bubbly and the edges are slightly dry.

Makes 10 to 12 four-inch pancakes.

Buckwheat Pancakes

1 cup buckwheat flour
1 cup whole wheat flour
½ teaspoon salt
1 tablespoon brown sugar
2 teaspoons baking
    powder
1 tablespoon oil
2 eggs, beaten
2 cups fresh milk

Sift the buckwheat flour (it tends to be lumpy) and stir the other dry ingredients in lightly with a fork.

Add the milk, beaten egg, and oil and mix briefly.

Cook the pancakes on a hot, lightly oiled griddle. These pancakes take a bit longer to cook than most, so wait until bubbles appear all over the surface before turning them.

Makes 18 four-inch pancakes.

Fresh Fruit Sauce

4 ripe bananas
1 orange, peeled
juice of 1 lemon
¼ cup raisins
¼ cup boiling water

The ways of the banana are such that this flavorful sauce should be eaten right away. Try it with Sarah's Sourdough Pancakes.

Pour boiling water over raisins and let stand until raisins are plump. Combine all ingredients in blender and purée until smooth.

Makes 1½ to 2 cups.

Applesauce

Core apples and cut into chunks. Add raisins and apple juice, bring to a boil, and simmer until done. To enhance flavor, add lemon juice to cooked apples.

Makes 3 or 4 cups.

6 winter apples
handful raisins
½ cup water or apple juice

OPTIONAL
lemon juice

Hot Orange Sauce

Melt Better-Butter in saucepan. Mix in flour, stirring over medium heat for 2 minutes. Stir in orange juice and bring to a boil. Simmer until thick and creamy. Add salt. Remove from heat and let cool. Stir in fresh oranges and mace if desired.

For a very creamy and somewhat sweeter version, blend powdered milk with the orange juice before adding to the flour and Better-Butter.

Makes 2 cups.

2 tablespoons Better-Butter or margarine
2 tablespoons whole wheat flour
1 cup orange juice
pinch salt
1 cup diced fresh oranges

OPTIONAL
pinch mace
¼ cup milk powder

Prune Whip Sauce

Remove prune pits, then combine all ingredients in a blender and purée. For a richer taste, bearing a resemblance to chocolate pudding, add 1 teaspoon brown sugar and 1 tablespoon carob powder.

1 cup unsweetened stewed prunes
½ cup juice from stewed prunes
2 tablespoons ground seeds or almonds
½ cup fresh milk
¼ cup dried skim milk

Breakfast Beans

½ cup dried whole or
  split peas
¼ cup lima beans
¼ cup garbanzos
1 teaspoon basil
¾ teaspoon salt
2 cups water

OPTIONAL
¼ onion, chopped
1 bay leaf

Electric slow cookers, available under several trade names, are perfect for cooking breakfast beans. Use the Red Bean or White Bean Mix (p. 257) or any other combination that appeals to you. Here is one we're currently fond of.

Follow instructions for use of your slow cooker. We put ours on high until the beans come to a boil, then turn it to low to cook overnight. More water often needs to be added in the morning. The joy of it all is that even the most resistant beans (like soybeans and garbanzos) are tender by breakfast time, using minimal electrical energy. Enjoy breakfast beans with whole-grain toast, corn bread, or hot cereal. Polenta and Red Bean Mix is a hard combination to beat.

Stewed Prunes

An old-fashioned favorite that we've revived, stewed prunes have become a regular item on our breakfast menu. Some of the few remaining prune orchards in California are just a morning's drive away, so we've been able to buy fresh dried prunes in bulk at a good price. A food cooperative would no doubt do as well.

Dried prunes are a healthful addition to lunch boxes. Stewed, they are enjoyable with hot cereal or yogurt. Their gently laxative properties are well known. Prunes are an excellent source of iron as well (especially if you stew them in an iron pot).

Simply cover a pound of dried prunes with cold water and bring to a boil. Simmer for about 20 minutes, then add a piece of cinnamon stick or half a well-scrubbed lemon, sliced, and cook for another 10 minutes.

Makes 3½ cups.

Stewed Dried Fruit Compote

Gather together your favorite dried fruits: prunes, apricots, apples, raisins, and pears, for example (leave out the dates and figs). Place about a pound in a good-sized pan and cover with water. Slice a well-scrubbed lemon or orange in thin rounds and add. Bring to a boil and simmer until done, about an hour. Traditionally, you would serve this in small cut-glass compote dishes. We think it's a natural with yogurt, and a great sweetener for pancakes.

Better-Butter

When we began to change our diet to whole, natural foods we made a surprising discovery: our most processed and refined food was margarine. What was the alternative? Why not make a combination of good vegetable oil and butter: oil for its high-quality unsaturated fat, butter because it's a natural food with unmatched flavor.

1 cup safflower, soy, or corn oil
1 cup butter (2 cubes)
2 tablespoons water
2 tablespoons dried skim milk
¼ teaspoon lecithin
½ teaspoon salt

Better-Butter has the same reduced amount of saturated fat as margarine without the processing or additives, and at a savings in cost. However, Better-Butter is one-half butter, so we would not recommend it for those who have to be especially strict about the amount of cholesterol in their diet.

An unpredicted charm of Better-Butter is that you need to use much less of it than margarine or butter because it spreads so easily; so it is ideal for the weight-watcher.

Use butter which is soft but not melted. One version of Better-Butter can be made by simply blending equal parts of oil and butter together, pouring into covered containers, and storing in the refrigerator. By including the other ingredients, though, you will have a spread that stays solid longer at room temperature. (Even at that, Better-Butter should be refrigerated when it is not in use.) For the "preferred" version, then, proceed as follows:

Dissolve salt in water in blender. Add all other ingredients and blend until smooth. Pour into containers and store in refrigerator.

Indian Breakfasts

When you've graduated from the dull school of "toast and a soft-boiled egg" breakfasts and have started to enjoy heartier items like beans, for example, you might like to try a traditional South Indian breakfast. Most of these recipes were given to us by our teacher's mother. If your American palate is still a little too sleepy at breakfast for these dishes, try them for dinner—but don't miss them. The basic dosa recipe is simple enough, and may be used in place of pancakes with your favorite pancake topping.

Uppuma

2 tablespoons oil
1 teaspoon black
   mustard seed
2 medium onions
1 green pepper
¼ teaspoon turmeric
   powder
1 teaspoon salt
2 cups cracked wheat
4 cups water
juice of 1 lemon

OPTIONAL
1 tablespoon finely
   minced fresh ginger
½ cup cashew pieces
½ cup raisins

This flavorful cracked wheat dish was our first exposure to South Indian cuisine, and it remains one of our favorites. Uppuma is popular in most of India for high tea, but it is quite suitable for breakfast, lunch, or dinner.

Heat oil in large, heavy pot—we prefer iron. When oil is hot, add mustard seed and place lid on pot for a few seconds while seeds are toasting. Add onions and green peppers which have been finely chopped. Sauté until soft. Add cracked wheat and allow to brown slightly, stirring so it doesn't stick. Cashew pieces, raisins, or both can be added at this point. Slowly pour in 4 cups hot water. Add turmeric powder and salt (and ginger if desired). Turn the heat to low and allow wheat to cook. It will need occasional stirring when the water is absorbed, and may need more water for longer cooking if the grain still isn't tender. It should be almost the consistency of pilaf, but not quite so flaky. Stir in lemon juice.

Makes 4½ to 5 cups.

VARIATIONS
❧ Add 1 cup finely chopped fresh coriander leaves.
❧ Stir in a cut-up tomato or leftover vegetables: green beans, carrots, or potatoes are all good. These may also be added to the pot raw, when you pour in the water, so that they cook along with the grain. This makes a great one-dish meal.

Dosas

Dosas are moist, tender griddle cakes in which the rice flour gets an added nutritional boost from soy flour. Dosas (pronounced "doshas") may be "stuffed" by placing ¼ cup of filling on one side and folding the other side over to make a semicircle. Filled, they are called *Masala Dosa* (*masala* means "spicy"). Masala Potatoes and Dal are excellent fillings, but they are fine dishes in their own right, too.

2 cups brown rice flour
½ cup soy flour
3 cups water
½ teaspoon salt

Mix all ingredients and allow to stand overnight to ferment. (Dosas may be made immediately, though, with good results.) The water and flour tend to separate, so stir the batter frequently as you prepare the cakes.

Ladle the batter onto a hot, lightly oiled skillet. With a wooden spoon, spread the batter quickly, as thin as possible. Make 1 dosa (about 7 inches across) at a time. Bubbles will appear immediately, but do not turn the dosa until it has dried out a little. With a sturdy spatula, loosen the dosa and turn it to cook on the opposite side. Dosas are tender and soft, so handle with care when turning them.

Makes about 12.

VARIATIONS

For a thicker, very tasty dosa reminiscent of Indian hand-ground dosa batters, try this cornmeal–whole wheat version, proceeding otherwise as above.

1⅓ cups cornmeal
⅔ cup whole wheat flour
2 to 2½ cups water
1 teaspoon salt

ADA

Here is an even chewier—and we think tastier—South Indian treat. It is practically a meal in itself, but may be served with chutney.

Put cracked wheat in a blender at high speed, or grind by hand, until it is a fine meal. Mix rice flour, cracked wheat, water, and salt and let stand overnight to soften. Add the coriander and onions at the last minute. Prepare as above.

2 cups cracked wheat
1 cup brown rice flour
3 cups water
½ teaspoon salt
½ cup coriander leaves, finely chopped
4 or 5 spring onions, minced

MASALA POTATOES

3 potatoes
2 tablespoons oil
1 tablespoon black
    mustard seed
1 large onion
1 medium green pepper
1 teaspoon turmeric
    powder
¼ teaspoon coriander
    powder
½ teaspoon salt
juice of 1 lemon

Boil potatoes in covered pot with as little water as possible. Don't overcook them. Remove their skins and cut into cubes. Heat oil in a covered pan. Add mustard seed to hot oil and brown but do not burn. Add finely chopped onion and green pepper and cook until soft. Stir in turmeric, coriander, and salt. Stir in potatoes and mix well to blend with spices. Cook for a few minutes. A couple of tablespoons of water may be necessary to keep potatoes from sticking. Mash potatoes or leave them in cubes. Stir in juice of 1 lemon and let stand covered until ready to serve.

Serves 4 to 6.

DAL

1½ cups yellow split
    peas
1 teaspoon salt
3 cups vegetable stock
    or water
2 tablespoons oil
1 tablespoon black
    mustard seed
½ green pepper
1 onion
1 teaspoon turmeric
    powder
½ teaspoon curry
    powder
juice of 1 lemon

In one form or another, this recipe is popular in many parts of India. Place ¼ cup on a dosa and fold into a semicircle, or serve a couple of tablespoons at a time directly on the plate.

Prepare yellow split peas by boiling in salted vegetable stock for about 30 minutes. Cook them until they are tender but not so long that they lose their shape. The peas should be rather dry, like mashed potatoes.

Chop onion and green pepper.

Heat oil in a large, heavy pan with a lid. Add mustard seed to hot oil and cover. Allow to brown, but not to burn. This takes a short time. Peek, but very carefully—the seeds jump like popcorn. Stir in turmeric, curry powder, onion, and green pepper. Sauté until vegetables are soft and add to peas along with the lemon juice.

Serves 6 to 8.

Spiced Indian Tea

The popular Indian blend of tea is 2 parts Darjeeling and 1 part Assam, but either may be used alone if you remember that Darjeeling is very strong. Ceylonese tea is especially good.

Bring water to rolling boil and pour over tea leaves. Some import shops carry ground tea spices which may be added to the pot with the tea, but you can do as well by tossing into the teapot the spices listed above. Be cautious with the anise and fennel seed unless you're sure you like their flavors. The spices will of course emerge more prominently if you boil them in the water for a few minutes before adding it to the tea.

Brew the tea for just 5 minutes—no more, no less—and strain immediately into a quart-size tea pot. Add very hot milk and a little sugar.

4 teaspoons black tea
1 pint boiling water
1 pint hot milk
cardamom
cloves
cinnamon
brown sugar

OPTIONAL
fennel and/or anise seed

About Dried Milk

Before we give you our yogurt recipe, a few words are in order about the chief ingredient, dried milk. As a beverage, fresh milk is somewhat more desirable in terms of nutrition—and taste. For yogurt and baked goods, though, and for adding extra protein to soups and sauces, powdered milk is best. *Nonfat, non-instant* powdered milk, preferably *spray-dried,* is the all-round best choice, for the following reasons:

[1] When whole milk is dried, one third of the solids is fat—making it more difficult to keep, because fat decomposes easily. Since most of us have ample fat in our diets, dried skim milk is more suitable. Because of the skim milk surplus from butter and cream manufacture, nonfat dried milk is more available and less expensive. It will have a slightly higher concentration of all the water-soluble nutrients (B-12, for example) than powdered whole milk.

[2] Instant milk powder is nutritionally as good as non-instant, and it certainly mixes into a liquid more easily. For most cooking purposes, though, it is not suitable: for yogurt-making, it is disastrous, and when added as a dry ingredient in cooking, it will cause lumps and chalkiness. All our recipes have been tested with non-instant skim milk powder.

[3] We've recommended spray-dried milk because it is processed at much lower temperatures than those used in the old roller-drying methods. If the equipment is up-to-date, roller-dried milk *can* preserve as many nutrients as the spray-dried variety does, but a good many plants are still using the old equipment.

To store powdered milk it is most important to protect it from moisture so that it maintains a moisture content under 5 percent. Keep it in a plastic bag in an airtight container which is in a cool place protected from light; whenever you open the bag, be sure to squeeze out all the air again before closing. In just one humid day the powder can take up as much as 10 percent moisture, which will cause it to deteriorate rapidly and render it unfit to eat: it won't mix well and it will smell bad.

To reconstitute powdered milk to the same strength as fresh skim milk, use 1 measure of powder to 4 measures of water, or 1 part by weight of powder to 7 parts by weight of water.

Foolproof Yogurt

After many trial and error batches of yogurt, we perfected a foolproof method for making yogurt at a fraction of the cost you pay for most commercial brands. We have culled from this experience some tips that will make your yogurt foolproof too, so before launching into the yogurt recipe look through the "Helpful Hints for Foolproof Yogurt" which follow.

Take two initial precautions. First, read the label on your commercial yogurt "starter." Don't use it if it contains stabilizers. Second, be sure the jars are very clean (see sterilizing instructions below).

Fill the jars with warm water from the tap to about 2 inches from the top. The water should be about 100°.

Put the heating pad on medium heat in a warm nook. We use a sheltered counter top which has a nearby electric outlet for the heating pad. Cover the pad with a towel.

We like to use dried (non-instant) milk rather than fresh because it's simpler than heating milk on the stove, and if the dried milk is of good quality, any nutritional loss will have been slight.

Pour 1 cup of warm water from one of the jars into the electric blender. Turn the blender on low and add 1 cup of non-instant dried skim milk and ¼ cup of the yogurt. The instant the milk-yogurt mixture is smooth turn the blender off and return the mixture to its jar. Repeat this procedure with the other jars. This method prevents the milk from foaming.

Place the filled jars on the heating pad and cover them with towels so no drafts can get at the yogurt. Newspapers over the towels help insulate too.

Leave the yogurt and check it after about 3½ hours. When it has set up, refrigerate it and try not to disturb or

1 cup plain yogurt, commercial or home-made
4 cups non-instant dried skim milk

EQUIPMENT
4 one-quart glass or plastic jars with lids
a heating pad
towels

bump it until it has cooled, since the whey is apt to separate. Yogurt is set when it resists a light touch of the finger even slightly.

HELPFUL HINTS FOR FOOLPROOF YOGURT

If the yogurt does not set up:

. . . the milk powder wasn't fresh enough. Buy it at a store which has a fairly rapid turnover in merchandise, and sweetly ask the proprietor if you can have a sniff before buying. Fresh powdered milk is odorless. The best buy in milk powder is from your local dairy, and several families can share a 100-pound sack. Keep your storage container sealed airtight.

. . . the temperature of the water was too high. Check it with a dairy thermometer next time. At 120° the bacteria die, and below 95° they are not active.

. . . the culture you used for a starter was inactive. Check the label on your commercial yogurt to see if it contains stabilizers, as they inactivate the bacteria, and try a different brand.

. . . you may have left some residual bleach in your yogurt container when you sterilized it, killing the bacteria.

If the yogurt tastes chalky:

. . . the powdered milk mixture was too concentrated. If you allow foam to build up when you're mixing the powdered milk, it will fill your container so that you can't add the necessary water. If you do get foam, skim it off with a slotted spoon and fill the container to the brim with water.

If the yogurt separates and tastes sour:

. . . it may have been exposed to too much heat. Take it off the heating pad sooner.

. . . it may not have chilled quickly enough. Be sure to leave room all around the yogurt containers in the refrigerator so that cold air can circulate freely.

. . . you've done the unthinkable and used instant powdered milk.

If the yogurt is cheesy:

   . . . it may have some stray bacteria in it. These are not dangerous, but will certainly affect flavor. Sterilize your containers and change the culture you're using.

   To prepare water for sterilizing utensils, add 1 tablespoon of 5% chlorine bleach to 2 gallons of warm (but not hot) water. Chlorine will evaporate from water that is hotter than 100° F. Soak the utensils for 30 seconds or more. (This procedure will sanitize eating utensils too.)

Sprouts

When a seed sprouts, its food value skyrockets. Vitamin C materializes as if by magic, and other nutrients increase several times over. The starches turn to sugar, so the flavor is quite sweet.

   Sprouts should be eaten soon after they are "ripened" to get the full nutritional benefit. They can take the place of lettuce in sandwiches, and they add a whole new dimension to salads. Add them whole to cooking vegetables for just the last few minutes.

   You may also blend or grind sprouted wheat berries and add them to bread dough. You'll notice the bread actually rises faster when you do, and the flavor is *very* special. When adding a cup of sprouted wheat berries, subtract ½ cup of flour and ½ cup of water from the recipe. You may leave the berries whole if you prefer, but watch for the ones lurking in the crust: they can be hard as rocks.

   The following method works, with some adaptations, for sprouting all kinds of things: mung beans, garbanzos, whole dried peas, lentils, alfalfa seeds, wheat berries, and, for a piquant addition to salads, mustard seeds (just a few).

[1] Soak 1 tablespoonful of seeds or ⅓ cup of beans in 1 quart of tepid water overnight. Be sure the seeds have not been chemically treated for planting. Your health food store is probably the best source of seeds for sprouting. This is the only time sprouts should actually soak, for if they are not completely drained hereafter, they will ferment unpleasantly.

[2] On the second day, rinse the seeds thoroughly in tepid water and drain. Place them in a quart jar and cover it with a dampened washcloth or piece of cheesecloth. Fasten with a rubber band and store in a dark cupboard.

[3] Continue to rinse the seeds or beans twice each day—three times if the weather is hot or you live in a dry climate. *Make sure excess moisture is drained off each time.*

[4] By the third day, if it's seeds you're sprouting, all the seeds which aren't going to sprout will sink to the bottom of the container when you fill it with rinse water. The growing sprouts will rise to the top and can be poured off into a colander, leaving the "dead" seeds behind to be thrown away.

[5] Sprouted mung beans and lentils (our two favorites) are ready in just three days. So are soybeans. Wheat berries take just two days to reach their peak nutritional value, while alfalfa seeds take four to five days.

When your sprouts are ready, place them in cold water briefly and disentangle them for easier use. Sprouted alfalfa seeds shed their "cases" at this point. The cases will float above the sprouts and can be skimmed off easily if you like. Store sprouts refrigerated in a covered container. To increase their nutritional value somewhat, and certainly their eye appeal, place them in the sun to green for a few hours before refrigerating.

[6] In hot weather, be sure to keep growing sprouts in a relatively cool place and keep the towel damp. They grow faster in hot weather, so don't fail to rinse them regularly.

[7] Be sure to sterilize the container before starting new seeds. A bleach solution will take care of it.

[8] One last suggestion: don't throw away the soaking water that first day. It will be yellow and murky and none too fragrant, but your houseplants will love it. Many a drooping coleus has taken a new lease on life after a dose of sprout water.

Alfalfa sprouts are probably the most popular. They are especially delicate—lovely for salads and sandwiches. Eaten in excess, though, they may not be the best thing. (Excess, in this case, can perhaps be defined by the practice of a friend who was so enamored of alfalfa sprouts that she used to pile her three breakfast toasts and her lunch sandwich too with great curly haystacks of them.) Alfalfa contains saponins, substances which, when eaten in large amounts, damage red blood cells. The saponins in alfalfa increase greatly during sprouting. Research in this area is not complete, and we admit to having eaten a lot of alfalfa sprouts ourselves with no apparent ill effects before we learned of the possible hazard. It *is* a well-known problem among cattle farmers, though, who have learned never to feed their cows a diet of straight alfalfa hay. The lesson in all this appears to be Moderation in All Things. There are toxins that occur in certain foods— natural foods *as well as* processed foods—which will do no harm as long as one does not eat them in abnormally large quantities. Once again, the need for variety in diet is underscored. So enjoy alfalfa sprouts—we certainly do—but in moderation.

Soybeans require special attention to sprout, for they mold very easily. Sort out the non-sprouters as soon as they've made themselves known. Rinse *at least* three times daily, and disentangle them often. Don't expect a long "tail" to develop. Sprouted soybeans are ready to eat after three or possibly four days. They should not be eaten raw, as they contain a protein-inhibiting enzyme which heat destroys. Steamed for 5 minutes or so they have a nutty savor and crunch that graces any mixed vegetable dish very nicely.

Soy Milk

A good number of vegetarians are interested in decreasing sharply or eliminating altogether their use of milk, cheese, and eggs—the so-called vegan diet. It is possible to do this and still be well nourished if the guidelines given in our nutrition section are observed carefully. Fortified soy milk is a great aid to those who wish to exclude all animal products from their diet.

Soy milk has the same amount of protein as cow's milk and only one third as much fat, most of which is unsaturated. Unlike milk, it has no carbohydrate, no vitamin B-12, and very little calcium, but these can easily be added. Soy milk fortified in this way can then replace milk as a beverage and as a base for soups, sauces, and desserts, sparing the vegan a good deal of worry about the adequacy of his or her diet.

Commercial soy milks are available, but we have found most of them unsatisfactory. Generally speaking, their flavor is either strong and "beany" or extremely sweet—too sweet by far to be used for anything but a beverage. Powdered soy milk often contains a remarkable number of unnecessary additives, too. Its cost is comparable to that of fresh milk, but considering how cheaply it can be made at home, starting from soybeans, the commercial kind is needlessly expensive.

The basic procedure for making soy milk is to soak the beans in water for 4 to 16 hours until they are saturated, and then grind them up fine with water in a blender. The "milk" is drained off, cooked, flavored, and refrigerated. This milk contains 65 percent of the total solids of the bean, more than 80 percent of its protein, and most of its oil.

The major problem with soy milk is that it has a strong, rather bitter taste which, until very recently, has prevented its widespread use. The bitter flavor develops because the enzyme lipoxidase, naturally present in soybeans, is released when the bean is ground in water; this enzyme in turn triggers chemical activity that affects flavor. Stop lipoxidase and you put an end to the bitter taste of soy.

Cornell University has developed a way of making soy milk that inactivates lipoxidase. They have made their technique a gift to the public in hopes that it will bring soy milk into the widespread use it deserves. After experimenting with soy pulp, flour, grits, and powder, we found the Cornell technique to be far and away the most successful. We present it here; for more information, write to Dr. W. B. Robinson, New York State Agricultural Experiment Station, Cornell University, Geneva, New York 14456, requesting the FAO/WHO/UNICEF Protein Advisory Group Bulletin no. 10, 1970, "Recent Advances in Soybean Milk Processing Technology." For recipes using soy milk, see the *Oats, Peas, Beans & Barley Cookbook,* by Edyth Cottrell (Woodbridge Press, 1974).

METHOD

The secret of the Cornell process is to grind the beans in *hot* water, 180° F, which inactivates the lipoxidase. (Cooking the bean first and *then* grinding it inactivates lipoxidase too, but the bean's protein is thereby rendered insoluble, so it won't make milk.) This boiling-water grinding process yields a soy milk that is bland and pleasant-tasting, but you have to be careful that the water you use is at a good rolling boil. It won't work even if you let the water boil and then set the kettle aside for a few minutes. This takes extra effort and time, but the result is well worth it.

Inspect the soybeans carefully, discarding any that are broken. Wash them thoroughly and soak in 3 cups cold water for 4 to 16 hours. The beans will double in size during soaking, so allow room in the container. If the water bubbles a bit, it means the beans have fermented slightly. No problem: just rinse them off before grinding. Drain the beans well.

Put a large kettle full of water on to boil. Divide the beans into three equal parts. Preheat the blender by blending 2 cups of boiling water for approximately 1 minute. Grind each portion of beans with 2 full cups of boiling water for 2 to 3 minutes. During the grinding, insulate the blender with newspaper to keep the temperature high.

Stainless steel blender tops are obviously the most desirable. Plastic ones cannot always stand boiling water. Glass tops should be warmed before pouring in boiling water, to prevent their cracking.

1 cup dry soybeans
6 cups boiling water
    (plus 2 cups boiling
    water to heat blender)
2 tablespoons oil
4 tablespoons honey
    OR
1 tablespoon honey
    and 3 tablespoons
    barley malt extract
1 tablespoon calcium
    carbonate (1800
    milligrams)
1 tablet vitamin B-12
    (25 or 50 micrograms)

Strain the mixture in a muslin bag to remove the insoluble residue. Squeeze the bag to get as much of the milk as you can.

Heat the milk for at least 30 minutes in an open saucepan set over boiling water to prevent scorching. Stir the milk occasionally to prevent a film from forming on the top. Take note of the original quantity of milk and after the cooking time is finished, add water to make up for the amount lost to evaporation. Fortify and refrigerate immediately.

One cup of dry beans will make 6 to 7 cups of milk.

FORTIFICATION

After the milk is cooked, we suggest blending in, for every *cup* of soy milk: 1 teaspoon oil, 2 teaspoons honey, and ½ teaspoon (300 milligrams) calcium carbonate.

To every *batch* add one 25- or 50-microgram tablet of vitamin B-12, crushed into a powder (use two spoons to crush the tablet).

Fortified in this manner, the soy milk has a fat content that is just a bit lower than that of cow's milk (and of course the fat is almost completely unsaturated). The carbohydrate level, too, is almost that of milk. (This is especially important for the vegetarian child who doesn't use milk products, since he may otherwise have trouble getting enough calories from a bulky, grain-based diet.) The calcium is just a shade higher than milk. B-12 content is much higher, but tablets smaller than 25 micrograms aren't sold—no harm done nutritionally.

Calcium carbonate is easily available in drugstores. It does not dissolve, so the soy milk should be stirred or shaken before every use. Calcium lactate, which *does* dissolve, can also be used, but if the soy milk is hot, it will curdle.

We think the flavor is excellent, but you may want to experiment with vanilla, brown sugar, or a pinch of cardamom or nutmeg. Barley malt extract used with a small amount of honey or brown sugar gives a pleasing flavor which is less sweet than sugar or honey. For use in soups and sauces, you might well like to use an unsweetened soy milk.

Lunch

When you're leading a busy life, and there are a hundred things you want to get done in a day, it's a temptation to skip lunch. Don't do it. Remember Adelle Davis's adage: "Breakfast like a king, lunch like a prince, and dine like a pauper." If you haven't eaten since breakfast, the low-blood-sugar grouchies are likely to set in something fierce just about the time your family's coming in the door. Not only that, but when you crawl to the supper table famished, you're likely to leave it crammed.

As great a danger as skipping lunch is the Constant Nibble. It's so easy to lose track of calories when we're grazing most of the day. Snacking blunts our appetite so that we're never quite sure we're really hungry.

Drs. Meyer Friedman and Ray Rosenman, authors of the thoughtful book *Type A Behavior and Your Heart,* see "hurry sickness" as one of the key factors in bringing on that number-one killer of Americans, heart disease. An important piece of advice they give us all is to arrest the pell-mell, often mindless rush of our daily activities by making a kind of island in the middle of every day, where we catch our balance, slow down, and try to center ourselves somewhat. Make lunchtime that kind of a break: deliberate, leisurely, and quiet.

For most of us, lunch means sandwiches, eaten at home or packed off to school or work. Make a point now and then of packing a sandwich for *yourself* while you're packing your husband's and children's, and then eating it at the usual time. It's pretty sobering to discover what can happen to a sandwich in a few hours, or worse yet, overnight—a little experiential knowledge goes a long way in motivating us to try a little harder.

Sandwich Ideas

Lentil Nut Loaf slices,
shredded lettuce, and
tomato slices
on Rye Bread

Soy Burgers,
fresh bean sprouts, and
Homemade Ketchup
on Whole Wheat French
Bread

Tofu Patty,
sliced raw mushrooms,
spinach leaves,
sesame salt, and
mayonnaise
on Cracked Wheat Bread

avocado slices sprinkled
with lemon juice
and a dash of salt,
thinly shredded cabbage,
and mayonnaise
on Black Bread

Soy Pâté,
thinly sliced cucumber,
fresh bean sprouts, and
Russian Dressing
on Pumpernickel

Whenever we talk to people who are trying to cut back on meat or eliminate it altogether, one of the knottiest questions seems to be, What do we do for sandwiches? Actually, there are a hundred and one possibilities. People think immediately of cheese, or egg salad. Well and good, but the first is high in saturated fat and both are full of cholesterol, so we prefer to mix cottage cheese (lower in saturated fat and cholesterol) with egg salad and serve it rather seldom. Hard cheese, too, can be grated and mixed with cottage cheese and other ingredients in a variety of ways. Imaginative use of beans, nuts, seeds, vegetables, and dried fruits opens the door to myriad combinations. Try our suggestions, and work out your own.

All of the suggested sandwiches travel well. In hot weather, though, or when you know the sandwich is going to sit around for more than four hours or so, it's wiser not to use Homemade Mayonnaise, as it is more susceptible to spoilage than the commercial variety.

To accompany the sandwiches, in the lunch box or picnic basket, here are some of our favorite "totables." Fresh fruit, of course, but fresh vegetables, too: carrot sticks, raw cauliflower pieces, green pepper rings, and raw zucchini. Lemon cucumbers are mild in flavor and most refreshing; grow them in your backyard. Cherry tomatoes are sturdy enough to pack, and tender sweet peas in their pods are a delicate treat. Stuff a celery boat with any of our spreads—cut it in half and wrap up the two halves face to face.

We like to reserve out-and-out desserts for special occasions, but Peanut Butter Bars are so packed with nutritional goodies, particularly when you cut the sweetener back to almost nothing, that we often pack them in the lunch box. Simpler still, send a packet of raisins mixed with other dried fruit, nuts, and toasted sunflower seeds.

Fresh milk or buttermilk, plain or blended with fresh fruit (see the Strawberry Buttermilk Cooler on p. 143), can be taken in thermoses. A wide-mouthed thermos is useful for yogurt, plain or fruity, and for hot soup or beans come winter.

Split Pea–Parmesan
  Spread,
crisp lettuce, and
green pepper rings
on Rye Bread

garden lettuce,
tomato slices, and
Russian Dressing
on Soy Bread

Garbanzo Spread,
sliced tomatoes and
cucumbers, and
mayonnaise
on Sour Corn-Rye Bread

cheddar cheese spread
topped with Vegetable
  Relish
on Rye Bread

ricotta cheese,
toasted walnuts,
sesame salt,
small bean sprouts, and
butter lettuce
on Black Bread

sieved cottage cheese,
chopped dried apricots,
toasted almonds, and
cinnamon
on High-Protein Bread

peanut butter,
sliced bananas, and
toasted sunflower seeds
on Oatmeal Bread

crunchy peanut butter,
lemon cucumber slices,
bean sprouts, and
mayonnaise
on Cracked Wheat Bread

chili beans,
grated cheese,
finely shredded lettuce,
and Creamy French
  Dressing
on Sour Corn-Rye Bread

At-Home Lunches

For at-home lunches, you may enjoy setting out a variety of spreads, breads, and garnishes as a buffet, so that people can combine what they like. Include a pot of hot soup, and make up a batch of corn bread or whole-grain crackers. Serve Rarebit (p. 142) on toast or use it as a fondue-like dip for chunks of french bread. Salads can be meals in themselves: see our Mexican Salad Bowl, for instance, or the Chef's Salad Bowl. Here are a few sample menus for well-balanced and very tasty lunches, drawn from our recipe collection.

Manybean Soup
Shades of Green Salad
Black Bread with Better-
  Butter
Fresh fruit

Cream of Tomato Soup
Provincial Salad
Crispy Seed Wafers with
  Garbanzo Spread

Vegetable Gumbo Soup
Celery boats stuffed with
  ricotta cheese
Corn Bread
Fresh fruit salad

Whole-grain toast with
  Swissy Spread and
  tomato slices, lightly
  grilled
Navy Bean & Cashew
  Salad
Fresh fruit

Soy Spread

1 cup cooked, ground
soybeans
½ teaspoon salt
1 tablespoon oil
¼ onion, minced
1 stalk celery, chopped
fine
1 teaspoon basil
½ teaspoon oregano
dash garlic
2 tablespoons tomato
paste

We developed these spreads as a way of incorporating soybeans into our families' diets, and they've been extremely successful. Soy Spread keeps for about a week. If you've made more than you can use up in sandwiches, add it to soups, casseroles, or patties, or make Pine Nut Pinwheels (p. 97).

Sauté onion and celery in oil until soft. Add seasonings and tomato paste. Simmer briefly. Add to ground beans. Correct seasonings.

Leftover tomato sauce may be used instead of all ingredients but the beans.

Makes 1 to 1½ cups.

SOY SPREAD WITH PARSLEY

Leave out tomato paste and herbs. Add ¼ cup parsley to onion and celery a minute before removing from heat. Add 1 teaspoon soy sauce and the juice of ½ to 1 lemon as you mix all ingredients together.

SOY PÂTÉ

Leave out tomato paste, celery, and herbs. Sauté onion in just 2 teaspoons oil. Add 1 cup toasted sunflower seeds, ground, and 2 tablespoons mayonnaise—a dash of garlic if you like.

Simplest Bean Spread

Just about any leftover beans can be made into tasty sandwich spreads, and except for garbanzos and soybeans, most of them can be used as is, without grinding or blending. A fork or a potato masher will usually do the job. Blend in two or more tablespoons of Homemade Ketchup (p. 228) or sauté minced onion and add. Chopped fresh parsley adds liveliness, and so do lemon juice and vinegar.

Cheese Spread

Cheese is costly and caloric, but the cost and the calories go down if you combine it with low-fat cottage cheese. An open-face cheese spread sandwich can be toasted under the broiler or served as is. Here is a list of optional ingredients and then an example of a particularly enjoyable version.

Mix the ingredients together and refrigerate until serving.

natural cheese (e.g.,
    Swiss, cheddar, or
    jack)
equal amount of low-fat
    cottage cheese
mayonnaise
OPTIONAL
celery, finely chopped
green pepper, finely
    chopped

parsley, minced
hard cooked egg, diced
chives, chopped
tomatoes, chopped
salt
pepper
dill weed
garlic
paprika
mustard powder

SWISSY SPREAD
½ cup grated Swiss
    cheese
½ cup cottage cheese
¼ cup chopped green
    pepper
½ teaspoon dill weed
salt and pepper to taste
1 tablespoon mayonnaise

Favorite Peanut Butter Spread

Mix all ingredients. If you have applesauce on hand, use it in place of the honey or molasses. The amount can vary with your preference. This makes a lighter-textured spread with a marvelous flavor.

Makes 1½ to 2 cups.

TOFU–PEANUT BUTTER SPREAD

Simply drain and mash ½ pound tofu (soy cheese) and blend with half of the Peanut Butter Spread recipe above. This makes a delicious, rather fluffy spread which should, of course, be refrigerated. Cottage cheese can be used in place of tofu, in the same proportion.

¼ cup toasted sunflower
    or sesame seeds,
    preferably ground
1 cup peanut butter
½ cup raisins, chopped
    dates, or other dried
    fruit
dash salt

OPTIONAL
2 tablespoons honey or
    molasses

Garbanzo Spread

½ onion, chopped
2 tablespoons oil
½ bunch parsley,
   chopped fine
salt to taste
1 teaspoon basil
½ teaspoon oregano
dash cumin
dash garlic
juice of 1 lemon
3 cups cooked garbanzo
   beans, mashed,
   ground, or blended
OPTIONAL
⅔ cup toasted sesame
   seeds, ground

This is one of our favorites for sandwiches and cracker dips. Try it as an open-face sandwich with cucumber and tomato slices, or thin it with a little vegetable or bean stock and serve it with whole wheat crackers.

Sauté onion in oil until soft. Add herbs and parsley at the last minute, just long enough to soften parsley. Mix all the ingredients together thoroughly with a fork.

Makes about 3 cups.

Jessica's Mock Rarebit

1 tablespoon Better-
   Butter or margarine
¾ cup low-fat cottage
   cheese
¾ cup grated cheddar
   cheese
½ cup milk
2 tablespoons dried skim
   milk
1 egg
¼ teaspoon salt
¼ teaspoon mustard
   powder
dash curry powder

Blend milk with milk powder and set aside.

Set up a double boiler or improvise one by placing a saucepan in a larger pan of boiling water. Melt Better-Butter over simmering water. Stir in the cheeses and seasonings of your choice. When cheese is melted, slowly add milk. Stir constantly until hot.

Beat the egg or, if time permits, separate it and slightly beat the yolk. Stir into mixture and continue to cook, stirring constantly until thickened.

Remove from heat and fold in stiffly beaten egg white if you separated the egg. Serve at once over toast, or as a dip for chunks of french bread.

Makes 1½ cups.

Split Pea Spreads

All three of the following recipes start out with cooked split peas and mayonnaise, but they produce three very different results, each one of which is simple and quite tasty. Leftover split pea soup may be used very nicely in all three, and may eliminate the need for salt.

Mash split peas and mix with other ingredients. Refrigerate.

SPLIT PEA—SUNSEED SPREAD

1 cup cooked green
    split peas
2 tablespoons
    mayonnaise
¾ to 1 cup toasted sun-
    flower seeds, ground
salt to taste
dash pepper

OPTIONAL
2 tablespoons lemon juice
2 tablespoons whole
    toasted sunflower
    seeds

SPLIT PEA—PARMESAN SPREAD

1 cup cooked green
    split peas
2 tablespoons
    mayonnaise
2 tablespoons Parmesan
    cheese
2 tablespoons low-fat
    cottage cheese
¼ teaspoon basil
½ teaspoon salt
dash pepper

SPLIT PEA—TOFU DIP

1 cup cooked green
    split peas
2 tablespoons
    mayonnaise
1 pound tofu
1 cup toasted sunflower
    or sesame seeds,
    ground
1 teaspoon salt
¼ teaspoon soy sauce

Strawberry Buttermilk Cooler

Blend your favorite fruit with buttermilk for a refreshing summertime beverage. Strawberries are super, but try fresh peaches, bananas, blackberries, or oranges—or a combination.

Plump the raisins in boiling water for a few moments, drain, and put in blender with strawberries and buttermilk. Blend and chill.

Makes 3 cups.

2 cups buttermilk
1 cup strawberries
½ cup raisins

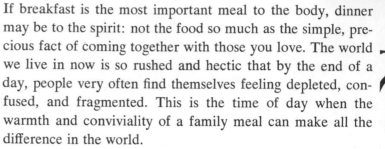

Dinner

If breakfast is the most important meal to the body, dinner may be to the spirit: not the food so much as the simple, precious fact of coming together with those you love. The world we live in now is so rushed and hectic that by the end of a day, people very often find themselves feeling depleted, confused, and fragmented. This is the time of day when the warmth and conviviality of a family meal can make all the difference in the world.

Be fierce as a mother lion to protect the sanctity of this hour. Fight football coaches, drama teachers, and scout leaders if you must, but keep the dinner hour intact. Actually, the most insidious opposition may well come from right within the home. By absorbing our attention so that we don't really see or hear one another, by filling our minds with the most ignoble trivia, and by giving our daily life a backdrop of continual violence, television exerts a ceaseless, disintegrating influence upon individual consciousness and family unity.

Strong language, and startling, maybe, in the middle of a cookbook. But people's lives are all of a piece—good health involves much more than B vitamins. Put your television set on dry ice for a month, by whatever ruse will work. Withdrawal symptoms are inevitable, and people will be at a loss for a while. Make a conscious effort, though, to foster activities that develop your minds and hands and draw you closer to one another. See whether at the end of the month you wouldn't like to pack the nuisance off for good.

Dinner should be a leisurely affair—slow, gracious, and calm. There are sound physiological reasons for eating slowly. One is obvious: eating in haste interferes with thorough digestion and assimilation of food. The other is more subtle, and of special interest to those of us who have to watch our weight. Many nutritionists believe that our appetite mechanism is regulated by the level of glucose in our bloodstream. As we eat a meal, the blood sugar level rises slowly, and when we've eaten what our body needs, the signal goes to the brain to stop

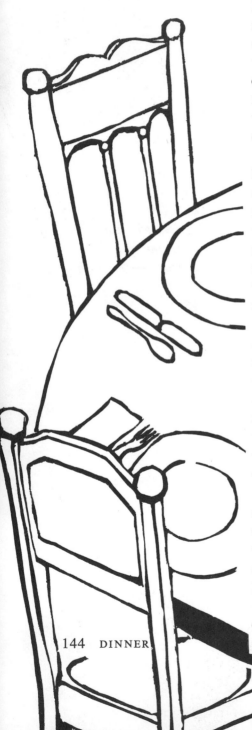

eating. If we eat very rapidly, we may outstrip the mechanism and overeat before the body can give a warning.

Tired nerves need time to relax, and laughter helps, so encourage family members to cull little stories from their day to share with one another. There's definitely an art to this, so don't be disappointed if the conversation falters a little at first. It seems so obvious, yet we have to remind ourselves continually how important it is to give our full attention to one another. The full, healthy development of children depends on their parents' capacity and willingness to do this. An eight-year-old's anecdote may be pretty roundabout, but an attentive listener, asking the right questions, will gradually make a fluent conversationalist out of him or her.

If the deeper purpose of the evening meal is to draw a family together, it stands to reason that they will want to eat the same food. However well-intentioned the effort might be, when we cater too solicitously to individual likes and dislikes we end up emphasizing the differences between family members at just the moment when we want to bring out their fellow feeling. We realize that this is not a popular line of reasoning. The restaurant business is bigger than ever now, and as if ordering from a restaurant menu didn't give full enough scope to personal preferences, we now have international restaurants in every town, where Junior can have a pizza while his mother eats crepes. A small thing, perhaps, but eating the same food is a quiet but effective force for family unity.

If the dinner hour is going to do all we've suggested, some leadership is obviously called for—and there's the rub. If both parents are frazzled and bone-weary from knocking about in the workaday world, and if both of them have the commuter's six p.m. blues, how can they carry it off? This is a question no one can answer for anyone else. The unspoken assumption now seems to be that both parents can work without imposing any strain on their family. Our own experience has led us in the opposite direction, towards an increasing awareness of what a privileged role a woman can have if she is willing to assume it.

Our teacher's teacher was his granny. An unlettered village woman, she was the spiritual leader through personal example of a joint family that numbered about a hundred. The advice she used to give the girls in their ancestral home is a source of endless inspiration to us. Every evening, he recalls, as the sun set, one of the women would light an oil lamp, and as she carried it, everyone would look up in quiet delight to see her soft black eyes and warm brown skin glowing above the polished brass lamp. The beauty of this simple ritual made unforgettable the words that Granny used to repeat time and time again: "Be a lamp in your home, my daughters—be a lamp to everyone around you."

It's with the evening meal that vegetarianism truly comes into its own. The possibilities are all but infinite. Dinner should not be heavy. Yet, since it's such an important time, you'll want the meal to be appealing in every way. Before we were vegetarians we tended to put our biggest efforts into the meat entrée and the dessert. We were rather perfunctory in salad and vegetable preparations. Now, though, we take special pains with these light but very nourishing foods and we find that preparing dinner is much more enjoyable now, because of the wealth of color, shape, and texture that's involved.

Our dinners always begin with a salad, but it's different each night, and we can never seem to serve too much. (Until you've done the salad justice, of course, it helps to keep the entrée out of sight!) From the salad on, the pattern will be different every night. Once you've eliminated meat, you've also shaken free of cut-and-dried menu patterns. The chief constraint now is the need for nutritional balance, and within that framework anything goes. Here are a few pointers on successful planning.

◄ Soups are a traditional starting point for the evening meal—but if you've come up with a good thick minestrone, why go any further? Add crackers and a green salad for a simple, delicious meal. If you're serving a one-vegetable blended soup, or a milk chowder, you can always lace the salad with a few other raw or cooked vegetables for variety, color, and nutritional benefits.

◄ Serve only one "hefty" dish: a casserole, perhaps, a bread, a thick bean stew, or a salad like Tabouli or potato salad.

◄ If a rich sauce accompanies the vegetables, use a light dressing for the salad. Similarly, if you're serving two vegetables and one is sauced, serve the other plain. Otherwise, it's easy to end up serving oil or butter in some form with every single course.

◄ Be artful in your use of color, texture, "family," raw or cooked, etc. For instance, don't serve yellow squash, carrots, and corn bread together—or coleslaw, potatoes, and cauliflower. Watch out that your sauces don't clash inordinately: for instance, Sweet and Sour Mustard Sauce is a bit much with Sesame Dressing (one of our more piquant offerings). Similarly, a cream sauce will lose some of its appeal if the salad dressing is milk-based also.

With this sort of cautionary note in mind, mix and match with a free and adventurous hand. Sometimes you'll be putting together a menu and find you've created a slot for something you have no recipe for, and that's when the fun starts ("I need a dark brown bread that's got a lot of crunch and isn't too sweet" or "a sauce that's mellow, pale, and not too heavy"). The menus on page 287 will get you started, but it won't take long at all for you to discover how much leeway you really have.

Salads

Serve them before your main course, as most Americans do, or afterwards, in the Italian tradition, but don't fail to serve a truly splendid salad with every supper. Green salads should be the general rule. Raw leafy greens are an important source of B vitamins that are sometimes lost in cooking—the darker green, the better, as a rule.

We used to begrudge the oil in salad dressings as an unnecessary source of calories. We've since learned, though, that it plays a valuable role. Most cold-pressed vegetable oils are well endowed with polyunsaturated fatty acids and vitamin E, and salad dressings may be the only uncooked source in your diet. Taking cost and flavor into account as well as food value, we prefer safflower oil for general use. Corn oil and sesame seed oil are fine too. Soy oil is inexpensive and good for you, but it's rather heavy for salads. Olive oil is expensive, but it certainly gives that air of authenticity to a Greek salad or a ratatouille. Keep a variety of cold-pressed vegetable oils around for different purposes (and don't neglect to refrigerate them—rancid oil is no joke).

Variety is the key, in fact, to serving salad bowls that get emptied every night, to the last leaf. Never be mechanical about the salad course, because there's always some little thing you can add at the last minute to give it heightened appeal. Our recipes suggest a number of delicious combinations of greens, vegetables, beans, cheeses, and croutons, and we encourage you to make up your own as well. Here are our suggestions for the perfect green salad.

❧ Use lettuce that is fresh, crisp, clean, cold, and dry. We dry it gently on a clean terry towel. You can wash and dry lettuce and put it in a bag or crisper in the refrigerator, then cut and dress it just before serving.

ళ Try several varieties of lettuce in one salad: romaine, red leaf, butter, and loose leaf make good combinations. You can probably grow them all in your backyard garden. Fresh spinach, watercress, and young, tender beet greens are all nice additions.

ళ Don't toss salads until you're ready to serve the meal. Use dressing at room temperature; it spreads further and coats the lettuce evenly.

ళ To make a salad into a light meal that's perfect for lunch or for dinner on a hot summer evening, select some of these additions:

> *Cooked, marinated garbanzo beans*
> *(or other beans)*
>
> *Small chunks of cheese or tofu*
>
> *Lightly cooked vegetables like fresh corn,*
> *string beans, sliced carrots, broccoli flowers,*
> *or beets (chill vegetables with or without*
> *marinade and add to salad before tossing)*
>
> *Raw vegetables like thinly sliced zucchini,*
> *celery, cucumber, cabbage, green pepper,*
> *parsley, finely grated carrot, fresh green peas,*
> *or avocado*
>
> *Croutons (see Soups)*

ళ Fresh herbs add so much to salads—and to other dishes as well. Grow them in a window box or in a plot near your kitchen that is shaded for part of the day. Mince fresh herbs thoroughly to bring out all their flavor. When using dried herbs, crush them first by rolling them between your hands; otherwise, the flavors stay locked in.

Dilled Cucumber & Yogurt Salad

1 head leafy lettuce or
    mixed greens
2 cucumbers, thinly sliced
1 cup water
¼ cup vinegar
1 teaspoon dill weed
1 slice raw onion
1 cup yogurt
⅛ teaspoon turmeric
dash pepper
½ teaspoon salt

OPTIONAL
¼ cup diced, cooked
    potatoes

Put water, vinegar, dill, and onion in large jar or bowl. Add cucumber slices and marinate 30 minutes or longer. Drain. Discard onion.

Mix yogurt, salt, pepper, and turmeric. Stir cucumbers and potatoes into the yogurt.

Serve over beds of fresh lettuce leaves which have been washed, dried, and torn into bite-size pieces.

Chef's Salad

1 head leafy lettuce or
    mixed greens
8 cherry tomatoes, halved
½ bell pepper, thinly
    sliced
½ cucumber, diced
½ cup cooked garbanzo
    beans
¼ cup marinade (p. 163)
½ cup diced jack or
    Swiss cheese
2 to 4 tablespoons French
    Dressing (p. 163)
pinch oregano

Chill garbanzos in marinade. Wash and dry lettuce and tear into bite-size pieces. Toss very well with dressing and oregano. Add tomatoes, drained marinated beans, and cucumbers. Toss lightly again, garnish with pepper rings, and sprinkle diced cheese over top.

Sunchoke Salad

Remember Jerusalem artichokes? Now they're called sunchokes.

Steam asparagus lightly and chill in marinade. Wash and dry lettuce and tear into bite-size pieces. Toss grated sunchoke with lemon juice; then add to lettuce along with drained asparagus. Dress, toss well, and serve with a sprinkle of almonds.

1 head leafy lettuce or
mixed greens
1 cup asparagus, cut in
1-inch slices
¼ cup marinade (p. 163)
1 cup grated sunchoke
1 tablespoon lemon juice
¼ cup or more Avocado
Dressing (p. 163)
½ cup toasted, slivered
almonds

Shades of Green Salad

Cook peas. Mix with limas in marinade and chill. Wash and dry greens and tear into bite-size pieces, removing stems from spinach. Drain vegetables and add with seeds to greens. Toss with dressing and serve.

1 head leafy lettuce or
mixed greens
½ bunch spinach
½ cup green peas
½ cup cooked lima
beans
¼ cup marinade (p. 163)
¼ cup toasted sunflower
seeds
¼ cup or more Green
Goddess Dressing
(p. 161)

Tomato Pepper Salad

If your tomatoes are fresh from the garden, this simplest of salads needs no dressing at all.

Use about 1 tomato and ⅓ green pepper per person. Cut tomatoes and peppers into bite-size pieces. Combine and sprinkle generously with basil or parsley, mixing well.

tomatoes, fresh and ripe
green peppers
parsley or fresh basil,
finely chopped

Navy Bean & Cashew Salad

1 head leafy lettuce or
   mixed greens
1 cup broccoli or
   cauliflower pieces
½ cup cooked navy
   beans
¼ cup toasted cashew
   bits
½ cup marinade (p. 163)
¼ cup Avocado Dressing
   (p. 163)
   OR
¼ cup Bleu Cheese
   Dressing (p. 160)

Steam broccoli or cauliflower until tender and combine with navy beans in marinade. Chill.

Wash and dry lettuce and tear into bite-size pieces. Drain marinade from vegetables and beans and add them to lettuce. Add cashew bits and dressing just before serving.

California Tossed Salad

1 head leafy lettuce or
   mixed greens
3 sprigs watercress
½ avocado, in bite-size
   pieces
½ cup sliced cucumber
8 cherry tomatoes, halved
1 cup herbed croutons
2 to 4 tablespoons French
   Dressing, p. 163
   (omit paprika)
dash garlic powder
2 tablespoons Parmesan
   cheese

Wash and dry lettuce and tear into bite-size pieces. Wash and dry watercress and remove stems. Toss the lettuce and watercress thoroughly with dressing and garlic. Add vegetables, croutons, and cheese. Toss lightly again and serve.

Greek Salad

Bake green pepper in oven (it takes an hour) or put under broiler (takes minutes) or toast with a fork over a gas flame until the skin turns black and peels off easily. Peel and chop coarsely. Chill.

Wash and dry lettuce and tear into bite-size pieces. Crumble cheese over the top and add the olives, tomatoes, cucumber, and green pepper.

Pour olive oil over salad and toss well to coat, then add the wine vinegar, salt, and pepper. Toss and serve.

1 head leafy lettuce or mixed greens
2 or more ounces feta cheese
1 handful black olives (Greek, if available)
1 tomato, chopped
½ cucumber, sliced
½ green pepper
2 tablespoons olive oil
2 teaspoons wine vinegar
salt and pepper to taste

Mexican Salad Bowl

Chill kidney beans in marinade. Wash and dry lettuce and tear into bite-size pieces. Toss well with dressing and seasonings. Add the vegetables and drained beans and toss lightly. Sprinkle cheese over top and serve.

1 head leafy lettuce or mixed greens
½ avocado, cubed
½ green pepper, diced small
½ cup chopped tomatoes
¾ cup cooked kidney beans
¼ cup marinade (p. 163)
½ cup grated cheddar cheese
2 to 4 tablespoons French Dressing (p. 163)
½ teaspoon oregano, crushed

OPTIONAL
dash cumin powder

Yogurt Rice

2 cups brown rice
4 cups water
1½ teaspoons salt
2 tablespoons finely
   minced fresh ginger
½ green pepper
2 cups yogurt

This is especially good for picnics and box lunches. Although usually served cold, it is just as good warmed up. If you heat it, a little water in the bottom of the pan will keep it from sticking.

Cook rice in salted water for about 45 minutes.

Chop green pepper fine and add to rice along with ginger and yogurt. Cool and allow rice and yogurt to marinate for a few hours.

Makes 4 cups.

Hot or Cold Potato Salad

4 or 5 potatoes
¼ cup water from
   cooking potatoes
2 tablespoons vinegar
½ teaspoon celery seed
1 tablespoon minced
   fresh onion
pinch rosemary
1 teaspoon salt
dash pepper
pinch mustard powder
1 grated carrot
3 stalks celery, diced
   small
2 tablespoons mayon-
   naise (p. 160)
2 tablespoons dried skim
   milk
2 tablespoons buttermilk

Scrub, cube, and boil potatoes until tender. Save water for bread.

Bring to a boil ¼ cup potato water, vinegar, onion, celery seed, and rosemary. Pour over potatoes.

Make a paste of buttermilk and milk powder, mix with mayonnaise, and stir into potatoes along with remaining ingredients. Serve hot or refrigerate overnight. If served the next day, adjust seasonings; you'll probably need more salt.

Serves 6.

Provincial Salad

Mix the green beans in marinade and chill along with potatoes and peas. While vegetables are chilling, wash and dry lettuce and tear into bite-size pieces. Toss well with dressing and tarragon. Drain vegetables and add to lettuce. Toss lightly.

*1 head leafy lettuce or
   mixed greens
⅔ cup cooked, diced
   potatoes
1 cup cooked green
   beans, 1-inch slices
¼ cup marinade (p. 163)
¼ cup cooked green peas
¼ cup Russian Dressing
   (p. 160)
¼ teaspoon tarragon*

Tabouli

This Lebanese bean and wheat salad makes a great luncheon dish. The combination of garlic and fresh mint gives it an unusual piquancy. Don't miss it!

Bring stock to a boil with salt. Add cracked wheat slowly and keep boiling for 5 minutes. Remove from heat, cover pot tightly, and set aside for 2 hours. If you use bulgur wheat, just bring to boil, cover, and set aside for 1 hour.

Drain off excess water and chill the grain. Toss thoroughly with all ingredients, taste for seasoning, and serve on bed of lettuce.

Makes 6 generous servings.

*1½ cups uncooked
   cracked wheat or
   bulgur wheat
3 cups vegetable stock
   or water
1 teaspoon salt
½ cup cooked white
   beans
2 tomatoes, chopped
3 tablespoons oil
pepper to taste
pinch garlic
2 tablespoons chopped
   chives
2 teaspoons chopped
   fresh mint leaves
juice of at least 2 lemons
¼ cup chopped parsley
lettuce*

Coleslaw

½ head cabbage, red
    and/or green
¼ cup mayonnaise
    (p. 160)
¼ cup fresh lemon juice
    or vinegar
salt to taste

OPTIONAL
buttermilk

Cabbage is a fine source of vitamin C and is available year-round at low cost. There was a time when our family was indifferent to coleslaw unless it was loaded with, say, fresh pineapple or raisins, but gradually they've developed a real fondness for even the simplest version.

Shred cabbage and dress. Unlike green salad, coleslaw can be dressed ahead of serving time, and is in fact still very good the next day. Use buttermilk if you enjoy a well-dressed slaw but want to keep the calorie count low. We're enthusiastic about all of the optional additions, but would caution you against including more than two at a time unless you're pretty sure what you're up to. The fruit additions aren't always compatible with the vegetables, except for carrots.

Serves 4.

VARY WITH
dill weed
tarragon
caraway seeds
poppy seeds
toasted sunflower seeds
chopped walnuts

slivered almonds
raisins or dates
chopped dried apricots
fresh pineapple or orange
    chunks
grated apples
cardamom (with fruit)

green beans, cooked
grated carrots
corn off the cob, cooked
minced green pepper
chopped celery
minced parsley
shoestring beets, cooked

Antipasto

With a simple soup and Whole Wheat French Bread, here's a summertime dinner that's unbeatable.

Peel broccoli stems and slice. Cut cauliflower into attractive flowerets and slice asparagus spears into 2-inch pieces. Snip ends off whole green beans. Steam the first group of vegetables briefly until tender but crisp. Give the beans a head start, then add others (asparagus and mushrooms last). Chill in marinade along with garbanzos for several hours.

Slice zucchini very thin and cut the pepper in thin rings. The celery sticks should be about 2 inches long. The zucchini, green pepper, celery, and tomato can be served raw, either plain or sprinkled lightly with oregano, olive oil, and vinegar.

Arrange vegetables, beans, olives, and cheese attractively on a large platter.

whole small mushrooms
broccoli, flowers and
    stems
cauliflower
asparagus spears
whole green beans
artichoke hearts
marinade (p. 163)

zucchini
green pepper
celery sticks
tomato wedges
olives
garbanzo or kidney beans,
    cooked
cubes of Italian cheese:
    fontinella, provolone,
    or mozzarella

OPTIONAL
crushed oregano leaves
olive oil
vinegar

Summer Salad

Take corn off cob and chill. Steam cabbage briefly, so it's still crunchy, and chill. Wash and dry spinach leaves and tear into bite-size pieces. Mix vegetables together, add dressing, and toss well.

1 large bunch spinach
3 ears corn, cooked
¼ to ½ head cabbage,
    shredded
2 to 4 tablespoons
    Orange-Sesame
    Dressing (p. 161)

Spinach & Mushroom Salad

1 pound fresh spinach
¼ pound raw mush-
    rooms, thinly sliced
1 to 2 tablespoons
    Parmesan cheese
½ cup garlic-flavored
    whole wheat croutons
French Dressing to taste
    (p. 163)

Wash and dry spinach leaves and tear into bite-size pieces. Add all ingredients and toss well with salad dressing.

Vegetable Relish

2 cups shredded green
    cabbage, packed
½ cup grated carrot,
    packed
¼ cup very thinly sliced
    onion
½ cup very thinly sliced
    green pepper
1 teaspoon salt
dash pepper
6 tablespoons vinegar

This crisp and tangy relish goes well in sandwiches, and just a spoonful can enliven very simple dinners.

Combine all vegetables. Mix salt, pepper, vinegar, and water. Stir together and refrigerate, tightly covered, overnight.

Makes 3½ cups.

Raita

1½ cups yogurt
1 cup finely chopped raw
    vegetables
2 teaspoons finely minced
    fresh ginger
dash cayenne
dash curry powder

Raita is an Indian salad, refreshing and low in calories. Two or three spoonfuls makes an ample serving.

Stir vegetables into yogurt, choosing two or more of these: radishes, cucumber, green pepper, green onions, tomatoes, or beets. Season with cayenne, curry powder, and fresh ginger.

Chutneys

If you've only eaten the heavy, sweet chutneys sold in the gourmet section of the supermarket, you won't recognize these much lighter, tangier condiments as chutneys. They are quite traditional, though. Enjoy them in small amounts with the vegetable dishes described on pages 220 to 223. Coriander, also known as cilantro and Chinese parsley, is an unusually delectable herb. It is available in many fresh produce markets, but if you take to it as enthusiastically as we have, you will want to grow it in your own garden.

COCONUT CHUTNEY

Blend coconut into a coarse, moist powder in a dry blender. Be sure the blades are more than covered by coconut. Stop and start the blender frequently to protect the motor. Add ginger, green onions, lemon juice, and a little salt if you like. Blend again.

Makes about 1 cup.

1 cup dried coconut
juice of 1 lemon
1 tablespoon finely minced fresh ginger
2 green onions, finely minced
OPTIONAL
salt

PEPPERMINT OR CORIANDER CHUTNEY

Chop onions, including tender part of tops. Wash and chop peppermint or coriander leaves. Put lemon juice into blender and add a small amount of leaves at a time, until a paste is formed. Blend onions and ginger with leaves, a little at a time.

Makes about ¾ cup.

juice of 3 lemons
2 cups peppermint or coriander leaves
3 or 4 green onions
1 tablespoon finely minced fresh ginger
OPTIONAL
salt

VARIATION

The combination of coconut chutney and peppermint or coriander chutney, thoroughly mixed, is excellent.

Homemade Mayonnaise

1 egg
½ teaspoon salt
½ teaspoon mustard
  powder
2 tablespoons cider
  vinegar
1 cup oil

Put egg, salt, mustard, and vinegar in blender with ¼ cup oil. Blend on low, uncover, and slowly but steadily pour in remaining oil.

Atmospheric conditions will occasionally cause mayonnaise to curdle as you're making it. If this should happen, remove it from blender, put another egg into the blender, turn it on, and slowly pour in curdled mayonnaise.

Makes 1¼ cups.

Russian Dressing

½ cup oil
2 tablespoons tomato
  paste
¼ cup mayonnaise
3 tablespoons vinegar
½ teaspoon salt
¼ teaspoon paprika
¼ teaspoon mustard
  powder

Mix all ingredients together very well. Makes 1 cup.

Bleu Cheese Dressing

1 ounce bleu cheese
2 tablespoons mayonnaise
2 tablespoons lemon juice
  or vinegar
2 tablespoons cottage
  cheese
2 tablespoons buttermilk
¼ teaspoon salt
dash dill weed
pinch garlic powder
pinch white pepper

Crumble bleu cheese with a fork and combine with remaining ingredients.

Makes a scant ½ cup.

Green Goddess Dressing

Good on cabbage as well as lettuce salads.

Blend everything except mayonnaise. Stir with mayonnaise.

Makes a little more than ½ cup.

½ cup mayonnaise
¼ cup yogurt
¼ cup chopped parsley
1 teaspoon chopped
    fresh chives
2 teaspoons vinegar
¼ teaspoon salt
dash pepper
½ teaspoon basil

Sesame Dressing

This dressing is fine with or without parsley. Put all ingredients in blender and blend until nearly smooth. Refrigerate.

Makes ½ to ¾ cup.

½ cup oil
¼ cup toasted sesame
    seeds
2 tablespoons lemon juice
½ teaspoon salt

OPTIONAL
1 cup chopped parsley

Orange-Sesame Dressing

Toast sesame seeds by heating in a dry frying pan on medium heat. Grind them in blender. Shake all ingredients together in a jar, or blend.

Makes ¾ to 1 cup.

ORANGE-CELERY DRESSING
Omit the sesame seeds and add ½ cup chopped celery leaves. Blend.

¼ cup sesame seeds
¼ cup oil
2 tablespoons lemon juice
1 tablespoon vinegar
½ teaspoon salt
⅛ teaspoon celery seed
⅛ teaspoon cumin
⅛ teaspoon paprika
½ orange, chopped

Lemon Parsley Dressing

½ cup oil
2 teaspoons cider
   vinegar
juice of 1 lemon
1 cup chopped parsley
½ teaspoon salt
¼ teaspoon marjoram
2 teaspoons chopped
   green pepper
dash pepper

Place all ingredients in blender and blend until parsley is fine.
   Makes almost 1 cup.

Broccoli Dressing

1 cup cooked broccoli,
   mainly flowers
¼ cup oil
¼ cup wine vinegar
pinch basil
dash each: dill weed,
   cumin, pepper
1 tablespoon tomato
   sauce
¼ teaspoon salt

This sounds strange, but it is one of our favorites. It bears a curious resemblance to guacamole.
   Blend all ingredients thoroughly in blender.
   Makes about 1 cup creamy green dressing.

Curry Dressing

1 cup oil
½ cup vinegar
½ teaspoon salt
½ teaspoon brown sugar
¼ teaspoon mustard
   powder
¼ teaspoon curry powder

Shake all ingredients together in covered jar. Makes 1⅓ cups.

French Dressing

Shake all ingredients together in a jar. Makes just over ½ cup.

½ cup oil
2 teaspoons lemon juice
2 tablespoons cider or
   wine vinegar
¼ teaspoon salt
¼ teaspoon mustard
   powder
¼ teaspoon paprika
dash pepper
OPTIONAL
¼ teaspoon basil
   or tarragon

CREAMY FRENCH DRESSING

Add 2 teaspoons tomato paste or 1 tablespoon ketchup (page 228) to French Dressing and whisk thoroughly until mixed.

OIL AND VINEGAR MARINADE

Omit lemon juice entirely and increase the vinegar to 3 tablespoons. More herbs may be added, or a slice of onion and/or a clove of garlic. Be sure to discard onion and garlic when you drain marinated foods. When you have marinated vegetables, you will find that the leftover marinade contains a good deal of vegetable juice, which is replete with water-soluble vitamins and minerals. Its flavor is mild, as the vegetables have absorbed most of the vinegar, so feel free to add it to soups and sauces.

Avocado Dressing

Mash avocado with fork. Shake all ingredients together in a jar or put everything into a blender and blend very briefly on low speed.

    Makes 1 cup.

2 tablespoons oil
1 large ripe avocado
3 tablespoons lemon juice
½ teaspoon salt
dash pepper
dash chili powder

OPTIONAL
dash garlic powder

Soups

A well-prepared soup can be the first course of a memorable meal, or it can be a delicious meal in its own right. We're partial to light suppers, so soup is likely to have top billing several nights a week.

In our pre-vegetarian days, we'd have sworn that meat or chicken stock was indispensable to a good soup—a prejudice that others must hold too, because a good many vegetarian cookbooks continue to call for beef-flavored bouillon cubes for soups. Nothing could be sillier. You can make excellent, full-flavored soup stock at home out of the snippets and trimmings from vegetables: tips of green beans and zucchini, winter squash peelings, pea pods, spinach and parsley stems, and carrot ends (and *especially* green tops). Remember, as vegetarians you're probably generating more of these little treasures than was your wont. Avoid the brassica family (cabbages, etc.), as they get a very strong flavor when boiled. Wash all vegetable trimmings and store them in a jar or plastic bag until you have a good quart or more. Put them in a pan, cover them with cold water, and add salt—it pulls the flavors into the stock. Place a lid on the pan and bring it to a boil. Simmer for 20 minutes or so, until the vegetables are cooked but not overcooked. Strain the stock immediately, cool, and refrigerate. Use this vegetable stock for soups and sauces and for cooking grains.

A nicely flavored stock adds a good deal to any soup—minerals and vitamins as well as flavor—but in fact, it *isn't* indispensable. Water can be used instead in most of our soup recipes. If you feel the need of a more savory broth, just sauté and add chopped onion or celery, or increase the parsley and other herbs. Do not (need we add?) use MSG. For milk soups, of course, no stock is needed. Pea and bean soups are good with or without it.

Try all of our soup recipes, but don't fail to develop your own as well. Here's a stripped-down, basic technique you might start with.

Basic Vegetable Soup

Sauté a chopped onion in oil or margarine until it is soft. Add some chopped celery or green pepper if you like. Pour in vegetable stock and herbs and bring the pot to a boil. Add whatever vegetables are in season, chopped attractively. Start with the slow-cooking ones like potatoes, carrots, and green beans, and end with delicate greens like spinach and chard. Leftover grains, beans, or noodles are always welcome. The more you add of starchy foods like potato, barley, or winter squash, the more body the broth itself will have. In fact, you may want to toss a handful of uncooked split peas or barley into the soup stock and cook *before* adding the vegetables.

You may prefer, especially if you're preparing soup for more than four people, to cook all or part of the vegetables separately, adding them to the pot at the last minute. This prevents their being overcooked and preserves their color. It's especially important when the stock is tomato-based.

This simple, basic vegetable soup is obviously a perfect way to use up little odds and ends from the garden, but made with a delicately flavored broth and just the right herbs, it can be a superb dish.

Minestrone

1 onion, finely chopped
¼ cup olive oil
1½ cups chopped celery
4 cups grated fresh
    tomatoes
      OR
1 large can tomatoes
    with juice
      OR
1 six-ounce can tomato
    paste & 3 cups vege-
    table stock
½ cup chopped parsley
salt to taste
dash pepper
1 or 2 bay leaves
1 teaspoon oregano
2 teaspoons basil
½ teaspoon rosemary
dash garlic
2 cups or more, chopped:
    carrot, zucchini, broc-
    coli, potato, green
    beans, green pepper,
    cabbage, peas, corn,
    sautéed mushrooms
1 cup cooked lima,
    kidney, pinto, black,
    or garbanzo beans, or
    sautéed mushrooms
½ cup raw whole wheat
    noodles or broken
    whole wheat spaghetti
½ cup cooked barley or
    whole wheat berries

Minestrone is a generic term for a richly flavored, tomato-based soup which welcomes infinite variation, according to your family's taste and needs. It can appear as a light, fragrant vegetable soup on summer evenings or, most memorably, as a hearty stew for a cold winter day. Either way, Minestrone is a wonderful meal in itself with green salad and Whole Wheat French Bread. Begin with this tomato soup recipe as a base and include any of the suggested grains, beans, and vegetables.

Sauté onion and celery in oil until soft. Add the tomatoes or tomato paste and stock, parsley, and seasonings. If you prefer a thicker soup, stir in the ground soybeans; if you like it thinner, add more stock. Simmer the soup while you prepare whatever grains, beans, and vegetables you wish to add.

At least 30 minutes before serving the soup, add the cooked beans, the raw noodles or spaghetti, and the cooked barley or wheat berries.

Cook the chopped vegetables until they are *nearly* done by steaming or cooking in as little water as possible. Combine with the soup about 10 minutes before serving, including any cooking water. The leafy greens should be added to the pot just 5 minutes before serving. Don't count them as part of the 2 cups of vegetables but add them in as extras, because they cook down to a fraction of their original volume.

After combining all the ingredients, bring the soup to a boil, then simmer for a minute or two while correcting the seasonings. If you like, garnish each bowl with a spoonful of Parmesan cheese.

Makes about 10 cups.

OPTIONAL
½ cup ground soybeans
    or Soy Spread (p. 140)
Parmesan cheese

spinach and/or chard,
    cut into bite-size
    pieces

Greek Lentil Soup

Mix all ingredients, except the vinegar, in a soup pot and cook until the lentils are very soft, about one hour. Add vinegar at the end and serve.

Makes about 8 cups.

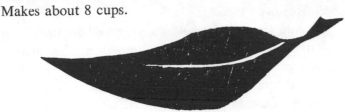

2 cups uncooked lentils
8 cups water or
  vegetable stock
½ onion, chopped
1 small carrot, chopped
1 celery stalk, chopped
1 small potato, chopped
2 tablespoons oil
2 bay leaves
1½ to 2 teaspoons salt
2 teaspoons vinegar

Black Bean Soup

Wash the turtle beans and put them in a saucepan along with the stock and 1 tablespoon of oil. Cover tightly, bring to a boil, and simmer for 2½ hours or so, until beans are quite tender.

Chop the onion and sauté in the remaining oil until soft. Chop the celery, including the leaves. Grate potato and carrot on large grater. Add celery, potato, and carrot to onion and cook over medium heat for several minutes, stirring all the while.

Add the vegetables to the beans, along with the seasonings, in the last hour of their cooking. Include garlic if desired. Bring the soup to a boil and lower the heat to simmer until the beans and vegetables are done.

Add the lemon juice and lemon slices when the soup has finished cooking.

Makes about 9 cups.

1½ cups black turtle
  beans
1½ quarts water or
  vegetable stock
2 tablespoons oil
1 carrot
1 onion
1 potato
2 stalks celery
1 bay leaf
1 teaspoon oregano
¼ teaspoon savory
2 teaspoons salt
⅛ teaspoon pepper
juice of 1 lemon
½ lemon, thinly sliced

OPTIONAL
pinch garlic powder

Vegetable Gumbo Soup

1 onion, chopped
2 tablespoons oil
3 cloves
1 green pepper, diced
2 cups tomatoes, diced
4 cups vegetable stock
1 cup cooked lima beans
1 cup fresh corn
1½ cups sliced okra
1 teaspoon salt
¼ teaspoon allspice

OPTIONAL
½ cup cooked brown
   rice

With a little luck, you'll find a produce market that carries fresh okra. *Vive la différence!*

Sauté the onion and cloves in oil until the onions are soft. Remove the cloves.

Add green pepper and stir over medium heat for several minutes. Then stir in the tomatoes. Bring the mixture to a boil, turn down the heat, and let it simmer for 5 minutes.

Add the rest of the ingredients. If you're using frozen okra, it should be partially thawed and then sliced (or better still, buy it already sliced). Bring soup to a boil again, cover, and simmer for 15 minutes. Add rice if desired.

Makes 8 to 9 cups.

Tomato Soup

3 cups fresh or canned
   tomatoes
1 medium onion
2 stalks celery
2 tablespoons oil or
   margarine
1 carrot
¾ teaspoon oregano
1½ teaspoons basil
1 quart hot vegetable
   stock
1½ teaspoons salt
pepper to taste

Here are two versions of tomato soup: one is plain and the other creamed. When you harvest your tomatoes from the garden you'll want to try both.

Chop the tomatoes into small pieces if you don't mind including the skins, or simply rub them over a grater to get the juice and pulp. Chop the onion and celery and grate the carrot.

Sauté the onion along with the celery and carrot. Cook these vegetables until the onion is soft.

Add oregano, basil, and tomatoes to the pot and simmer gently for 15 minutes. At this point, if you want a smooth, creamy texture, purée the soup in a blender or food mill.

Add the hot stock and bring the soup to a boil. Simmer on low heat for 5 minutes. Season with salt and pepper.

Makes 8 cups. For a thicker soup, use only 2 or 3 cups of stock and reduce seasonings.

Cream of Tomato Soup

Follow the tomato soup recipe, but tone down the herbs, using just ¼ teaspoon oregano, ½ teaspoon basil, and 1 teaspoon salt.

Blend 1 cup of dried skim milk with part of the stock or with the tomato mixture. Pour it back into the pot, add salt and pepper, and heat thoroughly. Do not boil. For a heartier soup, add a cup of cooked brown rice.

Makes 8 cups.

Dumplings

This fluffy, tender dumpling, which bears a faint resemblance to a matzo ball, turns any vegetable soup into a special dish.

The simplest way we know of for making bread crumbs is to use stale bread and grate it; crackers can be crumbled by hand or under a rolling pin.

Cook onions in oil and stock until soft.

Mix dry ingredients and seasonings together. Add very slightly beaten egg and onions. Stir well and refrigerate for at least 20 minutes.

Bring pot of stock to a gentle boil. Divide dumpling dough into 1½-inch balls—you'll get over a dozen. Roll them between your palms to make them smooth and round. Drop them into the stock. Cover the pot and simmer on low heat for 30 to 40 minutes.

Remove the dumplings with a slotted spoon and add them to the soup several minutes before serving. If the soup is very light and simple, you can drop the dumplings directly into the soup and cook as directed above.

Makes 14 to 16 dumplings.

½ cup whole wheat
cracker crumbs
¼ cup whole-grain
bread crumbs
¼ cup oil
¼ cup stock or water
4 green onions, chopped
2 eggs, slightly beaten
¼ cup nut or seed meal
2 teaspoons salt
½ teaspoon oregano
½ teaspoon basil
pot of lightly salted stock
or water

Creamy Green Soup

At its simplest, and some say its best, Creamy Green Soup is cooked, garden-fresh zucchini blended with salt, pepper, and Better-Butter or margarine. With this as a basis you can:

- ◄ enliven with bright red bell peppers or corn off the cob.

- ◄ enhance nutritionally by blending in one or more of the following:

  dried skim milk
  soy powder, ground cooked soybeans,
  *   or toasted soy flour*
  low-fat cottage cheese
  cooked green split peas
  ground sunflower or sesame seeds
  ground cashews or almonds
  2 tablespoons torula yeast
  1 or 2 tablespoons cornmeal soaked in
  *   boiling vegetable stock*

- ◄ vary the texture by blending some ingredients and leaving others chopped or shredded. Try thinning to taste with good vegetable stock or milk.

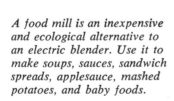

To complete its versatility, Green Soup can be served chilled: top it with a spoonful of yogurt, and add Whole Wheat Crackers with Garbanzo Spread for a refreshing supper on a hot summer evening.

The following version is our current favorite.

A food mill is an inexpensive and ecological alternative to an electric blender. Use it to make soups, sauces, sandwich spreads, applesauce, mashed potatoes, and baby foods.

Sauté the onion and celery in oil until soft. Add 4 cups of stock, split peas, and bay leaf. Bring to a boil, then cover and simmer over low heat for about 40 minutes.

Add zucchini, remaining stock, and seasonings. Cook for another 10 minutes.

Remove bay leaf and discard. Purée soup in a blender, sieve, or food mill. Return to the soup pot and stir in the spinach and parsley. Cook over medium heat for several minutes. Adjust seasonings and serve.

Makes 7 to 8 cups.

½ onion, chopped
2 stalks celery, diced
2 tablespoons oil
6 cups vegetable stock
¾ cup green split peas, rinsed
1 bay leaf
6 cups diced zucchini
¼ teaspoon basil
⅛ teaspoon pepper
2 teaspoons salt
1 pound spinach, washed and chopped
¼ cup chopped fresh parsley

Winter Squash Soup

This delicious soup is a great way to use leftover baked squash.

If you use raw squash or pumpkin, cook it in the broth until it is tender. Blend or purée the cooked squash and put it in your soup pot to heat.

Sauté the onion in the oil, and when the onion is soft, add the parsley. Cook just long enough to soften parsley, then add, along with the seasonings, to the squash in the soup pot.

Remove a cup of the soup and put it in the blender. Add the milk powder and yeast (torula preferably) and blend them until smooth. Pour this mixture back into the soup pot and bring the soup to a simmer. Don't boil or it will stick. For a lighter soup with a strangely satiny texture, omit the milk.

Squash and spinach are the best of friends, so at the very end of the cooking time, add fresh spinach, chopped bite-size, for a colorful and vitamin-rich variation.

Makes about 7 cups.

5 cups cubed raw winter squash
OR
3 cups cooked winter squash
2½ cups vegetable stock
¼ cup chopped onion
1 tablespoon oil
½ cup chopped parsley
2 teaspoons salt
1 teaspoon basil
1 cup dried skim milk
1 tablespoon torula yeast

OPTIONAL
1 pound fresh spinach

Corn Chowder

2 cups water
½ cup chopped onion
½ cup chopped celery
½ cup diced potato
1 cup fresh raw corn
½ cup chopped parsley
2 cups milk
   OR
2 cups light cream sauce
   (p. 230)
1 teaspoon salt
¼ teaspoon pepper
pinch garlic powder
Better-Butter or
   margarine

Simmer the water, onion, celery, potato, and parsley until half cooked, about 10 minutes.

Add the corn. Simmer gently with the other vegetables until nearly done, not more than a few minutes.

Add the 2 cups of milk and bring the soup just to the boiling point without actually boiling. Add seasonings and correct to taste.

Serve piping hot, with a dot of Better-Butter or margarine. Serves 4 to 6.

Asparagus Soup

2 tablespoons oil
2 cups vegetable stock
½ onion
1 medium potato
1½ pounds fresh
   asparagus
4 stalks celery
1½ teaspoons salt
⅛ teaspoon pepper
1 tablespoon whole
   wheat flour
1 cup fresh milk

Dice potato small and chop onion fine. Cook them in 1 cup of stock and 1 tablespoon of the oil for 5 to 10 minutes.

Wash the asparagus and snap off the tough ends. Cut in thin slices. Chop celery small, including leaves.

Add the asparagus, the celery, and remaining vegetable stock to the potatoes and onions. Cook this for 10 minutes, until the vegetables are quite tender. Add the seasonings and blend the whole mixture until it is smooth. Fill the blender no more than half full at a time.

Heat the remaining tablespoon of oil in a small saucepan. Stir in the flour and cook it over medium heat for 1 to 2 minutes. Stir in the milk, little by little, and bring the sauce to a boil. Continue cooking and stirring over medium heat until it just thickens, then add it to the soup and adjust the seasonings to taste.

For an elegant touch, set aside the asparagus tips and steam them separately. Stir them in just before serving, so they will float in the soup.

Makes 6 cups.

Cream of Celery Soup with Cabbage

Sauté onion in oil until soft. Stir in the flour and cook over moderate heat for 2 minutes. Add 2 cups of stock very slowly and bring the sauce just to a boil. Simmer, while stirring, until it thickens.

Blend the rest of the stock with the milk powder. Bring it to a boil in a heavy-bottomed pot. Stir frequently so the milk doesn't burn. Stir in the potatoes, celery, and celery seed. Cook on a low simmer, covered, for 10 to 15 minutes, until the vegetables are soft.

Cut the cabbage in small pieces and add to soup. Simmer again for 5 minutes.

Purée half of these vegetables in a blender or rub them through a sieve. Return them to the soup pot. Stir in the flour-stock mixture, the parsley, and the seasonings.

Makes 8½ cups.

½ onion, chopped
2 tablespoons oil
*2 tablespoons whole
    wheat flour*
*6 cups vegetable stock
    or water*
½ cup dried skim milk
2 medium potatoes, diced
½ bunch celery, diced
¼ teaspoon celery seed
¼ head cabbage
2 teaspoons salt
*¼ cup finely chopped
    parsley*
¼ teaspoon paprika

OPTIONAL
pinch pepper
dash garlic powder

Croutons

Croutons are a good way to use leftover bread ends or bread which is a little stale. They also provide a nutritious, attractive garnish for soups and salads.

Spread bread slices with Better-Butter or margarine, with or without herbs. Stack the slices and cut the stack into ¾-inch cubes. Distribute the cubes in a pie plate and toast in a preheated 250° oven for 30 to 60 minutes, or until crisp. The baking time depends on the age and dryness of the bread.

Makes about 2 cups.

*4 slices whole-grain
    bread*
*1 tablespoon Better-
    Butter or margarine*

OPTIONAL
¼ teaspoon basil
¼ teaspoon oregano
dash garlic powder

Hearty Pea Soup

1 onion, diced
2 tablespoons oil
1 bay leaf
1 teaspoon celery seed
1 cup green split peas
¼ cup barley
½ cup lima beans
10 cups water
2 teaspoons salt
dash pepper
½ teaspoon basil
½ teaspoon thyme
1 carrot, chopped
3 stalks celery, diced
½ cup chopped parsley
1 potato, diced

Sauté onion in oil until soft, along with bay leaf and celery seed. Stir in peas, barley, and limas. Add 10 cups cold water and bring to a boil. Cook on low heat, covered, for about 1 hour and 20 minutes.

Add salt, pepper, vegetables, and herbs. Turn heat down as low as possible and simmer another 30 to 45 minutes. Thin with additional water or stock if necessary.

Makes about 8 to 9 cups.

Whole Beet Borscht

8 beets with tops
1 medium potato, diced
1 small onion, chopped
2 quarts vegetable stock
2 tablespoons oil
2 tablespoons whole
    wheat flour
juice of 1 lemon
2 teaspoons salt
⅛ teaspoon pepper
2 teaspoons brown sugar

OPTIONAL
¼ teaspoon paprika
½ teaspoon dill weed

This borscht recipe takes advantage of the whole beet, including the tender green leafy top which is full of vitamins and minerals. Serve it hot or cold; it's delicious either way. As you're serving, put a spoonful of homemade yogurt in each soup bowl.

Wash the beets and the beet tops. Chop beet tops fine and set them aside. Peel and grate the beets and cook with the potato and onion in the vegetable broth. Simmer the vegetables until they are well cooked.

Mix the oil and flour and cook on low heat for 2 minutes. Add 1 cup of the soup mixture slowly and cook this sauce until it thickens, stirring constantly. Return the sauce to the soup pot.

Season the soup and add the lemon juice. Stir in the chopped beet greens and cook the soup for 5 to 10 minutes more. Taste and adjust the seasonings.

Makes about 3 quarts.

Vegetable Barley Soup

Cook the onions, carrots, celery, and other vegetables in the oil, covered, for about 10 minutes. Add the stock and bring to a boil.

Add the barley and bring to a boil again. Cover and turn down to a low simmer for 45 minutes.

Add the salt and other seasonings quickly, and continue cooking the soup for another 45 minutes. Chop chard or kale in bite-size pieces and add for last 10 minutes.

Stir in the parsley at the last minute and serve steaming hot. You can thin the soup with additional stock or a bit of milk.

Makes 10 to 12 cups.

½ onion, chopped
3 carrots, diced
2 stalks celery, diced
2 parsnips or turnips, diced
1 cup sliced green beans
OR
1 cup fresh green peas
¼ cup oil
½ pound chard or kale
2 quarts hot vegetable stock or hot water
1 cup whole barley, uncooked
2 teaspoons salt
⅛ teaspoon pepper
½ teaspoon marjoram
½ teaspoon thyme
2 tablespoons chopped parsley

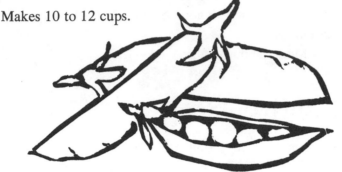

Xergis

On hot summer evenings, this flavorful Levantine beverage is a refreshing first course.

Peel cucumbers and remove seeds. Chop the cucumbers, onion, and garlic fine. Put cucumber, onion, and garlic in blender with part of yogurt, oil, dill weed, salt, and pepper. Blend. Pour out some of the mixture, add remaining yogurt, and blend again. Combine and chill.

Makes 6 cups.

3 cucumbers
1 onion
1 small clove garlic
OR
dash garlic powder
5 cups yogurt
1 teaspoon oil
4 teaspoons dill weed
1 teaspoon salt
dash pepper

Potato-Cheese Soup

4 cups sliced potatoes
2 cups water or vegetable
    stock
2 teaspoons salt
1 small onion, sliced
1 tablespoon oil
5 sprigs parsley
3 cups fresh milk
1 cup grated cheese
2 tablespoons margarine
    or Better-Butter
¼ teaspoon pepper
pinch garlic powder

Great for winter evenings, with a dark rye bread and a fine green salad.

Cook the potatoes in water with salt until tender. Reserve cooking water.

Sauté the onion in oil until it's soft. Then place some of the potatoes, the potato water, the onion, and parsley in a blender and purée with the blender no more than half full, until all the potatoes are smooth.

Return the potato mixture to the pot and add the milk. Stirring continuously, add the cheese, margarine, and seasonings. Heat until the cheese is melted and the soup is hot, but do not boil. Thin with additional stock if necessary and adjust seasonings.

Makes about 9 cups.

Manybean Soup

1 onion, chopped
¼ cup oil
1½ teaspoons paprika
1 cup pinto beans
8 to 10 cups water or
    vegetable stock
1 tablespoon celery seed
1 bay leaf
1 cup kidney beans
1 cup lima beans
1 cup yellow split peas
1½ teaspoons dill weed
4 teaspoons salt
¼ teaspoon pepper

OPTIONAL
chopped vegetables

Sauté onion lightly in oil, with paprika.

Rinse pinto beans in cold water and add them to the onion along with *4 cups* of the water or stock, celery seed, and bay leaf. Partially cover the pot and cook for about 1 hour.

Wash and add kidney beans and limas; add more liquid too if much has boiled away. Cook another hour, still partially covered.

Rinse and add the split peas, dill, salt, and pepper. Be sure there is enough liquid to keep the soup soupy. Cook another hour, partially covered. For Manybean Stew, you can add chunks of celery, carrot, and potato, or whatever vegetables you like, halfway through this hour. Correct the seasonings and serve.

Makes 8 to 10 cups of soup in about 3 hours.

Vegetables

During our early days of vegetarian cooking, our chief concern was just to fill the part of the plate that meat used to occupy. That meant casseroles. The vegetable side was still just a spoonful of cooked carrots, a mound of green beans.

Gradually, though, with the advent of a garden, vegetables crept to the forefront. Now they are the focal point of most of our dinners—as well they should be, considering the wealth of color, texture, taste, and food value they bring to a meal (not to mention the calories they *don't* bring).

We vastly prefer and recommend using only fresh vegetables. One obvious reason is that they are nutritionally superior to canned, dried, and frozen foods. Their flavor, too, is much livelier, and that's important: you can't expect people to be very enthusiastic about a vegetable plate made up of the flat, tasteless, months-old residents of a deep freeze.

If you have room to start a garden of your own, please do. The hours we spend in the fresh air, tending the plants that will nourish our family and friends, are among the most satisfying of each week. Even if you have no backyard, there may well be a vacant lot nearby where you could have a plot. All over the country now, bits and pieces of unused lands around churches and schools are turning into cooperative gardens. In fact, some businesses which are surrounded by open spaces are turning parcels over to their employees for lunch-hour gardening. So investigate all the possibilities. The only danger is that of addiction: you may quickly spoil your palate for anything short of the real garden-fresh thing.

Even the most vitamin-rich, mineral-rich, organically grown, vine-ripened tomato or string bean can be denuded of its nutritional value if we don't treat it properly. It starts with harvesting: when you're picking vegetables, don't allow them to stand in the sun and wilt. Whisk them into the refrigerator right away, or, if you're delayed, cover them up. If you're harvesting them from a supermarket, the principle is the same. Even if the price is right, don't buy wilted-looking produce. It's no bargain. Don't buy more than a few days' supply, either. Potatoes, carrots, winter squash, and the like can hang around for weeks if stored correctly. Most of the others aren't that sturdy, particularly the leafy greens. Make a practice of using the most delicate vegetables first. Store potatoes, onions, and uncut winter squashes outside the refrigerator in cool, well-ventilated cupboards or cellars. The atmosphere should be moist enough so they don't dry out, but not so damp they mold. To keep other vegetables crisp and vitamin-rich, store them airtight in the refrigerator, in plastic bags, or in a humidifier. Tomatoes that are not overripe may be stored at room temperature (that doesn't mean on a hot windowsill) for up to a week.

The nutrients in question here are the B vitamins and vitamin C, which are all water-soluble. Fat-soluble vitamins like A are in no hurry to take flight, but C and the B's have to be guarded carefully. Air (oxygen, to be exact), heat, and water are the three major vitamin thieves, so handling and cooking procedures for vegetables should minimize exposure to all three. Wash them quickly, and don't soak them, especially once they're cut. Be particularly vigilant in this regard with leafy greens. To avoid long exposure to air and light, cut vegetables just before you cook them, and if there's any delay at all, cover and refrigerate them. A good many vitamins are susceptible to bright light as well, so keep vegetables covered at all times.

The most frequently committed crime against fresh vegetables is peeling them. The only times you should peel a vegetable are when the peeling is unpalatably tough (most broccoli stems), bitter (turnips), or so rough-skinned it can't be thoroughly scrubbed (an infrequent gnarly carrot). Peeling vegetables doesn't just waste nutrients; it wastes your time.

Cutting vegetables in large chunks exposes minimal surface area to the three vitamin thieves, and preserves flavor and juices as well. On the other hand, smaller pieces cook more quickly, so if they're called for, chop away—especially if you're careful to preserve cooking liquids.

Some vegetables are so attractive in their native shape that it's good to steam them and serve them whole. Artichokes, of course, but tiny crookneck and patty pan squashes also, fall into this category. So does asparagus, and so do broccoli spears. Tender green beans can be cooked whole, with just the ends snipped off. Serve an assortment of these vegetables with Yeast Butter, Soy Gravy, or Cheese Sauce for an ultra-simple dinner.

When we take the time to cut vegetables carefully and evenly, the result is more appealing to the eye and therefore more appetizing. You can cut a carrot in at least eight ways, each one somehow more appropriate than the others for a particular dish. Vegetable chopping has never been quite the same for us since we watched a Japanese friend prepare a lavish supper for twenty-five people. As her knife flashed swiftly and rhythmically across the board, her expression was completely concentrated. She didn't say a word. In just half an hour, she had filled several big bowls with vegetables, all cut in pretty, perfectly uniform little shapes. In other parts of the world, like India or China, this humble art is taken for granted. The swiftness we don't need to worry about, but the artfulness we can certainly emulate, proof again that even the simplest daily act is worth our full, loving attention.

It might seem that eating vegetables raw would guarantee our getting the most nutrients, but it isn't quite that simple. Certainly, since vitamin C is particularly destructible by heat, some raw source of vitamin C should be eaten every day. On the other hand, cooking a vegetable breaks down its cellulose structure and makes other vitamins *more* accessible than they would be otherwise. Proper cooking methods can preserve well over 90 percent of the nutrients.

The cooking methods we prefer are steaming and the so-called waterless method, where vegetables actually cook in their own juices. In both these methods, steam fills the space in the pan around the vegetables, so that oxygen can't rob them of vitamins. Since the vegetables aren't standing in water, the water-soluble B vitamins and minerals stay put. The small amount of liquid left after cooking vegetables by the waterless method and the water used for steaming them should be kept and added to your vegetable stock supply.

Vegetables cooked in a pressure cooker can retain a greater percentage of certain vitamins than those cooked by other methods. Timing has to be very accurate, though, for cooking takes place so rapidly that vegetables are easily over-cooked. A few weeks' trial and error and the knack is easily picked up. So for cooks whose time is constrained, a pressure cooker can be a real lifesaver. Follow the instructions carefully, though—pressure cooker mishaps are quite unnecessary and no fun at all.

STEAMING VEGETABLES

Purchase a collapsible steamer basket—the kind that opens flowerlike to fit small or large pots. In fact, they're such treasures that you might purchase *two*. Nothing could be simpler to use. Bring an inch of water to boil in a saucepan. Plunk your magic basket into the pan, place the vegetables in the basket, put the lid on (a close-fitting one, please), and drop the heat to medium, just high enough to keep the water bubbling. Vegetables cook very quickly this way, and require minimal attention from the cook.

THE WATERLESS METHOD

Here, the vital piece of equipment is a pan which distributes heat evenly all around (sides and lid as well as bottom) and which has a close-fitting lid. Vegetables contain enough water to steam by themselves once they are heated if the heat is coming from all sides. We prefer iron pots. (We know that this entails loss of a certain amount of vitamin C, which reacts with iron; but the gain in usable iron is so great, and so needed, that we think it outweighs the partial loss of C.) Acidic foods like tomatoes are highly reactive in contact with iron, producing a harmless but unattractive change in color. For this reason, you shouldn't add lemon juice or vinegar to vegetables cooking in an iron pot.

Preheat the pot or pan and place two tablespoons of water in it, to provide steam until the vegetables release their own. When the water boils, add vegetables, cover, and turn the heat down low after a couple of minutes. Cooking time will be longer than with steaming.

In place of the water, you may put two tablespoons of oil or margarine into the preheated pan and stir the vegetables to coat them. The oil will seal in nutrients and will of course add to flavor. Remember, though, you're *not* frying them but sautéing them lightly. Be especially careful not to brown cabbage or its cousins (broccoli or brussels sprouts, for instance). When cooking any of these vegetables, add a small amount of water after you've stirred cut-up vegetables into the hot oil, cover, and proceed as above.

One thing should be kept in mind when using heavy cooking pots: they retain heat for a long time. So if you have to hold the vegetables for tardy biscuits or a late diner, take the pots off the flame well before the vegetables are cooked through. Left in the pots with the lid on, they will continue to cook gently.

COOKING IN MILK

Any strong-flavored vegetables, and greens in general, benefit from being cooked in milk. Strong flavors are evidence of acidity, which the alkalinity of milk neutralizes beautifully. You will be amazed to discover how sweet cabbage, turnips, and chard are when cooked in milk, and how much brighter their color is, too. The same goes for kale, spinach, brussels sprouts, cauliflower, and broccoli. The real surprise is that the milk too is sweet and flavorful. Not at all strong, it's a real asset for cream soups or sauces. Use reconstituted powdered milk for this. If you mix it only half strength, it will still do its job but won't be as likely to scorch (the one hazard in this method).

Here, too, heavy pans are helpful. Preheat the milk just to scalding, then add the vegetables, put the lid on, and simmer, stirring frequently with a wooden spoon. If you stir them often, you won't need to worry about completely immersing them.

COOKING TIMES

As you may have noticed, we are reluctant to recommend cooking times. The variables in vegetable cookery are considerable, and so are the variables in taste. Suppose you're cooking green beans. How old are they? How big? Are they tough and stringy? What size pieces have you cut them into?

What about the pan—how thick is it, and how even a conductor? Is your stove gas or electric? All these factors count, so that the cooking time might vary by as much as 10 minutes one way or the other.

Generally speaking, we encourage you to push back the timer little by little. You may find, as we certainly did, that you are missing a great deal of flavor and texture (to say nothing of vitamins) by overcooking vegetables. This is particularly so of the brassica family (cabbage, cauliflower, brussels sprouts), whose sulfur compounds break down with long cooking to release obnoxious flavors and aromas.

Cooking time for different vegetables will vary from 8 minutes for sliced asparagus, garden peas, or corn to roughly 10 minutes for ¼-inch pieces of zucchini. Try 12 minutes for ¼-inch pieces of carrot and broccoli stems, and up to 20 minutes for reasonably tender green beans or broccoli spears. Artichokes will take anywhere from 30 to 45 minutes.

When you are steaming *mixed* vegetables, simply cut the ones that require longer cooking times into thinner pieces. You can of course add them in order of their cooking time, but it's a shame to open the pot at intervals and release the steam.

We'd like now to introduce our favorite friends from the vegetable patch, one by one. In some parts of India, the proper response to an introduction is to say, "Sing me his praise." This is our intention: to proclaim the virtues of each and tell you how best we think they can be enjoyed.

In terms of sound nutrition and even aesthetics, *simplest* is best, especially if a vegetable is garden-grown. Freshly harvested spinach, for instance, is so sweet and delectable it seems almost a shame to cook it, let alone cream it. Growing your own vegetables is a good way to help your family enjoy them unadorned.

Another way is to serve a wide variety. Don't stop with spinach; explore all the hundred and one kinds of leafy greens. Even the strong ones like mustard greens hit the spot now and then. Bok choy is excellent, and so are kale and Swiss chard. When you see a stranger on display in the produce section, bring him home for dinner, no matter how odd he might look. If we hadn't, we'd never have met the jicama—a recent arrival from Mexico whose crisp, juicy texture and fine flavor make a real difference in tossed salads.

We haven't provided recipes for anywhere near all the vegetables we actually eat, largely because most of them are best cooked in a very straight forward style, by steaming or using the waterless method. Others we haven't given recipes for because they are often not available at a reasonable price. When we *do* purchase mushrooms, and when fresh peas *are* in season, we're never at a loss to know what to do with them, and we doubt you will be either. (Though while we're here, a plea is in order in the name of mushrooms: don't wash them; wipe them with a damp cloth. And don't overcook them, either. Slice them a good ¼ inch thick and sauté them briefly.)

Mingled here and there among the recipes and serving ideas that follow, you will find some intentionally rough outlines of recipes. These are meant for you to fill in and carry out as you like. Don't be frustrated at their vagueness. When amounts are unspecified, it's because you have quite a bit of latitude, and you probably know better than we do how much squash your family can eat at a sitting. We include these suggestions in an effort to convey to you our own habitual way of cooking vegetables, which has almost nothing to do with recipes. Once you've acquired a feel for the cooking times of particular vegetables—and that doesn't take long—you needn't be bound by recipes at all. Treat ours as points of departure. Make use of foods that are in season and prepare them with the tastes and special nutritional needs of your own family in mind.

We were tempted to cross-reference this section with reminders like "Don't miss Rutabaga Soup on page 32," but have decided that after all, that's what indexes are for. So before you decide what to do with that bumper harvest of chard, don't stop here—turn to the Index and alert yourself to *all* the possibilities. Whenever we capitalize the name of a sauce or other dish, that means it's one of our own recipes. Page references are given only when it's not obvious in what section that recipe will be found.

Artichokes

Artichokes are California's own. The highway south from Berkeley to Big Sur takes you through Watsonville, with its funky banner telling you that you've finally made it to the Artichoke Capital of the World. Well might they brag—they're on to a good thing.

It can take anywhere from a half hour to an hour to steam artichokes, depending on size and age. For a gourmet touch, slip a few drops of olive oil down into the leaves and hide a few slivers of garlic clove here and there before cooking. If you have a few minutes, trim the thorns with a sharp knife: the artichoke is much prettier without them, though of course they soften quite adequately with cooking. Serve artichokes hot or cold.

People seem to have rather strong opinions about how best to enjoy artichokes. Some like to have mayonnaise to dip the leaves in; others prefer drawn butter. Still others insist you miss the real joys of artichokes if you drench them in fat. In any case, don't forget to provide a bowl for the gnawed-up byproducts—though it's fascinating to see how differently people cope with them if you don't.

Asparagus

Asparagus ranks right alongside the hyacinth as a sure, spriggy herald of spring. Its season is so brief we never have time to tire of its delicate appeal.

Break the stalks off just above the white part, at the place where they choose to snap. If they're too long to lie across your steamer basket, stand them upright in a coffee pot, with just ½ inch of water in the bottom. Steam for no more than

20 minutes, if that. They should still be bright green, and flexible but not limp. Serve with Lemon Butter, or just lemon, or sprinkle lightly with Parmesan cheese. If you'd like the piquancy of hollandaise sauce without all its calories, try our Buttermilk Sauce or Sunshine Sauce.

For ASPARAGUS CHINOISE, slice asparagus diagonally into 2-inch lengths and sauté in a little oil; add sliced water chestnuts at the very last minute, and a few drops of soy sauce.

Give a new twist to Ratatouille (p. 216) by stirring in a cup of asparagus pieces for the last 10 minutes of cooking time—and before the season is past, make Asparagus Soup at least once.

Slivered and toasted almonds are an especially tasty garnish for cooked asparagus spears. They've found their way into the following recipe, too, in small but effective measure.

Asparagus Patties

Slice asparagus lengthwise and cut small. Steam just until tender.

Sauté onions in oil until soft. Add parsley; stir to wilt.

Combine almond meal, bread crumbs, salt, and cooked grain. Stir in beaten egg yolks. Add the steamed asparagus, making sure it has cooled somewhat so that it doesn't cook the eggs. Stir in the onions and herbs. Beat egg whites until stiff and fold into asparagus mixture.

Heat a lightly greased Teflon skillet or well-seasoned iron one. Drop batter by spoonfuls and spread to form patties. Brown on each side over medium heat.

Makes about 8 patties.

ZUCCHINI PATTIES

Substitute 2 cups coarsely grated zucchini for asparagus, and sunflower seed meal for almond meal. Increase bread crumbs to 1 cup.

1 pound asparagus
2 or 3 green onions,
  chopped
2 tablespoons oil
2 tablespoons chopped
  parsley or coriander
  leaves
1 teaspoon basil
¼ cup toasted almond
  meal
½ cup bread crumbs
½ teaspoon salt
¼ cup cooked bulgur
  wheat or rice
2 eggs, separated

Beets

Charmed by the rich red of the beet root, we've traditionally given too short shrift to the beet's greatest asset, its leaves, where an abundant store of vitamins and minerals is tucked away. Picked while they're still tender, beet tops are wonderful in salads. Richly endowed with red juice, the leaves share their color liberally when cooked with other vegetables. They can be used nicely, though, in any soup that already has a red base.

Mature beets can be dropped whole into boiling water, or steamed, until tender, when their jackets slip off in the most cooperative way you could imagine. Slice them and serve them hot, with a dollop of Mock Sour Cream perhaps. Chilled and marinated, they are fine cut up in a salad or served as is.

The following recipe is meant as a way to use beet thinnings from the garden. We like it so much that we now systematically pluck a good many more of our beets than we would normally, and just keep planting new ones. Mature beets, too, can be cut up and cooked in the same way.

Whole Beets

12 to 15 tiny beets,
tops and all
2 tablespoons oil
juice of 1 lemon
1 green onion, chopped
½ teaspoon dill weed
½ teaspoon tarragon
½ teaspoon salt

OPTIONAL
dash garlic powder

Wash beets well and remove inedible parts, but keep skin and leaves.

Heat oil, lemon juice, onion, and seasonings in a heavy pan with a tight-fitting lid. Add beets and steam over medium heat. Check after 5 minutes: if necessary, add a small amount of water to prevent burning. Cook until tender.

Serves 4 to 6.

Broccoli

We don't usually think of green vegetables as a source of protein, but 1 cup of steamed broccoli provides 5 grams. If you've only had frozen broccoli, you'll be amazed to find what sweet flavor it has when fresh. We enjoy it year-round, on its own or in mixed vegetable dishes.

Broccoli is one vegetable that needs peeling. The outer skin of the stalk can be quite fibrous and tough, and if you cook broccoli for a long time in hopes of tenderizing its skin you risk overcooking the other parts of the vegetable, destroying more vitamins in the process than you've saved by keeping the skin. Besides, here as with beets, the real hangout for vitamins and minerals is the leaves. Cook the leaves along with the spears and flowers, or, if they look untidy to you, snip them off, but add them to soup or casseroles. Don't discard them, for love nor money.

Here is one of our simplest and best-received broccoli recipes.

Broccoli Spears with Yeast Butter

Cut broccoli into spears. Peel the skin off the stalk (it is almost always tough) and trim nicely. If stalks are thick, slice them lengthwise so they will cook as quickly as the flowers. The leaves are vitamin-packed and delicious. Remove their stems and cook the leaves with the spears.

Steam until tender, about 15 minutes.

Drizzle with Yeast Butter just before serving.

Serves 4 to 6.

2 pounds broccoli
½ cup Yeast Butter
(p. 225)

If you peel the broccoli stem and cut it into ¼-inch slices, it will cook right along with the flowers in the same amount of time. Serve cut-up broccoli *or* spears with Lemon Butter, Cheese Sauce, Yeast Gravy, or Sunshine Sauce. But after you've tried all these, don't be surprised if you find yourself coming back to the simplest and best: bright green, perfectly cooked spears adorned by nothing but lemon wedges, salt, and pepper.

Brussels Sprouts

Have you ever seen brussels sprouts growing? They're easily the most fanciful things in the garden: sturdy, upright stalks, maybe three feet tall, all stuck over with round knobs that peek out from just where the leaves connect with the stem.

At their best they can be cooked intact, but if the core extends thick and tough, you will want to remove it. Score brussels sprouts by cutting an $\times$ in the bottom, ¼ inch deep. This makes for quicker and more even cooking time. The outermost leaves can go if they're yellow and spotty, but take it easy: some people are so zealous about this that they throw away over half the vegetable.

Steamed whole, or cooked in milk, brussels sprouts are delectable, and when they're first in season it never occurs to us to eat them any other way. After the initial thrill subsides, we start dressing them up. A light sprinkling of grated hard cheese never hurts, and a cream sauce with nutmeg or thyme complements perfectly their very special flavor.

One of our favorite winter dishes is BRUSSELS SPROUTS WITH CHESTNUTS. Simply roast chestnuts, peel them, cut them into chunks, and stir them into steamed sprouts with some Better-Butter. The mild, nutty flavor and somewhat mealy texture of the chestnuts complements the sprouts beautifully. Try both of the following recipes too—the first one has a real holiday air about it.

Brussels Sprout–Squash Casserole

Clean and trim brussels sprouts; cut large ones in half. Steam sprouts and squash separately until nearly done. Set aside.

Preheat oven to 350°.

While squash and sprouts cook, chop onion and celery. Sauté onion in margarine. Add flour and cook slowly for about 3 minutes. Add milk and spices slowly, stirring to keep mixture smooth. Bring to a boil and remove from heat. Correct seasonings. If extra protein and richer flavor are desired, blend ¼ cup dried skim milk with fresh milk before making sauce.

In a greased 8″ × 8″ baking dish, arrange cubed squash on bottom. Next, make an even layer of the brussels sprouts. Sprinkle chopped celery over the top. Pour the white sauce over the vegetables and sprinkle with nutmeg.

Bake for 30 minutes or so.

Serves 4 to 6.

1 pound brussels sprouts
1½ cups cubed winter squash
1 medium onion, minced
1 cup chopped celery
¼ cup margarine or Better-Butter
¼ cup whole wheat flour
2 cups milk
½ teaspoon salt
¼ teaspoon marjoram
dash pepper
dash nutmeg

OPTIONAL
¼ cup dried skim milk

Creamy Brussels Sprouts & Bell Peppers

Sweet red bell peppers make a perfect complement to brussels sprouts—what good fortune that their seasons coincide!

Clean and trim brussels sprouts. Cut large ones in half. Cut peppers into ½-inch pieces.

Sauté onion in oil with bay leaf until onion is soft.

Add the pepper pieces and stir for a few seconds. Add the brussels sprouts and stir again.

Add ¼ cup of stock and steam all until just tender. This is probably about 7 minutes, but keep checking.

Steam or boil the potato cubes separately and purée in blender with margarine and some of the juice from the vegetables. Stir together with the sprouts and peppers.

Season with salt.

Serves 4 to 6.

2 red bell peppers
¼ onion, chopped
1 bay leaf
2 tablespoons oil
1½ pounds brussels sprouts
1 potato, cubed
¼ cup stock
2 tablespoons margarine
salt to taste

Cabbage

We are enthusiastic fans of the lowly cabbage, as a glance at our index will reveal. Its nutritional pluses, versatility, and year-round low cost make it irresistible. Get acquainted with both the green and red varieties. We prefer green cabbage if we're stuffing it; red cabbage is at its best raw in salad, or cooked sweet and sour as in the following recipe. (Serve with your favorite potato dish.)

Sweet and Sour Cabbage

8 cups (1 small head) shredded cabbage, green or red
½ onion
2 tablespoons Better-Butter or margarine
1 medium apple
¾ cup stock or water
2 tablespoons whole wheat flour
2 tablespoons cider vinegar
1 tablespoon brown sugar
1 teaspoon salt

OPTIONAL
1 teaspoon caraway seed

Chop onion coarsely and sauté in Better-Butter until soft. Grate apple. Add to onion with cabbage and ¼ cup stock. Cook 5 minutes.

In jar shake together the whole wheat flour, vinegar, brown sugar, salt, and remaining ½ cup stock. Add caraway seed if desired. Stir into cabbage and cook another 5 to 10 minutes, until cabbage is just tender.

Serves 4 to 6.

VARIATIONS
Omit brown sugar. Cook ½ cup grated carrots and ½ cup grated beets with the cabbage. A very colorful dish.

Cabbage is usually served in a sweet or sweet and sour sauce or dressing that ameliorates its rather assertive flavor. People are often surprised to find that it does very well on its own. Cook it in milk and it can be as sweet and pleasing as you'd ever want a vegetable to be, but it does need to be cooked gently—not too hot and not too long. Simmered in milk and then tossed with Better-Butter, salt, pepper, and a handful of chopped parsley, cabbage gets surprised requests for seconds from devout cabbage-loathers.

The cabbage core, by the way, is strong-tasting and tough: discard it.

Chinese Cabbage

If you've never grown Chinese cabbage, don't wait another minute. On aesthetic grounds alone you're missing something. Taller, more elegant by far than its plump occidental cousins, Chinese cabbage has pale, curly leaves and a lighter, subtler flavor. It's delicious raw, but we also like to respect its origin and cook it Chinese style occasionally—sliced thin crosswise and sautéed lightly in oil with a little parsley and a drop or two of soy sauce.

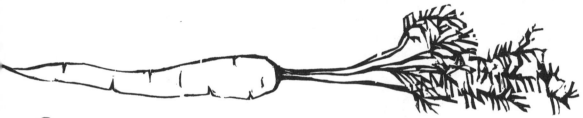

Carrots

You may be able to grow carrots year-round. Otherwise, when you have a choice, buy the young, slender ones (get the tops too, for soup stock).

Lemon juice gives a real boost to carrots that aren't garden fresh; add a tablespoonful for every 2 cups of carrots while you're cutting or grating. It enlivens their flavor considerably, and it keeps them from turning brown (though it does bleach them slightly, too).

Since carrots are always available and inexpensive, here are several more of our tried and true methods of preparing them:

᳇ Grate them and cook in a cream sauce seasoned

VEGETABLES 191

with tarragon, nutmeg, dill weed, or chervil. Use about a cup of cream sauce for a quart of grated carrots.

❧ Cut them in thin sticks and cook with the waterless method. Towards the end of their cooking time, stir in chopped parsley and add Lemon Butter just before serving.

❧ Grind in blender a spoonful each of sesame and poppy seeds. Add along with margarine for the last few minutes cooking time.

❧ Glaze cooked carrots very lightly with a tablespoon or two of warmed honey and stir in a few chopped walnuts—*after* the carrots are cooked and removed from the pan (especially if it's iron); walnuts have an odd trick of turning things black otherwise.

❧ Serve cooked carrots with a sauce of unsweetened applesauce and lemon juice, just enough to coat them.

❧ Sneak over to page 204 and try Hungarian Squash, substituting carrots for squash—delicious!

❧ Sauté chopped onion in oil, stir in cut carrots, cover, and cook on low until tender.

❧ Don't forget about CARROT RAISIN SALAD. Grate carrots and add lemon juice; then stir in raisins, chopped nuts, chopped apple, and Coleslaw Dressing (p. 156).

Baked Carrots

4 large carrots
1 tablespoon oil
½ cup bread crumbs
 and sesame meal
 OR
½ cup whole-grain
 cracker crumbs
½ teaspoon salt

The natural sweetness of carrots is fully developed with this method of cooking.

Preheat oven to 350°.

Cut carrots in half crosswise, then quarter each piece lengthwise. Toss with oil.

Put crumb mixture in paper bag. Shake carrots in bag to coat. Place in single layer in greased baking dish. Cover tightly.

Bake for 20 to 30 minutes.

Serves 6 to 8.

Cauliflower

Cauliflower became an entirely new vegetable for us when we first heard a friend from Virginia call it "collyflower"— as the word must surely be meant to be pronounced. Now cauliflower seems to occupy a unique botanical niche somewhere between hollyhock and cornflowers. Don't be fooled by its snowy-white color—it's a good choice nutritionally. Its color and shape are so unusual that it adds a lot to any mixed vegetable dish.

Steam a head of cauliflower whole and serve it with a generous topping of grated sharp cheddar cheese or a cheese sauce. Surrounded by green vegetables on a platter, it makes an impressive entrée.

Cauliflower cooks faster when broken into flowerets. If you cook it in milk, you can mix up a rather thick cream sauce while it's simmering and thin it at the end with the cooking milk. Add green peas—they cook in a flash—or chopped parsley, and perhaps some grated Swiss cheese.

Cauliflower takes beautifully to creamy sauces. Here are our favorite combinations:

Yeast Gravy with chopped peanuts on top

Cottage Cheese Cream Sauce and a sprinkling of toasted slivered almonds

Cashew Gravy and paprika

Buttermilk Sauce with herbs and toasted bread crumbs

Cauliflower is very tasty raw, too, or lightly cooked and marinated, served in salads and relish trays. Don't miss the Indian approach to cauliflower on page 222—and try the recipe which follows.

Greek Cauliflower

2 medium heads
 cauliflower
juice of 1 lemon
2 tablespoons oil
½ small onion
2 tomatoes, chopped
 OR
2 tablespoons tomato
 paste and 1 cup water
1 teaspoon salt
⅛ teaspoon pepper
1 teaspoon basil

Wash cauliflower and break into flowerets. Toss with lemon juice. Chop onion.

Heat oil in heavy saucepan with a lid. Sauté onion until soft. Stir in cauliflower.

Combine the tomatoes and seasonings. Add to cauliflower and stir well. Bring to a boil, cover, and simmer over medium heat until liquid is absorbed (about 15 minutes).

Serves 6 to 8.

Celery

Someone told us once that celery is the only food that takes more calories to eat than it provides, which makes celery a true friend of the weight-watcher. We find celery to be indispensable for soups, Chinese mixed vegetables, casseroles, sandwich spreads, and stuffings for this and that. Its flavor is strong, though, and considering its negligible nutritional contribution, we're not often tempted to give it a starring role. Of course, it can be delicious in a cream sauce, but let's face it— what isn't? If you do serve it creamed, season it with tarragon, a dash of nutmeg, and the lightest hint of garlic—and don't be surprised if your family asks you to serve it often.

Swiss Chard

So sheltered were we in our nonvegetarian days that we'd never encountered chard until a few years ago, so our boundless enthusiasm has something of a convert's zeal. Chard is a breeze to grow in most places, by the way, well into autumn or even winter. The red kind—green with red stems and veins—is quite beautiful. The white-stemmed chard is equally enjoyable, though.

You'll want to separate the leaves from the thicker part of the stem, but don't discard the stem. If you're using a steamer basket, slice the stem crosswise in ½-inch pieces and put them into the basket first, giving them a 5-minute head start on the leaves; then pile the cut-up leaves on top and finish steaming.

If you're following the waterless method, sauté the sliced stem lightly first, then lay the leaves across, whole or cut up; cover and cook without stirring for another 5 minutes or so. If you have no immediate designs on the stems, save them for mixed vegetable dishes or casseroles, cooking them as you would celery. Chard is delicious served with just a little vinegar or lemon juice, salt, and pepper. Try it cold, too.

A simple and very tasty chard dish is prepared as follows: sauté chopped onion; stir in chard (cut bite-size) and a handful of raisins. Cook until chard is tender, then toss in a handful of toasted sunflower seeds.

If you want to serve chard with a sauce, make it Sunshine Sauce. For special dinners, try Stuffed Chard Leaves (p. 241) or Chard Pita (p. 237). The following recipe is one we developed last summer, on finding our backyard knee-deep in chard.

Chard and Cheese Pie

1½ bunches Swiss chard
(about 3 pounds)
2 cups low-fat cottage
cheese
2 eggs, beaten
juice of 1 lemon
½ teaspoon salt
½ cup whole-grain
bread crumbs
paprika

OPTIONAL
2 tablespoons chopped
chives

Wash chard and remove the stems; then chop into bite-size pieces. Cook quickly in a heavy pan with no added water, stirring constantly until wilted. Drain very well, saving the juice for vegetable stock.

Preheat oven to 350°.

Beat together the cottage cheese, eggs, lemon, and salt. Stir a cup of this mixture into the chard. Put into a greased 8″×8″ pan and press down firmly with a fork. Spread remaining cottage cheese mixture evenly over the top and sprinkle with bread crumbs and paprika.

Bake for 30 minutes, or until set. Allow to stand several minutes before cutting into squares and serving.

Serves 6 to 8.

For a refreshing summertime supper, chill and serve with a garnish of crumbled bleu cheese, sliced tomatoes, and minced parsley.

Corn

Remember all that stuff about how the only way to eat corn is to pick it at five minutes to six, *run* from the garden, shucking all the way, drop it into a pot of boiling water, snatch it out again, and skid into the dining room by six sharp? Remember? Well, it's all true. Within a few minutes after the corn is picked, its sugars have begun to change into starch and the flavor declines accordingly. So if you can, do grow your own corn. It can be sumptuous. For the first week or two you'll want to eat it right off the cob, but when you've begun to slack off, you may gild the lily in any of the following ways. Be sure, when removing corn from the cob, that you scrape the cob thoroughly to get the germ—that's where extra vitamins lurk.

❧ Chop a bell pepper, an onion, and a tomato. Sauté the pepper and onion in oil until soft, then stir in fresh corn and tomato. Cover and cook briefly.

❧ Cream corn, adding sautéed onion and chopped

parsley. Creamed corn needn't have a full-fledged cream sauce, either: just blend up part of the corn with milk and add a little Better-Butter for flavor.

⋇ For a summer garden treat, sauté sliced snow peas and chopped green onions for a few minutes; then stir in fresh corn, cover, and cook until tender.

⋇ Cook corn in milk with grated cabbage and parsley.

Eggplant

Their color and shape are so pleasing that eggplants are almost as enjoyable just to have around and look at as they are to eat. A traditional substitute for meat, eggplant is quite spongy and soaks up whatever oils or juices it is cooked in—so look out for it if you're watching your waistline. The caloric impact of the following two recipes, though, is far below the usual level for eggplant recipes, mostly because they don't ask you to sauté the eggplant first. See also Ratatouille (p. 216) and Green Bean Stroganoff (p. 199).

Simple Stuffed Eggplant

Steam eggplant, whole, about 20 minutes until tender.

Preheat oven to 350°.

Sauté pepper, onion, and celery in the oil.

Cut steamed eggplant in half lengthwise and carefully remove pulp.

Cut pulp into small pieces. Combine with other ingredients (except crumbs and margarine). Heap into shells. Top with crumbs and dot with margarine.

Place in baking pan, adding water if needed to prevent sticking. Bake for 20 to 25 minutes.

Serves 6.

1 large, firm eggplant
1 tablespoon grated onion
3 tablespoons chopped green pepper
1 cup chopped celery
2 tablespoons olive oil
1 cup canned or fresh tomatoes
1 egg, beaten well
1 teaspoon salt
3 tablespoons margarine
½ cup whole-grain bread crumbs

VARIATIONS

Serve sliced with Tomato Sauce (p. 226) seasoned with a dash of cumin.

Eggplant Parmesan

1 medium-size eggplant
1½ cups Tomato Sauce
  (p. 226)
1 cup grated mozzarella
  cheese
½ cup grated Parmesan
  cheese
2½ cups crushed whole
  wheat crackers
2 eggs
¼ cup milk
½ cup whole wheat flour
1 teaspoon salt
dash pepper
¼ teaspoon oregano

This version is the most delicious eggplant Parmesan we have had—also the lowest in calories.

Prepare three bowls for dipping eggplant slices:

[1] ½ cup whole wheat flour
     ½ teaspoon salt
[2] 2 eggs, slightly beaten
     ¼ cup milk
[3] 2½ cups cracker crumbs
     ½ teaspoon salt, plus pepper and oregano

Preheat oven to 350°.

Cut eggplant into ¼-inch rounds. Dip slices in each mixture in turn, coating completely.

Layer in 9" × 13" glass dish. (Slices may overlap but should not cover each other completely.) Sprinkle each layer with tomato sauce and Parmesan cheese. Cover tightly and bake for 30 to 45 minutes, or until fork pierces middle slices easily.

Top with mozzarella and remaining Parmesan. Return uncovered to oven just until cheese melts.

Serves 4 to 6.

Green Beans

Green beans should give a juicy pop when you snap them— and they seldom do unless you've grown them yourself. Both ends should be removed. You used to have to string them too, but we haven't seen a stringy one in years, so the string of string beans has presumably been bred out. Cut them in inch-long slices—on the diagonal, if beans aren't super-tender. Spend a few more minutes and you can enjoy them French-cut—quartered lengthwise and then halved crosswise. Green beans may be steamed or cooked by the waterless method. Serve them with any number of different garnishes: sautéed mushrooms or onion, toasted almond slivers, or a good sprinkling of grated Parmesan cheese are all fine. If you have a leftover cooked sweet potato, regard it as a prize. Dice it up small and add it to green beans towards the end of their cooking time.

For a very special garnish, sauté sunflower seeds in oil with a dash of garlic salt and ½ teaspoon of curry powder. Stir into beans just before serving.

Sweet and Sour Mustard Sauce is exceptionally good with green beans. Lemon Butter and Yeast Butter are also very nice.

Green beans in Cream Sauce are an old favorite. Add lightly cooked sunchokes, a vegetable more people should know about (see below), and top with buttered bread crumbs. Bake in a 350° oven for 20 minutes and you have GREEN AND WHITE CASSEROLE—unusual and *very* tasty.

We decided stroganoff was too good a thing to be abandoned to nonvegetarians, so here is our own: Green Bean Stroganoff, followed by two other favorite bean recipes.

Green Bean Stroganoff

Wash green beans and cut into bite-size pieces. Steam until tender.

While beans cook, chop onion coarsely and sauté gently in 2 tablespoons margarine.

Slice mushrooms in thick pieces. Add to onion along with the remaining margarine, stirring frequently.

Cube eggplant, add to mushrooms, and sauté until tender—a very few minutes. Season with salt and pepper. Add hot green beans.

Stir in yogurt or yogurt-buttermilk mixture just before serving. Heat through, but don't boil or it will curdle (it's good anyway, though).

Serve over plain rice or bulgur wheat.

Serves 4 to 6.

1 pound green beans
½ large onion
4 tablespoons margarine
½ pound mushrooms
½ large eggplant
1 teaspoon salt
dash pepper
*2 cups yogurt or yogurt
  and buttermilk*

Creamy Sesame Beans & Celery

3 cups cut green beans
1 cup cut celery
½ onion, chopped
2 tablespoons whole
    wheat flour
1 teaspoon salt
1 cup yogurt
½ cup low-fat cottage
    cheese
⅛ teaspoon pepper
½ teaspoon oregano
dash garlic powder
¼ cup toasted sesame
    seeds, ground
¼ to ½ cup whole-
    grain bread crumbs
1 tablespoon margarine
    or Better-Butter

OPTIONAL
2 teaspoons brown sugar

Preheat oven to 350°.

Cut green beans into ¾-inch lengths. Cut celery into crescents.

Cook onion, beans, and celery in small amount of stock or water for 10 minutes, or until beans are barely tender. Drain, reserving liquid (if any) for soups or sauces.

Stir in whole wheat flour, salt, and sugar (if desired). Add yogurt. Pour into deep baking dish.

Mix seasonings with cottage cheese and spread over vegetables. Sprinkle with sesame meal and bread crumbs. Dot with margarine and bake for 30 minutes.

Serves 4.

Green Beans Hellenika

2 pounds green beans
1 onion
3 tomatoes
    OR
¼ cup tomato paste
½ bunch parsley
¼ cup oil
1 teaspoon salt
dash pepper
stock or water

Cut beans into bite-size pieces. Chop onion, tomatoes, and parsley.

Put all the ingredients into a heavy pot, cover, and cook until tender, at least 20 minutes. Add only as much stock or water as necessary to keep from sticking. Stir frequently.

Serves 4 to 6.

Parsnips

Just one request: *don't* steam parsnips. Sauté them in margarine, sliced about ½ inch thick or cut like matchsticks; then cover and cook on low heat for 12 minutes or so.

Bell Peppers, Green and Red

Everyone knows about green peppers, and how indispensable they are for any dish that wants to taste Spanish or Creole. The red ones are really special, though. They are the same vegetable, but riper, and hence much more quickly perishable. Their season is very brief—just a few months in autumn. Their bright, sweet tartness and lovely color combine perfectly with quieter autumn vegetables like squash and brussels sprouts.

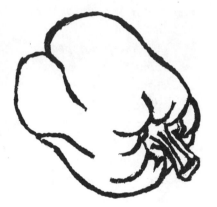

For much of the year peppers are pricey, so we often just use them for accent. When they're in season, though, we love to serve them stuffed. Spanish rice is the best-known filling, but you might try some of the other pilaf-type recipes in our Grains and Beans section as well. Fresh corn is a good choice too, either mixed with other vegetables or creamed.

Here are two recipes well worth your trying.

Spinach-Stuffed Peppers

Preheat oven to 350°.

Prepare peppers for stuffing as in following recipe.

Fill with creamed spinach and place in a greased baking dish. Pour extra filling around peppers. Top with bread crumbs and cheese.

Bake for about 15 minutes.

Serves 4.

SPINACH-STUFFED TOMATOES

Use 4 large, firm tomatoes. Do not precook them, but clean them out gently. Save centers for soups. Proceed as above.

4 bell peppers
2 cups Creamed
   Spinach (p. 206)
1 teaspoon basil
1 teaspoon tarragon
2 tablespoons bread
   crumbs
2 tablespoons grated
   Parmesan cheese

Stuffed Peppers

4 green peppers
1½ cups raw bulgur
  wheat
½ cup raw soy grits
1 bunch green onions
½ clove garlic
1 cup finely diced celery
¼ cup finely diced
  carrots
¼ cup finely sliced
  green beans
¼ cup fresh peas or corn
1 small tomato
½ cup finely chopped
  spinach
¼ cup oil
1 teaspoon minced
  ginger root
1 teaspoon salt
dash cayenne
¼ cup vegetable stock
  or water

Cook bulgur wheat and soy grits in 3½ cups of water with 1 teaspoon salt for 15 minutes.

Slice the tops off the peppers and remove the seeds. Place upside-down in a steamer basket in a pot of simmering water. Steam until barely tender, 5 to 7 minutes.

Chop green onions, ginger, garlic, and the tops of the peppers very fine and sauté gently in a little of the oil. Season with cayenne. Add vegetables and stock. Cover and cook for 5 to 10 minutes.

Preheat oven to 350°.

Combine cooked grain and vegetables with remaining oil. Salt to taste. Fill pepper cases and garnish the tops with slices of tomato. Bake for 15 minutes. Put any extra filling around the peppers on the serving platter.

Serves 4.

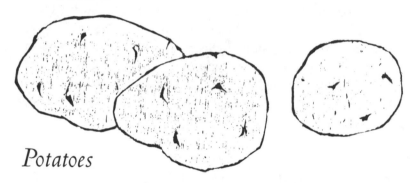

Potatoes

We doubt whether your becoming vegetarians will drastically affect the standing of potatoes at your house, and we doubt that you need to be told much about their preparation. Just a few observations, then:

Potatoes are not to be thought of as "strictly starch." Read their ratings on the nutritional chart and you'll be impressed with what they have to offer—not just in vitamins, but in minerals and protein as well. The vitamin C content of potatoes has warded off scurvy for whole populations that have never heard of orange juice. Baking potatoes is a particularly healthful idea, because the vitamin C stays inside the jacket.

Don't feel you have to say goodbye to potatoes and gravy (if your waistline can afford them) just because you've lost your taste for meat gravy. Try our gravy recipes or Mock Sour Cream.

New potatoes creamed with peas are superb. If you don't think it sacrilege, though, try treating big chunks of *any* potato in the same way. Fresh peas aren't easily available year-round, either, so chopped spinach or parsley are tasty substitutes.

The following recipes are designed to give you the nutritional benefits of the potato without piling on too many calories. Notice that in most of our potato recipes, here and elsewhere, potatoes are teamed up with milk or whole-grain foods for added protein. Colcannon is an exception, but look at all that kale!

Green Potatoes for Six

This is a simple recipe, *most* enthusiastically received by the children.

Preheat oven to 400°.

Scrub potatoes. Butter skins and make shallow slits around the middle as if you were cutting the potatoes in half lengthwise. Bake until done, 30 to 60 minutes, depending on size.

Peel broccoli stems. Steam whole stalks until just tender and chop fine.

Carefully slice the potatoes in half (the slit makes it easier) and scoop the insides into a bowl with the broccoli. Add ½ cup of the cheese and the margarine, salt, pepper, and milk. (Reconstituted dried skim milk may be used, regular strength or concentrated.) Mash all together until mixture is pale green with dark green flecks. Heap into the potato jackets and sprinkle with remaining cheese. Return to the oven to heat through (about 10 minutes).

Serves 6.

6 medium potatoes
3 stalks broccoli
¼ cup milk
¾ cup grated cheese
2 tablespoons margarine
1 teaspoon salt
⅛ teaspoon pepper

Colcannon

3 cups chopped kale
4 medium potatoes
6 green onions, chopped
⅓ cup milk
2 tablespoons Better-
    Butter or margarine
sprig parsley
1 teaspoon salt
⅛ teaspoon pepper

Cube potatoes and boil until tender. (Reserve water for baking.)

Preheat oven to 400°.

Stir kale and onions in a heavy pan over medium heat for 5 minutes. (The water that clings to the kale from washing is sufficient moisture for cooking.)

Mash potatoes with milk and margarine. Combine with kale, onions, parsley, salt, and pepper.

Bake for 15 to 20 minutes.

Serves 4 to 6.

Potato Latkes

1 tablespoon active dry
    yeast
1 cup warm milk, stock,
    or water
1 egg, beaten
1 tablespoon oil
1 cup coarsely grated
    potato
1 teaspoon salt
½ cup whole wheat flour
¼ cup wheat germ

OPTIONAL
1 tablespoon sautéed
    onion

These yeast-raised potato pancakes are very light and delicious, not at all greasy.

Dissolve yeast in liquid. Add egg and oil. Beat in potatoes, salt, flour, wheat germ, and onion (if desired).

Let rise 30 minutes. Stir down.

Cook over medium heat on lightly oiled griddle or dry Teflon pan until browned on each side.

Makes 8 pancakes.

Spinach

It's hard to figure out how spinach ever got such a bad press, because fresh spinach is an enormous hit among the people we know, *especially* with the children. Maybe we're just hung up on our primal recollection of canned spinach: gray, slimy, gritty stuff with its own unique bitterness.

Fresh spinach deserves to be handled with real delicacy. It's often quite muddy, so it needs to be washed with care— but oh, so briefly. Never soak it. If you do it will emerge limp, with dark, soggy patches where the vitamins have up and gone.

Real spinach devotees are content to just snip the pink root tips off a bunch, wash it, and steam it whole. A little lemon juice and salt, and we're pretty pleased. Others prefer to cut the stems off and cut the leaves into bite-size pieces and the stems into very short lengths before steaming. Do as you prefer. You can cook spinach using the waterless method, with just the water that clings to the leaves from washing.

If the acidity of spinach bothers you or yours, cook it in milk. Interestingly enough, when you're cooking spinach with other vegetables, the oxalic acid is seldom noticeable. It has something to do with alkalinity neutralizing acidity, and perhaps milk isn't the only food that can accomplish that.

Spinach and eggs have a long-standing affinity, so part of our weekly egg quota often goes into spinach dishes. Chopped hard-boiled egg is a traditional garnish for cooked spinach, along with a dash of vinegar. Here's another simple egg-and-spinach dish from a nine-year-old friend: Take a pile of cooked diced potatoes, about as many as a nine-year-old can eat and still have room for apple crisp; dot them with margarine and add a layer of cooked spinach. Top with a poached egg and you have it. It takes a child to pick up on something so simple and satisfying.

The hands-down favorite among spinach dishes is Spanakopita (p. 236), followed closely by Spinach Crepes (p. 247). The basis for the latter, and for many other dishes, is the following recipe for Creamed Spinach. Serve it over rice or noodles with a sprinkling of toasted almonds, stuff tomatoes or green peppers with it, or simply enjoy it as is.

Creamed Spinach

3 tablespoons whole
  wheat flour
3 tablespoons margarine
  or Better-Butter
½ small yellow onion
¾ cup milk
2 tablespoons non-
  instant powdered milk
3 quarts fresh spinach,
  washed and chopped
nutmeg and salt to taste

OPTIONAL
½ cup grated Swiss
  cheese
2 tablespoons Parmesan
  cheese
  OR
¼ cup crumbled cream
  cheese

Creaming greens is a traditional way of doing justice to one of nature's finest gifts. For a real delicacy, grow a garden plot of greens and pick them fresh for dinner.

Chop onion fine and sauté lightly in oil. Add flour and cook 2 minutes, stirring constantly; then add the blended mixture of powdered and fresh milk. Add cheese if desired.

A little at a time, stir in the chopped greens; you can keep stirring more into the pot as the greens cook down. Cook until tender and season with salt, nutmeg, and perhaps a pinch of white pepper for a stronger flavor. Serve plain or over hot biscuits as an entrée.

Makes 2½ full cups.

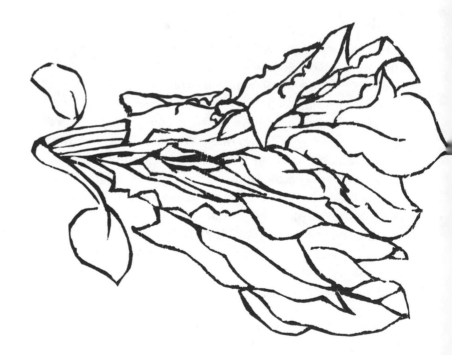

Summer Squash

Yellow crookneck squashes and patty pans are identical in texture to zucchini, so the same cooking instructions work for all three. In season, it's nice to cut all three in large chunks and cook them together with cut-up fresh tomato and sliced onion. Sauté onion first in margarine, lightly; then add squash and tomato, cover, and cook until done.

Yellow crookneck squashes are milder and sweeter than zucchini. We often use them willy-nilly along with zucchini for variety of color and shape. They look especially pretty in creole sauces. Yellow crooknecks are more perishable than other summer squashes, and have a shorter period of availability.

Patty pan squashes (the small green round ones with the scalloped rims) look and taste lovely when you scoop out the upper part, grate it, mingle it with Better-Butter, bread crumbs, and finely chopped onion. Stuff the squashes with this mixture and bake for half an hour. They are also very nice steamed whole, especially when you've harvested them from your own garden before they've gotten more than about two inches across. Serve them with Yeast Butter or enjoy their sweet, juicy savor as is.

Zucchini is the hardy perennial—available at low prices year-round. This is why you will find such a plethora of zucchini recipes here and in other sections. Before giving you some full-blown recipes, though, here are a couple of simple cooking ideas:

❧ Cut zucchini into shapes as much like cubes as you can, up to an inch thick. Sauté finely chopped onion briefly, then stir in zucchini while oil is quite hot. Cover and steam until tender. This searing seems to seal the juice inside so the zucchini holds its shape and flavor exceptionally well.

❧ Cut zucchini in half lengthwise and bake uncovered. Top with grated cheese, herbs, and paprika for just the last few minutes.

Greek Stuffed Zucchini

10 medium zucchini
½ cup raw brown rice
1 cup boiling water
1½ cups chopped onion
2 cups chopped celery
1 cup chopped parsley
2 to 3 teaspoons salt
½ cup olive oil
1 cup bread crumbs
3 lemons
2 eggs, separated
pepper

OPTIONAL
1½ cups chopped
    mushrooms
½ cup grated cheddar
    cheese

Hollow out the zucchini. Either make cylinders with an apple corer, or slice them in half lengthwise and scoop out the insides to make little boats. In either case, you will need a pan large enough to arrange them side by side for baking.

Chop all of the vegetables very small. Chop the insides of the zucchini too, but keep separate.

Cook the rice with the water, onion, celery, salt, pepper, and oil for 15 minutes.

Add the chopped zucchini and cook 5 minutes more.

Add breadcrumbs, parsley, juice from 2 of the lemons, and whites of the eggs. Add mushrooms and cheese if desired.

Preheat oven to 350°.

Put the filling into the scooped-out zucchini shells. (If you chose the cylinder style, pack the filling in firmly with your fingers, keeping a bowl of cold water nearby to cool your hands.)

Arrange zucchini in a baking dish. If there is extra filling, spread it over and around the zucchini. Cover and bake for about 40 minutes.

Beat the egg yolks with remaining lemon juice. Spoon out some of the juices from the baking dish. Pour slowly into egg yolk–lemon mixture, stirring briskly. Return this sauce to the zucchini and bake for another 5 minutes.

Serves 6 to 8.

Zucchini Provençal

Dice potatoes into ½-inch pieces and cut zucchini into 1-inch chunks. If using whole tomatoes, quarter and slice through again.

Using a large heavy pan, sauté onions, basil, and celery in oil. Add tomatoes, zucchini, and potatoes. Stir gently to coat with oil, then cover and steam until tender. Season with salt.

Serves 4 to 6.

5 large zucchini
2 medium potatoes
1 cup chopped celery
½ cup chopped green
  onions
½ teaspoon basil
2 tablespoons oil
2 tomatoes
  OR
½ cup Tomato Sauce
  (p. 226)
1 teaspoon salt

Zucchini Spinach Casserole

Preheat oven to 375°.

Cut zucchini into ¼-inch slices, and the greens into bite-size pieces.

Heat oil in heavy saucepan. Add zucchini and stir to coat with oil. Cover pan, and when zucchini begins to steam, turn down to simmer. Cook until half done (about 5 minutes).

Add greens and stir until wilted. Season with salt and nutmeg.

Layer half of the vegetables, half of the cheese, and all of the sprouts in a greased 9″ × 13″ baking dish. Repeat layers with remaining vegetables and cheese. Top with bread crumbs and dot with margarine. Bake for 15 minutes.

Serves 4 to 6.

1½ pounds zucchini (5
  medium zucchini)
1 bunch spinach or
  other greens
¾ cup grated cheese
¼ cup chopped parsley
½ cup bread crumbs
  and/or wheat germ
1 cup sprouted (or
  cooked) wheat berries
  OR
1 cup sprouted lentils
2 tablespoons oil
1 tablespoon margarine
1 teaspoon salt
¼ teaspoon nutmeg

VARIATIONS

For a one-dish meal, bake the vegetables and other ingredients on a bed of cooked millet or bulgur wheat.

Baked Zucchini

6 medium zucchini
½ onion, chopped
¼ cup chopped parsley
4 celery stalks, chopped
2 tablespoons margarine
1½ cups low-fat cottage
    cheese
⅓ cup buttermilk
2 eggs, beaten
½ teaspoon salt
⅛ teaspoon pepper
1 teaspoon oregano
½ cup grated cheddar
    cheese
    OR
¼ cup grated Parmesan
    cheese

OPTIONAL
whole wheat bread
    crumbs
dash garlic powder

Preheat oven to 350°.

Sauté onions and celery in margarine. Stir into cottage cheese. Add buttermilk, beaten eggs, and seasonings, including garlic if desired. Stir in parsley.

Slice zucchini in half lengthwise. Place halves, cut-side up, in a greased baking dish. Cover and bake until half done (about 15 minutes).

Spread with cottage cheese mixture and bread and bake again, uncovered, until done (about 15 minutes).

Sprinkle with grated cheese and let stand a few minutes. Serves 6.

Winter Squash

Harvest it in early autumn and enjoy it on through the winter: winter squash is an adaptable sort. You may treat it like a sweet potato, baked in big chunks with butter, brown sugar, and cinnamon, or you may cut it in small pieces and steam it along with other vegetables.

Since winter squashes of various kinds can be used almost interchangeably in many recipes, it's important to realize what a broad spectrum they represent calorically. The starchier, sweeter, more potatolike squashes are definitely more fattening. Acorn and butternut squash, for example, are on the high side—though they are also the tastiest ones in the patch.

When you grow your own squash, you will be fascinated at what variations there are between the different varieties and even between two squashes of the same variety picked at different stages of maturity: the squashes become more and more starchy as they mature. Lady Godiva squash is one of our current favorites, so named because its seeds are naked. One that we loved more for its name than anything else was the majestic Hungarian Mammoth, a pale blue-green in color outside, a deep red-orange inside.

It's a bit messy, but well worth the trouble, to sort out the squash seeds, wash them, and roast them in a low oven—a good source of protein, and very tasty.

A lighter than usual treatment of winter squash, simple and very tasty, is to cut the squash in small cubes and steam it. Add a handful of raisins for the last few minutes of cooking time, then stir in a cup of yogurt and heat.

Baked acorn squashes, when halved and seeded, make an excellent setting for creamed spinach. Fill them at the last minute, add a light crumb topping, and brown them ever so briefly under the broiler. Here's another version:

Stuffed Winter Squash

Use acorn squash, Lady Godiva, or any other small variety of winter squash.

Preheat oven to 350°.

Halve and clean squash. Bake for 25 to 45 minutes, depending on the variety.

Sauté onions in oil until soft. Add chopped celery. Cover and simmer on medium heat until just tender. Add spinach; stir to wilt.

Stuff squashes. Sprinkle with salted bread crumbs. Dot with margarine.

Return to oven for 10 to 15 minutes.

Serves 4 to 6, depending on size of squash.

3 small winter squashes
2 tablespoons oil
3 green onions, chopped
1 cup diced celery
1 bunch spinach,
*   coarsely chopped*
½ to 1 cup whole wheat
*   bread crumbs*
½ teaspoon salt
2 tablespoons margarine

The flavor of kasha blends beautifully with the sweetness of winter squash. Cut squash in small chunks and steam; while it's steaming, sauté chopped onion in margarine, add ½ cup cooked kasha, and stir into cooked squash.

The following two recipes both work best with squashes that are fully ripened—rather sweet and starchy.

Hungarian Squash

1 small onion, chopped
  fine
¼ cup Better-Butter or
  margarine
1 quart cubed winter
  squash
1 teaspoon paprika
1 teaspoon dill weed
2 tablespoons chopped
  parsley
1 cup yogurt
1 teaspoon salt
dash garlic powder

Cut winter squash into small cubes—about ¾ inch.

Sauté onion in Better-Butter. Add squash and cover; simmer for 15 to 20 minutes on low heat. (Very starchy squash might need ½ cup vegetable stock or water.) If any liquid is left after the squash is cooked, drain it off before adding yogurt.

When squash is tender, stir in remaining ingredients. Heat very gently until warmed through. If you heat it too much the yogurt will separate, which is just as tasty though less aesthetic.

Serves 4 to 6.

Simplest Squash Pie

baked 9″ pie shell
5 cups mashed cooked
  winter squash
¼ cup margarine
¼ cup raisins
¼ teaspoon salt
¼ teaspoon nutmeg
¼ teaspoon allspice

OPTIONAL
¼ cup brown sugar

Choose any of the starchier winter squashes. Since the sweetness of squash varies so much, you will want to adjust the amount of brown sugar—our butternut squashes were so sweet they didn't need any.

Mix squash and other ingredients and pile into pie shell. Dust with cinnamon. Serve warm or at room temperature.

Serves 6 to 8.

Vary by substituting chopped dried fruits or nuts for the ¼ cup raisins.

SAVORY SQUASH PIE

Omit brown sugar, raisins, and spices. Instead, add a sautéed minced onion and ½ teaspoon salt. Garnish generously with paprika. Excellent!

Sunchokes

Jerusalem artichokes are now billed in most places as "sun-chokes" because they aren't artichokes at all, but the roots of a kind of sunflower. In texture and appearance they will remind you of potatoes, though they contain virtually no starch and their flavor is more distinct. Uncooked or cooked just slightly, they have the crisp texture of water chestnuts and a very pleasing flavor, so that they can often be used where you would use water chestnuts.

Introduce your family to sunchokes gradually: a little bit in soups or mixed vegetables for a start. When cut in big chunks and steamed (don't peel them, but do go over them with a scrub brush), they are delightful in a cream sauce, especially with fresh peas. The key to enjoying sunchokes is not to overcook them, or their flavor gets rather strong.

Sweet Potatoes & Yams

Just for the record, yams (they're the darker orange ones) are considerably higher in calories than sweet potatoes. Minimum effort yields maximum delight when we bake either yams or sweet potatoes for dinner and serve them in their jackets, steaming hot, with a little Better-Butter tucked inside.

SWEET POTATOES AND APPLES

Slice sweet potatoes and place them in a baking dish, alternating with slices of apple and scattering raisins around as you go. (Chopped nuts, of course, are perfectly appropriate here too.) Sprinkle them with lemon juice, dot with margarine, and dust with cinnamon. Cover and bake in a medium oven for about an hour.

Tomatoes

September is traditionally a pretty euphoric month at our house, because for up to six weeks we have all the fresh tomatoes we can eat. The ones you buy in the store nowadays are the saddest, palest, poorest cousins that years of careful hybridization could produce. We don't often cook them—they're so marvelous raw, and such a good source of vitamins, that we've never seen too much point in developing elaborate tomato casseroles. Stuffed tomatoes, though, are too much of a treat to pass by: stuff them cold with cheese spread or potato salad, adding lots of finely chopped celery, or best of all, with Tabouli (p. 155)—chop up the insides of the tomato and add it to the filling. Creamed spinach or finely chopped garden vegetables make good fillings for oven-baked tomatoes. Try this version, too.

Stuffed Tomatoes

4 large or 6 medium
    tomatoes
1 onion
2 tablespoons oil
2 stalks celery
1 green pepper
1 cup fresh corn
½ cup chopped summer
    squash
½ cup chopped
    mushrooms
¼ cup or more bread
    crumbs
¼ cup grated sharp
    cheese
½ teaspoon salt

Choose firm and ripe tomatoes. Vary the vegetables according to season: asparagus and garden peas are delightful when available.

    Preheat oven to 350°.

    Cut tops off tomatoes and remove pulp carefully with a teaspoon, leaving the flesh around the sides. Salt the shell lightly and invert to drain. Chop the pulp.

    Sauté onion in oil. Add vegetables, including tomato pulp. When they are hot, add 2 tablespoons of the cheese and enough bread crumbs to hold the mixture together. Salt to taste.

    Fill tomatoes while the filling is still hot. Place any extra filling in a greased baking dish just large enough to hold the tomatoes and put them on top. Sprinkle with remaining cheese and bread crumbs.

    Bake for 15 minutes.
    Serves 4.

Mixed Vegetables

The remaining recipes in this section are for mixed vegetable dishes, most of which are from other cultures. Aside from these, and too simple to be treated as real recipes, are the many delicious combinations of garden-fresh vegetables that one stumbles upon from day to day as the seasons change. Cook them separately, or all together once you've picked up the knack of when to add what, or how much thinner the carrots need to be than the zucchini to cook in the same amount of time. Serve them in a glorious heap, just as they are, or accompanied by lemon wedges or soy sauce. Top them, if you like, with gomashio, chopped nuts, grated cheese, Lemon Butter, or your favorite sauce. Serve them with brown rice or millet, or a loaf of whole-grain bread. Add a salad, and your meal's complete.

You may choose to start with a sautéed onion, but from there on, almost anything goes, though most cooks prefer to keep the number of vegetables down to three. Choose with color, texture, *and* flavor in mind. Vary the way you cut the vegetables, and you'll be amazed at what a difference it can make. Chop them, dice them, slice them thin or thick, in rounds or diagonals, shred them or grate them—fix some one way, some another, but make them as attractive as you can.

The following combinations are a few that we enjoy often. Here again, though, please use our suggestions as a jumping-off place. Invent your own vegetable medleys—a different one each time.

- *Zucchini and stems of broccoli cut in thick rounds (flowers left intact), carrots in thinner rounds*
- *Cauliflower and green beans, with red bell pepper for accent*
- *Winter squash, cubed, with celery crescents and spinach or chard*
- *Green beans, diced potato, and sautéed onion*
- *Zucchini sliced very thin, with corn and parsley*
- *Carrots and zucchini grated large, with shredded cabbage and finely chopped parsley (add lemon juice at serving time)*

Ratatouille

1 large onion
1 green pepper
¼ cup olive oil
1 large eggplant
2 medium zucchini
3 tomatoes, chopped
        OR
5 tablespoons tomato
    paste & 3 tablespoons
    water
1 teaspoon salt
⅛ teaspoon pepper
½ teaspoon basil
½ teaspoon oregano
½ clove fresh garlic,
    minced

Ratatouille—the word means "stew" or "soup" in French—makes use of a savory vegetable combination which is a favorite the world round. See the exotic dishes which follow as variations on this basic theme.

Dice eggplant into 1-inch cubes and slice zucchini into ½-inch rounds. Chop onion coarsely and cut green pepper into squares.

Use a heavy-bottomed saucepan with a lid. Sauté the onion, garlic, and green pepper until they are soft; stir in eggplant and zucchini and sauté a few minutes more. Add tomato and seasonings. Cover and simmer gently for about 30 minutes or until all the vegetables are well cooked.

Uncover and turn the heat up to evaporate some of the liquid.

Serves 6 to 8.

IMAM BAYILDI

Preheat oven to 350°.

Add a large potato cut in chunks, some sliced mushrooms if you wish, and a cup of hot water or stock. Instead of simmering on top of the stove, bake in a covered dish for 45 minutes, and you will have what the Greeks and Turks call *Imam Bayildi*.

GVETCH

Include not only potato chunks and sliced mushrooms, but also 4 carrots sliced in rounds and the juice of 1 lemon. Use only 2 tablespoons water instead of a whole cup and bake as for *Imam Bayildi*. The result is a dish known in Israel and other Middle Eastern countries as *Gvetch*.

Chinese Vegetables & Tofu

This recipe is endlessly adaptable. There are a few fixed ingredients and some that may vary with seasonal changes and differing tastes. Where amounts are given, they are for 6 servings.

Allow at least 1 cup of vegetables per person. Cut them all in diagonal shapes. Cut the onion in thin wedges. If a vegetable doesn't lend itself to the diagonal cut (cabbage, for example), dice or cut in square pieces.

Heat the oil in heavy saucepan or wok. Sauté the onion, green pepper, ginger, and celery over medium heat for 5 minutes.

Add each of the longer-cooking vegetables in turn. Sauté for a few minutes between additions and stir occasionally.

Add some stock, put faster-cooking vegetables and leafy greens over other vegetables, and place cubes of tofu over this. Cover all and steam about 10 minutes until vegetables are just tender.

Gently stir in bean sprouts if desired. (Allow sprouted soybeans to cook a full 5 minutes.) Add soy sauce or salt to taste.

Sprinkle with coarsely ground sesame seeds and serve right away, with a steaming hot bowl of brown rice.

THE MUSTS
1 onion, preferably red
celery
green pepper
¼ cup oil
1 teaspoon chopped fresh ginger root
½ cup vegetable stock or water
tofu
soy sauce
OR
salt to taste

THE VARIABLES
green beans
carrots
broccoli
cauliflower
zucchini
snow peas
mushrooms
bok choy or chard
Chinese or Western cabbage
peas
bean sprouts
coarsely ground sesame seeds

Middle Eastern Vegetables

¼ onion, chopped
2 tablespoons oil
½ bay leaf
¾ teaspoon mustard
  seed
¼ teaspoon celery seed
½ teaspoon dill weed
1 potato
1 carrot
½ head cauliflower
1 medium green apple
1 tomato
2 zucchini
1 teaspoon salt
½ teaspoon paprika

Preheat oven to 375°.

Dice potato, carrot, and apple small. Separate cauliflower into small flowerets. Cut zucchini into chunks.

Sauté onion in oil with bay leaf, mustard seed, celery seed, and dill.

Stir in vegetables in this order, leaving 2 minutes or so between each addition: potato, carrots, cauliflower, apple.

Add tomato and zucchini. Heat quickly and transfer to oven for 20 minutes. Sprinkle with salt and paprika.

The trick of getting vegetables to bake evenly is to cut the longest-cooking vegetables (potato, carrot, and cauliflower) quite small.

Serves 4 to 6.

VARIATIONS

Try other vegetable combinations. The tomato and apple are essential, though, and the potato adds a good deal. A green pepper cut in chunks is a nice addition; so is a red bell pepper in season.

South Indian Recipes

We include the following recipes with special pleasure because they represent a cuisine that has been neglected in this country. South Indian food is distinct from that of other regional traditions in India. These recipes do not completely reflect their tradition, for we have modified them in the interests of sound nutrition. But we've grown very partial to this style of cooking, and we hope you do too.

A few words of caution are in order, though, first. Don't expect most of these dishes to blend gracefully with foods from other cuisines—they are too distinctively flavored and they complement each other so beautifully that they really should be served together. Also, several of these recipes include more coconut than you might want to eat frequently—coconut is replete with saturated fat. This and the fact that they are rather spicy suggest that you should serve South Indian food at rather widely spaced intervals.

There are various words in Indian languages for vegetable preparations—*bhāji, kootān, kolombu,* for example. *Curry,* the word the English in India used, covers a wide variety of dishes, all of which taste better after they stand for a while so that the flavors can permeate the whole preparation.

Serve any of these curries or bhājis with rice, chapathis, or dosas. Indians eat with their fingers, so to enjoy Aviyal or Palghat Stew in the traditional manner, break off pieces of chapathi or dosa and wrap them around chopped vegetables, never allowing the food to go beyond the second knuckle. There's an art to this, but once you've gotten used to it, you may well share the Indian's disdain for forks and spoons.

A good many South Indian recipes ask you to toast mustard seed. This is done by heating oil in a pan with a lid, adding mustard seed, covering, and continuing to heat until the seeds are brown. This takes just a minute or two, but it's rather tricky to brown the seeds without burning them. The problem is that they jump around like popcorn, so when you check on their progress, as check you must, do so gingerly.

Fresh whole spices ground at home are tastier than those you buy already ground. Fenugreek seeds and other spices can be ground in your blender or food grinder. If the spices mentioned are not available where you live, you may mail order them from specialty or import shops in the larger cities. One of the best is Haig's Delicacies, at 642 Clement, San Francisco, California 94118. Fresh coriander, or cilantro, is available in Chinese produce markets if you don't find it in the produce section of your usual grocery store.

Amma's Buttermilk Curry

¾ cup dried
    unsweetened coconut
1 quart buttermilk
½ cup water
1 teaspoon salt
1 potato
2 tablespoons oil
½ teaspoon black
    mustard seed
1 tablespoon finely
    minced onion
½ teaspoon turmeric
    powder
½ teaspoon curry
    powder

OPTIONAL
½ teaspoon powdered
    fenugreek seed
dash cayenne

The name of this traditional Kerala recipe is actually *kalan*. *Amma* is the word used in many parts of India for mother—in this case, our teacher's mother, who gave us most of our South Indian recipes.

Blend coconut with buttermilk and set aside.

Cut potato in chunks about ½″×½″×1″ and cook over low heat in ½ cup salted water. When potato is done but still slightly crisp, remove from heat.

Add buttermilk-coconut mixture to the potato and return to heat until preparation comes to a boil. Turn off heat and cover.

Heat oil in a small pan and cover. Add mustard seed when the oil is hot. Allow seeds to crackle and toast, but do not burn. Add minced onion, turmeric, curry powder, and, if you wish, cayenne and fenugreek. Pour this mixture into the pot with the buttermilk mixture.

This preparation is quite liquid; it is served with rice. The flavor is improved if it stands overnight.

Zucchini may be substituted for potatoes.

Serves 6 to 8.

Aviyal

Aviyal means "miscellaneous" in Malayalam. You may substitute asparagus, broccoli, or green pepper if green beans are not available. Eggplant may be added, or substituted for other vegetables.

Combine coconut, yogurt, and seasonings and set aside.

Cut vegetables into 2-inch strips the size of your little finger. Cook vegetables in as little water as possible. Start cooking the green beans first, then add carrots and potatoes after a few minutes. Zucchini should go in last, when the other vegetables are half cooked. Stir the vegetables from time to time so they will cook evenly, but be careful not to break them as they begin to get soft. Add water if necessary.

When all the vegetables are tender—not mushy, but just slightly crisp—remove from heat. There should be just a little water left.

Add the coconut-yogurt mixture and return to heat just long enough to warm it. Turn off heat. Add lemon juice.

This makes 6 cups or more. If any is left over, it tastes even better the next day.

Serves 4 to 6.

1 cup dried unsweetened coconut
1 cup yogurt
1 teaspoon salt
1 teaspoon turmeric powder
¼ teaspoon curry powder
2 large potatoes
2 medium zucchini
2 large carrots
¼ pound green beans
juice of 1 lemon

Cauliflower Eggplant Curry

1 cauliflower
1 eggplant
1 cup peas
2 potatoes
2 to 4 tablespoons oil
1 teaspoon black
    mustard seed
½ teaspoon turmeric
    powder
1 teaspoon curry powder
1 teaspoon salt
¼ cup water
1 tomato, chopped
    OR
1 tablespoon tomato
    paste
juice of 1 lemon

This combination of vegetables is popular all over India.

Remove thick stems of cauliflower and cut into small pieces. Separate carefully into flowerets and slice.

Cut eggplant into ½-inch cubes.

Heat oil in large, heavy pot with a lid. When hot add mustard seed and brown, covered. Be careful not to burn it. Stir in turmeric, curry powder, and salt.

Add cauliflower and stir to coat with spices and oil. Add ¼ cup water and eggplant. Cube potatoes and boil them separately until partially cooked before adding them.

Continue cooking over medium heat, adding 1 or 2 tablespoons of water from time to time, stirring gently. Peas should be added about 5 minutes before serving. At the last minute add a finely chopped tomato or tomato paste. Turn off heat and add lemon juice. The cooking time will depend on how crisp you like your vegetables.

Serves 6 to 8.

Green Bean Bhaji

4 cups green beans
2 tablespoons oil
1 teaspoon black
    mustard seed
1 teaspoon salt
1 teaspoon turmeric
    powder
2 to 4 tablespoons water

OPTIONAL
2 tablespoons chopped
    onion
⅓ to ½ cup dried
    unsweetened coconut

Remove ends from green beans. Place a handful at a time on a board and slice them into cross sections ⅛ to ¼ inch wide.

Heat oil in large, heavy pan with a lid. Add mustard seed to hot oil and cover. Allow to brown, but not to burn. Stir in turmeric and salt, and sauté onion if desired.

Add green beans and 2 to 4 tablespoons of water. Turn down the heat and cook until beans are tender. Add a little water as needed.

If you like, stir in coconut a few minutes before the vegetables finish cooking.

CABBAGE BHAJI

Shred cabbage as for coleslaw and follow directions for Green Bean Bhaji.

OKRA BHAJI

Slice okra into thin cross sections. Follow directions for Green Bean Bhaji, but don't add water. Instead, stir frequently. A few green onions may be sautéed just before adding okra.

ZUCCHINI BHAJI

Proceed as with Okra Bhaji.

Coconut Stew

Prepare coconut milk with dried coconut and boiling water as follows. Put coconut in blender—just enough at a time to cover the blade. Blend until coconut is powdery and a little moist. Remove to a pot and pour boiling water over it. Add salt and bay leaf.

Cut potatoes into ½-inch cubes and cook in the coconut milk.

While potatoes are cooking, heat oil in a heavy pot. Stir in fenugreek. Slice onions in thin wedges, chop green pepper, and add both to oil along with ginger.

When the onions are soft and the potatoes are cooked, combine the two and add coriander leaves. There should be enough coconut milk left with the potatoes to provide a little sauce. This curry is neither dry nor very liquid.

Serves 6 to 8.

2 cups dried
    unsweetened coconut
4 cups boiling water
2 teaspoons salt
1 bay leaf
5 potatoes
2 tablespoons oil
2 teaspoons powdered
    fenugreek seed
2 to 4 tablespoons
    minced fresh ginger
½ green pepper
2 medium onions
¼ cup finely chopped
    coriander leaves

Sauces

A tasty sauce is the simplest shortcut we know to a truly memorable dinner. The easily prepared and nutritious sauces we've collected here can be served with single or mixed vegetables, grains, noodles, or potatoes.

You will notice that many of our sauce recipes are departures from the basic Cream Sauce. There is almost no end to the variations you can develop. Cream Sauce becomes mushroom sauce, for example, with the addition of a cup of sautéed mushrooms, or an ultra-simple curry sauce if you stir in a spoonful of curry powder. Herbs and spices make all the difference in the world. Take Sunshine Sauce, for instance: when we have no coriander, we use a bit of mustard powder, and find it delicious. So please use these recipes as a starting point for your own creations, making good use of whatever you might have on hand. With a blender or food mill (see p. 170), almost any flavorful leftover can become part of an appetizing sauce. One of our all-time favorite salad dressings came about because we had a cup of cooked broccoli in the refrigerator.

We were at a loss for a good replacement for gravy (not relishing the meat-flavored, just barely vegetarian preparations sold in some health food stores) until we began cooking dried beans in quantity. The stock left from cooking beans (especially soybeans) makes a rich-tasting, thick brown gravy (see p. 229) that is not at all meaty, just the thing for baked potatoes. Soybean stock flavored with fresh ginger, a hint of garlic, and toasted sesame seeds makes a fine sauce for Chinese vegetables, thickened, if necessary, with cornstarch.

The most important thing to remember about sauces is that almost all of them are high in calories. We've marked the especially fattening ones, but all should be used with discretion. A few guidelines have helped us enjoy sauces with a free mind.

◆ Don't cook in oil or margarine any vegetable that's going to be sauced.

◆ Use sauces in small quantities: add them to the vegetables in the kitchen rather than serving them separately.

Their purpose is to enhance food, not to smother it. Stir in what seems a reasonable amount of sauce, or drizzle it over the serving dish with a light hand.

–{ By and large, use just one sauce per meal. If the carrots are creamed, for instance, serve lemon wedges with the broccoli, or sprinkle it with toasted sesame seeds—or let it stand on its own, cooked just right. The object here is not just to keep calories down, but to help your family learn to relish the wonderful range of flavors and textures that the vegetables have on their own, easily overlooked if they are always served with sauce.

A few tablespoonfuls of leftover sauce is well worth the keeping; add it to soups or casseroles. Sweet & Sour Mustard Sauce can enliven a cheese spread, and Green Sauce can turn leftover beans into a tasty spread. Some sauces, especially the cheesy ones, are quite good warmed slightly and spread on toast.

Yeast Butter

We know you don't believe it. It sounds like a health food addict's put-on. But in fact, we know of no simpler or more popular sauce than this, particularly over broccoli spears or petite patty pan squashes, steamed whole. Left in the refrigerator overnight, it will be firm in the morning and ready to spread on your breakfast toast. Not just any old yeast will do. In this case, flavor is all, and for good-flavored yeast, torula is hard to beat.

Melt margarine in a saucepan. Repeat, *margarine*—the flavor of Better-Butter somehow doesn't work here. Remove the pan from the heat as soon as the margarine melts. If you don't, it may lump or curdle with the yeast, and then you'll need to mix it in the blender. Stir in the yeast until the sauce is smooth.

Makes about ½ cup.

½ cup margarine
2 tablespoons nutritional
  yeast

Tomato Sauce

½ onion, chopped
1 clove garlic
2 tablespoons oil
1 small carrot, grated
2 tablespoons chopped
   green pepper
1 bay leaf
1 teaspoon oregano
½ teaspoon thyme
¼ teaspoon basil
2 tablespoons chopped
   fresh parsley
2 cups tomatoes, fresh
   or canned
1 six-ounce can tomato
   paste
1 teaspoon salt
¼ teaspoon brown sugar
⅛ teaspoon pepper

This sauce becomes tastier with time. Make up a large quantity and keep it on hand. Use vegetable stock to thin it to desired consistency for spaghetti, or use it as is for dishes like pizza.

Sauté onion and garlic clove in oil until onion is soft. Discard garlic.

Add carrot, green pepper, bay leaf, and herbs. Stir well, then add the tomatoes, tomato paste, and seasonings. Simmer for half an hour. Remove the bay leaf.

Makes a little more than 2 cups.

Potato Dill Sauce

½ onion, chopped
2 tablespoons oil
2 cups vegetable stock
4 potatoes, cubed
1 clove fresh garlic
   OR
scant ⅛ teaspoon garlic
   powder
2 teaspoons dill weed
2 tablespoons chopped
   parsley
⅛ teaspoon pepper
1½ teaspoons salt

Sauté onion in oil. Add stock, potatoes, garlic, and dill weed. Cook until potatoes are soft, then purée in blender until potatoes are smooth. Add seasonings and parsley.

Makes 3 cups.

Broccoli, chard, brussel sprouts, and the like take very kindly to this sauce.

Tomato Ginger Sauce

Vegetables and grain dishes alike take on a distinctly Oriental air when served with this flavorful sauce.

Sauté onions in oil until soft. Stir in flour and cook several minutes. Slowly add the stock and tomato paste, stirring all the time. Add ginger. Bring to a boil, then simmer gently for about 15 minutes. Add soy sauce and serve.

Makes about 2½ cups.

¼ cup oil
½ onion, cut in thin slices
¼ cup whole wheat flour
2 cups vegetable or soy-bean stock
2 tablespoons tomato paste
½ teaspoon finely minced fresh ginger root
soy sauce to taste

Curry Sauce

Combine the oil and flour in a saucepan over medium heat. Stirring constantly, add the stock, then the onions. Mix the juice and grated peel of the lemon with other ingredients, add to sauce, and cook until apples are soft.

Makes about 3 cups.

2 tablespoons oil
2 tablespoons whole wheat flour
2 onions, finely chopped
1 pint vegetable stock
2 apples, diced
¼ cup raisins
1 teaspoon brown sugar
1 to 3 teaspoons curry powder
1 lemon, well scrubbed
2 bay leaves
1½ teaspoons salt

Lemon Butter

This is one of the nicest things that could happen to a pile of fresh, steamed asparagus spears. Try it on carrots, too, and broccoli.

Juice the lemon and grate half of the peel. Melt the margarine and pour it into a blender along with the lemon juice and peel. Blend.

Makes about ⅔ cup.

1 lemon, well scrubbed
½ cup margarine or Better-Butter

Green Sauce

1 cup vegetable stock
6 tablespoons olive oil
1 green pepper, chopped
3 stalks celery with
    leaves, chopped
1 onion, chopped
1 head parsley, chopped
    (without stems)
1 to 1½ teaspoons salt
⅛ teaspoon garlic
1 teaspoon basil
1 teaspoon oregano
½ teaspoon rosemary or
    coriander

Try "green spaghetti" for an enjoyable change of pace. This is a rich sauce, but so flavorful that a little bit goes a long way. Try it on mixed vegetables, too, with a restrained hand.

Sauté onion in half the oil. Stir in herbs and vegetables. Add stock and simmer 5 to 10 minutes. Purée in blender. (If you like a texture to the sauce, blend only three-fourths of the vegetables.) Return sauce to pan with remainder of oil and seasonings. Continue to cook over low heat for 2 or 3 minutes.

Makes an ample 2 cups.

Homemade Ketchup

1 twelve-ounce can
    tomato paste
½ cup cider vinegar
½ cup water
½ teaspoon salt
1 teaspoon oregano
⅛ teaspoon cumin
⅛ teaspoon nutmeg
⅛ teaspoon pepper
½ teaspoon mustard
    powder
dash garlic powder

If you can do without it, fine, but some of us are so fond of it that we decided to make our own relatively wholesome and quite tasty version. Try it on Soy Burgers (p. 266) or Lentil Nut Loaf (p. 264) or add it to sandwiches.

Mix all the ingredients together very well.

Makes 1¾ cups.

Soy Stock Gravy

This unusual, fragrant sauce is so popular that we value the stock left over from cooking soybeans almost as much as the beans themselves. Try it over potatoes, grains, or vegetables.

Toast the flour in a dry pan using medium heat. Remove the flour and sauté the onion in the oil.

Stir in the flour and cook a few minutes. Add the stock slowly, stirring continuously. Let it come to a boil and thicken. Add the seasonings and simmer briefly.

Makes 2½ cups.

1 onion, chopped
¼ cup oil
¼ cup whole wheat flour
2 cups soy stock (cooking water from soybeans)
1 teaspoon salt
½ teaspoon marjoram
dash pepper
dash garlic powder

Cashew Gravy

This is a rich, unusually flavored sauce that turns simple, steamed vegetables into something special. About half a cupful of sauce nicely complements 4 servings of vegetables.

Sauté onion in oil until soft. Stir in flour and cashew nut meal and cook for three minutes, stirring all the time. Add the stock and salt and stir to blend all the ingredients. Bring the mixture to a boil, then simmer until thick.

If the sauce is not creamy and smooth, it may be blended briefly. Add the parsley.

Makes an ample 2 cups of gravy.

½ cup ground cashew nuts
3 tablespoons whole wheat flour
2 tablespoons oil
¼ onion, chopped
2 cups vegetable stock or water
¼ cup chopped parsley
1 teaspoon salt

Savory Yeast Gravy

Not quite as rich as Yeast Butter, this gravy is creamy and flavorful as can be, excellent on cabbage, cauliflower, broccoli, and greens.

Melt margarine in saucepan. Stir in yeast and flour. The mixture will be dry and crumbly. Continue to cook and stir this over medium heat for 3 minutes. Add the stock slowly. Cook, stirring constantly, over medium heat until sauce starts to boil and thicken. Stir in salt.

If a thinner sauce is desired, stir in more stock.

Makes 1½ cups.

2 tablespoons margarine
2 tablespoons whole wheat flour
2 tablespoons torula yeast
1 cup vegetable stock or water
¼ teaspoon salt

Cream Sauce

2 tablespoons margarine
  or Better-Butter
2 tablespoons whole
  wheat flour
1 cup milk (whole, skim,
  or reconstituted dried
  skim milk)
½ teaspoon salt
herbs or spices to taste

How bleak the old white sauces will look and taste once you have enjoyed the full-bodied flavor of cream sauces made from whole wheat flour. Here is our basic recipe for medium cream sauce.

Melt margarine in a saucepan. Stir in flour and cook 3 or 4 minutes over medium heat, stirring constantly. Add milk slowly, always stirring (a wooden spoon is best), and bring the sauce to boiling point to thicken. Add desired herbs or spices. A heavy-bottomed pan is helpful to prevent scorching or sticking. Adjust seasonings and serve.

Makes 1 cup.

VARIATIONS

Sauté ¼ cup finely chopped onions in the margarine until soft. Then add the flour and proceed as above.

Experiment with different herbs and seasonings to produce your own unique sauce: a bay leaf, a hint of nutmeg, basil, thyme, rosemary, or tarragon.

For a particularly smooth texture and lighter color, substitute corn flour for whole wheat flour.

If you will be serving the sauce with vegetables that tend to be juicy, blend ¼ cup or so of dried skim milk into the sauce to make it thicker but not richer. You may, in fact, replace part or all of the milk with vegetable stock: just drain your cooked vegetables and use the juice.

Light Cream Sauce: Use just 1 tablespoon whole wheat flour, 1 tablespoon margarine.

Heavy Cream Sauce: Use 3 tablespoons flour and 3 tablespoons margarine.

Brown Gravy: Toast flour in dry pan first and then proceed as above.

Sweet & Sour Mustard Sauce

This delicate and simple version of a culinary classic is best on steamed green beans, carrots, or Swiss chard.

    Dissolve mustard in vinegar. Stir all the ingredients together and heat.

    Makes 1 cup.

1 cup Cream Sauce
1 teaspoon mustard powder
1 teaspoon brown sugar
1½ teaspoons vinegar

Split Pea–Cheese Sauce

This is excellent on vegetables and grain dishes, and especially on vegetable-filled blintzes or crepes.

    Prepare cream sauce. Stir peas and cheese into sauce and cook over medium heat, stirring constantly, until the cheese melts and the sauce is smooth.

    Makes about 1½ cups.

1 cup Cream Sauce
½ cup well-cooked split peas
½ cup grated sharp cheddar cheese

Cheese Sauce

Add cheese to cream sauce just after it thickens and continue stirring until the cheese melts. Remove from heat.

    Makes 1½ cups.

1 cup Cream Sauce (made with only ¼ teaspoon salt)
½ cup grated sharp cheddar cheese
OR
½ cup grated Swiss cheese plus 1 tablespoon Parmesan

Cottage Cheese Cream Sauce

1/2 cup cottage cheese
1/4 cup Parmesan cheese
  OR
1/2 cup grated Swiss
  cheese
2 tablespoons margarine
  or Better-Butter
2 tablespoons whole
  wheat flour
1 cup skim milk
  OR
1/2 cup skim milk and
  1/2 cup vegetable stock
1/4 teaspoon salt
dash pepper

Grate Parmesan or Swiss and add to cottage cheese. Melt the margarine in a saucepan. Stir in the flour and cook for 3 or 4 minutes. Slowly add 1/4 cup of the skim milk. Stir well over medium heat until the sauce is smooth. Add salt and cheese and stir until the mixture melts. Bring sauce just to a boil and add the rest of the milk gradually. Add a dash of pepper and simmer a moment longer.

Makes 1 1/4 cups.

Buttermilk Sauce

A tangy departure from the norm that takes very happily to herbs. Some of us prefer it to the traditional cream sauces. Simply substitute buttermilk for milk in the light or medium cream sauce recipe, but *don't cook it*. Cook the flour in the margarine for a few minutes along with the herbs, then add the buttermilk, heating only to desired serving temperature. Overheating will cause it to curdle. Even if it separates a little, this is a delicious sauce.

TOMATO BUTTERMILK SAUCE

For a buttermilk sauce that goes quite nicely with cooked whole wheat noodles, sauté half a chopped onion in the margarine. Before you add the buttermilk, stir in 2 tablespoons of tomato paste, 1 teaspoon basil, and a dash of garlic powder. This is a big favorite with children.

Sunshine Sauce

Simmer green onions and coriander in stock for 5 minutes. Use a small covered saucepan. Set aside to cool.

Make a cream sauce with remaining ingredients; be careful not to let the buttermilk come to a boil or it will curdle. Slowly cook the sauce, stirring constantly, over medium heat until it thickens. Combine the sauce with the onions and coriander, and adjust seasonings to taste.

Makes 1 cup sauce.

2 green onions with tops, chopped
¼ cup vegetable stock
OPTIONAL
1 tablespoon finely chopped, fresh coriander

2 tablespoons oil
2 tablespoons whole wheat flour
1 cup buttermilk
½ teaspoon salt
⅛ teaspoon turmeric
OPTIONAL
1 tablespoon grated Parmesan cheese

Mock Sour Cream

This topping is low in saturated fat. It is great on baked potatoes, borscht, potato pancakes, or Black Bread (p. 93).

Mix all ingredients except chives in a blender until they are smooth and creamy. Add chives.

Makes about 1½ cups.

1 cup cottage cheese
1 tablespoon lemon juice
2 tablespoons oil
2 tablespoons mayonnaise
¼ teaspoon tarragon
¼ cup buttermilk
1 tablespoon vinegar
OPTIONAL
2 tablespoons chopped chives

Heartier Dishes

A few of these recipes include no vegetables at all, but most of them are for dishes that require no more than a well-wrought green salad to qualify as one-dish meals. Most of our foreign recipes come in here—for piroshkis, blintzes, pizzas, and the like. These are the ones you pull out when wary nonvegetarian relatives come to dinner.

In their traditional form, many of these dishes are laden with calories and high in saturated fat. They've all taken a turn for the better, though. Cheese is not used in large amounts, but when we do use it, we opt for the more flavorful kinds, like cheddar, Swiss, bleu, and Parmesan, because a small amount adds a lot of appeal. Low-fat milk products, whole wheat pastas, minimal eggs, and vegetable oil to replace butter: it all helps.

Whole-grain and soy pastas may be new to you. Search them out at health food stores and try all the varieties, including buckwheat noodles and the green ones made with spinach. One 8-ounce package of noodles or spaghetti makes about 4 cups cooked. For instructions on making homemade noodles, which are tender, delicious, and not nearly the production number you might think, see the recipes for Hungarian Noodles and Canneloni.

Try all of our pasta recipes, but please don't ignore the obvious: full-flavored whole-grain noodles served plain with Better-Butter and perhaps some finely chopped parsley. Most of the cream sauce variations from the previous section go well with noodles, and of course spaghetti calls for either Tomato Sauce or Green Sauce, and Neat Balls (p. 266).

Buckwheat noodles deserve special mention. After you have cooked and drained them, stir in a spoonful of sesame seed oil for an especially delicate flavor. Serve them with Chinese Vegetables (p. 217) or just stir into the cooked and drained noodles a cup or so of cooked, chopped vegetables (use onion, green pepper, celery, green beans, snow peas, cauliflower, and the like). Add soy sauce and top with Sesame Salt (p. 118).

Canneloni

These are large homemade noodles with a delicately fla-vored cheese filling. The saving grace of this admittedly time-consuming gourmet delight is that it can be done in several steps ahead of time. The whole dish can be assembled early and baked later.

To make the filling, combine Parmesan, mozzarella, and ricotta or cottage cheese with 1 beaten egg, nutmeg, and ¼ cup of the cream sauce. Reserve remaining cream sauce for topping.

Wash and dry spinach and chop it into bite-size pieces. Wilt it by steaming briefly. Combine with other filling ingre-dients and refrigerate.

To prepare noodles, mix flour and salt together and place in a mound on a flat surface. Make a well in the mound and drop in the 2 unbeaten eggs and the water. Use your fingers to work these ingredients together swiftly and knead well until smooth. This will take about 10 minutes.

Let the dough rest 10 minutes before rolling it out.

Bring 3 quarts of water to a boil and add a tablespoon of oil to keep the noodles from sticking together as they cook.

Divide dough into two balls. On a floured surface roll dough out paper-thin, turning it around and over frequently. Keep turning and rolling dough until it's about ¹⁄₁₆ inch thick.

Cut dough into ten 4″ × 6″ rectangles and drop into boiling water. Cook five at a time. Keep pushing the noodles back under the water. After 8 minutes, remove with slotted spoon or tongs. Drain and rinse.

Preheat oven to 350°.

Fill noodles with a generous ¼ cup of filling each and roll them up. Place them seam-side down in a greased casse-role. Spoon the remaining cream sauce on top and dribble Tomato Sauce over all. Sprinkle with parsley and bake for 20 minutes.

Serves 4 to 6.

1 cup Cream Sauce
  (p. 230) seasoned with
  1 bay leaf and a pinch
  of nutmeg
¾ cup grated Parmesan
  cheese
½ cup grated mozzarella
  cheese
2½ cups low-fat cottage
  cheese and/or ricotta
3 eggs
¼ teaspoon nutmeg
1 bunch spinach
1¾ cups whole wheat
  flour
½ teaspoon salt
4 tablespoons water
1 cup Tomato Sauce
  (p. 226)
½ cup chopped parsley

Spanakopita

2 or 3 bunches spinach
3 cups low-fat cottage
 cheese
3 eggs
1 teaspoon salt

2½ cups whole wheat
 flour
¼ cup oil
2 teaspoons salt
1 cup warm water
½ cup melted margarine
 or Better-Butter

Over the years, our friend Sultana's pita has gradually outstripped all contenders for the title of Most Requested Dish. There is a knack to making it, we admit, but it's a knack you'll be glad to have developed. You will need a pizza pan and a 4-foot piece of ¾- or 1-inch doweling to roll out the dough. If you have neither a pita pan nor a pizza pan, don't be daunted. Use pie plates or tins, and since you'll be working on a smaller scale, a rolling pin will do. One recipe will make two 9- or 10-inch "pies."

Wash and dry the spinach and chop it fine. Sprinkle with salt and squeeze or wring to wilt it. Add the cottage cheese and eggs. Mix very well and set aside.

Sift the flour and save the bran for tomorrow morning's porridge. Mix flour, salt, oil, and water, and knead briefly until you have a soft dough.

Divide dough into two balls, one larger than the other. Pat the larger ball flat and roll it into an 8-inch circle, using a rolling pin. Now, beginning with the edge closest to you, roll the dough over the dowel as shown. Use the sifted flour only as needed to keep dough from sticking.

Start with your hands in the center and move them forward and backward, working outward, towards the ends of the dowel. When your hands reach the edge of the dough, unroll it gently so that it is flat again. Turn the crust (larger now, but lopsided) a ⅛ turn, and repeat this rolling operation until the dough is very round, paper-thin, even, and 3 inches bigger all around than your pan. The tricky part is to do all this without making holes in the dough.

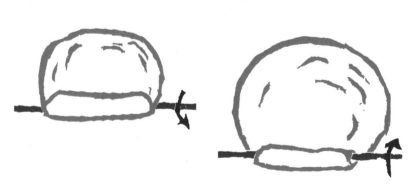

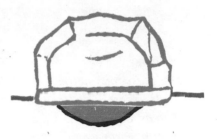

Grease a pizza pan. Preheat oven to 400°.

Place the dowel with the dough wrapped around it on one edge of the pan, and unroll the dough over the pan. Gently fold the excess edge of the crust in, towards the center, so that it won't break while you're preparing the second crust.

Now roll the smaller ball similarly, until it is slightly smaller than the other. Set it aside carefully.

Unfold the edges of the dough in the pan and spread with a tablespoonful or two of the melted margarine. Put in the filling and drizzle again with a little margarine. Place the second piece of dough over the top, leaving it loose with plenty of wrinkles. Pour half the remaining margarine over the edges and fold the under-crust edge around the upper-crust edge as shown.

Drizzle the last of the margarine over the top, particularly around the edges. Be sure to poke holes all over the top crust with a fork or a sharp paring knife.

Bake the pita on the bottom rack of the oven for 45 minutes, until just brown. Cover it with a towel and let it stand for 10 minutes before serving. Cut in wedges.

Serves 6 to 8.

CHARD PITA

We're very fond of chard, which grows abundantly in our gardens. With a few changes, the spanakopita recipe adapts very nicely. The crust is the same; here is the filling.

Sauté green onions in a large pan until soft. Add the chopped chard and cook until wilted. Drain off the liquid (save it for soup). Combine all ingredients and mix well. Prepare crust and then fill and bake just as you would spanakopita.

6 green onions, chopped
3 tablespoons melted margarine
4 quarts chopped chard leaves
3 cups low-fat cottage cheese
3 eggs
1 teaspoon salt
pinch pepper
3 tablespoons grated Parmesan or other sharp cheese

Piroshki

DOUGH

*1½ teaspoons active
    dry yeast*

¼ teaspoon brown sugar

¾ cup warm water

1 egg

2 tablespoons oil

1 teaspoon salt

*2 or more cups whole
    wheat flour*

We've given two of our favorite fillings for these vegetable turnovers, but you may want to invent your own.

Dissolve sugar and yeast in water. Beat egg and oil together and add to yeast. Stir in salt and start beating in flour a half cup at a time until the dough is too stiff to mix with a spoon. Knead in the rest of the flour and add even more if necessary to make a fairly stiff dough. Knead about 10 minutes on a floured surface.

Let dough rise in a greased bowl until it has doubled in size. You can also start the dough early in the day and refrigerate it in a covered container. If you do this very early in the morning, you may need to punch the dough down around noon. An hour before you need to roll it out, remove the dough from the refrigerator.

Roll the dough on a floured surface until it's about ⅛ inch thick. Cut with a 4-inch cookie or pastry cutter. Roll each of these circles thinner still, to about ¹⁄₁₆ inch. They should be large enough to be filled and folded, but not too fragile to manipulate. Re-roll the dough scraps or make little dinner rolls from them.

Preheat oven to 400°.

Put a heaping tablespoon of filling in center of the circle of dough. Dip a pastry brush into cold water or milk and wet edges of dough. Fold over in a half-circle and seal the edges by pressing with the tines of a fork.

Bake on lightly greased cookie sheet for 20 minutes. Brush with melted margarine or Better-Butter when done.

Serves 6 to 8.

For a sturdier variation, convenient for picnic lunches, simply roll the dough into ⅛-inch thickness and cut in 5-inch circles. Do not roll thinner. Fill and proceed as above.

ASPARAGUS FILLING

Chop green onions with tender part of tops. Dice green pepper and chop squash. Snap tough ends from asparagus and cut into ¼-inch slices.

Sauté green onions in oil and 2 tablespoons stock until soft. Add 2 more tablespoons stock along with the patty pan squash and cook, covered, until soft—5 to 10 minutes. In another pan steam the sliced asparagus and diced green pepper in remaining stock. Purée the first mixture in the blender with just a spoonful or two of the asparagus mixture and the seasonings. Combine.

Makes 1¼ cups.

2 green onions
½ green pepper
1 patty pan squash
10 asparagus spears
½ teaspoon salt
pinch garlic powder
pinch savory
2 tablespoons oil
¼ cup water or
*   vegetable stock*

CHARD FILLING

Sauté the onions and celery in oil and stock until soft. Add chopped chard and cook, covered, for 5 to 10 minutes, until chard is tender. Stir in Sunshine Sauce.

Makes 1⅓ cups.

For a fine variation, use spinach instead of chard, and Cottage Cheese Cream Sauce (p. 232) instead of Sunshine Sauce.

2 green onions, chopped
2 stalks celery, diced
1 tablespoon chopped
*   parsley or coriander*
*   leaves*
1 bunch chard leaves,
*   chopped*
2 tablespoons oil
1 tablespoon stock or
*   water*
1 recipe Sunshine Sauce
*   (p. 233) prepared with*
*   just ½ cup buttermilk*

Stuffed Cabbage Rolls

1 large head cabbage

FILLING

2 tablespoons minced
    onion
1 tablespoon oil
1 cup raw brown rice
1½ cups vegetable stock
2 tablespoons raisins
¼ cup toasted almonds,
    slivered, or sunflower
    seeds
½ teaspoon cinnamon
½ teaspoon salt
dash pepper

SAUCE

2 tablespoons oil
1 onion, thinly sliced
1 tablespoon whole
    wheat flour
2 cups fresh or canned
    tomatoes, chopped,
    and 1 cup tomato juice
    OR
3 cups vegetable stock
⅛ teaspoon pepper
½ teaspoon salt
OPTIONAL
¼ teaspoon powdered
    cloves

GARNISH
¼ cup lemon juice
2 tablespoons raisins

Not to be undertaken when you're pressed for time—a delicious dish, though, well worth the effort.

To make filling, sauté onion in oil, then stir in rice and sauté a few minutes longer. Add stock, nuts, raisins, and seasonings. (Nuts may be replaced with any crunchy vegetable, like carrot or celery, chopped.) Bring to a boil, cover, lower heat, and cook for 45 minutes.

To prepare sauce, sauté onion in oil until soft. Stir in flour and cook 2 or 3 minutes. Gradually add tomatoes or stock and seasonings, stirring constantly. Simmer 30 minutes.

Remove core from the cabbage and steam for 5 minutes over boiling water. Carefully peel off 18 or so of the outer leaves.

Preheat oven to 350° if you wish to bake the rolls.

Place 2 tablespoons filling on each leaf, tuck in sides, and roll up.

Lightly grease a baking dish or a large pot with a lid. Spread the sauce in the bottom and place the stuffed leaves seam-side down over the sauce, in several layers if necessary. Cover and bake for 45 minutes or simmer gently on top of the stove for 45 minutes. Halfway through the cooking time, pour lemon juice and raisins over the rolls.

Serves 6 to 8.

Lasagna al Forno

This version has all the flavor and eye appeal of traditional lasagna but is not nearly so devastating to the figure. If whole wheat–soy lasagna noodles are hard to find, substitute any kind of whole-grain noodle.

Cook noodles in boiling, salted water until tender, and drain.

Preheat oven to 350°. Toast nuts or seeds in oven, stirring frequently. Wash and dry spinach and chop into bite-size pieces.

Spread ¾ cup of sauce in bottom of an 8″ × 8″ baking dish. Place one third of the noodles on top. Cover with one third of the spinach, one fourth of the nuts, ¼ cup cottage cheese, 1 tablespoon Parmesan cheese, and a layer of mozzarella slices. Repeat layers twice. Spread the last cup of sauce and the remaining nuts and cheeses on top.

Bake for 40 minutes, and let stand for 10 minutes before cutting.

Serves 4 to 6.

3 cups Tomato Sauce
  (p. 226)
¾ pound whole wheat–
  soy lasagna noodles
½ cup chopped walnuts,
  almonds, or sunflower
  seeds
1 medium bunch spinach
12 thin slices mozzarella
  or Swiss cheese
¼ cup grated Parmesan
  cheese
1 cup cottage cheese
  OR
¾ cup ricotta cheese
  softened with ½ cup
  skim milk

Stuffed Chard Leaves

Preheat oven to 350°.

Sauté onion in oil. Mix all ingredients except chard.

Wash and dry chard leaves and remove stems. Place 2 tablespoons of filling on the underside of the leaf, a third of the way from the bottom. Fold over the sides of the leaf and roll up into a square packet. Place seam-side down in a greased casserole. Cover and bake for about 30 minutes, or steam in a steamer basket over boiling water until the leaves are tender, about 20 minutes. Bake any extra filling and serve with stuffed leaves.

Serves 6 to 8.

16 large leaves Swiss
  chard
2½ cups cooked brown
  rice
1 onion, chopped
¼ cup oil
1½ cups low-fat cottage
  cheese
1 egg, beaten
½ cup chopped parsley
¾ cup raisins
1 teaspoon dill weed
¾ teaspoon salt

VARIATION
Stuff chard with Bulgur Wheat Pilaf (p. 269) and serve with Sunshine Sauce (p. 233).

Vegetables, Macaroni, & Cheese

¼ cup margarine

2 green onions, sliced

3 tablespoons whole wheat flour

2 cups milk

¼ cup chopped parsley

1½ teaspoons salt

½ teaspoon pepper

¼ teaspoon thyme

dash garlic

dash nutmeg

1 cup low-fat cottage cheese

4 cups cooked whole wheat or whole wheat–soy macaroni or noodles (8-ounce package)

¼ cup toasted wheat germ

3 cups cut-up cooked vegetables

1 cup grated cheddar or Swiss cheese

1 cup whole-grain bread crumbs

Preheat oven to 350°.

Sauté onions in margarine until soft. Blend in flour and cook over medium heat several minutes, stirring constantly. Slowly add the milk, continuing to stir. Add the cottage cheese and seasonings. Cook until sauce thickens. Combine noodles, vegetables, and sauce, and pour into greased 2½-quart baking dish. Top with cheese and bread crumbs. Bake until piping hot and bubbly (15 to 20 minutes).

Serves 6 to 8.

Zucchini Oat-flake Loaf

Preheat oven to 375°.

    Sauté onion in oil until soft. Combine with other ingredients and press into a well-greased loaf pan. Bake for 30 minutes.

    Serves 6.

2 cups uncooked rolled oats
3 cups grated zucchini
½ cup grated Swiss or cheddar cheese
2 eggs, beaten
½ cup soy meal
   OR
½ cup wheat germ
½ cup chopped onion
3 tablespoons oil
½ cup toasted sunflower seeds
¼ teaspoon nutmeg
1 teaspoon salt

Potato Carrot Kugel

A kugel is a pudding, and comes in many forms. Serve this tasty version with a lavish green salad.

    Preheat oven to 300°.

    Cook carrots and onion in stock and margarine for several minutes, until tender. Grate potatoes and add immediately. Remove from heat and stir in beaten egg yolks.

    Mix together the flour, wheat germ, baking powder, and seasonings and add to vegetables. Beat egg whites stiff and fold into vegetable mixture. Pour into a greased baking dish and bake for 1 hour.

    Serves 4 to 6.

1 cup grated carrots
2 tablespoons chopped onion
¾ cup vegetable stock or water
¼ cup margarine
3 cups grated potatoes
2 eggs, separated
¼ cup whole wheat flour
¼ cup raw wheat germ
pinch pepper
dash garlic
1½ teaspoons salt
1 teaspoon baking powder

Hungarian Noodles

NOODLES

¾ cup whole wheat flour
1 egg
1 tablespoon water
½ teaspoon salt
1 teaspoon oil
dash garlic
dash pepper
  OR 2 cups cooked
  whole wheat noodles
  (half an 8-ounce
  package)

SAUCE

1½ cups diced vege-
  tables: fresh artichoke
  hearts, garden peas,
  carrots, asparagus,
  etc.
1 large onion
¼ cup margarine
3 tablespoons whole
  wheat flour
2½ cups thick buttermilk
2 cups low-fat cottage
  cheese
¼ cup grated Parmesan
  cheese
¼ cup chopped
  coriander leaves
1 teaspoon salt

Homemade noodles and fresh coriander put this dish in a class by itself. Even with purchased whole wheat noodles, though, it's extremely good. If you can't get fresh coriander, use 2 teaspoons of dill weed for an admittedly more authentic Hungarian flavor.

To make noodles, measure flour into good-sized bowl. Combine the egg with the water, salt, pepper, garlic, and oil, but just barely: the "stringiness" of the egg helps hold the dough together. Drop the egg mixture into the flour and work dough together until ingredients are well mixed.

Turn out onto a large, lightly floured surface and continue to knead as if it were bread, for a full 10 minutes. Set dough aside for an hour, covered.

Divide the dough into three balls for ease in handling. Use a rolling pin to roll them out into long, paper-thin rectangles. The board should be generously floured. Keep turning the dough around and over as you roll. When the dough is thin enough to be translucent, let it dry for about 30 minutes—hung over cloths on the backs of kitchen chairs, for example.

While the dough is still pliable, cut it into ribbons about ½ inch wide. Cook in a large pot of rapidly boiling salted water for 5 minutes and drain. Toss with a bit of margarine to keep noodles from sticking together while you are preparing remaining ingredients. You will have about 2 cups of cooked noodles.

Preheat oven to 350°.

Steam the diced vegetables lightly, until just done. If you have garden peas, you may not even need to cook them.

Cut the onion into thin slivers and sauté in the margarine until the onion is soft. Add the flour and cook, stirring frequently, for 2 minutes. Stir in cottage cheese, buttermilk, Parmesan cheese, coriander, and salt, but do not boil. Combine with noodles and vegetables.

Bake about 15 minutes.

Serves 4.

Vegetable Bean Noodle Bake

This very colorful casserole relies on neither cheese nor eggs for its appeal. We think there's something special about the combination of noodles, corn, and soybeans, and for nutritional value, it can't be topped.

Cook soybeans early in day. Cook noodles and drain.

Prepare all vegetables: dice the celery and onion, grate the carrots and potato, remove the corn from the cobs, chop one tomato and slice the remaining three.

Sauté onions and celery in oil until soft. Stir in flour and cook several minutes, stirring over medium heat. Slowly add soybean stock, stirring constantly. Keep heat low. Add carrots, potato, corn, chopped tomato, and seasonings. Bring to boil to thicken, stirring all the while, and remove from heat.

Preheat oven to 350°.

In a greased 9″×13″ baking dish, alternate layers of beans and noodles, pouring some of the vegetable gravy over each layer. Liquid should come almost to top of mixture. Arrange tomato slices over top of casserole and sprinkle with parsley. Bake for 40 minutes.

Serves 8.

3 cups cooked whole wheat noodles (6 ounces uncooked)
2 cups cooked soybeans (1 cup uncooked)
1 onion
½ head celery
2 carrots
1 potato
2 ears fresh corn
4 tomatoes
4 tablespoons oil
5 tablespoons whole wheat flour
3 cups soybean stock
1 teaspoon salt
¼ teaspoon pepper
¼ teaspoon mustard powder
½ teaspoon sage
2 teaspoons basil
⅓ cup minced parsley

Blintzes

CREPE

1 cup skim milk

¾ cup whole wheat flour

2 eggs (plus 1 white if you use a yolk in filling)

1 tablespoon oil

½ teaspoon salt

CHEESE FILLING

2 cups baker's cheese, ricotta cheese, or low-fat cottage cheese

1 tablespoon brown sugar

1 tablespoon melted margarine or Better-Butter

½ teaspoon salt

2 tablespoons chopped toasted almonds

1 egg yolk (add white to crepe batter)

1 tablespoon raisins

We like to serve the cheese-filled blintzes with yogurt and applesauce. Split Pea–Cheese Sauce (p. 231) goes well with either the savory or the simple vegetable fillings. Mock Sour Cream (p. 233) is a fine topping for all three versions—for the cheese-filled blintzes, omit the chives.

Put all ingredients in blender and mix on low speed, or use an electric or rotary beater.

Grease lightly a 7-inch skillet, Teflon pan, or griddle. Heat over medium-high flame as for pancakes.

Pour a scant ¼ cup of batter on the pan. Tilt the pan as you pour so the batter spreads evenly on the bottom. Brown the bottom of the crepe lightly, and as the top becomes visibly dry, remove from pan. Turn cooked side up onto a tabletop or counter covered with a smooth cloth. Make remaining crepes in the same manner; do not stack them. Makes about 15 crepes.

Preheat oven to 400°.

Put a rounded tablespoon of filling on the cooked side of each crepe. Turn in opposite sides and then roll up. Place seam-side down in a greased baking pan. Bake for 20 minutes. After 10 or 15 minutes, when the bottom is browned, turn to brown other side. Some filling may escape from the crepes, but they will be just as good. Instead of baking the blintzes, you may brown them on a Teflon or iron skillet if you prefer.

Choose the cheese, the savory, or the simple vegetable filling. Each recipe makes enough filling for about 15 crepes, which will serve 4 to 6.

CHEESE FILLING

Vary cheese filling as follows:

◄ Add either ½ teaspoon cinnamon, ½ teaspoon vanilla, or 1 tablespoon lemon juice.

◄ Substitute a dash of pepper and ½ teaspoon paprika for sugar and raisins.

SAVORY FILLING

Sauté onions in oil just lightly. Stir in green beans. Add stock and bring to a boil. Simmer for 10 minutes or more, until beans are tender. If there is too much liquid, drain and save for the sauce topping.

Combine beans and onions with remaining ingredients. Cool until ready to fill the blintzes.

This filling makes an excellent vegetable dish on its own.

SIMPLE VEGETABLE FILLING

Prepare 1½ cups of your favorite combinations of vegetables. Cut them quite small or grate them. Cook and season to taste. Try any of these:

Creamed spinach and celery
Asparagus and green onion
Green pepper and eggplant or okra
Shredded cabbage, carrots, and onions
Fresh corn, green onion, and parsley

SAVORY FILLING

3 small green onions, sliced fine
1 tablespoon oil
1 cup finely cut green beans
¼ cup vegetable stock or water
½ cup baker's cheese, ricotta cheese, or low-fat cottage cheese
½ teaspoon salt
2 tablespoons grated Parmesan cheese
½ cup well-cooked green split peas

Spinach Crepes

Crepes are in French cuisine what blintzes are in Jewish cooking. Up to a point they are alike in ingredients and preparation.

Prepare the batter and pour onto pan as directed in the Blintz recipe. When the crepe is lightly browned underneath (in about one minute) turn with a spatula and cook second side for half a minute. It will have browned only in spots. Now turn the crepe onto a platter with the second side up, and make the remaining crepes in the same manner.

Preheat oven to 400°.

Place a generous ¼ cup of creamed spinach on lower part of each crepe and roll into a cylinder. Place the stuffed crepes side by side in a shallow baking pan. Pour the remaining creamed spinach (thinned with a little milk if necessary) down the center of the row of crepes. Sprinkle with grated cheese and heat through in oven for 5 to 10 minutes.

Makes 15 crepes.

1 recipe Blintz batter
1 double recipe Creamed Spinach (p. 206)

OPTIONAL
grated Parmesan or Swiss cheese

Vegetable Enchiladas

1 dozen Tortillas
  (p. 109)
3 to 4 cups Tomato
  Sauce or Green Sauce
  (p. 228)
½ to 1 teaspoon cumin
½ teaspoon chili powder
3 tablespoons oil

FILLING
1 onion, minced
1 green pepper, chopped
  fine
3 stalks celery, chopped
  fine
1 cup chopped parsley
  OR
¼ cup chopped coriander
2 cups coarsely grated
  zucchini
2 cups green beans,
  chopped small
corn flour
1 teaspoon salt
dash cumin
dash chili powder
dash garlic
1 cup grated cheddar
  and/or jack cheese

Season Tomato Sauce or Green Sauce with cumin and chili powder.

Sauté onion, pepper, celery, and parsley in oil. Add vegetables and cook, covered, until tender. If they are very wet, thicken with corn flour. Add ¾ cup of the sauce and adjust seasonings. Set aside.

Preheat oven to 350°.

Soften tortillas as instructed on page 109 and fill at once with a generous ⅓ cup of the vegetable mixture for each one. Roll them up and place in a baking dish, seam-side down, rather close together, and cover with sauce. Top with cheese. Heat until the sauce bubbles.

Serves 6.

VARIATIONS

Replace the zucchini and green beans with whatever vegetable you choose, grated coarsely or chopped fine.

CHEESE ENCHILADAS
Leave out half the zucchini and add 1 cup of cheese in its place.

HEARTY BEAN ENCHILADAS
Replace part or all of the vegetables with 2 cups cooked and seasoned pinto, kidney, or other beans.

Zucchini and Green Rice

Slice zucchini in ¼-inch rounds. Steam until done but still firm.

Preheat oven to 350°.

Mix rice with lemon juice, parsley, and seasonings. In a greased casserole make a layer each of rice mixture, cottage cheese, and zucchini. Top with grated cheese. Bake uncovered for 10 to 15 minutes. Sprinkle with Parmesan cheese.

Serves 4 to 6.

1½ pounds zucchini
¾ cup chopped parsley
juice of 1 lemon
1 cup low-fat cottage cheese
1 teaspoon salt
pinch pepper
1 teaspoon basil
2 tablespoons oil
2 cups cooked brown rice
½ cup grated cheddar cheese
2 tablespoons grated Parmesan cheese

Vegetable Rice Soufflé

Cook carrots, celery, and onion in 1 tablespoon of the margarine and ½ cup of the stock for 10 minutes.

Make a cream sauce (p. 230) with the remaining 3 tablespoons of margarine, the flour, the remaining ½ cup of stock, and the milk.

Preheat oven to 375°.

Mix vegetables, rice, seasonings, sauce, and egg yolks together. Beat egg whites until stiff and gently fold into the mixture. Pour into a deep, well-greased baking dish and bake for 30 to 40 minutes. Serve at once.

Serves 6.

1½ cups cooked brown rice
1 cup diced celery
1 cup grated carrots
2 tablespoons minced onion
1 cup vegetable stock or water
4 tablespoons margarine
¼ cup whole wheat flour
½ cup milk
3 eggs, separated
1 teaspoon salt
½ teaspoon powdered ginger
2 teaspoons brown sugar

MUSHROOM BEAN SOUFFLÉ

Omit ginger and sugar. Substitute 1 cup of ¼-inch sliced green beans and 1 cup of chopped mushrooms for the carrots and celery. Add ½ teaspoon marjoram.

VEGETABLE RICE PUDDING

Use either combination of vegetables. Substitute 2 beaten eggs for the 3 separated eggs. Simply stir them into the other ingredients and bake.

Good Shepherd's Pie

TOPPING

2 cups leftover mashed
    potatoes
    OR
3 medium potatoes,
¼ cup milk,
1 tablespoon margarine
    or Better-Butter, and
½ teaspoon salt

pinch paprika

FILLING

1 onion, chopped
    coarsely
2 tablespoons oil
1 pound broccoli
1 bunch spinach or Swiss
    chard
1 green pepper, diced
1 pound or 4 medium
    carrots, diced
¾ cup chopped fresh
    tomatoes
    OR
¼ cup tomato paste and
    ½ cup water
1 bay leaf
½ teaspoon basil
1 teaspoon salt

Here's a happy home for leftover mashed potatoes. Vary the vegetables according to the season. A small amount of leftover lentil, pea, or bean soup may be stirred in with the vegetables to good advantage.

Unless you have leftover mashed potatoes, cook potato chunks in fast-boiling water until soft. Mash well with margarine, milk, and salt. Save the potato water for breadmaking.

Cut broccoli into flowers and stems. Peel and slice the stems in ¼-inch rounds. Wash spinach thoroughly and cut into bite-size pieces.

Preheat oven to 350°.

Sauté onion in oil. Add broccoli, green pepper, and carrots and then the basil and bay leaf. Stir well and add tomatoes. Bring to a boil, cover, turn heat to low, and simmer for 15 minutes or until vegetables are just tender. Stir in spinach. Add salt.

Put vegetables into a 9″ × 13″ baking dish. Spread potatoes over top and bake for 10 or 15 minutes, until the potatoes are piping hot. Shake paprika over top before serving.

Serves 4 to 6.

Vegetable Cobbler

Leftover soups and vegetables are transformed into a hearty, savory cobbler in a trice.

Preheat oven to 425°.

Heat vegetables in stock, and pour them into a greased 9″×13″ baking dish.

Stir dry ingredients together. Add eggs and milk and mix just until ingredients are well distributed.

Spread batter over top of vegetables. Bake for 20 to 25 minutes. Sprinkle with cheese if desired.

Serves 6 to 8.

4 cups cooked vegetables
  (or very thick soup)
1½ cups stock
herbs and seasonings
  to taste
1 cup whole wheat
  flour
1½ teaspoons baking
  powder
½ teaspoon salt
½ cup cornmeal
2 eggs, beaten
1 cup milk or broth

Cabbage Kuchen

Preheat oven to 375°.

To make topping, slice onions thinly and sauté with cabbage in margarine. Mix in other topping ingredients and set aside.

Stir flour, baking powder, and salt lightly with a fork. Combine egg, milk, and margarine and stir briefly into dry ingredients.

Spread in greased 8″×8″ baking pan. Spread with topping and bake for 35 minutes.

Serves 6 to 8.

TOPPING
2 onions
4 cups shredded cabbage
2 tablespoons margarine
1 cup yogurt
2 eggs, beaten
½ teaspoon salt
⅛ teaspoon black pepper
1 tablespoon caraway
  seed
DOUGH (KUCHEN)
2 cups whole wheat flour
2 teaspoons baking
  powder
½ teaspoon salt
1 egg, beaten
1 cup milk
2 tablespoons margarine,
  melted

Pizza

1 tablespoon active dry
    yeast
1¼ cups warm water
pinch brown sugar
2 tablespoons olive oil
¼ teaspoon pepper
1½ teaspoons salt
3 or more cups whole
    wheat flour
2 to 3 cups Tomato
    Sauce (p. 226)
½ pound grated mozza-
    rella, cheddar, jack, or
    Swiss cheese
¼ cup Parmesan cheese

Dissolve yeast in water with sugar. When it bubbles to surface, add olive oil, pepper, and salt. Add flour by the half cup, increasing amount if necessary to make a stiff dough. Knead well and set to rise, covered, in a warm place. Let the dough rise once only, about 1½ hours.

Preheat oven to 425°.

Punch dough down and knead well. Roll out for two 14-inch pizzas if thin, crisp crust is desired, or only one if thicker, breadier crust is preferred. Ease onto lightly greased pizza pans and push up a little edge to keep the sauce in.

Spread with Tomato Sauce and bake for 15 minutes. Sprinkle with cheeses and whatever garnishes you like: some of our favorites are sliced mushrooms and olives, sautéed onions, green pepper rings, grated zucchini, and crumbled bits of Soy Paté (p. 140). Return to oven until cheese has melted.

Makes one or two 14-inch pizzas.

Quiche

1 whole wheat piecrust
    (p. 284), partially
    baked
3 eggs, slightly beaten
2 cups warm milk
½ teaspoon salt
pinch pepper
pinch nutmeg
¾ cup grated Swiss
    cheese
margarine or Better-
    Butter

"Cheese pie" just doesn't do justice to this classic of French cuisine. Delicate and delicious as it is, quiche takes happily to the addition of sautéed mushrooms, cooked spinach, or other vegetables.

Preheat oven to 350°.

Scald the milk if it is raw, and let it cool. Combine eggs, milk, salt, and pepper. Spread the cheese evenly in the bottom of the pie shell and pour the milk mixture over it. Sprinkle the top with nutmeg and dot with margarine. Place pie plate on a cookie sheet. Bake for 30 minutes, or until set. If the middle is not quite firm, don't worry. Quiche needs to stand for 10 minutes before serving, and it should be firm after that.

Serves 6.

One cup (no more) of almost any leftover or freshly cooked vegetables can be added to the filling, provided they are tasty and not overcooked. Asparagus is particularly pleasant. Drain vegetables well, though, or the filling won't set.

Chillaquillas

Very unusual, and rather rich, Chillaquillas came to us by way of a Mexican friend. They are traditionally made with tortillas that are several days old, as fresh tortillas tend to disintegrate in the sauce.

Tear tortillas into pieces 2 inches square. Sauté the onions in oil in a heavy 10- or 12-inch skillet until soft. Add chili powder, oregano, and tortilla pieces. Stir frequently until the tortilla pieces are soft and lightly coated with oil. Blend cottage cheese with Tomato Sauce. When smooth, pour over tortillas, sprinkle with salt, and top with grated cheese. Cover the skillet and heat through until the cheese is melted and the sauce is bubbly.

Serves 6 to 8.

*1 dozen Tortillas
(p. 109)*
*½ pound jack cheese
(about 2½ cups
grated)*
*1½ cups Tomato Sauce
(p. 226)*
*1½ cups low-fat cottage
cheese*
*½ cup chopped green
onions, with tops*
2 teaspoons chili powder
*½ teaspoon crushed
oregano*
¼ cup oil
1 teaspoon salt

Spoon Bread

Perfected under the tutelage of a beloved Virginian who knows her spoon breads, this simple dish is one of the irreplaceables. Allow for a half hour pause part of the way through to let the hot cornmeal mixture cool to lukewarm. Serve immediately after baking.

Put the cornmeal and 1 cup of the milk in a heavy saucepan. Bring to a boil, stirring in the rest of the milk in cupfuls as the mixture thickens.

Stir in the margarine. Pour the mixture into another pan and refrigerate for about ½ hour or until lukewarm.

Preheat oven to 400°. Add the salt and eggs to the cornmeal mixture and beat the batter thoroughly. Pour it into a deep, well-greased 2-quart baking dish or casserole.

Bake for 30 minutes, or until the spoon bread turns a golden brown on top.

Serves 6.

1 quart fresh whole milk
1 cup coarse cornmeal
*2 tablespoons margarine
or Better-Butter*
3 eggs, beaten
1½ teaspoons salt

Grains & Beans

Whole-grain and bean cookery is one of the most pleasurable and important discoveries to be made by anyone newly turned vegetarian. These unrefined foods play a critical nutritional role for vegetarians, because they supply the greatest share of the protein and certain B vitamins in the meatless diet, as well as carbohydrate and a good many minerals.

As we mentioned in discussing the Four Food Groups, yeast-raised bread is the ideal way to fill most of the grains and beans requirement. To include a wide selection of these foods, though, and to allow for more flexibility in menu planning, it's helpful to have a good repertoire of grain and bean dishes. Preparing whole-grain cereals and beans is quite easy, and the cooking chart on page 260 will make it even easier. Little needs to be said about the storage of grains and beans, for they are quite hardy. Stored in a cool, dry place and sealed in airtight containers to keep out moisture and insects, they will keep for a full year. Any deterioration or infestation will be evident to nose and eye. You *will* notice with both beans and grains that the longer they've been stored, the longer they will take to cook.

Grains

Try to purchase grains that are grown organically, and explore the full variety. Natural brown rice is sure to please, but keep going from there. Cracked wheat and bulgur wheat can be used interchangeably in most recipes. Bulgur wheat has been parboiled, dried, and broken up, so it has lost a few nutrients along the way. Still, it's an excellent food with a fine, nutty flavor.

Kasha, or buckwheat groats, isn't a member of the cereal grass family at all. It's a staple in the Russian and Eurasian diet—so much so that according to legend, a Russian athletic team slated to compete in an international event near Paris packed their bags and went home when they learned that not a restaurant in town served kasha. If the kasha you buy is brown, it's already roasted; but if it's pale in color, pan-roast it briefly before cooking to bring out its hearty flavor.

Wild rice is actually not rice. It's a seed, native to America. Costly, yes, but so full-flavored and expansive is wild rice that a little goes a long way when mixed with brown rice (see our recipe). We like to reserve this gourmet favorite for holidays.

Get acquainted with all these grains, plus barley, millet, and coarse cornmeal. Each represents the single most important staple food for one population or another, so the wide selection that is available to Americans is truly a luxury.

COOKING METHOD

Rinse grain in cold water and drain well. Bring water to a boil (stock or milk may be used instead). Pour grain in slowly, stirring as you do, and add salt (¼ to ½ teaspoon per cup of grain). Let the water come to a boil again, then turn the heat down to the lowest possible temperature. Cook slowly until all the water is absorbed.

If you have cooked the grain the full time and it still seems hard or tough, add a little boiling water, cover, and continue cooking. Do not stir it any more than absolutely necessary, or it will be gummy.

The times we have suggested are necessarily approximate. Heavy pans with close-fitting lids retain heat and moisture so well that usually a shorter cooking time and less water are called for. Polenta, though, can stick and scorch rather easily if cooked in this way, so we prefer to use a double boiler or to cook it uncovered, stirring continually. Double boilers, in fact, work very nicely for *all* kinds of grains. Pressure cookers are fine for whole grains—whole barley, millet, brown rice, for example—but *not* for those that have been broken up, like polenta or cracked wheat, which can easily clog up the vent of the cooker.

All of these grains stand up very nicely on their own. Serve them plain, with just a dab of Better-Butter to bring out their full yet delicate flavors. Here are some other suggestions:

◅ Sauté raw grain in oil with chopped onion until onion is soft before adding boiling water. Celery and green pepper fit in very nicely too.

◅ Don't forget herbs and spices. Saffron rice is an elegant case in point. Just sauté rice with chopped onion and garlic; bring water or stock to boil with a pinch of saffron and cook as usual.

◅ Dice assorted vegetables and cook along with grain.

◅ Combine grains. Rice and barley go well together and cook in about the same time. Whole wheat berries add texture and color to millet or rice. Give the wheat berries a long head start, though. Kasha's very up-front flavor calms down a bit when you cook it with bulgur wheat or cracked wheat.

◅ Stir ground toasted sesame seeds into cooked grain (especially rice) for nutritional benefit and marvelous flavor.

◅ Sprinkle cooked grain with chopped toasted nuts.

◅ Add a tablespoon of lemon juice to cooked grain.

◅ Do any or many of the above, and stir in yogurt just before serving. This is a Middle Eastern touch, absolutely delicious. A few raisins can be good here, also, but they should be added to the hot grain before the yogurt, in time to "plump."

◅ Serve grains with sauces or gravies. In Italy, where it is a staple food, polenta is often accompanied by tomato sauce.

◅ Stir cream sauce or a variation thereof into cooked grain, top with bread crumbs, chopped nuts or seeds, grated cheese, and chopped parsley, and bake for 20 minutes to half an hour. This is just the ticket for using up oddments of leftover grain and pasta (and even potato or beans). To add a bit of crunch, stir in some lightly steamed diced celery. If anyone asks you, it's called GRAIN DELIGHT.

Beans

Even if you weren't interested in cooking them, you'd probably like to have several jars of beans around for decorative value alone. Their rich, earthen colors are a feast for the eye. Our Red Bean Mix is designed to maximize nutritional value, but its appearance would delight the most exacting artist.

It may be because during the Depression people could afford nothing else, but a good many people have a mental block against beans. We did at first, but it quickly gave way with a little experimentation. They are such a versatile food; you can make soups, salads, casseroles, sandwich spreads, and cracker dips with them—or you can add them in small quantities wherever you want extra body, texture, and nutritional "oomph." We have one friend who cooks up soybeans in large quantity, then freezes them in ice-cube trays so she can just pull out a few cubes when she wants to add them to soups or main dishes. This is useful for very small families, but the practical habit for larger families is just to cook up a pot of beans once or twice a week and draw on them for all kinds of uses.

A glance at the nutrition charts will show you that the various legumes differ slightly in their nutritional profile. It's a good idea, for that reason, to eat a wide variety of beans and peas. Try all of them, and try mixing several varieties together. See the Breakfast Beans combination on page 122, or try the two at the right. In Red Bean Mix, there is a wide divergence in cooking time among the different beans, but if you use an electric slow cooker there is no difficulty. The result is a nice, stewy blend that takes beautifully to your favorite herbs or vegetables.

If you aren't used to eating legumes, they may cause flatulence at first. Split peas, limas, and lentils are easier to digest than the others, so start out with them. Take small servings at first and give your tummy a few weeks' time to adjust. Many people have no trouble with them at all, but even those of us who did at first do fine now, perhaps because of a gradual change in intestinal flora. Some people feel that presoaked beans are less digestible. Thorough cooking, though, is the

RED BEAN MIX
1¼ cups pinto beans
1¼ cups kidney beans
1 cup black beans
⅓ cup mung beans
⅓ cup green split peas

WHITE BEAN MIX
2 cups limas
2 cups small white beans
½ cup yellow split peas

most important factor, especially for soybeans. To determine whether soybeans are done, put one on your tongue and press it against the roof of your mouth. If you can't mash it, continue cooking the beans until you can.

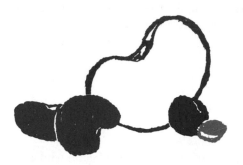

COOKING INSTRUCTIONS

Beans come to us direct from the fields, so we need to sort through them to remove any rocks and moldy or discolored beans. Then rinse them well. Overnight presoaking will cut down the cooking time on any legume by a good half hour or so. Soybeans should be refrigerated during presoaking time to prevent fermentation.

We like to use iron pots for cooking beans; pressure cookers are fine, but certain beans—limas, black beans, and soybeans—get foamy and can clog the vent.

Cover beans with water, bring them to a boil, and let them simmer until the beans are tender. Check them occasionally and add more water if needed. Don't add salt or oil until the beans are tender. Use about ½ teaspoon salt per cup of beans. Keep the pot partially covered at all times; they usually boil over if covered tightly.

The amount of water recommended is very loose. The important thing is to keep the beans covered with liquid at all times. If you want extra bean stock for sauces or soups, just add more water. Be sure to save and use this flavorful stock; it contains a rich supply of B vitamins and minerals.

The amount of cooking time we've suggested is also rather loose. If you are cooking beans to be used for a salad, or any dish where they should be intact, you will cook them just until tender; for soups, they can be cooked a good deal longer.

Here are some of the tricks that will help you make beans as popular with your family as they are with ours.

◄§ Add vinegar or lemon juice to cooked beans. Lentils are especially appreciative of vinegar; lemon juice is a natural with black beans. Start with a tablespoonful and adjust to taste.

◄§ Turn a bean pot into a stew pot by stirring in chopped vegetables for the last half hour of cooking.

◄§ For a more elegant dish, cook up a mixture of limas and red beans. Use the bean stock to make a rich gravy, flavored with tomato paste, onions, bay leaf, garlic, basil, a pinch of sage, and a good red wine vinegar. Stir this gravy back into the bean pot along with a few cups of chopped vegetables. Try potatoes and any combination of carrots, green beans, peas, corn, and asparagus. Simmer until vegetables are done. We call it BEANS BOURGUIGNON and serve it with hot biscuits, rice, or Whole Wheat French Bread.

◄§ Experiment with different combinations of herbs. Dill weed, celery seed, and bay leaf are splendid. Any old pot of red or pinto or kidney beans can become fine-tasting chili beans if you cook them with chopped onion and green pepper, chili powder, cumin, and garlic.

◄§ The Greeks have a very straightforward and delicious way of preparing white beans. Cover a cup of beans with water and add a carrot, an onion, a stalk of celery (all chopped coarsely), and a hearty pinch of oregano. When the beans are tender, stir in 2 tablespoons of oil, ½ teaspoon of salt, and a pinch of paprika. GREEK BEANS are hard to beat.

◄§ Serve lima beans with Tomato Sauce, or garbanzos with Cream Sauce and your favorite herbs.

◄§ Black-eyed peas come to life when cooked with tomato, chopped onion, and soy sauce.

Cooking Times & Proportions for Dinner Grains

Grain (1 cup dry measure)	Water	Cooking time	Yield
Barley (whole)	3 cups	1 hour 15 minutes	3½ cups
Brown rice	2 cups	1 hour	3 cups
Buckwheat (kasha)	2 cups	15 minutes	2½ cups
Bulgur wheat	2 cups	15–20 minutes	2½ cups
Cracked wheat	2 cups	25 minutes	2⅓ cups
Millet	3 cups	45 minutes	3½ cups
Coarse cornmeal (polenta)	4 cups	25 minutes	3 cups
Wild rice	3 cups	1 hour or more	4 cups
Whole wheat berries	3 cups	2 hours	2⅔ cups
Black beans	4 cups	1½ hours	2 cups
Black-eyed peas	3 cups	1 hour	2 cups
Garbanzos (chickpeas)	4 cups	3 hours	2 cups
Great northern beans	3½ cups	2 hours	2 cups
Kidney beans	3 cups	1½ hours	2 cups
Lentils & split peas	3 cups	1 hour	2¼ cups
Limas	2 cups	1½ hours	1¼ cups
Baby limas	2 cups	1½ hours	1¾ cups
Pinto beans	3 cups	2½ hours	2 cups
Red beans	3 cups	3 hours	2 cups
Small white beans (navy, etc.)	3 cups	1½ hours	2 cups
Soybeans	4 cups	3 hours or more	2 cups
Soy grits	2 cups	15 minutes	2 cups

Grains and Beans Together

Not only do they balance one another well nutritionally; grains and beans taste great together too.

◆ Cook lentils along with barley or rice.

◆ Cook split peas with cracked or bulgur wheat.

◆ Add cracked wheat to chili beans, or serve chili beans with polenta.

◆ Leftover rice and cooked beans (drained well) can be combined with mayonnaise and chopped vegetables (pepper, celery, green onion, grated carrot) to make an unusually good luncheon salad.

◆ Rice combines beautifully with beans of all kinds: soybeans in Asia, chili beans in the American Southwest, black-eyed peas in the South. Cuba has a particularly good idea, though. Cook black beans with chopped green pepper and onion, bay leaf, and garlic (traditionally the dish is rather fiery—we like to use a gentle hand). When beans are tender stir in a couple of tablespoons of oil and vinegar. Serve them on a bed of cooked rice, garnished with tomato wedges and chopped parsley or green onion. BLACK BEANS AND RICE is one of the most colorful, tasty, and nourishing dishes we know of.

Chili con Elote

3 tablespoons oil
1 onion, chopped
1 clove garlic
1 green pepper, diced
2 cups vegetable stock
1 cup chopped tomato
    OR
2 tablespoons tomato
    paste
1 cup fresh corn
4 cups cooked kidney or
    pinto beans
½ teaspoon chili powder
¼ teaspoon cumin
    powder
1½ teaspoons salt
1 teaspoon oregano

Chili con *what*? *Elote* means "corn"—a colorful and tasty addition to a traditional favorite.

Sauté onion and garlic clove in oil until onion is soft. Discard garlic clove. Add green pepper. Sauté another 2 or 3 minutes. Add stock, tomatoes, and corn. Mash 2 cups of the kidney beans and add to pot along with whole beans and seasonings. Simmer 30 minutes. If too watery, remove cover and cook another 10 minutes.

Serves 6.

Tennessee Corn Pone

4 cups very juicy cooked
    and seasoned beans
    (especially pinto or
    kidney)
2 cups cornmeal
2 teaspoons baking soda
1 teaspoon salt
1 quart buttermilk
2 eggs, slightly beaten
¼ cup margarine

A homesick friend from Knoxville described a dish his grandma used to make. After several false starts, we came up with this—a dead ringer, he says, and certainly one of our favorites.

Heat beans until quite hot and pour into a lightly greased 9″ × 13″ baking dish.

Preheat oven to 450°.

Mix the cornmeal, baking soda, and salt in a large bowl. Melt the margarine and combine with buttermilk and eggs.

Stir the wet and dry ingredients together until smooth and pour them over the hot beans. Bake on the top rack of your oven until bread is a rich golden color and the sides of the corn bread pull away from the sides of the pan. This takes about 30 minutes.

Serves 10 to 12.

Falafel

Traditionally, falafel (garbanzo balls) are served as a filling for Arab Bread (p. 98) with fresh shredded vegetables and yogurt. The result is somewhat like a taco, but with its own quite distinctive savour.

Cook and mash potato and set aside. Mince leaves of parsley.

Preheat oven to 350°.

Chop onions fine and sauté in oil until soft. Stir in parsley and cook briefly. Add to ground beans. Mix well with remaining ingredients. Form into balls or shape into patties, using about 2 tablespoons of the mixture for each one. Place on greased cookie sheets and bake for 10 minutes on each side.

Makes about 24.

1 medium potato
1 large bunch parsley or coriander
2 small onions
3 tablespoons oil
3 cups cooked, ground garbanzo beans
¼ cup sesame seed meal
1 tablespoon yogurt
⅛ teaspoon garlic powder
1 tablespoon salt
dash cayenne
⅛ teaspoon pepper
1 teaspoon paprika
juice of 1 lemon

New England Baked Beans

Navy, pinto, or kidney beans may be used, or any favorite combination.

Preheat oven to 350°.

Sauté onion in oil for 3 minutes. Add apples and carrots and cook over very low heat, keeping tightly covered, for 5 minutes. Mix with remaining ingredients. Bake covered for 45 minutes.

Serves 6.

4 cups cooked dried beans
½ onion, chopped
1 carrot, grated
1 apple, grated
2 tablespoons oil
1 teaspoon salt
1 teaspoon dry mustard powder
½ cup Homemade Ketchup (p. 228)
¾ cup vegetable stock or water

Lentil Nut Loaf

1 small onion, chopped
  fine
3 tablespoons oil
½ cup wheat germ
2 cups cooked, drained
  lentils
½ cup whole wheat
  bread crumbs
½ cup sunflower seeds
  or walnut pieces
½ teaspoon sage or
  thyme
2 tablespoons torula yeast
2 tablespoons soy flour
2 eggs, beaten
½ cup vegetable stock
  or water
1 tablespoon vinegar
sesame seeds

Preheat oven to 350°.

Sauté onion in oil until soft.

Mix ingredients and place in large, greased loaf pan. Sprinkle generously with sesame seeds. Bake for 30 minutes, covered with aluminum foil or a cookie sheet, and then for 10 minutes uncovered.

Serves 6.

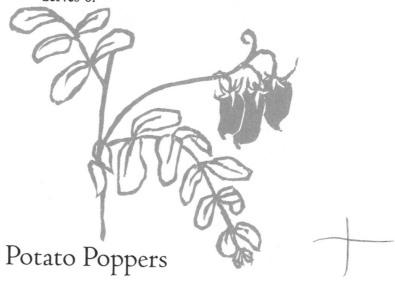

Potato Poppers

½ onion, chopped
1 tablespoon margarine
½ cup mashed potato
1 cup cooked brown rice
1 tablespoon tomato
  paste
½ teaspoon salt
½ cup whole-grain
  bread crumbs
¼ cup grated Parmesan
  cheese

Preheat oven to 350°.

Sauté onion in margarine. Combine all ingredients and form into 1½-inch balls. Bake until delicately browned.

Makes about 12.

Savory Dinner Loaf

A very flexible and tasty way to use leftover vegetables, grains, and sauces.

Preheat oven to 350°.

Mix all ingredients together, reserving ½ cup sauce for topping. Adjust amount of sauce to wetness of mixture—it needs to be moist but not runny. Grease a 9″ × 5″ loaf pan and dust with wheat germ or cornmeal. Bake loaf for 1 hour. Let stand 15 minutes before cutting.

Serves 6.

1 cup cooked bulgur wheat
1 cup cooked soy grits
⅓ cup sesame or sunflower seeds, ground
1⅔ cups whole wheat bread crumbs
2 eggs, beaten
2 tablespoons oil
1 to 2 cups well-seasoned Tomato Sauce (p. 226) or Soy Gravy (p. 229)
2 cups chopped leftover vegetables
1 to 2 teaspoons salt
dash pepper
dash sage

Wild Rice

Chop celery and carrots in ¼-inch cubes. Chop green onions and sauté them in margarine. Add stock and bring to a boil. Stir in the remaining ingredients (except the almonds). Bring to a boil, cover, reduce heat, and cook gently for an hour or more, until the rice is tender. Chop the almonds and add them about 20 minutes before serving.

Makes about 5 cups.

1 cup wild rice
⅓ cup brown rice
5 cups stock or water
1 carrot
1 large stalk celery
6 green onions
2 tablespoons oil
1 teaspoon marjoram
¼ teaspoon rosemary
¼ teaspoon thyme
1 teaspoon salt
dash pepper
pinch garlic
⅓ cup toasted almonds

Soy Burgers

2 tablespoons oil
2 tablespoons chopped
    green onions
1 cup cooked soy pulp,
    or coarsely chopped
    soybeans
1 cup cooked brown rice
½ cup grated cheese
1 cup toasted sesame
    and/or sunflower
    seeds, ground
⅓ cup whole wheat
    flour
2 eggs, beaten
1 teaspoon salt
2 teaspoons soy sauce
½ teaspoon basil

Sauté onions in oil and mix into remaining ingredients. Shape into patties and cook on a griddle or in a skillet. You can also bake patties in a 350° oven for 20 minutes. To keep them from sticking, sprinkle griddle or baking dish with sesame seeds.

Makes 8.

Neat Balls

1 cup cooked bulgur
    wheat or brown rice
½ cup Soy Spread
    (p. 140)
¼ cup cottage cheese or
    grated Swiss cheese
½ cup whole-grain bread
    crumbs
½ teaspoon salt
1 teaspoon soy sauce

Try them with Tomato Sauce (p. 226) and whole wheat spaghetti noodles, or top with Soy Gravy (p. 229), or serve them plain. If you don't have Soy Spread on hand, put cooked soybeans through a food mill with a little tomato paste or Homemade Ketchup (p. 228) and some sautéed onions.

Preheat oven to 350°.

Combine all ingredients and form into 1½-inch balls. Bake on a greased cookie sheet for 10 minutes on each side.

Makes 15 to 18.

Tofu Patties

Chop the onion, celery, and green pepper fine and sauté in oil until soft. Drain the tofu in a strainer; then mash it with a fork and mix in the egg, flour, salt, and soy sauce. Add vegetables and either the curry powder or the cheese. Form into small patties and roll them in the wheat germ. Brown on a griddle or skillet, or bake in a 350° oven.

Makes about 2 dozen.

½ onion, minced
1 stalk celery, finely chopped
½ green pepper, finely chopped
2 tablespoons oil
1 package tofu (about 20 ounces)
1 egg, beaten
2 tablespoons whole wheat flour
½ teaspoon salt
2 tablespoons soy sauce
2 teaspoons curry powder
OR
½ cup grated cheddar cheese
wheat germ, cornmeal, or sesame seeds

Green Rice Casserole

Preheat oven to 350°. Dice onion and sauté in oil until soft. Combine remaining ingredients and add to onion. Bake in a greased 2-quart casserole for about 30 minutes, or until bubbly around the sides.

Serves 4 to 6.

VARIATION

A more nutritious version, and certainly as tasty, substitutes 2 cups cooked bulgur wheat and ½ cup cooked soy grits for the rice. See the charts on page 260 for cooking instructions.

2½ cups cooked brown rice
2 tablespoons oil
1 small onion
½ cup chopped parsley
1 cup grated Swiss cheese
2 eggs, beaten
2 cups milk
1 teaspoon salt
½ teaspoon dill weed
pinch garlic

Pilaf Avgolemeno

4 cups cooked brown rice
or millet
3 tablespoons margarine
2 tablespoons whole
wheat flour
½ cup milk
½ cup hot vegetable
stock or water
½ teaspoon salt
1 egg
juice of ½ lemon
⅓ cup Parmesan cheese

Make cream sauce (p. 230) with 2 tablespoons of the margarine and the flour, milk, stock, and salt. Remove from heat and cool slightly.

Beat egg with lemon juice and slowly add to sauce, stirring constantly. Return pan to stove. Continue stirring and cooking until sauce thickens. Stir in the remaining tablespoon of margarine and half of the cheese. Pour sauce over grain and sprinkle with remaining cheese.

Serves 4 to 6.

Spanish Rice

1 cup raw brown rice
1 onion, minced
1 teaspoon oil
2 cups vegetable stock
or water
4 stalks celery, diced
small
1 large green pepper,
diced
3 medium fresh or 1 cup
canned tomatoes,
chopped
1 teaspoon salt
½ teaspoon oregano
½ teaspoon basil
dash pepper
pinch chili powder
OPTIONAL
½ cup grated cheddar
or jack cheese

Bring the stock, oil, onions, and rice to a boil. Cover and simmer on low heat for 25 minutes. Add remaining ingredients except cheese. Simmer another 20 minutes or until rice is well cooked. Sprinkle cheese on top if desired.

Makes 4 cups.

Rice Lentil Polou

Chop onion and sauté in 2 tablespoons of the oil until soft. Add rice and cook, stirring, for several minutes. Combine tomato paste with water and cinnamon. Add this mixture, along with the lentils, to the rice. Bring to a boil, cover tightly, turn heat very low, and simmer for 30 minutes.

Preheat oven to 350°.

Stir in salt, nuts, and raisins. Coat a baking dish with the remaining tablespoon of oil and 1 tablespoon of hot water. Pour in rice mixture. Cover and bake for 20 to 30 minutes.

Serves 4 to 6.

½ medium onion
3 tablespoons oil
1 cup raw brown rice
¼ cup raw lentils
¼ teaspoon cinnamon
2½ cups water or vegetable stock
1 tablespoon tomato paste
1 teaspoon salt
½ cup raisins
½ cup pine nuts, sunflower seeds, or chopped almonds

Bulgur Wheat Pilaf

Pilaf can be made with just about any grain. Try millet, cracked wheat, rice, or triticale in this dish, or a partial substitution of barley for any of these. See the cooking chart on page 260 to adjust cooking instructions.

Dice carrot, celery (the leaves, too), green pepper, and onions. Place the oil in a heavy pot with a close-fitting lid. Add all the vegetables and the bay leaf and stir over medium heat for several minutes. Pour in the stock, bring to a boil, and simmer for 5 minutes, covered.

Add wheat and salt and bring to a fast boil again. Cook, covered, over very low heat for 15 minutes. If too moist, uncover and simmer another few minutes until the liquid diminishes.

1¾ cups vegetable stock or water
1 small carrot
1 medium stalk celery
½ green pepper
¼ cup chopped mushrooms
2 green onions
1 bay leaf
1½ tablespoons oil
1 cup raw bulgur wheat
1 teaspoon salt

VARIATION

For special occasions add 1 cup garden peas towards the very end of the cooking time, and ¼ cup toasted pine nuts or chopped almonds.

Serves 4.

Tamale Pie

GROUP I
2 cups cooked pinto or
 kidney beans
2 tablespoons oil
½ cup chopped onion
¼ teaspoon garlic
 powder
1 teaspoon chili powder
1 teaspoon salt
1 tablespoon tomato
 paste
3 tablespoons water
¼ cup sliced ripe olives
½ cup fresh corn
½ green pepper, chopped
¼ cup chopped parsley
½ cup chopped celery

GROUP II
2½ cups cold water
1½ cups cornmeal
1 teaspoon salt
½ teaspoon chili powder
¼ cup grated cheddar
 cheese (more if
 desired)

Tamale Pie is one of those staff-of-life dishes: nutritionally it is an excellent combination of ingredients which complement one another in proteins, and its rich, full flavor of beans and corn makes it a family favorite.

Grind beans in blender or mash in food mill. Mix tomato paste with water. In a skillet sauté onion in oil and combine all Group I ingredients. Let these cook over medium heat; if the beans were hot to begin with, no more than five minutes' cooking is needed. Keep stirring the mixture since beans tend to stick to the pan. Adjust seasonings to taste.

Combine the ingredients of Group II except for cheese in a heavy pan, and cook over medium heat until cornmeal thickens and comes to a boil. You have to stir this constantly or the cornmeal will stick.

Grease an 8″ × 8″ pan and spread two thirds of the cornmeal mixture over the bottom and sides; then pour the bean mixture into this cornmeal crust and spread the remaining one third of the cornmeal on the top. Sprinkle the top crust with grated cheddar cheese and cook in a 350° oven for half an hour.

Kichadi

This is very much like pilaf—perhaps not so fluffy. It makes a good luncheon or dinner dish.

Sauté spices in 2 tablespoons oil, in a large, heavy-bottomed pot. If the spices are not available, use 2 teaspoons curry powder instead. Add finely chopped onions and green pepper and stir until onions are soft.

Stir in the rice and continue to cook for about 5 minutes, or until rice begins to turn white. Add water and salt and bring to a boil. Cover and cook on low heat for 20 minutes.

Sauté yellow split peas in remaining 2 tablespoons oil. Add split peas to the cooking rice and continue cooking for 30 minutes more.

Makes 6 cups.

4 tablespoons oil
2 cloves
very small piece
    cinnamon stick
cardamom seeds from
    3 pods
dash turmeric powder
2 teaspoons ground
    fenugreek seeds
2 onions
1 green pepper
2 cups brown rice
6 cups water
2 teaspoons salt
1 cup yellow split peas

VARIATION

Add chopped cooked vegetables or a diced raw tomato at end of cooking time.

SIMPLE KICHADI

A simpler version is eaten for breakfast in many parts of India, but it is quite suitable for dinner or lunch. You may substitute any beans or lentils that combine well with rice, but add them *after* the rice if they cook in much less than an hour.

Add rice and peas to salted boiling water in heavy pot. Cover, turn heat as low as possible, and simmer gently for just under an hour.

Serves 4 to 6.

1 cup brown rice
½ cup blackeyed peas
3 cups water
1 teaspoon salt

Dessert

More than a hundred pounds a year: that's how much sugar each of us is eating now. It comes to about a pound of sugar every three days. Can you believe it? Some authorities cite this as our number-one nutritional problem. (For a full discussion of the matter, please see our nutrition section.) The implications for our collection of dessert recipes are clear. All of us need to cut back dramatically on our families' sugar intake.

This is an area where you will have to proceed gradually and let yourself be guided by the present eating habits and attitudes of your family members. A sudden and complete ban on desserts can easily backfire. Our palates have been conditioned to large daily doses of sugar, and protest they will when that pattern is threatened. Be prepared for some dragging of heels, but don't give up the campaign, even if it takes years. The first step is to cut out sugary snacks and at least confine sweets to mealtimes: pancakes with fruit sauce for breakfast, a lunchbox cookie, or a dessert with dinner—one in a day, not all three! After a short time, start serving desserts just once or twice a week. Meanwhile, make a variety of delectable fresh fruits available. Eventually you may find you can back off entirely and serve desserts only on special occasions. It's amazing to discover that after just a month or so with minimal sugar, or none, you no longer enjoy some of the intensely sweet desserts you used to go for. Our children have recognized this too, with a measure of real astonishment.

Admittedly, as long as we move about in an environment that urges us to "boost our energy" with hourly chocolate bars and soft drinks, the change of heart we're proposing won't come easily. It *is* within our reach, though, and sometimes the example of one family is enough to influence many others. We know of one kindergarten teacher who got so frustrated at the array of candy bars her pupils brought for snack time that she wrote all their parents, requesting very firmly that they send only healthy snacks. Her concern for the children was so obviously genuine that the appeal worked. The result: twenty-five little ones spared for the time being the terrible effects of sugar addiction.

When you do serve a dessert, there's no reason why it has to be a total loss. The recipes we've included here are for desserts that have nutritional plus points. Old-fashioned milk puddings, bread puddings, and rice puddings, for instance, call for relatively little sweetener, and they are made from otherwise quite useful foods.

One of the problems with overconsumption of sugar is that it raises our requirement for the particular B vitamins which metabolize carbohydrates. Thus, deficiencies can arise. With this in mind, we have added wheat germ—a B-vitamin gold mine—to our dessert recipes wherever it was appropriate.

The recipes have been tested repeatedly until each includes just enough sweetener to keep it in the dessert camp but much less than most conventional recipes call for. This is of course a question of individual taste. You may well want to cut it back even further.

As for the *kind* of sweetener, you will notice that our recipes call more often for brown sugar than for honey, though honey can certainly be used in most cases. It is about twice as sweet as sugar, however, so use less, and if you are sweetening something that is to be baked, keep a close eye on it as it will tend to brown very quickly. Honey is a liquid ingredient, so you might want to cut back other liquids slightly. To mix honey with other ingredients easily, it helps to have it at room temperature or warmer.

Our use of brown sugar instead of honey might come as a shock to some, because honey has a pretty good name for itself in health food circles. Certainly, honey is among the tastiest foods around: it's great fun to explore the wide variety of flavors, each subtly distinct from the others. Nutritionally speaking, though, honey seems to have no real advantages over sugar, and its cost is significantly higher. The real nutritional issue here is *amount,* after all, and not kind. It's a very common tendency among people new to natural foods to fall upon honey with such verve that they end up eating far more of it than they might previously have been eating of sugar (says one who knows). Sugar is sugar is sugar, whether it's

been extracted from sugar cane, sugar beets, or beehives. If you like the taste of honey enough to be willing to pay the extra cost, well and good, but don't lose sight of what's really in question.

Genuine raw sugar does have a slight edge over refined sugar. The brown sugar that is sold now, though, is not raw at all; rather, it is refined sugar with a bit of molasses added— or, sadly enough, a bit of caramelized refined sugar. The kind with molasses added is the one with the edge, for molasses does have certain valuable minerals. We use it for this reason, and because its quite distinct flavor puts a certain automatic brake on its use (white sugar, in contrast, has a way of sneaking in all over the place).

When you come down to it, fresh fruit is undoubtedly the pleasantest and most wholesome dessert of all. Ripe fruit is sweet as can be, but its sugar is mingled with vitamins and minerals as well. Our Four Food Groups recommendation is for at least one serving of fruit a day. Of course, even a good thing can be taken too far (sugar is sugar is sugar), so keep your daily intake down to four pieces at most.

More than any other dessert, fruit has tremendous eye appeal. Explore the variety that abounds in spring, summer, and early fall. By and large, apples, oranges, and bananas are the cheapest and most easily available year-round. Keep them around for general use; but for dessert, surprise your family often with a bowl of apricots, wedges of honeydew or crenshaw melon, or a small basket of fresh figs. A pineapple might seem like a luxury, but compare its cost to that of a frozen pie or a devil's food cake—and then check the food charts if any doubt is left.

Fresh fruit salad is always a treat. Oranges cut up with bananas and decked with toasted coconut or chopped dates are a big favorite. Apples, grapes, and bananas sprinkled with toasted walnuts or sunflower seeds are equally popular. In summer, of course, the sky's the limit: take full advantage of the berries, grapes, peaches, melons, cherries, and apricots that come with the sunniest months. Yogurt, buttermilk, cottage cheese, or ricotta cheese are good accompaniments to a fruit salad. A handful of toasted wheat germ on top makes for flavor appeal, and of course greater nutritional value.

Strawberry or peach shortcakes are a summertime classic: made with Stratford Hall Biscuits (p. 105), they have a particularly down-home appeal. For a sweeter shortcake, use our Pound Cake instead and top it with Vanilla Pudding.

Autumn and winter have their compensations, of course: persimmons, for instance, which only induce that characteristic pucker if they aren't ripe yet (ripe means deep red-orange, translucent, and softer than you can believe). In late autumn, enjoy juicy pears served with a soft, nutty cheese. Pomegranates come along in late November. The charms of a good-sized pomegranate can keep two small children occupied for a good long time, though it's only advisable if they're out of doors and dressed in their oldest T-shirts!

On winter evenings, when we're enjoying ourselves so much that it seems a shame to leave the table quite yet, we put out a bowl of nuts for dessert—not shelled, because it's too easy to take in more calories than you need that way, but with nutcrackers and picks. The accumulation of shells on the plate is a helpful reminder of how many you've eaten.

Hopefully, you're sufficiently warmed by now to the Who Needs It approach to desserts that you've decided you can live without them. If you aren't—or more likely, if you sense some resistance among the rank and file—please try these recipes, knowing that they are thoroughly appealing and just about as nourishing as they could be and still be called desserts.

Diana's Apple Crisp

8 apples (green pippins
    are best)
juice of 1 lemon
1 teaspoon cinnamon
2 tablespoons whole
    wheat flour
¾ cup raisins
water or apple juice

TOPPING
1 cup rolled oats
⅓ cup toasted wheat
    germ
½ cup whole wheat flour
½ teaspoon salt
2 teaspoons cinnamon
½ cup brown sugar
½ cup margarine

Preheat oven to 375°. Slice apples until you have enough to fill a greased 9″ × 13″ baking dish. Mix the apples in a bowl with lemon juice, cinnamon, flour, and raisins. Return them to the baking dish, adding enough water or apple juice to cover the bottom.

Mix topping in a bowl and press onto top of apples. Bake for 25 minutes, or until apples are soft.

Serves 8.

Carrot Fruitcake

1 cup grated carrots
1 cup raisins
¾ cup honey
1 teaspoon cinnamon
1 teaspoon allspice
1 teaspoon salt
½ teaspoon nutmeg
¼ teaspoon cloves
2 tablespoons margarine
1½ cups water
1½ cups whole wheat
    flour
1 teaspoon baking soda
½ cup wheat germ
½ cup chopped walnuts

Moist, rich, and spicy—a favorite for festive occasions.

Preheat oven to 300°.

Cook carrots, raisins, honey, margarine, and spices in the water for 10 minutes, then allow to cool.

Mix together the flour, baking soda, wheat germ, and walnuts and combine with the other ingredients. Pour into two small, well-greased loaf pans.

Bake for 45 minutes.

Makes 2 small loaves.

Banana Bread

Preheat oven to 375°.

Mash bananas and mix them with lemon juice until they are smooth.

Cream margarine and sugar together and add the banana mix, stirring well.

In a separate bowl stir together the dry ingredients. Add to the banana mix and stir in the dates and nuts if desired.

The dough will be very stiff. Turn it into a greased loaf pan and bake for 30 to 45 minutes. To test for doneness, insert a knife into the loaf; if it comes out clean, the bread is done.

Makes 1 loaf.

juice of 1 lemon
3 very ripe bananas
½ cup brown sugar
½ cup margarine
1½ cups whole wheat flour
½ cup wheat germ
½ teaspoon salt
½ teaspoon baking powder
½ teaspoon baking soda

OPTIONAL
1 cup chopped dates
1 cup nuts, toasted sunflower seeds, or coconut

Pound Cake

The traditional versions of this recipe are much higher in calories and cholesterol than most of us are willing to go along with; this version is far less rich, but thoroughly enjoyable. We like to frost one loaf and use the other one later in the week, sliced and toasted, with fresh fruit and yogurt.

Preheat oven to 350°.

Ingredients should be at room temperature. Sift flour before measuring, then sift with baking powder, baking soda, and salt.

Cream sugar and margarine. Add vanilla.

Separate eggs. Whip egg whites until stiff. Beat yolks and add to sugar and margarine. Add sifted ingredients to this mixture, a third at a time, alternating with buttermilk.

Fold in egg whites and turn into two well-greased small loaf pans, or one large one.

Bake 30 to 40 minutes.

Makes 2 small loaves or 1 large one.

2¼ cups whole wheat pastry flour
1½ teaspoons baking powder
½ teaspoon baking soda
½ teaspoon salt
1 teaspoon vanilla
¾ cup brown sugar, packed
¾ cup margarine
2 eggs
1 cup buttermilk

Creamy Frosting

1 teaspoon flour
1 teaspoon margarine
¼ cup milk
½ cup ricotta cheese
¼ cup brown sugar
1 teaspoon vanilla
pinch salt

Melt margarine. Stir in flour and cook 2 minutes. Add milk and ricotta cheese and stir. Cook until thickened. Add sugar and a pinch of salt and stir until it melts. Remove from stove. Let cool a bit and add vanilla.

Makes about ¾ cup.

Pal Payasam

1 quart milk
4 tablespoons rice meal
*   or rice flour*
3 tablespoons brown
*   sugar*
⅓ cup raisins
3 cardamom pods
*   OR pinch saffron*
⅓ cup toasted cashews
*   or almond pieces*

This rather liquid milk pudding is an essential dessert in any Indian feast.

To make rice meal, grind raw brown rice in grinder or dry blender. Fine wheat meal or flour may be substituted, but rice is more delicate in flavor.

Make a paste with rice meal and ½ cup cold milk.

Heat remaining milk. Stir in rice mixture and continue stirring until it comes to a boil. Add brown sugar, raisins, and the seeds from the cardamom pods or the saffron. You may add the nuts at this point or stir them in just before serving if you like them crisp.

Reduce heat and simmer 5 to 10 minutes until pudding thickens a little.

Serve cold. It will continue to thicken somewhat as it cools, but it remains a thin pudding.

Serves 4 to 6.

Rice Cream Pudding

Cook rice for 30 minutes in water and oil by bringing to a rolling boil, covering tightly, and turning down to a low simmer.

Add milk and raisins and bring to a boil again. Cover and simmer for another 15 minutes. Stir in sugar and salt.

Stir the flour with 1 cup of the rice mixture. Return to pot and simmer 5 minutes more, stirring constantly. If the flour forms lumps, beat with rotary beater for a minute.

Cool slightly. Stir in vanilla and sprinkle nuts over top. Serve warm or cold.

Makes about 4 cups.

½ cup uncooked brown rice
1 cup water
1 teaspoon oil
2½ cups milk, whole or skim
¼ cup brown sugar
¼ teaspoon salt
3 tablespoons whole wheat flour
1 teaspoon vanilla
½ cup raisins

OPTIONAL
¼ cup chopped nuts

Bread Pudding

Preheat oven to 350°.

Mix lemon juice with the grated apples.

Put one third of the bread in bottom of a greased 8″ × 8″ baking dish and cover with 1 cup of apples, ¼ cup cottage cheese, half of the raisins, and some of the cinnamon.

Blend the milk, milk powder, egg, and sugar together, or beat with hand beater until smooth. Pour 1 cup of this mixture over the ingredients in the baking dish. Now repeat the layers of bread, apples, and liquid, ending with the bread. Pour the last of the milk mixture over the top, sprinkle with cinnamon, and dot with margarine.

Let the pudding sit for 20 minutes or longer. Bake, covered, for 45 minutes. Let it stand for 10 to 20 minutes at room temperature before serving.

Serves 8.

2 cups grated apples
juice of 1 lemon
4 cups whole-grain bread, cubed small
½ cup low-fat cottage cheese
⅓ cup raisins
¼ teaspoon cinnamon
2 cups milk
¼ cup dried skim milk
1 egg
¼ cup brown sugar
1 tablespoon margarine

Fruit Tzimmes

1 pound (3 cups) dried
    fruits, including
    raisins, prunes, and
    apricots, but not dates
    or figs
1 teaspoon salt
2 grated carrots
1 or 2 grated apples
1 lemon or lime, thinly
    sliced
2 tablespoons margarine
water for soaking fruit

Serve tzimmes with pancakes (especially Potato Latkes, page 204), toast, or as a chutney with vegetables and grains.

Wash dried fruit and soak in water, covered, for 1 hour. Drain water and reserve. Combine all ingredients in a pot with ½ cup of the liquid. Bring to a boil, then cook over very low heat for 1 or 2 hours, adding more liquid as needed.

Makes 4 cups.

Peanut Butter Bars

2 to 3 cups peanut butter
    (crunchy is best)
1 cup High-Protein
    Granola (p. 117)
    OR
1 cup toasted wheat germ

1 cup dried skim milk
½ cup brown sugar
¼ teaspoon salt
1 cup toasted, unsweet-
    ened dried coconut
    OR
1 cup toasted sesame
    seeds
½ cup raisins
OPTIONAL
chopped dried fruit
toasted sunflower seeds
chopped nuts

An energy-packed treat, these are affectionately known as P-B Bars. Use peanut butter that's 100 percent peanuts, with no extra sugar or salt—and not hydrogenated. The amount you need to use varies considerably, depending on how oily or stiff the peanut butter is. If the jar is fresh, the peanut butter off the top will be a good deal runnier than that from the bottom.

Mix cereal, milk powder, sugar, raisins, salt, and optional ingredients. Add enough peanut butter to make the mixture stiff but not crumbly.

Roll the mixture into balls, or press on a flat surface by hand or with a rolling pin until it's about ½ inch thick. Cut into 1½–inch squares. Cover the balls or squares with the coconut or sesame seeds. Store in a covered container in the refrigerator.

Makes about 5 dozen bars.

Date Sandwich Cookies

Preheat oven to 325°. Combine dry ingredients. Cut in the margarine with a pastry cutter or two knives. Using your fingers, crumble the mixture until it's the size of small peas. Stir in buttermilk with swift strokes.

Turn onto lightly floured surface and roll into a ⅛-inch sheet. Cut with a 2-inch biscuit cutter and place on greased cookie sheets. Bake for 10 to 12 minutes.

Cook dates and water in double boiler over boiling water until the mixture becomes thick and smooth. Stir a few times while cooking, then set aside to cool.

When cookies and filling have cooled, make them into sandwiches.

Makes 2 dozen.

½ cup brown sugar
2 cups rolled oats
2 cups whole wheat flour
½ cup wheat germ
1 teaspoon baking powder
1 cup margarine
½ cup buttermilk
½ pound dates, pitted and chopped (2 cups)
½ cup water

Oatmeal School Cookies

Preheat oven to 375°. Cream together the margarine and sugar. Add the egg, vanilla, and salt and beat well.

Stir flour, baking powder, wheat germ, and rolled oats together with a fork. Blend well with other ingredients, adding a tablespoon or more of water if necessary to hold the mixture together.

Place by tablespoonful on greased cookie sheets. Flatten them slightly. Bake for 10 to 12 minutes.

Makes about 3 dozen.

½ cup margarine
¾ cup brown sugar
1 egg, slightly beaten
1½ teaspoons vanilla
½ teaspoon salt
½ cup whole wheat flour
¾ teaspoon baking powder
1 cup wheat germ
1½ cups rolled oats
¾ cup raisins
½ cup toasted sunflower seeds or chopped nuts

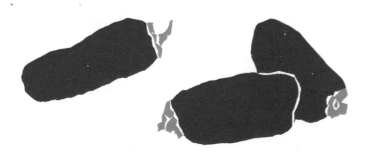

Graham Crackers

2 cups whole wheat flour
½ cup wheat bran
½ cup wheat germ
1 teaspoon baking
    powder
½ teaspoon baking soda
¼ teaspoon salt
½ cup margarine
½ cup brown sugar
½ cup milk

These are remarkably similar to the ones we remember from childhood, but are more full-bodied in flavor and healthful besides. They are crisp the first day, but must be sealed airtight to stay that way.

Stir together the dry ingredients. Cream the margarine and brown sugar until fluffy. Add flour mixture alternately with milk, mixing well after each addition.

Chill dough for several hours or overnight.

Preheat oven to 350°. Roll dough out extremely thin directly onto greased cookie sheets, and cut into squares. Prick with fork and bake 10 to 12 minutes, until brown.

Makes 24 crackers, about 2½ by 5 inches.

Vanilla Pudding

2 cups fresh milk
2 tablespoons cornstarch
    or arrowroot
¼ cup brown sugar
⅛ teaspoon salt
1 teaspoon vanilla

OPTIONAL
2 well-beaten eggs
toasted coconut
chopped nuts

Serve this simplest of wholesome desserts with fresh peaches or berries, bananas or orange slices. It's a boon for the low-cholesterol set, and a helpful replacement for the packaged and (praised be technology) canned puddings.

Gently heat 1½ cups of the milk in a heavy pan.

Combine cornstarch or arrowroot with reserved milk. Add to milk in pan when hot. Stir in remaining ingredients and cook over very low heat until thick. (A double boiler is good for this.) Reduce heat further and cook gently about 8 minutes more.

For a richer version, mix 1 cup of the pudding with 1 or 2 well-beaten eggs. Return to pan and heat thoroughly, stirring constantly.

Serve warm or pour into bowls and chill. Garnish with toasted coconut or chopped nuts.

Makes 2 to 2½ cups.

Italian Cheese Dessert

Good with Graham Crackers or fresh fruit slices.

Whip all ingredients except lemon together in a blender or with a hand beater. Add grated lemon peel from a well-washed lemon and a teaspoon or more of lemon juice, to taste.

Makes a little over 2 cups.

2 cups ricotta cheese
1 egg yolk, beaten
1 tablespoon melted
    margarine or Better-
    Butter
⅛ teaspoon salt
2 tablespoons brown
    sugar
1 lemon

Fresh Strawberry Yogurt

A pleasant answer to the over-sweetened commercial product.

Simmer raisins in apple juice 5 minutes and cool.

Purée raisin mixture in blender with half the strawberries and 1 cup yogurt. Stir in remaining strawberries and serve over, or mixed with, the remaining yogurt.

Makes about 5 cups.

½ cup unsweetened
    apple juice
½ cup raisins
1 box strawberries,
    washed and sliced
3 cups homemade yogurt

French Apple Yogurt

Cook the apples in ½ cup water 5 to 10 minutes, or until soft. Reserve 1 cup and put rest into blender with 1 cup yogurt, vanilla, cinnamon, and sugar. Blend very briefly. Mix all ingredients together.

Makes 1 quart.

3 cups diced or sliced
    apples
2 cups homemade yogurt
1 teaspoon vanilla
½ teaspoon cinnamon
2 teaspoons brown sugar
    if apples are tart

Piecrust

1½ cups whole wheat flour

OR

combination of whole wheat and whole wheat pastry flour
½ cup wheat germ
10 tablespoons margarine
1 teaspoon salt
4 to 6 tablespoons cold water

There's no getting around it: whole wheat piecrust is a little trickier to work with than those you're used to, but it is certainly tastier too.

Stir together the flour, wheat germ, and salt. Cut the margarine into the dry ingredients with two knives or a pastry cutter. When dough is the consistency of rolled oats, sprinkle with the water, using just enough to hold the dough together. Using cupped fingers, work the dough together quickly and gently. As soon as it will hold together, form into a ball. For best results, refrigerate for at least a half hour, or even overnight, but be sure to remove from refrigerator an hour before rolling it out.

Preheat oven to 400°.

Press the dough out into a thick disc. Roll to size on a lightly floured surface, or between sheets of waxed paper, or on a pastry cloth. Gently roll the dough over the rolling pin and onto the pie plate, easing it loosely into the plate. If it should stick to the table, slide a long, sharp knife underneath, and if it should tear, patch with extra dough once it is in place. Gently press the dough into the plate so there are no air pockets. Cut off the excess with a sharp knife, but be sure to make the rim extra thick so it won't burn. If you are going to fill the pie before baking, you may use the extra dough for lattice; otherwise, sprinkle with a bit of sugar and cinnamon and bake along with the pie as an impromptu cookie.

Form an attractive rim as shown, and prick the pie shell all over with a fork.

Bake for 10 to 12 minutes, cool, and fill. Bake for just 7 minutes if your recipe calls for a partially baked crust.

Makes one 10-inch crust *or* crust and lattice for one 8-inch pie.

Mock Mince Pie

Mincemeat pies are traditionally nonvegetarian. This simple meatless recipe is our Thanksgiving standby.

Pare and slice apples, chop raisins, and mix with apple juice. Scrub the orange well, juice it, and grate the peel. Simmer together in a covered pan until the apples are very soft. Stir in the sugar, cinnamon, cloves, and brandy extract. This mixture will keep for several days.

Preheat oven to 450°.

Line a 9-inch pie pan with crust, and reserve extra dough for lattice. Reheat the filling and pour it in hot. Cover with lattice.

Bake for 30 minutes.

Makes one 9-inch pie.

*dough for a 10-inch
   piecrust*
½ cup raisins
4 medium apples
⅓ cup apple juice
1 orange
¾ cup brown sugar
½ teaspoon cinnamon
½ teaspoon cloves

OPTIONAL
*½ teaspoon brandy
   extract*

Berry Pudding Pie

For a gala summertime dessert, bake a 10-inch piecrust and fill it with fresh blackberries, raspberries, strawberries, blueberries, or sliced peaches—3 cups or so. Pour Vanilla Pudding (p. 282) over them while it's still warm. Sprinkle with toasted nuts if you like, and chill.

Banana Cheese Pie

FILLING

1 cup low-fat cottage
    cheese
2 medium bananas, ripe
1 cup yogurt
2 eggs
juice of ½ lemon
3 tablespoons honey
¼ teaspoon salt
¼ cup whole wheat flour
1 teaspoon vanilla

CRUMB CRUST

¾ cup whole wheat
    bread crumbs
¼ cup dried skim milk
¾ teaspoon cinnamon
¼ cup High-Protein
    Granola (p. 117)
    OR
¼ cup combined oats,
    wheat germ, and
    seed meal
¼ cup melted margarine
2 teaspoons honey

OPTIONAL

toasted coconut

This light and very tasty dessert comes with a crumb crust. Filling and crust alike are highly nutritious. Serve with berries or sliced peaches for special dinners.

Preheat oven to 350°.

Slice bananas.

To prepare filling, blend eggs, yogurt, cottage cheese, lemon, and vanilla in blender. When mixed, add flour and salt, keeping blender on low speed. Add honey, by the tablespoon, and finally the bananas. If you prefer, put bananas and cottage cheese through a food mill, mixing these by hand with the remaining ingredients.

Combine the crust ingredients and press into a greased 9-inch pie plate.

Pour filling into crust and bake for about 25 to 30 minutes. Sprinkle with toasted coconut if desired.

BANANA CHEESE PUDDING

Instead of making a crust, simply dust a greased 9-inch pie plate with wheat germ. This is an even lighter dessert, and blessedly simple!

Menus

Changing over to a diet of whole, natural, vegetarian foods does force us to rethink our accustomed ways of putting together a meal, or a day's meals. We've actually found that there is much greater flexibility to our menu patterns now than we ever had before, but it took us a little while to realize this and take full advantage of it. To help you through the initial period of adjustment, we've put together a whole week's worth of meatless menus, followed by a number of dinner menus (actually some could be served as lunches) based on foods from other cultures. The first set of menus is carefully planned so that the Four Food Groups guidelines are followed within each day. The other menus are just for single meals, so the nutritional strengths and weaknesses of each meal should be balanced over the whole day.

Most of the items in these menus represent our own recipes. All are easy to prepare, though of course cooking with whole foods takes more time than cooking with convenience food does. Some of the most satisfying dinners take almost no time: garden vegetables steamed just right, a tossed salad, and a bowl of brown rice, with fresh fruit for dessert. Add a tasty sauce if you like—some of our sauces can be prepared in just ten minutes. Obviously, too, most of us are not likely to make up as many lunches from scratch as are mentioned on the pages which follow. Salad plates made up of whatever's on hand, peanut butter and lettuce sandwiches, or a bowl of last night's minestrone (always better the next day) are perhaps more typical of our at-home lunch fare. These menus are meant rather as patterns, to suggest what needs to be included overall.

Our foreign food menus are designed to give good nutrition a distinct edge over authenticity. In the South Indian menu, for example, we have included Raita, a salad that is not typically South Indian at all. Despite our tinkering, some of these menus are still a bit on the rich or spicy side, and will probably be most appreciated if used only at intervals. Eggs, cheese, and coconut all appear more frequently here than they do in our everyday menus. We've worked hard, though, to

adapt these traditional foreign dishes to present-day nutritional needs, so when you look at the recipes themselves, you will be pleasantly surprised to see how much of this delicious and out-of-the-ordinary food your family can enjoy without fear of raising cholesterol or calorie levels.

Vary the pattern of your meals often—serve soups as dinners, beans for breakfast, casseroles for lunch. As long as you include the simple requirements of the Four Food Groups, just about anything goes.

One Week's Meals

First Day

Buckwheat Pancakes
Cinnamon-flavored Applesauce, toasted almonds,
   and cottage cheese
Red clover blossom tea

Sandwich of Soy Paté, cucumber slices,
   and alfalfa sprouts on whole-grain bread
Melon basket
Milk

Steamed greens with Lemon Butter
Savory Squash Pie and yogurt
Navy Bean & Cashew Salad

Second Day

English Muffins split, toasted, and spread with Better-Butter
Yogurt topped with orange and banana slices,
   toasted seeds or nuts, and raisins
Mint tea

Cream of Tomato Soup with rice
Sally's Savory Crackers
Celery sticks and Split Pea–Tofu Dip
Milk

Tennessee Corn Pone
Steamed broccoli spears
Tossed salad with Creamy French Dressing
Diana's Apple Crisp
Lemon grass tea

Third Day

BREAKFAST
Polenta and red beans
Cottage cheese sprinkled with toasted sunflower seeds
Half a grapefruit
Lemon grass tea

LUNCH
Sandwich of whole-grain bread filled with
  Split Pea–Parmesan Spread, green pepper rings,
  and tomato slices
Potato Salad
Milk or buttermilk

DINNER
Steamed beets, sliced and buttered
Creamed Spinach over split Stratford Hall Biscuits
Tossed green salad with Avocado Dressing
Diana's Apple Crisp

Fourth Day

BREAKFAST
All in One Cereal with milk and sliced peaches
Whole-grain bread toasted and spread with peanut butter
Sassafras tea

LUNCH
Manybean Soup
Corn Bread
Coleslaw

DINNER
Creamy Sesame Beans & Celery
Potato Poppers
Chef's Salad
Milk or buttermilk

Fifth Day

Oatmeal with hot milk
Apple Bran Muffins
Rose hips tea

Soy Burger sandwich with Vegetable Relish, lettuce,
   and mayonnaise on whole-grain bread
Strawberry Buttermilk Cooler

Corn Chowder
Shades of Green Salad
Crispy Seed Wafers
Basket of fresh fruit

Sixth Day

Sarah's Sourdough Pancakes with Hot Orange Sauce
   and yogurt
Gandhi's Coffee

Jessica's Mock Rarebit over whole-grain toast
Fruit salad with dates and walnuts

New England Baked Beans
Asparagus spears
Boston Brown Bread
Summer Salad
Buttermilk

Seventh Day

BREAKFAST   *Cracked wheat cereal with Stewed Prunes and milk*
Postum
Whole-grain bread, toasted, with Better-Butter

LUNCH   *Black Bean Soup with herbed whole wheat croutons*
Yogurt with cashews and fresh orange slices

DINNER   *Whole patty pan squashes with Savory Yeast Gravy*
Baked Carrots
Steamed brown rice with parsley and sesame salt
Spinach & Mushroom Salad
Milk

Vegetarian Cooking
with an International Flavor

French

Quiche
Zucchini Provencal
Spinach salad with Creamy French Dressing
Fresh fruit basket

Ratatouille
Whole Wheat French Bread
Tossed green salad with Bleu Cheese Dressing
French Apple Yogurt

Greek

Spanakopita (spinach pie)
Greek Salad
Green Beans Hellenika
Rice Cream Pudding and fresh fruit

Pilaf Avgolemono
Dilled Cucumber & Yogurt Salad
Grapes

Italian

Spaghetti and Neat Balls with Tomato Sauce
Sautéed zucchini slices
Spinach & Mushroom Salad
Fresh fruit

Minestrone soup
Breadsticks
Tossed green salad
Italian Cheese Dessert and fresh fruit slices

Eggplant Parmesan
Herbed green beans
Tossed salad
Apples and almonds

Lasagna al Forno or Canneloni
Steamed broccoli
Green salad with marinated garbanzo beans
Fresh fruit

Pizza
Chef's Salad
Cantaloupe

Middle Eastern

Imam Bayildi (eggplant stew)
Tabouli (Lebanese wheat and white bean salad)
   on beds of lettuce
Bowl of yogurt
Fresh pears and figs

Arab Bread filled with Falafel (garbanzo bean balls),
   shredded lettuce, cucumbers, chopped parsley, and yogurt
Spinach with sautéed onions and pine nuts
Orange and date fruit salad

Mexican

Vegetable Enchiladas
Green beans cooked in lemon juice
Mexican Salad Bowl
Fresh pineapple slices

Chili con Elote
Tacos filled with shredded lettuce, chopped tomatoes,
*   green peppers, and grated cheddar cheese*
Tropical fruit salad sprinkled with fresh lime juice
*   and toasted coconut*

Jewish

Stuffed Cabbage Rolls
Potato Carrot Kugel
Dilled Cucumber & Yogurt Salad
Apple slices and walnuts

Potato Latkes with Mock Sour Cream and Applesauce
Braised kale
Coleslaw

Hot or chilled Whole Beet Borscht
Sour Corn Rye Bread spread with Houmous
*   (garbanzo sesame spread)*
Raw vegetable sticks and olives

Piroshki
Buttered whole wheat noodles
Tossed salad
Assorted nuts and fresh fruits

South Indian

Chapathis
Rice
Aviyal
Cabbage Bhaji
Raita
Pal Payasam

Thanksgiving Dinner

Creamed Spinach with mushrooms
Stuffed Winter Squash
Buttered brussels sprouts with roasted chestnuts
Wheat Berry Dinner Rolls and Better-Butter
Tossed green salad with French Dressing and
    grated Parmesan cheese
Mock Mince Pie with honey-flavored natural ice cream
Basket of assorted nuts and fresh fruits

Christmas Dinner

Green Bean Stroganoff
Lentil Nut Loaf and Brown Gravy
Baked acorn squash
Grilled tomato halves with chopped parsley
Spinach and watercress salad with fresh pineapple pieces
    and Sesame Dressing
Carrot Fruitcake with Creamy Frosting
Lemon grass tea

Feeding Your Dog

Remember those figures we cited on how much it would cost to stave off world famine for one year? For 1974, according to the World Food Conference that year in Rome, it came to about two billion dollars. Well, that same year Americans were spending two and a *half* billion dollars a year on commercially prepared pet food. Furthermore, most of that pet food is meat: fish, chicken, and beef, processed and preserved as elaborately as the most picky canine could require.

A great many committed vegetarians go right on feeding commercial meat preparations to their dogs under the impression that dogs are implacable carnivores. We'd like to raise a clamorous voice to the contrary. You don't have to support even this branch of the meat-producing industry. We count among our close friends two dogs who, except for an occasional and surely forgivable foray into neighboring garbage cans, have been complete vegetarians for about five years now. Both dogs are gleaming of coat and teeth, very outgoing and energetic. The larger one is eight years old. The middle-sized one is of indeterminate age (he was abandoned in our neighborhood), but every year when we take him to the veterinarian's for shots, the vet estimates his age at two years old, even though we've been going there for over five years.

Morning is the best time to feed dogs, and a once-a-day feeding is quite adequate. Let your pet's size and activity determine the amount you feed him—about two quarts of the basic dinner mixture seems right for an active seventy-five-pound dog. Some owners like to cut back on the breakfast and provide a snack later in the day: dogs like bread and peanut butter as much as kids do. The B vitamins in the nutritional yeast (wheat germ is good too) will help protect your pup against fleas, and the egg will keep his coat shiny. Don't worry about the yolks—dogs apparently have no cholesterol worries!

BASIC 'DOGGIE DINNER'

2 tablespoons oil
1 cooked egg
2 cups cooked vegetables, blended unless very soft
1 tablespoon nutritional yeast
1 cup milk
bread ends and leftover cooked cereals and beans

Nutrition for a Meatless Diet

Tables and Charts

Contents of This Section

Part I:
Nourishment & the
Vegetarian Diet

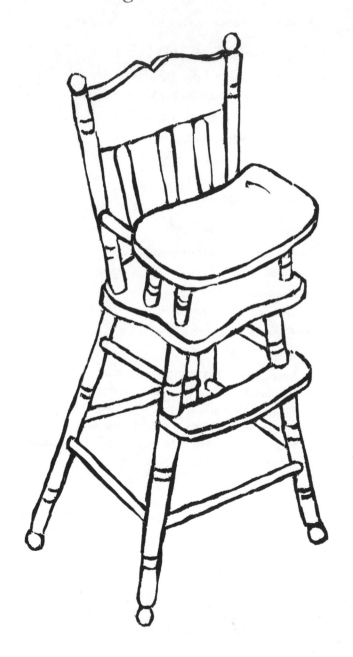

Food as Nourishment

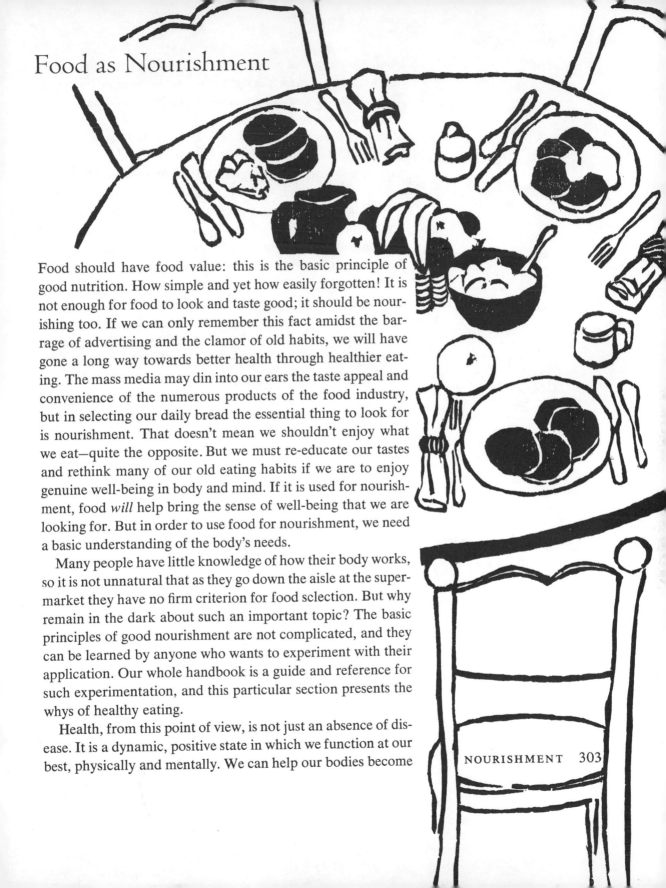

Food should have food value: this is the basic principle of good nutrition. How simple and yet how easily forgotten! It is not enough for food to look and taste good; it should be nourishing too. If we can only remember this fact amidst the barrage of advertising and the clamor of old habits, we will have gone a long way towards better health through healthier eating. The mass media may din into our ears the taste appeal and convenience of the numerous products of the food industry, but in selecting our daily bread the essential thing to look for is nourishment. That doesn't mean we shouldn't enjoy what we eat—quite the opposite. But we must re-educate our tastes and rethink many of our old eating habits if we are to enjoy genuine well-being in body and mind. If it is used for nourishment, food *will* help bring the sense of well-being that we are looking for. But in order to use food for nourishment, we need a basic understanding of the body's needs.

Many people have little knowledge of how their body works, so it is not unnatural that as they go down the aisle at the supermarket they have no firm criterion for food selection. But why remain in the dark about such an important topic? The basic principles of good nourishment are not complicated, and they can be learned by anyone who wants to experiment with their application. Our whole handbook is a guide and reference for such experimentation, and this particular section presents the whys of healthy eating.

Health, from this point of view, is not just an absence of disease. It is a dynamic, positive state in which we function at our best, physically and mentally. We can help our bodies become healthy, strong, and beautiful by eating the right kind of food, in the right amount, at the right time, and in the right company. Translated into daily life, this means eating wholesome, nourishing food in moderate amounts, in the relaxed company of family or friends. It doesn't take long for the entire body to begin to feel better and look better for such care, and soon our old ways of eating begin to lose their appeal. There may still be an occasional desire for banana cream pie or french-fried potatoes, but by and large we would just rather now eat what is really good for the body. In fact, we may find even these old favorites giving us up one day—suddenly we discover that the old habits have simply disappeared for good.

The rising tide of nutrition-related problems suggests that we Americans simply aren't feeding ourselves very well. We have allowed the advertisers to dictate our likes and dislikes by playing up an endless series of "foods" which look good or taste good or even *sound* good, but which unfortunately have little food value. Young people fill up on soft drinks and fast food; older people seek out rich gourmet dishes which please the palate but slowly poison the body with too much cholesterol and fat. Have we come to value the sensations of eating and drinking more than good health and joyous living? We seem to eat highly spiced, deep-fried, overrefined food under the mistaken impression that it will make us feel better, but in the long run it only makes us sick.

But habits *can* be changed, and through re-educating our tastes we can learn to enjoy greatly every food that nourishes the body. Green salad may be a complete stranger, but soon we find we are able to eat a huge plate of it, especially if it comes from our own vegetable garden. Just knowing that it is good for the body makes green salad a gourmet delight. When we start retraining our sense of taste in this way, nourishing food becomes the greatest of delicacies.

The wise choice of food is only part of what the body needs to keep itself well and strong. Some of our other ways, like sleep and exercise, are equally important. Exercise is so closely connected with diet that it can almost be considered a nutrient. Yet in our commuter's life we have forgotten that the body is meant for motion—motion fueled by the food we eat. We have almost forgotten how to walk, but if we learn again, by walking whenever we get a chance—to the post office, to work, to the store, on the beach—walking becomes not only easy but enjoyable. Interestingly enough, the fast walk invigorates; the slow walk does not. Fast walking sends the blood surging through our veins as more and more cells of the lungs come into play.

Without exercise, the body loses its capacity to regulate the appetite. This is the principle of feedlots, where animals are penned without exercise for the last few months of their life. Unable to adjust their eating to their needs, they overeat and grow fat. Exercising just before a meal sharpens the appetite, and a subtle sense of satisfaction comes when the body has had enough. By balancing exercise with moderate eating, we can maintain our ideal weight throughout life.

A Variety of Whole Foods in Moderation

Wise choices in eating depend upon understanding the basic principles of good nourishment. There are three principles which can give a firm foundation to all our experimentation: variety, whole foods, and moderation. Keeping these three in mind makes it possible to avoid food faddism on the one hand and simply sliding back into our old habits on the other.

VARIETY

No one food or food family supplies all the nutrients we need to maintain good health. Variety assures you not only of good-quality, balanced protein in a meatless diet, but also of elusive nutrients like vitamins and trace minerals. Trace minerals, for example, are needed only in small quantities, and the amount of them in foods varies greatly from one food to another. It is impossible to know how well the carrots we had for dinner last night met our trace mineral needs. But if we eat a variety of vegetables, each one will have taken up different nutrients from the soil, and whatever might have been left out of the diet on one day will very likely show up the day after.

Great concern over getting all the subtle trace nutrients has led many people to vitamin pills and a frantic study of nutrient charts. Actually, the most successful way to plan for these vitamin and mineral needs is simply diversity in the diet. That is the point of our Four Food Groups for a Meatless Diet: a balanced diet through planned variety.

Variety, of course, is important not just to nutrition alone; it makes for appetizing meals as well. Even staple foods can be worked into your menus in a wide variety of ways: one week you add a little cornmeal to your bread dough, for example, the next week a little buckwheat. Our Four Food Groups are designed to encourage such variety and experimentation, as you will see in the next chapter. Many foods working together combine for sound nutrition, and you can rest content that your nutritional needs are being fulfilled.

WHOLE FOODS

The second principle of good nourishment, relying on whole foods, has been sorely neglected for the last two decades. Many of us have only vague notions about what our food was like in its fresh and natural state. Between the fresh, natural, whole food and its refined, fractioned commercial product there is an abyss of lost nourishment, even when the refined food has been enriched. In whole foods there is a balance between calories and other nutrients, a certain density of nourishment that is lacking in many refined foods. The basic requirements of human nutrition are water, carbohydrate, protein, a broad range of vitamins and minerals, and a little fat or oil. Whole foods contribute to many of these needs at once; refined foods often contribute to only one or two.

Wheat is a perfect example of how nature has packed the nutrients carefully into our food. The whole kernel's interior, or endosperm, contains starch and a protein called gluten, which find their way into white flour, bread, and pastries. The vitamins and minerals found in the germ—B-1, niacin, B-6, iron, and zinc—are all needed by the body before it can utilize this starch and protein to produce energy and repair tissues, but all are lost in the process of refinement. Also lost in the wheat germ by refinement is the amino acid lysine, without which the gluten protein is severely imbalanced. The hull of the wheat, also removed in processing, contains valuable fiber, a nutrient which is now receiving new respect for its apparent role in keeping the digestive system healthy.

The soybean is another example of a food which Americans commonly eat in its fractioned form. We take the oil out and use it in large amounts as margarine, then buy the protein concentrate to supplement our diet. When the oil is extracted, the fat-soluble nutrients are lost; when the carbohydrate is washed from the protein, the water-soluble nutrients go too. And of the trace minerals present in foods in sometimes microscopic quantities but absolutely essential for health, it is impossible to say how many are missing from the artificially enriched protein concentrate we finally eat. The sum of the parts never quite adds up to the whole.

It is much better to eat corn than corn syrup, whole grain flour than milled flour, whole beans and seeds than their separated oils and protein concentrates. Cultivating what is whole, fresh, and natural in eating is a skill that leads to a simple but extremely satisfying diet.

MODERATION

We have become conditioned to consume things in the hope that they can make us feel better: more vitamins, more herbs, more drugs, more food. Often, however, what we refrain from putting in is as important as what we put in. The third principle of good nourishment, therefore, is moderation—moderation both in the total amount of food we eat and in individual foods.

Most of us do not need as much food as we think. One of the finer points of eating is to stop just when we find that everything is so good we'd like to have just a little more. Instead we usually decide that we might as well stay on at the table for five minutes more—forgetting that those five minutes will probably be followed by five hours of stomachache at night. Real gourmet judgment lies in stopping short of a stomachache.

Eating slowly makes moderation easier because it gives us a chance to know when we have had enough. There is a physiological basis for this. Normally, the sugar products of digestion enter the blood during the course of a meal and flow through a center in the brain which sends a signal of satiety when the body's needs have been filled. When we eat too fast, we get ahead of the digestive process and may eat too much before the signal is even sent. Eating slowly and peacefully allows time to know when this subtle signal comes, and feel satisfied.

Moderation applies to single foods too. A small amount of sugar taken on a special occasion does no harm, but in large, frequent amounts, it can upset the body's energy cycle and may even precipitate diabetes.

For us and many of our friends, changing our orientation towards food has accompanied a simplification of our lifestyle on many fronts. Breadmaking, for example, requires time—and that may mean withdrawing from other activities, doing fewer things better instead of many things superficially. The time we take to be thoughtful about how we live is extra time for living better. And as our kitchen experiment grows, the principles of good nourishment grow wider in their application, for they are to be tested for their validity in our own experience.

The chapters which follow present the nutritional foundation on which our recipes and menus are based. The first part, on the nutrition of the meatless diet, discusses in greater detail the Four Food Groups mentioned at the beginning of the recipe section and presents a special food-group plan for the vegan or all-plant diet. Later chapters give guidelines for meeting the special nutritional requirements of pregnant mothers, growing children, and those who want to lose weight.

The second part, on the nutrients themselves, is intended to be a basic nutrition reference for your kitchen shelf. The emphasis is practical rather than theoretical, encouraging intelligent choices in food and explaining the whys of healthy eating. The introductory overview called What Makes a Food provides a general background for understanding how the nutrients work together in the body. The chapters on carbohydrate, fat, and protein explain the purpose each of these foodstuffs serves in our diet and how each is commonly misunderstood or misused. The chapters on vitamins and minerals present these tiny, unseen nutrients in a positive light—what they do *for* us more than what lack of them does *to* us. Accompanying the discussion of each vitamin and mineral in the text is a list of foods in descending order of those which supply that nutrient best. In its own way, each kind of nutrient—carbohydrate, fat, protein, vitamins, or minerals—illustrates why the emphasis throughout this book is on eating a variety of whole foods in moderation.

Tables giving the nutrient composition of foods, including many of the more important recipes in this book, follow at the very end of this section. You may turn to the discussion of each nutrient as you become interested in it through studying the food composition tables for the foods you eat, or you may prefer to work in the other direction: read about a nutrient, then look at the tables to see how well what you are eating provides the amount of that nutrient you need. Two sets of standards provide the background for such comparisons. The Recommended Daily Dietary Allowances or RDA figures on page 454 are established by the National Research Council of the National Academy of Sciences—and are *not*, incidentally, the same as the U.S. RDA, the government standards for nutritional labeling which you see on cans and packages. The Recommended Intakes of Nutrients on page 454 originate from expert committees of the Food and Agriculture Organization (FAO) and the World Health Organization (WHO) of the United Nations.

One aspect of nutrition which we do *not* discuss is the effect of substances which have entered our food, whether by intent or by accident, as a result of our technology: colorings, flavorings, preservatives, and pesticides, many of which are adding to the pollution of our food. The diet presented here minimizes such pollution by emphasizing food that is as close as possible to its natural state. For those who are interested in reading more about food additives, we recommend Michael Jacobson's *Eater's Digest* (Doubleday, Anchor Books, 1972) as a good household reference.

Four Food Groups for a Meatless Diet: A Daily Guide

Grains, Legumes, Nuts, & Seeds

Six servings or more. Include several slices of yeast-raised, whole-grain bread, a serving of beans, and a few nuts or seeds.

Vegetables

Three servings or more. Include one or more servings of dark leafy greens, like romaine, spinach, or chard.

Fruit

One to four pieces. Include a raw source of vitamin C, like citrus fruits, strawberries, or cantaloupe.

Milk & Eggs

Two or more glasses of fresh milk for adults, three or more for children. (Children under nine use smaller glasses.) Other dairy products or an egg may be used to meet part of the milk requirement. Eggs are optional—up to four per week.

Four Food Groups
for a Meatless Diet

Outlining categories of food and specifying quantities in each category can provide a general pattern of eating that assures both balance and diversity. In a meatless diet, these groups are designed to maximize protein balance; the recommended quantities in each group are then determined by the daily requirements for vitamins and minerals. Rather than dealing with specific quantities of specific nutrients, our Four Food Groups balance *foods*. If you want to know how well a particular vegetable meets your needs for vitamin A, you can refer to the charts at the back of this book. But all you need of all the nutrients can be obtained just by intelligently selecting foods from each of these four groups.

The basic four food groups of the U. S. Department of Agriculture present meat as a basic food. This leaves us with the impression that something important is being left out of the vegetarian diet, even though the fine print includes nonmeat items in this category too. Actually, the basic food of the vegetarian diet is grain—and for the cook, a grain-based diet means a very different orientation from that of a meat-based diet from which meat has been subtracted. To the vegetarian cook, grains are not necessarily made into meat-replacing dishes on the menu. Instead, the breads and vegetables formerly served on the side now come into the limelight. In place of the basic meat-based main dish, vegetarians have a wonderful variety of foods to choose from for the focal point of any meal—and many more ways of preparing these foods than are normally contemplated in a meat-based menu, too.

An adequate meatless diet depends upon whole foods. Many Americans have avoided gross deficiencies while following poor nutritional practices because they eat extremely large quantities of meat, which is a concentrated source of nutrients—especially B vitamins and trace minerals. But grains and legumes provide many of these same nutrients as long as they are not fractioned and refined. Milling and fractioning grains and legumes, in fact, removes the very nutrients which are most commonly marginal in the American diet: vitamin B-6, folacin, iron, and zinc.

Grains (such as breads and cereals) and legumes (such as peas and beans) become staples for the vegetarian. Since they contain generous carbohydrate along with their protein and other important nutrients, changing to a meatless diet means developing a new respect for carbohydrate. Many people think of carbohydrate as a weight-producing substance to be avoided whenever possible. Actually, starchy carbohydrate is the body's ideal fuel. It is weight-producing only when the total caloric content of the diet is excessive, and no more so than the equivalent number of calories of protein or fat. A diet will have plenty of room for whole-grain bread and beans if they are not crowded out by empty-calorie "foods" like sugar and alcohol, or by too much fat. Whole foods also contain a lot of a different kind of carbohydrate which, though not absorbed, is of great nutritional importance: fiber. In addition to its importance to digestion, the fiber in these foods also makes them filling—but since fiber is not absorbed, it cannot turn into fat. So, even though they eat their fill, many people actually lose weight after switching to a cereal-based diet.

Since good sources of protein are usually good sources of other nutrients too, our Four Food Groups are designed to provide an optimum amount of high-quality, balanced protein—usually the prospective vegetarian's first concern. No additional planning for protein is necessary. The details are in our chapter on protein; here it is enough to say that the body can balance the amino acids from its food by drawing from the pool of amino acids in the digestive tract, so it needs only a general balance of food from day to day and not an exact balance of amino acids at every meal. The general obsession with protein which dates back many decades is, no doubt, overdone: if you meet your caloric or energy needs with a reasonable variety of whole foods, you should be getting all the protein you need.

A generalization as broad as grouping all foods into four categories leaves room for misinterpretation. One could conceivably choose all the wrong foods from each group and come up with an inadequate diet. The details of the outline on page 310, therefore, are essential. Six servings from the staple group—Grains, Legumes, Nuts, and Seeds—including several slices of yeast-raised or naturally leavened bread, a serving of beans, and a few nuts and seeds, will provide most of the protein and the scarcer nutrients that we need. Three servings a day of vegetables makes a large contribution to the rest of our requirements, for vegetables, including dark green leaves, are a rich source of vitamins and minerals, especially vitamin A and folacin. A serving of citrus fruit gives all the vitamin C that we need. And two glasses of fresh milk or their equivalent will provide vitamin B-12 and round out the diet's protein, calcium, and riboflavin content. The additional foods that each person needs to get enough calories can come from any of the groups, as well as from a little added oil to bring out the flavor and appeal of foods.

Grains, Legumes, Nuts, and Seeds

Grains, legumes, nuts, and seeds are really all seeds—embryonic plants containing enough nourishment to last through the first stages of growth. These substantial little packages of nourishment go a long way toward meeting our needs too. When they are the major source of calories in a diet, they contain starch and protein roughly in proportion to our energy and protein needs, and many of the vitamins that the body needs in order to metabolize that starch and protein also.

Most people are unaware of the substantial amount of protein which whole grains contribute to the diet. Actually, the best protein sources in the plant kingdom are found in this

IMPORTANT SOURCES OF:
Protein
Carbohydrate
Fat
Thiamin
Niacin
Vitamin B-6 (Pyridoxine)
Folacin
Vitamin E
Iron
Zinc
Magnesium
Cereal fiber

group. To make the most efficient use of this protein, however, it is important to understand how these foods work with each other and with the milk foods. One plant protein does not meet human needs by itself as efficiently as it does in combination with a complementary plant protein or with an animal protein. Grains and legumes, for example, complement each other's protein deficiencies to make a complete, high-quality protein. Similarly, a glass of milk at every meal will balance the protein from any plant source. With only two glasses of milk a day or the equivalent, a serving of beans is required to complete all the grain protein of a meatless diet. Combining grains, legumes, and milk products in this way maximizes their protein balance.

Although it is possible to balance grain protein entirely with liberal quantities of milk products, the grains, legumes, nuts, and seeds are still needed in substantially larger quantities than milk foods to balance the diet because of some of the scarcer nutrients that grains contain. Of the long list of vitamins and minerals they provide us, vitamin B-6 (pyridoxine), folacin, iron, and zinc are among the most important. Of course, most of these nutrients are seriously reduced in refined and milled products, and not all are included in enrichment formulas.

Whole-grain bread is an essential part of the meatless diet. Fortunately, bread is a familiar food to all of us, though its use has been declining steadily over the last century—not surprising when you realize that the "balloon bread" manufactured commercially is pretty drab compared with the variety of textures and flavors you can produce in your own kitchen. The whole-grain flours in bread are virtually as nourishing as the whole grain is when left intact. In addition, yeast-raised or naturally leavened bread makes one important contribution of its own: the leavening process releases important minerals like iron and zinc which are bound up in whole cereals and legumes by a substance called phytic acid, so that they cannot be absorbed into the body. During leavening, time and the right conditions of heat and moisture allow an enzyme to destroy much of the phytic acid, and the minerals are liberated. (More information about phytic acid is given on page 426.)

Beans are more concentrated in all nutrients than the other foods in this group. They have a higher protein and B vitamin content than cereals do, and round out the protein balance for the rest of the plant kingdom. So although they aren't an essential food when at least three glasses of milk a day are included in your diet, they are nonetheless highly desirable. We discovered the versatility of beans in the kitchen only after several years of experimentation, but once we introduced them our families took to them with great enthusiasm. Afterwards we became much less dependent upon the "superfoods" like wheat germ and rice polishings: beans are such a basic and simple food by comparison. Take your time in making their acquaintance—"I can't digest beans" is a common complaint. Start with smaller quantities at a simple meal; don't sit down to a huge bowlful on the first day. It's important to cook them well; cooking for a long time at a lower heat helps to reduce their flatulence-causing properties. When eaten early, as for breakfast or lunch, they are good fuel for the day's activity. Using the many tips in our Recipes and Menus section, you can gradually work them into your usual diet. Eventually you may find, as we have, that they have become almost as essential a part of your day as bread.

Nuts and seeds add important variety to the meatless diet. Sunflower seeds are particularly high in vitamin B-6, and are not too expensive. Unhulled sesame seeds, which are brown in color, are an exceptional source of calcium. And don't discard your squash and pumpkin seeds—they're delicious roasted, and a good source of protein.

When beginning to use whole grains, nuts, and seeds, keep in mind that they come in a hard kernel which is often encased in a hull. Although the hull itself contains valuable nourishment and fiber, the digestive system beyond the teeth may not be able to get at the nutrients in the kernel if the food is not chewed extremely well or ground up. Children especially do not chew very well, and in some parts of the world they are weaned onto a grain-based diet only to suffer deficiencies simply because the grind of grain which nourishes adults is too coarse for them to digest. The granola foods that are popular in this country should be used judiciously with this in mind.

Ground-up seed meals, on the other hand, are easily digested. They are a versatile food which may be made into sandwich spreads or sprinkled on other dishes for a nutty flavor.

Vegetables

IMPORTANT SOURCES OF:
Vitamin A
Folacin
Riboflavin
Vitamin C
Calcium

The roots, shoots, stems, leaves, flowerets, and fruits of plants become the foods we know as vegetables. Ideally they are the freshest food in our diet, especially if we can pluck them out of our own kitchen garden just before dinner. Vegetables are usually low in calories, so their most important contribution is the vitamins and minerals they contain. The fresher the vegetable, the better will be its vitamin content.

Vitamin C is the traditional guage of how well we've stored and cooked vegetables, since it is easily destroyed by improper care. Cabbage-type greens (broccoli, brussels sprouts, collards, and kale) and mustard and turnip greens are so high in vitamin C that they have more C than citrus fruits if cooked carefully.

Folacin, too, is easily destroyed, and is a commonly marginal nutrient in the American diet. Its name is derived from the same word as *foliage,* for fresh dark green leaves are its most important source. Nutritionally, in fact, dark leafy greens are the king of vegetables, so a generous portion of them every day is quite important. The leaves of a plant are its chemical factories which, with the aid of chlorophyll and sunlight, make the nutrients necessary for life. They are a good source of high-quality protein and are rich not only in folacin but also in provitamin A (carotene), vitamin C, riboflavin, calcium, and iron. The greener the leaf, the richer it is in vitamins and minerals. For those who don't drink milk, green leaves are especially important because of their calcium and riboflavin content. However, a few leafy greens—spinach, chard, sorrel, pigweed, parsley, and beet greens (as well as rhubarb and chocolate)—contain a substance called oxalic acid that binds up their minerals just as phytic acid does in grains. They still have many nutritional pluses to make them worthwhile foods, but you cannot utilize all their calcium and iron.

The yellow and dark green vegetables are the most important source of vitamin A in the diet. Again, the deeper the color, the richer the vitamin content.

Because of their freshness and color, the cook can do a lot with vegetables to make a meal more appealing: bright red tomatoes set off dark green leaves; brightly colored carrots and green peas liven up a dish of rich brown grains. With a sauce that's not too high in calories, vegetables in all their variety are the ideal basis for a light evening meal.

Fruit

Often in nutrition fruits and vegetables are considered together, because many fruits and vegetables are alike in being high in vitamins A and C as well as fiber. In fact, some of the foods we usually think of as vegetables—pumpkins, winter squash, and tomatoes—really *are* fruits. In our grouping, however, fruits get a food group of their own, because in the kitchen the foods we all commonly call fruit are quite different from vegetables. They are usually (and most nutritiously) eaten raw, and are quite sweet. Their sugar content, in fact, makes them much higher in calories than most vegetables—though we tend to forget this because the sugar is dissolved in juice, so they, like vegetables, are not heavy in the stomach. More than four pieces of fruit a day will give a lot of calories and sugar, more than you may be aware of. In our view, fruits should be considered a treat. They make an ideal dessert.

Eating a piece of fresh, raw citrus fruit is the best way to be sure you've met your vitamin C requirement. The citric acid in these fruits helps to preserve their vitamin C, which is more readily destroyed in other foods. Since vitamin C is also easily destroyed by heat during cooking, especially cooking in iron pots, a raw source will assure that the need is met—most inexpensively by an orange or two tomatoes. If you don't eat these foods, fresh strawberries, cantaloupe, papaya, honeydew melon, or vegetables like raw cabbage, broccoli, brussels sprouts, collards, kale, and mustard greens will all help meet the requirement.

Besides vitamin C, citrus fruits contain some calcium and thiamin. Orange and red fruits also have provitamin A.

IMPORTANT SOURCES OF:
Vitamin C
Vitamin A
Sugar (not essential)

Milk and Eggs

IMPORTANT SOURCES OF:
Protein
Vitamin B-12
Riboflavin
Calcium

MILK ALSO HAS:
Milk sugar
Butterfat

In our own experimentation with meatless cookery, we used to think of milk as *the* basic food in our diet. Now we have come to feel it was a bit overrated. If you use dairy products to replace part of your daily allotment of bread, beans, and seeds, you may well end up shy of some of the scarcer nutrients, especially B vitamins and certain trace minerals like iron. Milk can't be dropped completely from the meatless diet without great caution and care, but in the diet we present here, its real role is supplemental.

A little milk drunk regularly makes a substantial contribution to the nutritional value of a diet. People who live traditionally on cereal-based diets almost always eat yogurt or some other supplementary animal food. Milk products and eggs, as animal foods, give us the one essential nutrient which for practical purposes is totally lacking from the all-plant diet: vitamin

IMPORTANT NUTRIENTS IN MILK & EGGS

	Vit. B-12	Calcium	Riboflavin	Protein
RDA:	2*–3 µg	600*–800 mg	1.6 mg	50 g
Milk, fresh, *1 cup*	1.0	290	.41	8.5
Skim milk powder, *4 tablespoons (1 cup liq.)*	1.0	390	.54	11
Cottage cheese, creamed, *1 cup packed*	2.5	230	.61	33
Cheddar cheese, *1-ounce slice*	.3	210	.13	7.1
Buttermilk, *1 cup*	.5	300	.44	8.8
Yogurt, low-fat, *1 cup*	.3	290	.44	8.3
Egg, *1 large*	1.0	27	.15	6.5
Soy milk (our recipe), *1 cup*	4.0	350	.07	7.5

U. N. recommended intakes, 1974 (see pp. 454–455).

B-12. One cup of fresh liquid milk, whole or skimmed, or one egg will supply half of the 2-microgram allowance recommended by United Nations standards. The allowance recommended by the U.S. National Research Council is higher, 3 micrograms, but you will be safe in meeting the lower standard since the minimum requirement is a good bit less. (See the discussion of vitamin B-12 on page 410.) As you can see in the table on the facing page, some cultured milk products like buttermilk and yogurt have less vitamin B-12 than fresh milk does, so you need to eat more of them to get the same amount of that particular nutrient.

The Milk and Eggs group is an important source of other nutrients, too, especially calcium and riboflavin. Calcium is what makes bones and teeth hard, so milk is important for growing children. But older people need milk also, since too little calcium is one reason why many of them get brittle bones, especially on a high protein diet. Riboflavin, incidentally, is the one B vitamin of which milk is the mainstay, and it is destroyed by light, so milk should be protected from light to preserve it.

In a balanced diet, two glasses of fresh milk supply a minimum amount of all the milk-important nutrients, with the remainder easily supplied by other foods. The table here is designed to help you see how other foods in this group compare to fresh milk in meeting the same needs.

Some people turning to a meatless diet increase their intake of milk only to find that after drinking a glass or two they get a stomachache, feel bloated and gaseous, and have diarrhea. These are symptoms of lactose intolerance, an inability to digest milk sugar or lactose. Lactose intolerance is most common among people who are not of Northern European stock, except for children who have been drinking milk since birth. Even older people who react to large amounts of milk, however, can usually take one-fourth to one cup at a time without any problem. Cultured milk products like cheese, yogurt, cottage cheese, and buttermilk have most of their lactose already "digested" by bacteria, so they are more easily tolerated.

Being animal products, milk and eggs contain animal protein, which is very close in its composition to human protein.

Milk protein, therefore, provides all the materials needed to build and repair proteins in the body, and is referred to as "complete" protein. If a person meets half of his protein requirement with animal protein—about three glasses of milk for an adult—that will supply enough protein material to balance any "incomplete" plant protein eaten during the day. Less milk than this requires at least one serving of beans a day as well.

Eggs are a very nourishing food, and small children and young women particularly benefit by eating them occasionally. But eggs are also one of nature's richest sources of cholesterol—more so even than most meats. Those who are better off not having large amounts of cholesterol in their system— adolescent boys and adult men fall into this category more often than other people—would do well to keep the eggs they eat to a minimum. Many people, however, don't fall in either the "high-risk" or the definitely safe category on the cholesterol issue, particularly since there is quite a lot of disagreement among the experts as to who is actually safe eating foods rich in cholesterol. We feel that a cautious approach is reasonable at this time, and include eggs in our diet in moderation. To keep track of your family's egg consumption, buy enough for each person to have four in a week: when they're gone, that's it until next week. Those family members on cholesterol-restricted diets can avoid eggs at breakfast and enjoy them in smaller quantities in the wide variety of dishes where they work magic for the cook.

Four Food Groups for the Vegan

The diet of the vegan (pronounced *vej-an* as in *veg*etable) is the vegetarian diet in its purest form, made up exclusively of plant foods without any foods of animal origin at all. It represents a direction in diet which many people find more and more appealing with the passage of time, as they become less dependent on animal foods and more aware that it is possible to be completely well nourished without dairy products and eggs. It is, however, a diet with limitations which can be serious. These limitations must be completely understood and carefully compensated for.

As we have seen, plant foods can be balanced so that their protein pattern is more than adequate in meeting human needs. A diet which gets 60 percent of its protein from grains, 35 percent from legumes, and 5 percent from leafy green vegetables will be adequately balanced with respect to protein.* If you get the total *amount* of protein you need in these proportions, there will be essential amino acids to spare.

Because legume protein is necessary for balancing grain protein in the absence of animal foods, legumes must be a staple in the vegan's diet. The Four Food Groups for the vegan, then, are Grains, Legumes, Vegetables, and Fruit. From these groups the vegan must be careful to select foods rich in the nutrients which are usually best supplied by milk—specifically, calcium and riboflavin. The diet *must* be supplemented with vitamin B-12.

Grains should be the predominating food in the vegan's diet, as in the diet of any vegetarian. Yeast-raised or naturally leavened whole-grain bread should be eaten generously, as it is a dependable source of many scarce minerals like iron and zinc. Of course, the total amount of grain foods needed to provide the necessary 60 percent of the diet's protein will depend on the protein concentration in the foods chosen. Grains vary greatly in their protein concentration, from about 8 percent protein for uncooked rice and corn to about 14 percent for uncooked hard spring wheat. More calories must be eaten of the foods low in protein to get the same 60 percent of your protein requirement. This presents no problem as long as the whole diet has enough calories to meet your energy needs. In the example on the following page, about two and a half cups of various grains and four slices of bread supply the average male vegan's grain protein needs. When calories are restricted, however, as they are in a low calorie weight-reducing diet, getting enough grain protein is more of a problem, and the person should concentrate on the higher-protein grains. Nut and

*Conversation with Doris H. Calloway, Professor of Nutrition, University of California, Berkeley, 6 November 1974.

Four Food Groups for the Vegan

BALANCING PROTEIN

For the vegan, the four food groups and their proportions are determined by the formula for vegan protein balance:

	Men	Women
60% from grains	33 g	28 g
35% from legumes	20	16
5% from leafy greens	3	2
Total protein RDA	56 g	46 g

Grains

33 grams grain protein for men; 28 grams for women. Include 4 slices of bread, 3 to 5 servings of grain, and 1 serving of nuts or seeds seeds every day.

EXAMPLE:

	Protein(g)	Calories
1 cup oatmeal	5	132
1 cup brown rice	5	232
½ cup cracked wheat	3	108
¼ cup sesame meal	4	130
2 slices commercial whole wheat bread	5	122
2 slices Rye Bread (our recipe)	11	244
	33	968

Legumes

20 grams legume protein for men; 16 for women. Include ⅓ cup beans and 2 cups fortified soybean milk OR

1 ¼ cups beans plus other sources of vitamin B-12 and calcium every day.

EXAMPLE:

	Protein(g)	Calories
2 cups soy milk	15	312
⅓ cup navy beans	5	75
	20	387

Vegetables

4 or more servings of good-quality vegetables every day (3 grams of protein). Include 2 substantial servings of dark leafy greens for calcium and riboflavin.

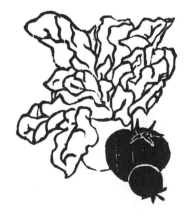

Fruit

1 to 4 servings a day. Include a raw source of vitamin C.

LIMITED NUTRIENTS & GOOD SOURCES

Vitamin B-12   *Two cups fortified soy milk, fortified nutritional yeast, or a vitamin pill*

Calcium   *Fortified soy milk, leafy greens without oxalates, sunflower seeds, unhulled sesame seeds, blackstrap molasses*

Riboflavin   *Beans, green leaves, certain nuts, nutritional yeast, wheat germ* seed protein may be counted as grain protein because it has similar strengths and weaknesses.

One cup of cooked beans has enough protein to supply the legume protein requirement (35 percent of the total requirement) for most people. Beans have a higher concentration of protein than grains (uncooked, about 20 percent) and they only double their size when cooked, whereas grains triple. So the one-to-three ratio of bean to grain *protein* becomes more like a one-to-six ratio of *servings* of cooked beans to grains. Soy milk, which is high in protein, is often a staple food for vegans. Two cups of it can nearly meet the need for beans. If it is fortified with vitamin B-12 and calcium, it can make a great contribution to the nutritional safety of the vegan diet as well as make it more interesting.

The vegan will want to eat plenty of fresh dark green vegetables. One serving is enough to round out the protein balance of the diet, but leafy greens are also good sources of riboflavin, a nutrient usually supplied most efficiently by milk. In addition, the dark green leafy vegetables without oxalic acid—mustard, turnip, and dandelion greens, collards and kale, and both romaine and loose-leaf lettuce—supply another milk-concentrated nutrient, calcium. They also supply iron.

Fruits, of course, are important to the vegan for vitamin C, just as to anyone else.

Vitamin B-12 is the really critical nutrient in the vegan diet, since it cannot be found in any plant food in sufficient quantities to meet human needs—and B-12 deficiency, as you can see from the details on page 411, is a serious matter. A simple way to get your B-12 is in fortified soy milk. However, commercial soy milk products are often designed primarily for the meat-eating child who is allergic to milk rather than for the vegan, so check the label to see what percent of the recommended dietary allowance (RDA) for B-12 is met by a glass of that particular product. If it is 10 percent, you'll need ten glasses to meet the RDA, and you can suspect that the manufacturer had the allergic child in mind. Because commercial products are expensive and heavily sugared, you may wish to make your own soy milk, which you can flavor and fortify yourself. (Our recipe is given on page 134.) If you prefer, alternative ways of getting vitamin B-12 are to use nutritional yeast which has been grown on B-12 enriched media or to take a vitamin pill. Pills generally come in high dosages, so you may need only one a week. The RDA level may also be supplied by daily multiple vitamin pills: again, check the label to see that it lists at least 2 micrograms of B-12.

Because the pure vegetarian diet contains a lot of vegetable fiber, many people have trouble eating enough food to meet their caloric needs. While a carefully chosen whole-food diet can be adequate for adults, children probably need supplemental sources of calories from easily digested, non-bulky foods. One of the most effective ways to supply this is to add sweetener to your soy milk. Another is to use oil in cooking, and margarine on your bread. Adequate calories keep the body from burning its protein supply for energy.

To those who are just entering the widely varied world of meatless cookery, the vegan's diet may seem a little odd. Cooking with soy milk for soup bases and making grain dishes without eggs is a real challenge to your cooking skill. But more and more of our friends have been experimenting with this challenge—and finding that with loving care, the vegan diet can be not only nourishing but delicious as well.

Pregnancy, Infancy, and Early Childhood

THE DIET DURING PREGNANCY

During pregnancy you eat not just for one but for two. Whatever you take in, or don't take in, will affect not only you but your baby too. You show love for your baby by eating what nourishes him or her and avoiding what does not. This applies not only to food but to alcohol, nicotine, and other substances which are harmful to the tiny fetus. Amounts that you can easily tolerate may be an overdose for your baby.

The need for all the nutrients increases during pregnancy. In fact, the mother who is well nourished *before* pregnancy will be in the best position to nourish her baby from conception on. The baby has first priority for any nutrients that your body has, and if your diet doesn't supply them, your body stores will be depleted. So the pregnant woman needs to eat a higher than normal level of all the nutrients in a well-rounded diet. Many women experience nausea during the first three months of pregnancy, making it very difficult for them to increase their nourishment. By eating smaller meals more often, eating well when the nausea is least, and always getting good food (especially foods that are rich in protein), you can stay very well nourished during the first three months of pregnancy in spite of nausea.

Just as at other times, your energy or calorie needs during pregnancy must be met so that the protein you eat won't be burned for fuel and can provide the raw materials the baby needs to grow. Twenty years ago a restricted calorie diet was thought to be good for pregnancy. Now, however, it is accepted that pregnancy and lactation are not the best times to reduce weight, because your baby will be in danger of being deprived. If you are overweight when you conceive, you are better off increasing your exercise to prevent too large a weight

HIGH-PROTEIN DRINK

Blend in a blender:
3 tbsp. whole soy powder
3 tbsp. noninstant
skim milk powder
½ ripe banana
1 rounded tablespoon
peanut butter
8 oz. (1 cup) fresh
skim milk
YIELD: *12 ounces or 1½*
cups (28 grams protein)

OPTIONAL:
1 tbsp. toasted wheat germ
½ teaspoon torula yeast
½ teaspoon carob powder
YIELD: *1⅔ cups (30*
grams protein)

For a supply of the dry
ingredients, mix:
1½ cups soy powder
1½ cups skim milk
powder
½ cup toasted wheat
germ
4 tbsp. torula yeast
4 tbsp. carob powder
Add ½ cup of dry ingre-
dients to each cup of milk
if all are used, OR *add ⅓*
cup if only the soy and
milk powder are used.

gain during pregnancy than restricting your calories below your energy needs, which are increased under these circumstances. The ideal weight gain during pregnancy varies from woman to woman. Young women, those in their first pregnancy, and those who are fairly thin tend to gain more than older, heavier women or those who already have children. A gain of 25 to 30 pounds is not at all unreasonable.

An additional 30 grams of protein should be added to the normal daily protein requirement during pregnancy. Protein needs are now thought to be fairly high during the beginning of pregnancy as well as the end. Although the baby doesn't require as much initially, your body probably is storing protein in its tissues which the baby can draw from later on.[1]

Adequate protein intake is also thought to protect against the development of a condition called toxemia during the second half of pregnancy. One symptom of this condition is high blood pressure, so if your doctor finds your blood pressure to be a little high, he may ask you, among other things, to increase your protein intake substantially.

Pure protein concentrates processed from soybeans are not the best way to get this extra protein, because too many important nutrients are lost in their processing. Although commercial soy protein products are often packed with artificial vitamins, it simply isn't possible to say what trace elements we miss or what balances we may be throwing off by eating artificial concentrates instead of whole foods. Here is a recipe for a high-protein drink made from nourishing supplementary foods—intended to be added to a normal diet when a person has special needs, not to replace some of its basic foods! You can mix up a week's supply of the powdered ingredients at a time and then blend the proper amounts of this mixture with fresh milk, banana, and peanut butter just before serving. Each 12-ounce drink contains a whopping 28 grams of protein; the wheat germ and torula yeast add many vitamins and the very important mineral iron.

It is recommended that the pregnant woman drink four glasses of skim milk a day or get the equivalent in low-fat dairy products. (The fat in whole milk will give you a lot of extra calories which you should be eating in a more nourishing form.) This supplies a large amount of good-quality protein, important for the baby's rapid growth, and ensures that calcium needs are met as well: your baby needs calcium to form strong teeth and bones. Drinking milk is a habit you may continue after the baby is born, throughout the period of breast-feeding. You need a substantial amount of extra fluid to produce milk, and getting this fluid as milk provides extra calcium, phosphorus, and protein for your baby too.

The most common nutritional problem during pregnancy is anemia, usually due to a deficiency of either iron or folacin, so during pregnancy you should include extra amounts of foods rich in these nutrients in your diet. Adequate iron ensures that the baby will be born with a good store of iron to last the first six months of life when his milk-based diet is iron-poor. And if you are anemic during childbirth, you will be more prone to excessive blood loss.[2] Generally it is whole grains, beans, and dark green vegetables that are rich in iron and folacin, but be sure to study the lists of foods high in these nutrients on page 434 (iron) and page 412 (folacin). The added insurance of a vitamin-mineral pill daily during pregnancy is easily justified because of the importance of preventing deficiencies in critical nutrients like iron.

NUTRITION DURING THE FIRST YEAR OF LIFE
During the first months of life the mother's milk is a perfect and complete food for the newborn baby. A tiny baby can thrive on other milks like specially fortified cow's milk or soy milk, but there is resounding agreement among the experts that nothing is equal to mother's milk for nourishing a newborn baby. The evidence for this is so convincing that formulas are now available which simulate mother's milk in every way that technology can. Cow's milk, for instance, has three times as much sodium and protein as human milk—perfect for the calf, which doubles its birthweight three times as fast as a human baby does, but undoubtedly more than the human baby needs. The protein and fat in human milk are more readily digested by a baby than the protein and fat in substitutes. (Cow's milk, in fact, is more likely to irritate the allergy-prone infant than any other substance, partly because a newborn baby's

digestive system is very delicate until it has had a chance to mature.) The protein, fat, and sugar in mother's milk also provide the right balance of calories and protein for optimal growth. Human milk has more sugar (lactose) than the milk of other animals, too—perhaps because the human brain grows larger than that of any other animal in proportion to body weight, and sugar is the form of food which the brain utilizes. (Milk, remember, is the infant's only food, and the sugar and fat in the milk or formula are his primary source of energy.)

Nutrient qualities aside, mother's milk also contains substances which protect the baby from infection. In addition, the baby who nurses is more in control of how much he eats—he simply stops eating when he is satisfied. Bottle-fed babies, on the other hand, are more easily overfed: the mother can measure the formula and will usually have in mind a certain amount she wants her baby to finish. Perhaps the most important point of all in favor of breast-feeding, however, is that the mother must always be close by to feed her baby, so that he always has the security of her presence. Unfortunately, in light of all these advantages, only one in four babies in the United States today is breast-fed for any length of time.

If your diet is supplying enough calories to maintain your weight and a somewhat higher than usual level of protein, vitamins, minerals, and fluids, your milk will most likely provide all the nourishment your baby needs. If you are getting enough vitamin C, for example, your baby will get the vitamin C he needs in his milk. One possible exception to this principle is vitamin D. Both mother *and* child should have a good supply of this vitamin, which can be gotten by sunning a little every day during warm weather. The vitamin D produced by the sunlight is then stored in the body throughout the cold season. (See the discussion of vitamin D on page 398.)

Perhaps the most important nutrient which milk cannot supply is iron. By about six months the baby uses up the supply of iron with which he was born and needs to get iron from his food.* Six months old is really the latest that solid foods

---

* Breast-fed babies are less likely to develop iron deficiency anemia than bottle-fed babies if they are started on solid foods at the appropriate time.[3]

should be introduced. However, babies develop differently and between the ages of three and six months your baby's caloric needs might increase so that milk no longer satisfies his appetite. If he suddenly increases his demand to be fed and requires more frequent nursing for several days, he probably is ready for solid food.

Because a baby's digestive system is developing and is too delicate to handle just anything, foods should be carefully selected and added to the diet one at a time, not more than once a week. A small spoonful of a new food is enough for the first time; the amount may be increased gradually until the baby is eating as much as he wants. This enables the baby to get used to each new food, and you can better tell whether or not it agrees with him. If he develops intestinal symptoms such as diarrhea, stomach discomfort, or vomiting, you should temporarily eliminate that food. Various kinds of skin rashes and other allergy problems can also be associated with food allergy, especially in infancy. If your baby remains on mother's milk until he is truly hungry for more food, he is less apt to become allergic than if he starts solids in the first few months.

Give the first few feedings between nursings so that the baby is not so hungry that he is too impatient to try something new. If you hold him in a sitting position in your lap, reclining him only slightly, you can slip a small amount of food into his mouth from the tip of a spoon or from your finger. It will take him a little while to get used to this new way of eating.

It is easier for a tiny baby to swallow a fairly thin, dilute food, so foods should be prepared with some liquid to achieve this consistency. Ripe banana (it should be very ripe) mashed with a little water is a nutritious first food for babies; they like its taste and smooth consistency. Whole-grain cereals should be given next; they are an excellent food for supplying iron. Use a full variety of them: first try rice, as it is easily digested and rich in iron; then give barley and millet; later add corn and oats. Because the baby doesn't chew, whole-grain cereals must be thoroughly ground up. Cook the grain as if you were going to eat it yourself; then blend it with some liquid to make it fairly thin and smooth. You may find it more convenient to prepare a supply of baby cereals by grinding the grain raw in a grain grinder or blender and then cooking what you need at each meal, making the same smooth, semiliquid food. Bread, too, may be given at this time, cut into pieces that the baby can hold, although many doctors recommend making wheat the last cereal to be added because older babies are less likely to develop wheat allergy than younger ones.

After your baby is well established with cereals he will enjoy potatoes and sweet potatoes mashed smooth with a little liquid. Vegetables should be added at this time, cooked fresh and mashed well or blended; offer those with a mild flavor first. Next your baby will be equal to munching on a peeled, ripe apple, peach, or pear.

Around the age of seven or eight months (or even later if milk allergy runs in your family) slowly introduce whole milk, from a cup, once or twice a day. It takes a baby a while to learn to manage a cup. Gradually give a little butter and peanut butter too.

Some pediatricians suggest that egg, chocolate, berries, and citrus fruits not be given until the end of the first year to lessen the chances of developing allergy to them. Such foods should be started in small amounts—citrus juices, for example, may be diluted at first with two parts of water. The time that a baby is most likely to become sensitive to these foods, as well as to cow's milk and certain cereal grains, is when the intestine is inflamed from diarrhea, so during intestinal illnesses it is best to avoid these foods and feed your baby only those foods which are known to be nonirritating, like apple juice, rice, bananas, and low-fat cottage cheese.

Around six or eight months old the baby may be very interested in gumming. Hard whole wheat biscuits or stale bread crusts, a stalk of celery, or a raw carrot are good for this purpose. (Our babies like to chew on soft-bristle toothbrushes.)

It is possible to overfeed a baby. If you are feeding him in a calm and attentive atmosphere, when he turns his head away and clamps his mouth shut he is saying that he has had enough. His body's fat cells are being made only during this first year and possibly during early adolescence, and they have come to stay: though they will vary in size later on, their number will never be reduced. Since an adult with too many fat cells is at a great disadvantage in trying to keep a normal weight, your doctor will watch your baby's growth curve when he weighs him and will tell you if your baby is getting too fat. Activity, of course, also helps to determine your baby's weight, just as it does yours.

Don't salt your baby's food to your own taste. All the salt he needs is naturally present in his food already, and studies strongly suggest that adding salt to a baby's diet predisposes him to high blood pressure in later life. Also, don't get him started on sugared foods: he needs them even less than we do, for he is growing rapidly and deserves the best possible nourishment.

Once your baby has a good start with solid foods, you can select most of his foods from your family menu, mashing them or cutting them up to suit his needs.

FEEDING THE YOUNG CHILD

From age two to five the child's rate of growth is constantly slowing and the number of calories he needs per pound is less, so he may not show quite so much interest in food as he did as a baby. Because his activity varies a great deal, his appetite fluctuates with seeming inconsistency. Generally a normal child can be trusted to select a balanced diet if you provide him with a wide variety of wholesome foods.

A little child may be hungry and ask for food at times that seem odd to you. There's no reason for not letting him eat at these times as long as he's given good, nourishing food. He should also join the family's meals, and though the amounts he eats may be quite small, they will be adequate. He may need help in selecting small amounts so that a great deal is not wasted on his plate. To free yourself from constantly feeding him between meals, give him finger-foods he can easily handle, like small sandwiches, vegetable sticks, and fruit sections. Also, since he may not be able to sit still the entire length of a family meal, it's really not reasonable to expect him to.

By keeping our food group scheme in mind you can be sure that your child is not skipping whole categories of food, such as fruits or vegetables. Because growing people need extra protein of high quality and ample calcium, milk is the one food which is traditionally recommended in a larger proportion than for adults. The vitamin D with which milk is fortified is also much more important for the child than the adult, especially if he doesn't get much sun. But the vegan child who doesn't drink milk can also do well by following the vegan regimen we outline in an earlier chapter. Figure his protein needs from the protein allowance for his age, and be sure that he is getting enough calories, calcium, vitamin D, and vitamin B-12.

Because many of America's children now show blood cholesterol levels which are much higher than the average in societies where problems like heart disease do not exist, skim milk, low in cholesterol, is now preferred by some doctors for children over two. After the second year a child doesn't need milk's fat for energy, so it is a good time to switch to skim. Dr. Jeremiah Stamler, a prominent cardiologist from Chicago, even questions whether children need the large amounts of milk we are accustomed to giving them. He points out that children raised in other food traditions grow quite healthily on much less milk.

If a small child dislikes a few foods, no harm is done by skipping them. If it is something the whole family is having, you can offer a nutritional substitute at another meal. A child's sense of taste is much more acute than ours, so he may find highly flavored mixtures of food too strong even when the same foods are delicious to him when cooked separately without seasonings. By gradually giving new foods on a take-it-or-leave-it basis, showing unconcern if they are refused, meals don't take on an unpleasant atmosphere. Encourage your child to enjoy his food—even if that means you have a mess to clean up afterwards.

SOURCE REFERENCES

1. National Research Council, Food and Nutrition Board, *Recommended dietary allowances,* 8th rev. ed. (Washington, National Academy of Sciences, 1974), p. 41.

2. National Research Council, Committee on Maternal Nutrition [Food and Nutrition Board], *Maternal nutrition and the course of pregnancy: summary report* (Rockville, Md., U. S. Maternal and Child Health Services, 1970), p. 5.

3. La Leche League International, Anemia: rare in breastfed babies (Franklin Park, Ill., 1970); reprinted from *La Leche League News.*

Keeping Your Weight under Control

Forty percent of Americans, including the majority of those who are middle-aged, are overweight. Of children and adolescents, it is likely that more than 20 percent are already too heavy.

Obesity, or clinical overweight, is defined as a total body fat content of more than 25 to 30 percent of body weight for men and more than 30 to 35 percent for women. It is important to think in terms of body fat rather than total weight, since some people who are overweight according to the height-weight charts—like college athletes—may actually be underfat. On the other hand, sedentary people of "normal" weight may be overfat. A good way to measure your body fat is to pinch between your thumb and forefinger as much as you can on your tummy below the navel. If what you pinch up measures more than one inch across, you are overfat.

Because of all the hazards associated with obesity, your ideal weight throughout life is what your weight was when you were twenty-five if you are a man and what it was when you were twenty-two if you are a woman—provided you were not obese at that time! Even if you maintain the same weight throughout life, however, some of your active tissue will progressively be replaced with fat. Some French physicians, consequently, encourage their patients to "age dry"—that is, to lose weight gradually as they grow older. Certainly your calorie needs lessen with the passage of time, for fatty tissue requires less sustenance than more active muscle tissue.

There are many possible causes of obesity. Heredity is important: less than 10 percent of children of normal-weight parents are fat, 40 to 50 percent of children are obese when one parent is, and 80 percent of the children of two obese parents are also obese. A number of hormones, too, influence food intake and fat metabolism. However, hormones like thyroid should never be taken unless the gland really does not function well—and only a small percentage of overweight Americans suffer from a true hormonal or endocrinal disorder. The artificial hormone will turn off the gland's natural secretions, and since it is extremely slow and uncomfortable to reactivate these secretions, the person becomes dependent on synthetic substitutes. Most overweight people have a basal metabolism similar to that of normal people; the main difference is that they are less active. In fact, they may not be eating any more than their more active, thinner friends.

Inactivity, in fact, may be even a more important cause of obesity in this country than overeating. Many people believe that physical exercise will only increase their appetite and make their weight problem worse. Actually, the mechanisms which adjust appetite to energy needs are regulated by physical activity, so sedentary living only causes the appetite to go out of control. If you are reasonably active, you will find it much easier to keep your appetite in line with what your body actually needs. On the other hand, if you are trying to reduce without exercising, you will have to go very hungry most of the time in order to achieve your goal. Don't feel discouraged at the amount of exercise required to burn off a few calories during a day: the calories you burn up in exercise not only help you control your appetite; they also add up significantly. An hour a day of brisk walking burns 250 to 300 calories—thirty pounds of body fat a year. (One pound of body fat is equivalent to 3500 calories.)

No matter what the cause, you can only put on fat when you eat more food than your body actually burns. Once it is on, fat is extremely difficult to get off, as experience overwhelmingly shows. An ounce of prevention is truly worth a pound of cure. So whether or not you are trying to reduce, be sure to get in an hour of brisk walking every day. Park your car a fifteen-minute walk away from work. Get in another fifteen minutes during lunch or coffee break. Walk to the mailbox instead of driving your car. Keep company with others by walking together; it's delightful. And walk briskly—the calories burned increase with the intensity of the exercise.

THE HAZARDS OF OBESITY

People who are overweight are already familiar with discomforts like backache, shortness of breath at the top of the stairs, and the general burden of their extra pounds. Long-range hazards are much more serious; they include diabetes, hypertension, heart disease, and stroke.

Probably the largest single health hazard of middle-age obesity is maturity-onset (middle-age) diabetes. This type of diabetes often responds dramatically to weight reduction. In one large study 75 percent of the diabetics of this type who achieved their desired weight had their blood sugar levels return to normal.

Also closely associated with obesity is high blood pressure or hypertension. An estimated 23 million Americans are afflicted with hypertension, and half of them are unaware of it. One fifth to one third of all hypertensive adults in the United States are markedly overweight. These people have more illnesses and earlier deaths and run an especially greater risk of heart disease than either hypertensive people who are not obese or obese people who are not hypertensive.

Excess weight increases the work load of the cardiovascular system. Consequently, though it is not true for all, the blood pressure of many people goes down when they lose weight. Weight loss also improves the life expectancy of people who have had heart attacks, and often favorably affects angina pectoris or heart pains. There is also a significant association between obesity and gall bladder disease, especially in women, but in this case losing weight does not improve the condition once it has developed.

THE FAT CHILD

As we have already mentioned, it is likely that more than 20 percent of our children are obese. This is a great liability with which to start life, as a fat child will most likely continue to be fat as an adult, with all the accompanying problems.

Evidence is now accumulating that adults who were fat as

children have more fat cells in their body than those who were normal-weight children.[1,2,3] Because reducing doesn't decrease the number of fat cells but only their fat content, the person with excessive numbers of fat cells who is trying to reduce is at a tremendous disadvantage: he or she will have to shrink each cell much smaller than is normal in order to achieve a normal weight. The theory goes that the fat cells will then be "hungry" unless they can again attain their full size.

It is believed that the two periods after birth during which fat cells multiply are the first year of life and early adolescence. This implies taking care not to force a baby to overeat, and keeping an eye on his growth curve by weighing him regularly on the doctor's scales.

Activity will also greatly affect a baby's weight, just as it does at all other times in life. Activity, in fact, is one of the most critical factors in determining the weight of a child. In a study of 160 obese children, about 80 percent of them were inactive. Such children may spend only one third as much time on their feet as their more active peers; yet their caloric intake may be normal or even low. If the child is isolated socially, perhaps spending a great deal of time inside the house watching TV, he may get into the vicious cycle of eating food which is close at hand in an attempt to meet his emotional needs.

A restricted-calorie diet is a poor way to try to change the course of childhood obesity, because children are growing and need good nourishment. Chances are instead that the *type* of food which is eaten can be vastly improved. In particular, no unnourishing or "empty" food should be eaten at all, for such foods will only crowd out the real foods the child needs for nourishment. With a change in eating habits and a program of vigorous daily exercise for a long enough period every day to burn up calories, a child can grow naturally into his or her proper weight. Instead of discussing weight with the child as a problem, the parents should provide him with good food and spend time with him regularly in vigorous activity.

Because obesity among children is such a widespread problem, Dr. Jean Mayer suggests that comprehensive programs be developed to work with these children within schools. Smaller children don't mind being in a "fat group" as much as older children. If such children are clinically identified for such a group in school, special provision can be made for daily exercise, preferably with a team rather than in one-to-one competition, and the group can be taught about the importance of eating right.

DIETING

What is the best vegetarian reducing diet? Many people with a weight problem have experimented with a hundred and one approaches: the Grapefruit Diet, the Fiber Diet, appetite suppressant pills, hormone clinics, high protein–low carbohydrate diets, and so on. The weight goes on and off—alas, never staying off for long.

Fortunately, if you have a weight problem and are now beginning to experiment with nutritious vegetarian foods, you have already begun to turn your back on high calorie, nutrient-free foods, and already have the basis of a workable reducing diet. Furthermore, since the food is healthy and nutritious, it is also satisfying, even when you cut your portions back to the level where you lose weight.

The key to permanent success in losing weight is a change in attitude and life style, and vegetarianism is a natural partner to many such changes. Instead of grimly avoiding things which are harmful—not just foods but activities too—it helps immensely to seek out what is healthful and beneficial, cultivate it, and enjoy it in the company of friends who share similar purposes. Walking, for example, is not only an essential part of our reducing diet; it is also a delightful way to spend time with friends—and a lot easier on the environment than going for a drive.

Changes in life style accompany a growing awareness of the choices which lie before us. In diet this means not only a new awareness of which foods to eat and which not, but also a new respect for sensibly meeting our own emotional and physical needs. For example, a moderate amount of good, nourishing food eaten slowly with enjoyment is much more satisfying than large quantities of nutritionless "treats." Although we eat such foods in the hope that they will satisfy us, by the time we have sampled all that appeals to our taste we feel slightly bloated and are probably building up guilt feelings for eating more than is good for us, more than we wanted. Even the fine edge of enjoyment is dulled by heavy indulgence. It is worth some effort and practice to retrain ourselves to hear the subtle signals the body sends out about what it really needs. If you are tired, no amount of coffee can give you the same lift as a short nap or getting to bed earlier at night. After a day of sitting at a desk, no amount of candy or ice cream can restore to your body the sense of well-being you would get from a brisk walk home.

The real trouble is being trapped into eating things that do not meet our physical and emotional needs. Often the craving for more food doesn't arise from physical hunger, but from some frustration or sense of lack which food is expected to soothe and comfort. Do you eat as a transition activity? When switching from one job to another, particularly when it is something you do not like to do, a little snack is often eaten to compensate for having to do something you dislike. Actually, jumping into a job with concentration is the best way to make it enjoyable, and the craving for food simultaneously falls away. Try to meet your needs more directly. There *is* a choice.

Dwelling on what you have eaten, especially if the quantity has been larger than what you would have liked, can cause a lot of agitation. Instead of looking back with regret on your wrong habits of eating, from now onward see that you eat only healthy, nourishing food and then forget about the past. To help you do this, we have translated our Four Food Groups into a Basic Daily Diet for Reducing. The basic foods listed here can be adapted in menus and cooking by substituting their other forms for variety and interest. The beans and seeds, for example, can be made into sandwich spreads, or the skim milk can be taken as low-fat yogurt, buttermilk, or cottage cheese, or used in a hot drink. Bread, one of the most satisfying foods the world over (especially when fresh out of the oven), is still the staff of life, no less to the vegetarian on a reducing diet than to anyone else.

Crucial to making this diet work for you is adjusting your portion sizes so that you lose weight slowly, steadily, and in good health. With the right balance of food and regular daily exercise, the pounds *must* come off. Once you start losing weight on a healthy regime, the extra energy and vitality you have will encourage you to go on. Relishing your new freedom, you won't want to overeat.

As you cut back your portion sizes you may be meeting your needs for all the nutrients only marginally. Your best insurance is variety—vary your beans, vary your vegetables, and you will get everything in, avoiding the need for vitamin pills. You should continue to meet your recommended dietary allowances for all the essential nutrients but particularly for protein, because as you eat less calories, some protein calories will be burned for energy. The full protein allowance (roughly 50 grams for an adult) or even a little extra is necessary to meet your body's maintenance and repair needs. If you eat a balance of whole, natural foods, cutting out first of all sugar, large amounts of fat, and alcohol, you will probably have no trouble getting enough protein. In the portions given here, the Basic Daily Diet supplies about 1200 calories, and it meets all your nutritional needs.

BASIC DAILY DIET FOR REDUCING

Calories

74	*½ cup cooked whole-grain cereal*
354	*4 slices whole-grain bread*
86	*1 tablespoon peanut butter*
84	*2 tablespoons seeds*
204	*⅔ cup beans*
176	*2 cups skim milk*
75	*1½ cups cooked vegetables*
90	*1 cup green salad with 1 tablespoon dressing*
75	*1 orange*
1218	TOTAL CALORIES

Many people who try to reduce and do not lose weight have poor eating habits. Not only do they eat the wrong foods but they eat at the wrong times. They eat little throughout the day, eat a large dinner, nibble in the evening, and have no appetite for breakfast. Anyone who has tried to reduce knows this pattern only too well. In the morning, when your blood sugar is still high from what you've eaten the night before, your willpower is strong and your resolutions firm. So you skip, or merely sample, breakfast and lunch. Later, when your blood sugar drops, you become exhausted, irritable, and acutely hungry. Your undoing was not that you ate too much, but ate too little. If you eat at least one third of the day's food for breakfast and another third for lunch, the food you eat will be there when your body needs it to fuel its activities.

Sensibly followed, the Basic Daily Diet for Reducing frees you from the prison of being "on a diet." Your diet is *normal*, adjusted in quantity to meet your body's needs. Since you allow yourself to eat what you like within reason, you don't have to sneak away to eat it. You'll eat it anyway, so why not just plan a meal around it? If you can't have your bread without butter, a little of our Better-Butter (page 123) goes a long way. Remember that a teaspoon of Better-Butter—quite a lot—is only about 35 calories, an almost negligible amount. One teaspoonful can be spread on two pieces of bread easily without a caloric high. You might as well enjoy the butter on your bread at meals instead of saving up the desire for butter for a few days and then devouring three pieces of toast drowned in it one afternoon.

There are other interesting ways in which you can keep the palate on the path. When it is craving candy or a hot fudge sundae, go for a fast walk and bargain for time with your mind by telling it, "In two hours when we are going home we can go to an ice cream parlor for a deluxe sundae." Two hours later the mind has forgotten about ice cream sundaes and is thinking about the movie it will enjoy tomorrow evening. All you need to do is to put just a little break of time between desire and eating, for you can count on the mind to change its desires. Another technique, whenever the mind asks for some unnutritious delicacy like a chocolate candy bar, is to give it raisins instead. Very soon it will stop asking for candy.

Playing these little tricks on the mind will do no harm, but do not be violent with it. Treat it gently, patiently, and compassionately; it has been allowed to run loose for so many years that it is not fair to expect it to come to heel in a day or two. Occasionally, however, when there is a first-rate conflict, it is helpful to skip a meal. When this is done with discrimination, taking particular care that the body is not deprived of its energy, you will find that not only are the cravings easier to control, but the body benefits too.

Out-and-out fasting, however, does not yield many benefits in the long run. It may not be as easy as feasting, but after a while it is not too different. Both are extremes. It is not hard to go to extremes; what requires real artistry is neither to fast nor to feast, but to be moderate. Instead of suppressing our cravings, we train ourselves to harness them for our growth.

Weigh yourself once every week or two and keep a graph of your progress. If you weigh daily you will get an uneven graph: the course of your diet won't be as clear because you will register the water retention that initially replaces fat. Fat loss registers on the scale only after a delay.

If after a conscientious few months with the Basic Daily Diet your graph shows that you are not making much progress, you should take a serious and careful look at your calories. The calorie content for many foods, including some of our own recipes, is listed in the first column of the food charts in the back of this book. Keep track of what you eat for a couple of days and add up the calories. In order to do this at all accurately, you must measure your servings in cups, teaspoons, or whatever is relevant. Only such careful measurement will enable you to calculate the calories with reasonable accuracy. If you don't want to use these measurements, use a kitchen scale and go by weight—the important thing is to measure, accurately and consistently. Then compare the calories you are eating with what your needs are, following the steps on page 342. By eating 500 calories a day less than you expend in energy, you lose 1 pound a week, which is an ideal rate for getting

How to Estimate Calories
for Your Reducing Diet

1. Determine your ideal weight.
   (Lean weight at age 25 for men, age 22 for women.)

2. For each pound of ideal weight, figure:

	Women	*Men*
if you're under 45:	10 calories	11 calories
if you're over 45:	9 calories	10 calories

   This represents your basal metabolism—breathing,
   heartbeat, digestion, etc.

3. Take this figure and add ½ that number of calories.
   This represents your daily activity, including moderate
   exercise like normal activity and an hour's brisk walk or
   or a half-hour swim. The total is the amount of calories
   you'll need to maintain your ideal weight once you attain it.

4. To lose 1 pound per week, subtract 500 calories.
   To lose 2 pounds per week, subtract 1000 calories. BUT:

5. *Don't go below:* 1600 calories per day for a man,
   1200 calories per day for a woman,
   1400 calories per day for an adolescent girl.

   EXAMPLE (WOMAN, AGE 30):   115 pounds *ideal weight*
   $115 \times 10 = 1150$ calories
   $\frac{1}{2} \times 1150 = 575$ calories
   $1150 + 575 = 1725$ calories
   needed to maintain ideal weight.

   To lose 1 pound per week:
   $1725 - 500 = 1225$ cals./day

   This method is taken from the writings of Jean Mayer.

weight off to stay off. If you are eager to lose more quickly, 1000 calories less than you expend is the ideal maximum; however, men should not go below 1600 calories a day, women should not go below 1200 calories, and adolescent girls should not go below 1400 calories. A weight loss of more than 2 pounds a week is not possible without great hunger, low energy, and poor nourishment. You end up needing extra food just to get yourself back in shape.

Keep on measuring your portions at least until you become thoroughly familiar with their size and calorie content. Even after that you may continue to use the measure to set your serving size. This will keep you from getting that little extra which prevents you from losing. When your calories are below the energy you expend, the pounds *must* come off—there is no alternative. If you reduce your weight like this through good, intentional eating, you can increase your portions just enough to maintain your ideal weight once you have achieved your goal. The pounds stay off.

This diet is appealing, nourishing, and effective. It increases your health and your sense of well-being, and continues to be perfect for all occasions—good, in fact, for a lifetime.

ACKNOWLEDGMENT

The authors are indebted for most of the technical material in this chapter to the essays on obesity by Dr. Jean Mayer in his book *Human nutrition: Its physiological, medical and social aspects* (Springfield, Ill., Thomas, 1972).

SOURCE REFERENCES

1. Jules Hirsch and Jerome L. Knittle, Cellularity of obese and non-obese human adipose tissue. *Federation Proceedings* 29:1516–1521, 1970.

2. C. G. D. Brook, Evidence for a sensitive period in adipose-cell replication in man, *Lancet* 2:624–627, 1972.

3. Jules Hirsch, Can we modify the number of adipose cells?, *Postgraduate Medicine* 51(5):83–86, 1972.

Three Days of Reducing Menus

First Day

calories:		
	84	½ cup hot oatmeal topped with	BREAKFAST
	32	1 tablespoon toasted sunflower seed meal,
	27	1 tablespoon raisins, and
	44	½ cup skim milk
	176	2 slices whole-grain toast spread with
	86	½ tablespoon peanut butter each
471	22	hot beverage with 2 ounces skim milk*

	203	⅔ cup hot baked kidney beans OR	LUNCH
		⅔ cup kidney bean salad with
	54	2 teaspoons Oil and Vinegar Marinade on a
	4	crisp lettuce bed
	118	1 slice Sour Corn–Rye Bread spread with
	38	1 teaspoon Better-Butter
	82	1 grapefruit
521	22	hot beverage with 2 ounces skim milk*

	44	1 baked tomato	DINNER
	142	½ cup Creamed Spinach
	91	1 Lynne's Muffin spread with
	38	1 teaspoon Better-Butter
	124	½ cup Cole Slaw with poppy seeds and herbs
	61	½ cup yogurt
522	22	hot beverage with 2 ounces skim milk*

1514 total calories

Second Day

	122	1 cup yogurt topped with	BREAKFAST
	71	3 unsweetened cooked prunes and their juice
	224	2 slices Soy Bread toast with
	115	2 teaspoons almond butter each
615	83	6 ounces orange juice

*If you are not partial to hot beverages with milk, they may be replaced by a 6-ounce glass of skim milk or buttermilk midmorning, afternoon, at bedtime, or with one of the meals.

	176	2 slices whole-grain bread filled with	LUNCH
	78	3 tablespoons Cheese Spread	
	10	a slice of tomato	
	10	several cucumber slices and lettuce	
340	66	6 ounces skim milk	

	141	4 steamed broccoli spears tossed with	DINNER
	71	2 teaspoons Yeast Butter	
	154	1 cup Black Bean Soup	
557	191	Provincial Salad from ¼ head leafy lettuce	

1512 total calories

Third Day

	88	1 slice whole wheat bread topped with	BREAKFAST
	162	½ cup hot Red Bean Mix and juice	
	88	1 slice whole wheat toast spread with	
	86	1 tablespoon peanut butter	
	76	1 medium orange	
544	44	hot cereal beverage with ½ cup skim milk	

	208	2 slices Black Bread filled with	LUNCH
	74	2 tablespoons Garbanzo Spread and	
	6	¼ cup crisp alfalfa sprouts	
	200	1 cup low-fat cottage cheese	
546	58	1 small apple	

	16	½ cup green beans sprinkled with	DINNER
	55	1 tablespoon slivered almonds	
	13	½ cup cauliflowerets baked with	
	78	3 tablespoons grated cheese topping	
	204	½ cup Bulgur Wheat Pilaf,	
	10	1 cup greens tossed with	
457	81	1 tablespoon Creamy French Dressing	

1547 total calories

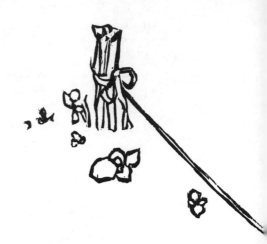

What Makes a Food

The story of food begins with the green plant and the sun. When the plant combines carbon dioxide from the air and water from the earth, it captures some of the sun's energy in the newly-formed chemical bonds. This is the process called photosynthesis, on which all life depends. The compounds that are formed are carbohydrates—hydrogen and oxygen atoms strung out along chains of carbon. These chains are the backbone of all organic compounds, including the constituents of living tissue. When such compounds are used for food within our bodies, oxygen from the air is used to "burn" their carbohydrate portions, releasing the energy from the sun trapped in their atomic bonds—and, to complete the cycle, the carbon dioxide which plants need for further photosynthesis.

Thus the story of food is a story of energy. In the living organism every cell is constantly active to maintain the processes of life, so that there is a continuous flow of energy, ultimately derived from the sun, through all living matter—in contrast to inert objects like metal or stone in which molecular energy is bound and static. In animals (including humans) this energy enters the body as food and is broken down in digestion into constituents small enough to be absorbed into the rest of the body through the intestinal wall. These absorbed compounds and elements are then remade into the compounds the body needs and carried by the blood to all systems of the body. The chemical changes involved in these processes are called metabolism. Overall, the body's metabolism is a constant and amazingly efficient cycle of building up and breaking apart for recycling all the substances in every cell of the body.

In each of these processes, substances called enzymes bring

together the necessary ingredients so that the required chemical reactions can take place—reactions that would take eons if simply left to chance. Assisted by vitamins from food, enzymes are involved in virtually every step of the body's metabolism, and without them, even with plenty of food available, there would be no energy to make the body run.

Even when we are doing nothing, there is a constant flow of energy through the body to maintain the basic processes of life: the beating of the heart, the tone of the muscles, the activity of the brain. Together these processes are called *basal metabolism*, and the energy they require is the rock-bottom foundation of our daily requirement for energy, which is measured in calories—or, more accurately, kilocalories. Any additional energy we might require over the day depends on the amount of our activity. Together, activity and basal metabolism make up our total energy needs, and food for energy makes up the largest part of our requirement for food.

FOOD FOR ENERGY: THE THREE FOODSTUFFS

Carbohydrate, fat, and protein make up the "foodstuffs" that are the bulk of our food. All three are found together, though in varying proportions, in most whole foods, and all are able to supply the body with energy, for all have in common a "burnable" chemical makeup of oxygen and hydrogen attached to carbon chains. Carbohydrate and fat, though they behave quite differently, both play a basically energy-giving role. Protein, however, is distinctively different, for it has a unique nitrogen group in its structure which enables it to link together with other proteins in an incredible number and variety of structures to provide the basic stuff of which our bodies are made.

In the body, the carbohydrate, fat, and protein from food become the building blocks of energy-giving substances and body tissues. Carbohydrate circulates in the blood in the form of the sugar glucose, which is taken up by the tissues as fuel for energy. The brain and central nervous system normally can use no other fuel. Fat, too, is an efficient fuel, especially for muscles, which demand the greatest part of our energy. Because fat is fairly insoluble, it does not dissolve in the body's fluids. This makes it the ideal substance for energy storage, for it supplies more than twice the calories that carbohydrate or protein can for the same weight: about 9 calories per gram as opposed to carbohydrate or protein's 4. Whenever we eat more of the foodstuffs than we need, whether protein, fat, or carbohydrate, the extra is greedily converted and stored as fat.

If fat and carbohydrate in the diet are too low to meet energy needs, protein from food or body tissues will be broken down for energy, since energy needs take priority over tissue building. If the diet is already supplying enough energy, any extra protein we eat is simply stored as fat. In either case, the nitrogen necessary for building tissue is simply thrown away. So carbohydrate—and fat, to a lesser extent—both spare protein in the diet for its proper function of maintenance and repair. Fortunately, as nutrition begins to ascribe proper, balanced roles to each of these three foodstuffs, the fear of never being able to get enough protein—the "protein paranoia" which has dominated our national dietary thinking for years—is now gradually fading away.

THE BALANCE OF FOODSTUFFS IN THE DIET

The body has an immense capacity to adapt what we give it to what it needs. Through an amazing variety of mechanisms, it can selectively absorb the nutrients it needs and leave behind those it does not; it can put other nutrients in storage or take them out again on demand; and with its task force of regulators (hormones and enzymes) it can see that everything goes just where it is needed.

So, incredibly, our bodies do not require just certain foods or one particular diet in favor of any others. The foodstuffs, vitamins, and minerals it needs can come from an extremely wide variety of sources over a wide range of proportions, and good health is possible throughout the spectrum, from the rice-based diets of Asia to the old-fashioned farm diet of the United States.

It is interesting, in fact, to see how the diets of the world vary in response to national wealth, for the natural presupposition is that health goes hand in hand with wealth and that our own national diet must therefore be some kind of model.

The following chart shows how international patterns in the distribution of the three foodstuffs differ according to wealth. As people become wealthier, more and more of their calories seem to come from fat, and the sources shift from whole-food oils to separated and animal fats as cooking practices shift from boiling to frying. Starch from staple food sources yields to a marked increase in refined sugar. The percentage of calories from protein remains fairly constant, but the sources shift from vegetable protein to animal protein, and the *amount* of protein eaten rises from an average of 50 grams per day to 90 grams per day as the total calories in the diet rise from 2000 to 3000. We may be tempted to think such changes beneficial, for our own national diet seems to foster maximum size, early maturity, an active sex life, and maximum muscular development—the classic American virtues of "more and faster." But a diet that fosters such attributes doesn't necessarily foster longevity[1] or even health, and the wealthy nations' diets—including that of the United States—seem to go hand in hand also with the diseases of excess: obesity, diabetes, and heart disease, to name a few.

NATIONAL DIETS & NATIONAL WEALTH

Calories from fats, carbohydrates, and proteins as percentages of total calories in the diet, according to national income. (Correlation based on 85 countries, 1962. Redrawn from Périsse et al. 1969)

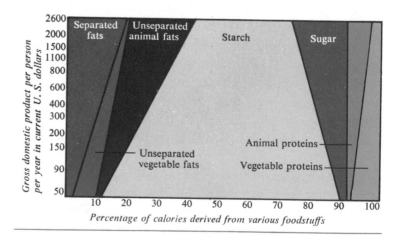

Percentage of calories derived from various foodstuffs

With just a little thoughtfulness and care we can give our bodies close to what they need within a broad latitude of individual variation. The amounts and proportions of each foodstuff we choose to eat will probably vary greatly, for age, sex, activity, inherited characteristics, environmental influences, and stress all change our needs for nutrients. The ideal diet for one person may be totally different from the ideal diet for another. This is the main reason why the recommended dietary allowance (RDA) for each nutrient, given at the end of this book, incorporate such a wide margin of safety over the minimum daily requirements. Normally, however, the basic pattern is quite simple: just enough protein to meet your needs for body repair and maintenance (and, for the child, growth) and just enough calories to meet your needs for energy, with most of the calories coming from the carbohydrate and fat which occur naturally in whole foods. If you meet these requirements from a reasonable variety of such foods—which is the purpose of our Four Food Groups—your diet should be very close to the ideal diet for you.

THE "MICRONUTRIENTS": VITAMINS AND MINERALS

Vitamins and minerals are the unseen dynamos of the food we eat. They are minute compared to the major foodstuffs, yet they are extremely versatile and just as essential for life. Because their concentration in food and in our bodies is so small, the vitamins and most minerals are called micronutrients. We measure them not in grams as we do other foodstuffs, but in thousandths or even millionths of a gram. Their role in the body's metabolism, however, is anything but small.

These micronutrients are regulators. They speed up or make possible millions of the chemical reactions which break down and store food, utilize it for energy, or synthesize from its components our bodies' tissues. They are as active as hormones and often work in concert with them. But, unlike hormones, our bodies cannot make them. Vitamins must come to us prefabricated, made in the cells of the food we eat; minerals are supplied by plants which have absorbed them from the soil.

Most of these nutrients serve not one but many functions. Vitamin B-6 (pyridoxine) is required both for synthesizing proteins and for breaking down proteins for fuel. Calcium, a mineral, is not only required for the coagulation of blood in the scab over a wound which stops it from bleeding; it also forms the deposits in bones and teeth which make them hard.

Perhaps because they are so inconspicuous and their functions so delicate and widespread throughout the body, it is only relatively recently that these nutrients have been recognized. Not until the early twentieth century did it occur to anyone that the now-famous syndromes of malnutrition like beriberi and pellagra might be deficiency diseases—diseases caused by the *absence* of something in the diet. As scientific investigation has brought the micronutrients to light, we've largely been able to protect ourselves from deficiencies and have come to understand more about what these nutrients do. But for many of us, the deficiency symptoms still provide the best clue we can get to the personalities of these mysterious little substances.

Lately, popular interest in the micronutrients has increased almost frantically as more and more people become aware that our dietary practices and food technology do not conserve them very well. Refined, highly processed foods may well be contributing to marginal deficiencies in whole sectors of our population. Again, those of us who get the calories we need from fresh, whole, natural foods probably have little cause for concern, for these foods generally provide the micronutrients in even richer supply than we need.

In the following chapters, the foodstuffs, vitamins, and minerals are discussed in a little more detail. We have tried to present a very basic background for each nutrient and then go a little deeper into some of the practical questions associated with each, especially if these relate to a meatless diet. Human nutrition is a complicated subject, however, and many of these questions are still being hotly debated. In some cases, up-to-date evidence has led us to conclusions which, though reasonable, are not what you will see in most popular presentations of nutrition. We have tried to show how we arrived at our conclusions even when this meant going into a little more detail, since these are all questions of immediate practical importance for someone trying to change the way he or she eats. Ultimately, however, the interpretation of these conclusions—how you translate them into what you actually eat—is up to you. Within the limits of what you can learn and simple common sense, we encourage you to experiment: good eating, like everything else in life, is essentially a matter of wise choices.

SOURCE REFERENCES

1. Robert S. Goodhart, Criteria of an adequate diet, in *Modern nutrition in health and disease: Dietotherapy,* 5th ed., ed. Robert S. Goodhart and Maurice E. Shils (Philadelphia, Lea & Febiger, 1973), p. 403.

The Foodstuffs: Carbohydrate

There is a popular myth that carbohydrates are fattening and should be avoided, since the carbohydrate in our food is almost entirely either sugars or starch. Actually, along with fat, carbohydrate is the body's major fuel, and the carbohydrate in whole foods is a perfect source of energy. The trouble arises with carbohydrates that are separated or refined: "empty calorie" foods like sugar, white-flour pastries, and alcohol, which are high in calories and low (at best) in everything else. Refining whole-grain carbohydrates has another drawback, too: besides stripping off many of the original nutrients, it removes the fiber encasing it, an indigestible but important carbohydrate whose absence from our national diet seems to be contributing to intestinal disorders, elevated cholesterol levels, and colon cancer.

Starch, an Ideal Source of Energy

The body can burn any of the three foodstuffs for energy, but starch is easily digested into the body's most efficient fuel: glucose, one of the simplest sugars, which is the primary fuel carried by the blood to all the cells of the body. Starch consists entirely of chains of glucose, and needs only to be broken down in digestion to become an excellent source of energy for the human body.

The nutrient "packaging" surrounding the starch in whole grains, legumes, and vegetables makes a perfect vehicle for this fuel, helping to supply other nutritional requirements while satisfying our need for energy. The carbohydrate in white flour or table sugar, on the other hand, provides fuel and virtually nothing else. Since the body needs certain vitamins to metabolize foods for fuel, eating large amounts of carbohydrate devoid of vitamins is a little like gathering the logs and kindling for a fire but not having any matches with which to light it. Since the body's appetite is satisfied by calories alone, large amounts of "empty calorie" foods crowd out other foods needed for decent nourishment. This "crowdout syndrome" is probably the single largest cause of marginal deficiencies in this country.

Whole grains and legumes offer the advantage of supplying, along with starch, the proper proportion of the B vitamins the body needs in order to burn glucose as fuel.[1] In addition, the fat and protein in the package, and its indigestible fiber covering, slow down the digestive process and give the sugars from carbohydrate digestion a little longer time in which to enter the blood. These foods are such an efficient package of nutrition that you can get virtually all the calories and protein you need from them. So don't be surprised to see in this book that grains and legumes are the mainstay not only of our Four Food Groups but also of our reducing diet! Because they satisfy your appetite and your nutritional needs at the same time, it is possible to eat them in moderation and still lose weight.

Sugar

Table sugar is one of the most familiar carbohydrates for all of us, but it is only one of the several kinds of sugar the body encounters every day. As the chart at the right shows, all the simplest carbohydrates are sugars in the chemical sense—some found naturally in fruits, milk, and vegetables, others found only in the body as the end products of digestion.

In the body, the simple sugars called monosaccharides play several all-important roles, such as being the body's major source of fuel. In the diet, however, sugar is a different matter. Within reasonable limits, the sugars occurring naturally in fruits and vegetables can be handled by the body quite easily. But refined table sugar, in all its forms, is a clear health hazard

SOME COMMON CARBOHYDRATES & THEIR SOURCES

MONOSACCHARIDES (SINGLE SUGARS)

GLUCOSE: *corn syrup, grape sugar, vegetables, honey*
FRUCTOSE: *honey, fruits, vegetables*
GALACTOSE: *product of lactose after digestion*

DISACCHARIDES (DOUBLE SUGARS)

SUCROSE (*glucose + fructose*): *cane, beet, maple, sorghum sugars; fruits & vegetables*
LACTOSE (*galactose + glucose*): *milk*
MALTOSE (*glucose + glucose*): *sprouting grains, beer*

POLYSACCHARIDES (CHAINS OF SIMPLE SINGLE SUGARS)

STARCH: *grains, legumes, vegetables*
GLYCOGEN: *in liver & muscle for energy storage; not found in plant or dairy foods*
CELLULOSE: *plants (indigestible structural components)*
PECTINS: *ripe fruits (absorb water & form jel as in fruit jellies)*

*Expressed as percentages
of sucrose or table sugar*

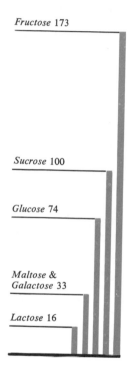

Fructose 173

Sucrose 100

Glucose 74

Maltose &
Galactose 33

Lactose 16

to millions of Americans, and is now being blamed for a wide spectrum of maladies from indigestion to heart disease.

One hundred years ago the average consumption of sugar in this country was 40 pounds per person per year. Now it has jumped to at least 100 pounds per year of table sugar and 15 pounds of corn syrup—about 500 calories of sugar per person every day. You may not think that *you* eat this amount—but do you know that aside from the obvious desserts, soft drinks, and sugar-coated breakfast cereals, sugar is also added to canned and frozen vegetables, soups, mayonnaise, peanut butter, baby foods, flavored yogurt, and many, many other products? Under the current labeling laws, added sugar does not even have to be listed on the labels of many foods because their legal definition includes the extra sweetener. Yet some physicians are claiming that sugar should be listed on the labels of *all* such foods, not simply as another ingredient but as a potentially dangerous additive.

Many of the detrimental effects of table sugar can be attributed to its chemical composition. Contrary to long—established opinion, table sugar (or sucrose, as it is called chemically) is not metabolized in the body in the same way as starch and other carbohydrates. In digestion, sucrose is immediately broken down into its two component simple sugars, glucose and fructose. The body has a well-developed capacity for handling large amounts of glucose, which is its primary fuel. But its capacity for metabolizing fructose is rather limited, and it may develop "fructose overload" when flooded with this sugar in large amounts.[2,3] It appears that we are probably not adapted to burn large amounts of refined sugar as fuel.

Among other physiological problems, sucrose metabolism has been connected with increased blood pressure, a higher likelihood of blood clotting in the veins, and elevated levels of blood fats called triglycerides which, like cholesterol, are implicated in heart disease. Some scientists now believe that sucrose is even more to blame than fat for the degeneration in our health that is associated with too rich diets. For example, sugar increases the blood level of insulin, the hormone by which the body regulates the amount of glucose for fuel that is supplied to all its cells. Insulin stimulates the cells to take up glucose from the bloodstream. In the disease of diabetes mellitus, from which middle-aged Americans are increasingly suffering, the cells of the body gradually become unresponsive to insulin. The pancreas produces more and more insulin in an attempt to overcome this insensitivity, but eventually it simply fails to meet the body's needs. Although there is plenty of glucose in the blood, the cells are unable to take it in—starvation in the midst of plenty. It is not unlikely that habitually eating too much sugar aggravates this process, and caloric restrictions like giving up sugar and alcohol can actually *reverse* the disease process if it is detected in time.

Although diseases of excess associated with too rich diets do not usually appear until adulthood, the patterns of eating responsible for such diseases often begin much earlier. Sugar-eating has been called the alcoholism of children because of the craving that thousands have developed for it. The trend seems to peak among teenagers: the average adolescent eats just a little less than three pounds of sugar a week, more than an American in any other age group. The English physician John Yudkin, who has participated in much of the research on sugar, estimates that some children in the United States and Great Britain get one quarter of their calories from sugar; some are getting as much as half. Sparing children from such large amounts of sugar will help to protect them in later years from obesity, diabetes, and tooth decay, and perhaps from heart disease as well. In addition, it is the best first step in making room in their diet for the foods they need for proper energy and growth.

THE 'ELEVEN A.M. BLAHS' — & HOW TO GET OFF SUGAR
Have you ever rushed off to work without time for a good breakfast, settling for white toast with jelly or maybe just orange juice or coffee, only to find after a busy three hours of work that you're so let down you can scarcely imagine making it through the rest of the day? That's the "eleven a.m. blahs," and it happens to many people who don't eat a good breakfast—especially if they eat quite a bit of sugar and drink large amounts of coffee, exaggerating their energy ups and downs.

The reason for eating a substantial meal—especially a substantial breakfast—is to provide the energy required for sustaining the day's activities. When basic, wholesome foods are eaten together at the same meal, food is released from the stomach gradually, so that it can be digested and absorbed into the blood over a period of several hours. However, when the "meal" consists primarily of refined carbohydrates like white bread or sugar, it is digested and absorbed much more rapidly, and what is not actually needed for fuel at the moment is greedily converted to fat for energy storage. Feeling let down and drained when this source of "quick energy" is spent is not a symptom of a disease; it is a perfectly normal reaction to wrong eating. Doughnuts or coffee, especially with sugar, in the middle of the morning can bring only temporary relief and may well exaggerate the letdown that follows, for after the first rush of sugar-energy and the nervous stimulation of the caffeine, the body is left again without adequate fuel to meet its needs. For many people, coffee undoubtedly plays an important part in such energy ups and downs. It is a powerful stimulant with many addicting effects, which even habitual coffee drinkers often fail to recognize or appreciate.

For most of us, erratic fluctuations in energy level and all the other disturbing consequences of a high-sugar diet can be avoided by taking three simple steps: (1) get plenty of good-tasting *whole* foods at every meal, (2) avoid sugar and other refined carbohydrates like "balloon bread," white-flour pastries, and commercial snack foods, and (3) eliminate between-meal sweets altogether. A good breakfast is especially important, for without it you'll be behind on energy all day long. So treat yourself to at least one third of your daily protein requirement every morning and enough calories to get you through till lunch. For your break, or for dessert at lunch, try fresh fruit instead of pastry; it's an excellent source of vitamin C, trace minerals, and fiber, and very sweet. If you really want to banish the eleven a. m. blahs, though, you won't eat more than three or four pieces of fruit a day. Many fruits have more sugar than most people realize, and three oranges, two apples, and a banana—not an uncommon amount of fruit for some vegetarians—add up to more than 500 calories of sugar, as much as the average American consumes in table sugar every day.

Sometimes honey, brown sugar, or molasses is offered as the answer to white sugar. Natural and less refined sugars do contain chromium, a trace metal which seems to offer a little protection against moderate amounts of natural sugar by enhancing insulin function. It is doubtful, however, if chromium offers protection against large quantities of sugar, no matter how unrefined, and beyond such marginal advantages, natural sugars have very little to offer. "Sugar is sugar is sugar . . ." Honey, for all practical purposes, is still straight sugar. Real raw sugar is no longer available on the market, and the brown sugar you see in stores is actually white sugar colored with burnt white sugar (which gives it a butterscotch flavor) or molasses. The slight advantage the second kind of brown sugar may have over straight white sugar is entirely due to the little molasses that colors it. Actually, blackstrap molasses is the only sugar with anything to offer of nutritional value. Blackstrap is the dark, strong-tasting residue from the last stage of refinement of white sugar, so it does contain some minerals from the original sugar cane plus calcium and iron from the processing. Its iron content is variable, however, depending on whether the company uses iron vats for processing and how long the molasses sits in them, so check the label.

The emphasis in our plan for getting off sugar is on *whole* foods. Not only do such foods provide nourishment and appetite satisfaction; they continue to supply energy for hours after they are eaten. If you're not convinced, try a whole-food diet for a couple of weeks and notice the stabilizing effect on your energy supply. During the transition period, be sure your diet includes foods that are high in protein—and, if you can afford the calories, foods that are high in fat as well. Cheese, nuts, and peanut butter are high in both, and foods like these at every meal can help the transition go more smoothly because they stay with you throughout the day.

Alcohol

Like separated sugar, the alcohol in beverages is a carbohydrate whose abuse has widespread adverse effects on health. Here we will just be talking about the effects of alcohol on nutrition alone, though it also has very serious effects on the brain and on behavior.

Like sugar, alcohol has a lot of calories for fuel—7 calories per gram, as compared to sugar's 4—but virtually no other nourishment. Since this high caloric content easily satisfies the appetite, alcohol often crowds out some or most of the foods we need for nourishment. Often, during drinking bouts, a heavy drinker will eat practically nothing at all. Many of the nutrients in what *is* eaten never get used, for alcohol reduces the absorption of some of the vitamins[5] and washes out minerals in the urine. The body quickly depletes its nutritional stores, so that in prolonged drinking there is a constant danger of protein, B complex, and mineral malnutrition. The water-soluble B vitamins are the first to be depleted, and the symptoms of thiamin (B-1) deficiency in the lower parts of the body—muscle cramps and weakness, numbness and tingling, pains and other discomforts of the feet—are common in alcoholics and usually go unrecognized as the danger signals they are.

Alcohol abuse also has a directly toxic or poisonous effect on the liver. This is true even when there is adequate protein in the diet; but when protein consumption is low (as is often the case when alcohol intake is high) this poisoning process is accelerated, for the liver requires protein to prepare fats for transport in the blood. Without protein the fat simply accumulates in the liver, contributing to the condition called "fatty liver" which usually leads to cirrhosis.

Finally, if you have a high level of blood fats (triglycerides)—a condition similar to high blood cholesterol that may be a significant risk factor in heart disease—drinking alcohol will raise them even further.[6] So, though intelligent eating helps a little to minimize the adverse *nutritional* effects of alcohol, even the amounts normally consumed in social drinking can, over a period of time, lead to liver, heart, and brain damage *in spite of* a good diet. In short—not surprisingly—it isn't possible to drink much and be healthy or even just well nourished at the same time. If you possibly can, avoid it.

360   CARBOHYDRATE

Fiber

Cellulose or fiber, the structural part of plants, is not properly a nutrient, since it is neither digested nor absorbed. But it is probably an essential part of a good diet, for it is the cellulose in our food that provides the bulk or "roughage" which helps the intestine move its contents along in digestion.

It is now thought that the fiber found in whole-grain cereals, including the hulls called bran, is of greater importance to the intestine than that in fruits and vegetables. In addition to providing bulk, cereal fiber has the capacity to absorb water, keeping the stool moist and soft as well as bulky. Unfortunately, fiber is one of the first parts of a whole food to be removed in the process of refining. In the United States, flour has been roller-milled since about 1880, and most of its bran is removed in the process. Before that period, the average American probably ate 1.1 to 2.8 grams of fiber every day in bread. It has been estimated that we get only one-tenth to one-twentieth that amount of cereal fiber today.[7]

The effects of this change in diet are only now beginning to be recognized in the medical world. Commercial interests have filled the vacuum and cashed in on the discomforts that have resulted from low-fiber diets, filling a whole aisle in every drug store and supermarket with various remedies for constipation. Meanwhile people are in the hospital requiring surgery for appendicitis, diverticulitis, hemorrhoids, varicose veins, and bowel cancer: all disorders which may be caused in part by constipation,[8] which in turn stems not only from unhealthy habits like lack of exercise but also, it appears, from lack of dietary fiber and fluid.

When there is little bulk in the diet, the intestinal wall thickens, increasing the pressure within. After many years the intestinal surface becomes irregular and may temporarily close completely, creating terrific pressures and cramps and causing little pockets to bulge out in the weak areas of the intestinal wall. This is diverticular disease, which affects an estimated forty million Americans, or one out of every three people over the age of forty.

There is some evidence that a very low fiber diet contributes also to elevated blood cholesterol. Bile salts, which are made of cholesterol, are excreted from the gall bladder into the intestine. When elimination is normal, cholesterol-containing salts are passed out of the body entirely, but with too little fiber in the diet, elimination is sluggish and these bile salts are reabsorbed into the blood.[8]

If you are young, eating plenty of whole-grain cereals and fresh fruits and vegetables every day should contribute greatly to preventing the outbreak of these problems in later years. You can use the tables in the back to compare how much fiber you're getting now with the 1 to 3 grams your ancestors got back in 1870. But for those who have lived on a highly refined diet for years—young as well as old—many physicians are now recommending adding unprocessed bran to prevent disease or to relieve the symptoms of constipation and diverticular disease once they develop. Two teaspoonfuls of bran three times a day with meals is the suggested way to start; the amount may be increased gradually until soft stools are passed once or twice a day.[7]

SOURCE REFERENCES

1. Rachmiel Levine, Carbohydrates, in *Modern nutrition in health and disease: Dietotherapy,* 5th ed., ed. Robert S. Goodhart and Maurice E. Shils (Philadelphia, Lea & Febiger, 1973), p. 112.

2. George M. Briggs, Sugar, nutrition and disease; addendum to testimony at hearing on alternative sources of funding for nutrition education programs before the California Senate Subcommittee on Agriculture, Food and Nutrition, 8 October 1974, in San Francisco.

3. Richard A. Ahrens, Sucrose, hypertension, and heart disease: an historical perspective, *American Journal of Clinical Nutrition* 27:403–422, 1974.

4. National Research Council, Food and Nutrition Board, *Recommended dietary allowances,* 8th rev. ed. (Washington, National Academy of Sciences, 1974), p. 101.

5. U. S. Department of Health, Education, and Welfare, National Institute on Alcohol Abuse and Alcoholism, *First special report to the U. S. Congress on alcohol and health,* DHEW Publication no. HSM 72-9099 (Washington, Govt. Printing Office, 1971 [i.e., 1972]), p. 52.

6. J. H. Mendelson and N. K. Mello, Significance of alcohol-induced hypertriglyceridemia in patients with Type IV hyperlipoproteinemia, *Annals of Internal Medicine* 80:270–271, 1974.

7. Alex G. Shulman, High bulk diet for diverticular disease of the colon, *Western Journal of Medicine* 120:278–281, 1974.

8. D. P. Burkitt, A. R. P. Walker, and N. S. Painter, Dietary fiber and disease, *Journal of the American Medical Association* 229:1068–1074, 1974.

The Foodstuffs: Fat

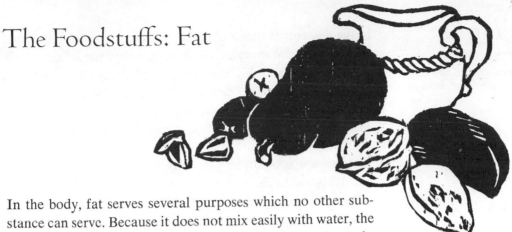

In the body, fat serves several purposes which no other substance can serve. Because it does not mix easily with water, the fatty tissues of the body can store and transport other substances like the fat-soluble vitamins which otherwise could not be carried by the blood. Also, fat can be burned for fuel to give more than twice as much energy as an equal weight of carbohydrate or protein, and because it cannot be washed away by body fluids, it is the ideal vehicle for storing energy. Normally, this stored fat is continually being burned for energy and replaced within the body, even when caloric intake is at the right level and there is no gain in weight.

Fat in the body, therefore, is indispensible. In the standard American diet, however, the fat in foods has taken a position all out of proportion to its necessary role: for most Americans it supplies more than 40 percent of their calories. Yet very little fat is really required for nourishment, and because saturated fats and the fatlike substance called cholesterol are linked so closely with heart disease, eating too much fat can have serious consequences for our health.

TOO MUCH FAT

Every cook can appreciate the qualities fat adds to foods. It has an amazing ability to absorb flavor—one of the reasons why convenience-food manufacturers often add a coating of oil or margarine to their foods—and a unique capacity for satisfying the appetite, not only becauce it is packed with calories but also because it slows down digestion so that your stomach stays full longer.

For the most part, food supplies three different kinds of fat, saturated, monounsaturated, and polyunsaturated, according

SATURATED

has maximum number of hydrogen atoms

predominant in animal fats

usually solid at room temperature

MONOUNSATURATED

2 hydrogen atoms short of saturation, forming 1 double bond

common in vegetable oils

liquid at room temperature

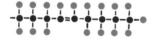

POLYUNSATURATED

4 or more hydrogen atoms short of saturation, forming 2 or more double bonds

common in vegetable oils

usually liquid at room temperature

● *carbon atom*

● *hydrogen atom*

to the makeup of their fatty acid chains. As you can see from the table in the margin, these apparently minor molecular differences make a big difference in physical characteristics. Probably the most apparent difference in the kitchen is the fact that saturated fats are usually solid at room temperature, like lard, while unsaturated fats are usually liquids or oils. In the discussion of fat and heart disease that follows, we shall see that there is a big difference between saturated and unsaturated fats within the body as well.

Whether saturated or unsaturated, two fifths of the fat in most Americans' diets is undisguised: butter, salad oil, mayonnaise, and the like. The rest, a full three fifths, is "hidden fat": the fat that lurks in meat, milk, dairy products, convenience foods, pastries, cream sauces, nuts, and so on. Even many vegetarians share this national tendency to get not only much more fat than they need but more than they even know.

HOW MUCH FAT DO WE REALLY NEED?

Some fat in the diet is absolutely necessary to provide one essential nutrient which no other source can provide: the polyunsaturated fatty acid called linoleic acid. The other fatty acids the body needs can be synthesized from other foodstuffs if linoleic acid is present, but linoleic acid itself must be supplied by what we eat.

Only 1 to 2 percent of our total caloric requirement as linoleic acid, however, is enough to prevent deficiency—just one tablespoonful per day of almost any polyunsaturated oil, even ignoring what is already supplied by a whole-food diet. With this minimum amount of fat and no more, you may grow lean and your skin will probably be less oily, but your body will be doing fine. Most Americans, however, pad this minimum a little too generously—adding not only to their own padding, but to the likelihood of heart disease as well.

Cardiovascular disease, of which heart attack and stroke are examples, has reached epidemic proportions in Western countries. In the last decade in the United States, it has been the cause of more deaths than all other causes combined, including all types of cancer.

Underlying cardiovascular disease is the condition called

LINOLEIC ACID CONTENT OF FATS & OILS
Grams of linoleic acid in 1 tablespoon of fat or oil

	Linoleic acid	Calories
Corn oil	7	124
Cottonseed oil	7	124
Olive oil	1	124
Peanut oil	4	124
Safflower oil	10	124
Sesame oil	6	124
Soy oil	7	124
Better-Butter (made with safflower oil)	5	113
Better-Butter (made with soy oil)	3	113
Margarine (first ingred. liquid oil)	4	100
Margarine (first ingred. hydrogenated oil)	2	100
Butter	trace	100
Peanut butter (with vegetable shortening)	2	86
Mayonnaise (soy, cottonseed, & corn oils, & egg)	6	102

Adapted from Watt & Merrill 1964 (Ag. Handbook no. 8)

atherosclerosis, in which fatty accumulations on the walls of the arteries narrow the passageways through which blood must pass and eventually cause the arteries to become rigid. Such diseased arteries may suddenly fail to deliver blood to the heart muscle, so that part of its tissues die. This is a myocardial infarction, commonly known as a heart attack.

The epidemic of heart disease now rages most mercilessly among younger men—men between the ages of 40 and 65, who are in the prime of their lives as husbands, fathers, and workers. This is called premature heart disease, and it spares no social or economic class. In men, the physiological changes involved probably begin as early as adolescence. Women seem to have been virtually immune until after menopause, but as they subject themselves to more risk factors they too are becoming increasingly susceptible at younger ages.

Conventional medical methods are incapable of dealing with heart disease adequately. Fatty arteries develop insidiously, the heart attack or stroke comes suddenly and severely, and medical treatment is simply unable to reverse the damage that has already been done. The only really practical approach to heart disease is prevention, and for prevention, all the contributing factors must be reduced to a minimum.

Research evidence consistently points to three major risk factors: a high level of the fatlike substance called cholesterol in the blood, high blood pressure, and smoking, all of which contribute directly to artery damage. Other risk factors include a diet rich in saturated fats (and maybe sugar), too little exercise, diabetes, and possibly time-driven, compulsively competitive behavior or "hurry sickness." In combination, two or three of these factors aggravate the damage of the others, often to a deadly degree.[1]

CHOLESTEROL AND DIET

Some of these risk factors are still controversial. Almost all researchers, however, agree that cholesterol is somehow associated with the atherosclerotic process, though quite likely not an essential condition or cause of it. As one researcher says, cholesterol seems to be the thread running through the web of circumstances that results in a heart attack or stroke.[2]

Cholesterol is a waxy, fatlike substance which is found in every cell of the body, where it is an essential component of the cell membranes. But though it is required for human and animal life, there is no need to get it in the diet, for the body can synthesize all the cholesterol it needs—primarily in the liver, where cholesterol is produced for transport through the bloodstream to the body cells.

Some cholesterol in the blood, therefore, is not only natural but essential. It is only above a certain level that blood cholesterol becomes a risk factor, contributing in some still unknown way to the likelihood of heart disease.

Opinions differ on what constitutes too high a level of cholesterol in the blood. However, since the body can make whatever it needs, no one has been known to suffer from a level that is too low, and the average American cholesterol count— 225 to 250 milligrams of cholesterol per 100 milliliters of blood serum—is far above the average in countries where there is little arterial disease (150 to 175). Tragically, this difference is now reflected even in the blood cholesterol levels of our children.[3]

There are many factors that can raise the level of cholesterol in the blood, though no one yet understands just how the change is brought about. Eating too much cholesterol, for example, can raise blood cholesterol levels, as can eating too much saturated fat.[4] If you are fortunate, *not* eating such foods will lower your blood cholesterol—but not necessarily, for diet is only a contributing factor. But if you are interested in keeping your cholesterol level down—and almost everyone in the United States has reason to be so interested—large amounts of cholesterol-rich foods and saturated fat have no place in your diet.

A LOW-CHOLESTEROL MEATLESS DIET

Fortunately for vegetarians, cholesterol comes almost entirely from animal foods—meat, eggs, and the butterfat in dairy products—so a meatless diet is a great help in keeping your cholesterol intake low. But you may be eating no meat and still be getting more cholesterol than you want.

If your blood cholesterol level is not dangerously high—and remember that the national average of 225 to 250 milligrams percent is already much higher than may be safe—the American Heart Association recommends an absolute maximum of 300 milligrams of cholesterol a day in the food you eat. You can use the table which follows to estimate how much you are getting now. If it is too much, or more than you want it to be, you can stay within the AHA maximum on a meatless diet simply by eating as few eggs as possible. Eggs, as you can see from the table, are one of nature's richest sources of cholesterol, and they add up fast.

If you have already suffered a heart attack, however, or if your blood cholesterol is above the national average, *any* cholesterol in your diet is an unnecessary risk. As a vegetarian, you can keep your cholesterol intake incredibly low by not only cutting out eggs but using low-fat and skim milk products and avoiding foods that are high in butterfat, like butter, cheese, and cream.

Saturated fats, too, raise blood cholesterol. However, the same foods that are high in cholesterol—animal fats—are also high in saturated fat, so controlling the one in your diet serves to control the other as well. In a meatless diet, dairy products will be your main source of saturated fat, for with the exception of coconut oil (which is mostly saturated) and olive and

CHOLESTEROL CONTENT OF FOODS

Figures to the left of food names give cholesterol content in milligrams.

DAIRY FOODS & EGGS

35	butter, *1 tablespoon*
282	*½ cup or 1 stick*
22	whipped, *1 tablespoon*
190	*½ cup*
5	buttermilk, *1 cup*
	cheese:
25	American, *1-oz. slice*
24	bleu, *1 ounce*
117	*1 cup crumbled*
25	brick, *1 ounce*
26	Camembert, *1 ounce*
35	*1⅓-ounce piece*
28	cheddar, *1 ounce*
112	*1 cup shredded*
27	Colby, *1 ounce*
23	cottage: low-fat, *1 cup packed*
48	creamed, *1 cup packed*
13	uncreamed, *1 cup packed*
16	cream cheese, *1 tbsp.*
94	*3-ounce package*
29	Edam, *1 ounce*
28	Limburger, *1 ounce*
27	mozzarella, *1 ounce*
18	part skim, *1 ounce*
25	Muenster, *1 ounce*
64	Neufchatel, *3-oz. pkg.*
27	Parmesan, *1 ounce*
113	grated, *1 cup*
28	Provolone, *1 ounce*
14	ricotta, *1 ounce*
9	part skim, *1 ounce*

	cheese (*cont.*):
35	Swiss, *1¼-ounce slice*
26	processed, *1-oz. slice*
6	cream: half & half, *1 tbsp*
105	*1 cup*
10	light, *1 tablespoon*
158	*1 cup*
20	heavy, *1 tablespoon*
316	*1 cup*
8	sour, *1 tablespoon*
152	*1 cup*
252	egg, whole, *1 large*
252	yolk, *1 large*
53	ice cream, *1 cup*
85	rich, *1 cup*
26	ice milk, hardened, *1 cup*
36	soft-serve, *1 cup*
0	margarine, vegetable fat
34	milk, fluid: whole, *1 cup*
22	low-fat(2%), *1 cup*
5	nonfat, *1 cup*
79	evaporated, *1 cup*
105	condensed, *1 cup*
	milk, dry instant:
31	whole, *¼ cup*
3	skim, *¼ cup*
10	mayonnaise, *1 tbsp.*
154	*1 cup*
50	noodles, egg, *1 cup ckd.*
36	white sauce: thin, *1 cup*
33	medium, *1 cup*
30	thick, *1 cup*
17	yogurt, nonfat, *8 ounces*
15	fruit-flavored, *8 oz.*

MEATS

80	beef, *3 ounces, cooked*
2000	brains, *3½ ounces, raw*
48	caviar, *1 tablespoon*
63	chicken, *½ breast, ckd.*
47	*1 drumstick, cooked*
114	clams, *1 cup meat*
125	crab, *1 cup cooked*
34	frankfurter, *1, cooked*
75	halibut, *1 fillet, cooked*
335	heart, chicken, *cooked, 1 cup diced*
1125	kidneys, *1 cup slices, ckd*
83	lamb, *3 ounces, cooked*
195	lard, *1 cup*
372	liver, *3 ounces, cooked*
123	lobster, *1 cup cubes, ckd.*
106	mackerel, *1 fillet, cooked*
120	oysters, *1 cup, raw*
76	pork, *3 ounces, cooked*
129	sardines, *1 can*
192	shrimp, *1 cup, canned*
102	tuna, *5½-ounce can*
65	turkey: light, *3 oz., ckd.*
86	dark, *3 ounces, cooked*
86	veal, *3 ounces, cooked*

Source: Feeley et al. 1972

sesame oil (mostly monounsaturated), vegetable oils are almost entirely polyunsaturated. Watch out, though, for "hydrogenated" fats—oils that have been artificially saturated for commercial reasons, such as to keep the oil from separating in a jar of peanut butter or to turn liquid vegetable oils into solid margarine. Once hydrogenated, an originally unsaturated fat acts just like a saturated fat in the body; so when you select a margarine, be sure that the first ingredient on the label is listed as "*liquid* vegetable oil." If your blood cholesterol is high, get the softer tub margarine (it's usually the least hydrogenated) and use liquid vegetable oils for cooking whenever margarine or butter is called for.

Interestingly enough, monounsaturated fats do not affect the blood cholesterol at all, and polyunsaturated fats will actually lower it. Because of this, many doctors now advise patients with high blood cholesterol to eat twice as much polyunsaturated fat as saturated.*[5] But large quantities of polyunsaturated oils may have long-term adverse effects too,[6,7] so the question of how much fat (and how much of each kind) it is safe to eat remains confused and unanswered.

To us, the common-sense position is simply not to eat too much fat at all. Virtually all doctors and nutritionists agree that more than one third of your calories as fat is too much, but considering that the rock-bottom minimum is only 1 or 2 percent, there is certainly room for a little thinning down. A safe, easy way to do this is to concentrate on the fat that comes naturally in whole foods—whole-grain flours, milk, nuts and seeds, and so on. This provides a natural limit to your fat intake in a good-tasting package, and retains the whole-food nutrients like the fat-soluble vitamins, many of which are lost when fats (including oils) are refined.

A diet rich in whole foods can be satisfying enough that you can cut back on the separated fats, polyunsaturated as well as

*Occasionally this advice has been dangerously misinterpreted as a rationale for eating large quantities of cholesterol-laden foods and hoping to wash out their effects with vegetable oils. Sometimes, too, an emulsifying substance called lecithin is credited with similar properties, though there is no controlled study to show that lecithin in the diet can lower cholesterol in the blood. A high-cholesterol diet remains an unnecessary risk.

saturated, that form the bulk of Americans' not so hidden fat—extra mayonnaise, butter, margarine, and oils. Food, after all, is still enjoyable with a little less fat than we're used to—a teaspoon of it will do just as much for a piece of bread as a tablespoon. And who needs a diet that gets more than one third of its calories from pure grease?

SOURCE REFERENCES

1. Robert I. Levy and Nancy Ernst, Diet, hyperlipidemia and atherosclerosis, in *Modern nutrition in health and disease: Dietotherapy,* 5th ed., ed. Robert S. Goodhart and Maurice E. Shils (Philadelphia, Lea & Febiger, 1973), p. 901.

2. William B. Kannel, The role of cholesterol in coronary atherogenesis, *Medical Clinics of North America* 58:363–379, 1974.

3. John P. Kane and Mary J. Malloy, The early prevention of atherosclerosis, *Western Journal of Medicine* 122:328–329, 1975.

4. Levy and Ernst, Diet, hyperlipidemia and atherosclerosis, p. 897.

5. Robert I. Levy, Joel Morganroth, and Basil M. Rifkind, Treatment of hyperlipidemia (Medical Intelligence), *New England Journal of Medicine* 290:1295–1301, 1974.

6. Richard A. L. Sturdevant, M. L. Pearce, and S. Dayton, Increased prevalence of cholelithiasis in men ingesting a serum-cholesterol-lowering diet, *New England Journal of Medicine* 288:24–27, 1973.

7. Geoffrey Rose et al., Colon cancer and blood cholesterol, *Lancet* 1:181–183, 1974.

Fat Content of Foods

Legend:
- Saturated fats
- Monounsaturated fats
- Polyunsaturated fats
- Unidentified fats
- Nonfat components

	% fat	% total fat of:*		
		Saturated fats	Monounsaturated fats	Polyunsaturated fats
FATS & OILS				
Corn oil	100	10	28	53
Cottonseed oil	100	25	21	50
Olive oil	100	11	76	7
Peanut oil	100	18	47	29
Safflower oil	100	8	15	72
Sesame oil	100	14	38	42
Soybean oil	100	15	20	52
Margarine: 1st ingred. liq. oil	81	23	38	36
1st ingred. hydrogenated oil	81	22	58	17
Mayonnaise (soybean, cottonseed, & corn oils, & egg)	80	17	21	50
Better-Butter: safflower oil & butter	90	33	25	37
soy oil & butter	90	37	27	27
Butter	81	57	34	2
NUTS & SEEDS				
Almond	54	8	68	19
Brazil nut	68	25	33	37
Cashew	46	20	58	16
Coconut	36	88	6	2
Filbert (hazelnut)	65	7	77	10
Macadamia nut	76	14	76	3
Peanut	50	19	46	30
Pecan	71	8	60	25
Pilinut	63	39	47	10
Pine nut	51	12	38	44
Pistachio	54	14	68	13
Sesame seed, whole	49	14	39	43
Sunflower seed	47	13	19	63
Walnut, black	60	8	18	68
Walnut, English	63	11	15	66

*Figures do not add up to 100% because values are not available for some of the minor fatty acids in each group.

	% fat	% total fat of:*		
		Sat. fats	*Mono. fats*	*Poly. fats*
DAIRY PRODUCTS				
Butter	81	57	34	2
Cheese:				
American	29	62	29	3
bleu	30	64	28	3
brick	29	61	31	3
Camembert	26	63	29	3
cheddar	33	62	30	3
pasteurized process	30	62	29	4
Colby	31	63	29	3
cottage, creamed	4	65	27	3
uncreamed	0.4	50	22	2
cream	34	63	28	4
Edam	28	65	28	2
farmer's (from whole milk)	18	60	31	3
feta	25	70	22	3
fontina	30	62	28	5
gjetost	30	65	27	3
Gouda	27	64	28	2
Gruyère	32	58	31	5
Leyden	24	63	30	3
Limburger	27	62	32	2
mozzarella	19	61	30	3
part skim, low-moisture	16	62	28	3
whole, low-moisture	26	63	28	3
Muenster	30	64	29	2
Neufchatel	24	64	29	3
Parmesan	26	63	29	2
port	30	59	33	3
provolone	26	63	28	3
ricotta, whole milk	15	64	28	3
part skim	9	60	29	3
Roquefort	34	63	28	4
Samsoe	21	63	29	3
Swiss	28	64	28	4
pasteurized process	24	64	29	2
Tilsit	29	65	27	3

Figures do not add up to 100% because values are not available for some of the minor fatty acids in each group.

	% fat	% total fat of:*		
		Sat. fats	Mono. fats	Poly. fats
Cream:				
half and half	12	62	29	4
light cream	21	62	29	4
heavy cream	38	62	29	4
sour cream	18	62	29	4
Egg, chicken's, whole	11	30	40	12
yolk	34	30	40	12
Ice cream, vanilla	12	63	29	4
Ice milk, vanilla	5	63	29	4
Milk, cow's:				
fluid, whole	3.5	63	29	4
low-fat	2	60	29	4
evaporated, canned	8	61	31	3
condensed, canned	9	63	28	4
dry, whole	27	62	30	2
skim, regular or instant	0.8	62	29	4
Yogurt: from whole milk	3.4	65	27	3
from low-fat milk	1.5	67	27	3
GRAINS & LEGUMES				
Cornmeal, whole-grain, raw	4	Tr	26	51
Garbanzos, raw	5	Tr	42	42
Millet, whole-grain, raw	3	33	33	33
Soybeans, raw	18	17	23	51
cooked	6	17	17	53
Soybean flour	20	15	20	54
Tofu (soy curd)	4	24	24	48
Wheat germ	11	18	27	46
OTHER				
Avocado	16	18	43	12
Chocolate, bitter or baking	53	57	38	2
Cocoa powder, medium-fat	19	58	37	Tr

*Figures do not add up to 100% because values are not available for some of the minor fatty acids in each group.

Adapted from Posati et al. 1975 and Watt & Merrill 1964 (Ag. Handbook no. 8)

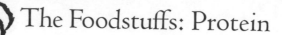

The Foodstuffs: Protein

Proteins are immense clusters of amino acids—chains of carbon, hydrogen, and oxygen like fats and carbohydrates but with one crucial additional element, nitrogen. It is the nitrogen group at the end of amino acid chains which enables amino acids to link on to each other to form the long, intricate protein structures from which living tissue is built. As the twenty-six letters in our alphabet can combine to represent an unlimited number of words, the more than twenty amino acids in the body can combine to form countless varieties of protein, making possible a whole language whose literature is the complex tissues of life.

All living tissue, both plant and animal, contains protein. Over half the body, excluding its water, is protein. Proteins are essential for tissue maintenance and growth, and provide the framework of many body structures: muscle and connective tissue, plasma and hemoglobin circulating in the blood, keratin in the skin, nails, and hair. Enzymes, hormones, and antibodies, which regulate many of the body's most important functions, are mostly protein. DNA and RNA, the substances in every cell which carry the genetic code by which cells replicate their proteins in the processes of growth and repair, themselves require protein enzymes for their formation. We need protein in our diet to maintain all these body proteins, and children need proportionately much more to provide the raw material for growth.

For many decades Americans have worried about the protein content of their diet. Yet the average of 90 to 100 grams of protein that each person in this country eats each day is almost double what he or she needs. Contrary to popular belief,

Americans have been eating this much protein ever since the first part of this century; it is only that today two thirds of our protein comes from animal sources, whereas earlier in the century the proportion was only one half.[1] Actually, a good diet of basic, whole foods is usually more than adequate in its protein content, and many whole foods which people do not usually associate with protein—bread, beans, and many vegetables, for instance—are capable of meeting our protein needs completely when eaten together in adequate amounts.

THE BODY'S NEED FOR PROTEIN

In the well-fed person, the proportion of protein in the body is kept fairly constant. The protein tissues themselves, however, are not static but in a state of constant turnover, being continuously degraded and rebuilt throughout the day. In this process the body efficiently recycles the nitrogen portions of those degraded proteins for use in making new protein structures, so that none of this critical element is lost in tissue turnover. The only nitrogen which actually leaves the body's total protein mass is a small but steady amount in sloughed-off skin, growing hair and nails, and various secretions and excretions like sweat and feces. The amino acids and nitrogen lost in this way must be replaced by the protein we eat. During digestion this protein is broken down into its component amino acids, which enter the body to join the amino acids from the turnover of body proteins to form a common amino acid pool.[2] The body can then draw on this pool twenty-four hours a day to get the raw materials it needs to make new proteins for growth and tissue repair.

To make new proteins, all the necessary amino acids must be present at the same time. About half of them can be assembled in the body from almost any source of nitrogen, usually just by rearranging the components of other amino acids. But there are nine amino acids which the human body cannot synthesize in adequate amounts.* These are called the *essential* amino acids, because they can be supplied only through

* The ninth amino acid, histidine, is known to be essential for infants and should be considered essential for adults as well unless proof is obtained to the contrary.[3,4]

what we eat. A short supply of any one of these nutrients in our diet can limit how much new protein our bodies can make.

Our need for protein in the diet, therefore, is twofold. First, there is a specific requirement for each of the essential amino acids, in the fixed proportion or pattern which protein synthesis demands. Second, above this, there is a nonspecific requirement for amino nitrogen in general, to provide the rest of the raw material for protein synthesis.[5] Since most whole-food proteins contain both essential and nonessential amino acids, though in different proportions, these two requirements can be covered at once by a nonspecific requirement for total quantity of protein from a planned variety of foods.

HOW MUCH PROTEIN DO WE NEED?

The amount of protein a person needs is never static. The use of protein in the body varies greatly from person to person, and even in the same person it fluctuates in response to both internal and external factors. On the one hand, age and the general state of health and nutrition both alter the amount of protein we need. On the other hand, the body is able to satisfy the need for widely differing amounts of protein at even a very low level of protein intake, through complex regulatory mechanisms which keep its internal environment as constant as possible despite changes in the environment outside.

In many different ways, the body accustoms itself to its usual environment. This is true also of protein metabolism: in a relatively stable dietary environment, the body adjusts the mechanisms of protein metabolism to suit the amount of protein it usually gets in food. Normal variations above or below this basic level of intake may then be handled easily by fine-tuning mechanisms which make the final adjustments to what the body needs. An extreme variation in the amount of protein one gets, of course, may temporarily overwhelm the body's capacities. But given time, it can adapt even to markedly unfavorable circumstances with great versatility, increasing its capacities and maintaining the best level of functioning it can.

Unlike fat and carbohydrate, protein cannot be stored. Excess protein is simply broken down and burned for energy or stored as fat, and its nitrogen is wasted, passing out in the urine. When protein is in short supply, however, its nitrogen is carefully conserved for tissue building, as long as there are enough calories in the rest of the diet to meet energy needs. In this way, under normal conditions, the body is able to maintain its protein content at a constant level all the time, simply by adjusting the efficiency with which it uses the nitrogen in protein foods.

All this means that the body can accommodate wide variations in the amount of protein it gets and still meet its needs for energy and protein synthesis. Despite this, however, it *is* possible to talk about a functional minimum of protein intake. An approximate measure of this minimum may be determined in the laboratory by nitrogen balance studies. Such studies are the basis of the current RDA for protein, which, as we shall see, is a rough but safe and simple guide for planning the amount of protein you need.

Nitrogen balance studies are based on the fact that normally, the amount of nitrogen we consume in protein is equal to the amount we excrete, both in sloughed-off body protein and in what is wasted from the excess protein we eat. The body is then said to be in nitrogen balance or nitrogen equilibrium. When nitrogen is retained to make new tissues, as it is during pregnancy and growth, the body is said to be in positive nitrogen balance. But when there is not enough protein in the diet, or not enough calories to keep the protein from being burned as fuel, the body falls into negative nitrogen balance—a highly undesirable state in which the body begins to feed upon its own protein, and more nitrogen is eliminated than is consumed.

The minimum amount of protein necessary to restore equilibrium after the body has fallen into negative nitrogen balance, averaged over a number of subjects, is the basis of the current recommended dietary allowance for protein. This amount is greater than the amount of protein that is actually lost from body tissues, because the body uses nitrogen in food with only about 70 percent efficiency when it is getting the minimum it needs to maintain equilibrium.[7] This gives the body a margin for greater efficiency in case the protein supply should suddenly drop. Nitrogen balance studies, therefore, automatically reflect some of the body's flexibility with respect to the protein it needs.

In determining a safe daily recommendation for protein, two upward adjustments are made to this basic experimental figure. First, an increase of 30 percent allows for the variation in protein needs from individual to individual. Second, this adjusted figure is further increased by one third to allow for diets in which protein is not as well utilized as the high-quality protein in the experimental diets—an allowance that covers diets with no other source of protein than the lower-quality protein in plant foods. The recommended figure comes to about 0.8 grams of protein per day for every kilogram of *ideal* (lean) body weight—56 grams of protein per day for a 77-kilogram (170-pound) man, 46 grams for a 58-kilogram (128-pound) woman.

Of course, because of the variation in individual needs, protein nutrition does not conform to some average or standard state. The RDA for protein is simply a guide for providing a safe amount of protein under normal circumstances. The two upward adjustments from the experimental minimum build plenty of protection into the RDA figure. There *are* times when this amount might not cover your need: pregnancy, lactation, and major trauma like surgery, for example, all require more protein for tissue building; fever and profuse sweating cause the loss of excessive amounts of nitrogen which must be replaced by extra protein; low-calorie diets require additional protein to allow for what will be burned as fuel. But if you have enough energy, your resistance to infection is good, your hair and nails are strong, your scratches and cuts heal easily, and your menstrual periods are regular, you can be pretty sure that you're getting the protein you need.

BUT IS IT COMPLETE PROTEIN?

By now, every vegetarian or prospective vegetarian has been told at least once that simple quantity of protein is not enough: plant protein is just not as high in quality as animal protein. In reference to diets with only one source of protein, this is true; but for the cook, who is preparing several foods to be eaten together, it is much more appropriate to talk instead about the quality or balance of the entire diet. But the question of plant protein quality is so often discussed that it is important for vegetarians to understand what is involved—and why they don't have to worry about it beyond the planned variety of a balanced diet.

Protein quality refers basically to how well a protein serves human needs. It is a function of two factors: how thoroughly the protein can be digested in the human body and how well it can supply the essential amino acids required for protein synthesis. Plant proteins are less well digested than animal proteins, but nevertheless they are digested well enough, especially when the foods supplying them are well cooked and, in some instances, well ground. The critical question is that of *completeness:* to what extent a food has enough of the essential amino acids for all its digested protein to be used.

Experiments have shown that protein synthesis requires all of the nine essential amino acids to be present in basically the same proportion. The requirement for essential amino acids thus forms a *pattern* which is characteristic of all human beings. It is a part of the total daily protein requirement, increasing or decreasing proportionately as the need for total quantity of protein rises or falls, and it provides a standard by which the completeness of a protein may be determined by comparing that protein's amino acid pattern with the ideal. The pattern shown on the following page is that recommended by the National Research Council in 1974, and is very similar to what U.N. agencies recommended in 1973.*[9]

The critical part of this pattern is a subpattern of three amino acids, the three on the right side of our chart. These are the *limiting amino acids*, the ones which really determine the completeness of a food or diet. A limiting amino acid is one which is in short supply—the one which will run out first

*Earlier standards, recommended by the U.N. in 1965[10] and still quoted today, were based on the "egg standard": the idea that the amino acid pattern in egg white was the perfect pattern for human needs. The pattern we show reflects the not surprising discovery that the amino acid pattern of eggs is actually just right for the chick: for human beings, a much more appropriate pattern (a good deal lower) is found instead in milk.

when the body is making protein. Once it is used up, all the remaining amino acids are useless as far as making new protein goes.

THE ESSENTIAL AMINO ACIDS PATTERN
Requirements are in mg per g of protein

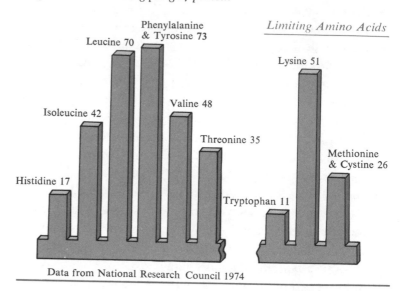

Limiting Amino Acids

Phenylalanine & Tyrosine 73

Leucine 70

Valine 48

Isoleucine 42

Threonine 35

Lysine 51

Methionine & Cystine 26

Histidine 17

Tryptophan 11

Data from National Research Council 1974

Though all the nine amino acids are equally essential, it is only these three limiting amino acids—tryptophan, lysine, and methionine*—that are critical in a real-life diet, for these are the three you can throw off when you severely unbalance your diet by selecting, or getting, the wrong foods.†[11] Conversely, if you eat foods which supply enough of these three amino acids in the ideal pattern, you will get the necessary amounts of all the other essential amino acids too. So this pattern of *three* essential amino acids is the real key to protein completeness, and provides a standard against which we may compare a food, or a meal, or a whole diet.

*The amino acid cystine is convertible in the body to the essential amino acid methionine, so the two are frequently represented together in foods as the "total sulfur-containing amino acids." Similarly, tyresine spares phenylalanine, so these two are often referred to collectively as the "total aromatic amino acids."

†Foods can also have other limiting amino acids, such as threonine in some grains and isoleucine in some vegetables, but these are naturally compensated for when the three critical amino acids are adequate in the diet.

In comparing single foods to this pattern, it is not surprising to find that animal foods compare favorably. Animal bodies are so like our own in composition that they contain the essential amino acids in very much the same proportions that our own bodies require. Soybean protein, too, is complete protein; its amino acid pattern conforms closely to that of milk. Most plant foods, however, are incomplete proteins, short on one or two of the three limiting amino acids. Wheat and rice, for example, like most other grains, are limited in lysine. With no other source of protein, a man would have to eat almost four cups of cooked whole wheat berries or five cups of cooked brown rice to get the lysine he needs for protein synthesis.

Fortunately, of course, it is only under laboratory conditions or in a severe food crisis that we have only one source of protein. Ordinarily, it is much more appropriate to consider the completeness of proteins eaten together—in other words, to compare the ideal amino acid pattern to the pattern of the whole diet rather than to that of individual foods. When this is done, the picture changes radically. Because some plant foods have generous amounts of the same amino acid in which others are deficient, they complement each other's amino acid deficiencies and can be used to supplement each other in the diet. Put together in the right proportions, they make up a source of high-quality protein. This is the principle of protein complementarity, first publicized widely by Frances Moore Lappé in *Diet for a Small Planet* in 1971, and its announcement has greatly benefited vegetarians. Through complementarity, meals can be planned so that the proteins in their foods balance each other to make protein which is complete in all the limiting amino acids. In such combinations, foods like corn and beans or bread and a little milk are high-quality protein sources, for their combined amino acid pattern has no deficiencies: all the digestible protein in both is available for body use.

For practical purposes, balancing protein does not mean you have to balance the amino acids found in each food item. In the kitchen it is enough to balance food *families*, because the members of families like grains, legumes, and milk products share similar amino acid strengths and deficiencies. For

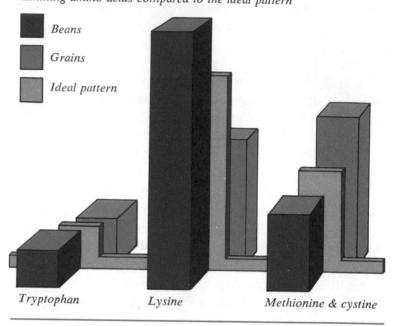

PROTEIN COMPLEMENTARITY: GRAINS & BEANS
Limiting amino acids compared to the ideal pattern

- ■ Beans
- ▨ Grains
- ▦ Ideal pattern

Tryptophan   Lysine   Methionine & cystine

example, grains are low in lysine and high in methionine, while legumes are just the opposite: low in methionine and high in lysine. In a particular proportion, almost any two members of these two families will complement each other adequately.* In practice, that is, the foods themselves should be balanced—part of a diet with a planned variety of foods.

Food-group planning makes it easy to balance a diet for high-quality protein. All that is necessary is to keep in mind what proportions of the food groups are needed to produce the ideal pattern shown above. In its simplest application, this means that if half your protein requirement is supplied by animal products—the Milk and Eggs group of the meatless diet—the other half can come from any source whatsoever and still be adequately complemented.[12] A glass of milk at each meal, for example, will balance all the rest of the plant protein that

---

*These groups do have a maverick member or two. Peanuts, for example, are a little lower in lysine than the rest of the legumes. By itself, peanut flour has been shown to supplement a grain diet well enough for good protein nutriture, but its contribution is enhanced by a variety of other protein foods, such as sesame seeds, milk, and other legumes.

is eaten with it. If only a third of the daily protein requirement is met with animal proteins (the equivalent of two glasses of milk a day for adults), a serving of legumes is necessary to supplement the grains. Most dramatic, however, is the application of food group balance to an all-plant or vegan diet. A diet whose protein comes 60 percent from grain, 35 percent from legumes, and 5 percent from dark leafy green vegetables will have a desirable amino acid pattern for meeting human needs, even without the addition of animal products like milk or eggs.*[13]

In our presentation, food group balance is applied not to individual meals but to the whole diet, on a day to day basis. This would not be possible if it were necessary to supply the body with essential amino acids in the exact pattern at every meal, as has been thought. Actually, since protein synthesis is always going on, the body needs a supply of balanced amino acids not just three times a day but almost constantly, and there is considerable evidence that it can maintain a balanced pattern in the amino acids it gets from food by complementing them with amino acids from body proteins in its own pool.

The key to this self-regulatory mechanism seems to be the digestive tract itself. First, the cells that make up the intestinal lining are being replaced continuously and very rapidly—the entire lining, in fact, is replaced every two to four days. As the old cells are cast off they are digested, and their protein is reabsorbed. Secondly, the protein enzymes of digestion are themselves digested, adding another source of protein in the intestine from the body itself. Together, these two sources may add as much as 90 grams a day of pure, complete protein to the intestinal contents.[14] When you remember the 56-gram daily protein requirement for the average male, it is clear what an effective buffer this process provides. Altogether, of the total protein digested and absorbed from the intestine after a meal, perhaps twice as much is supplied by the body itself as by the food just eaten.[15] By drawing on this pool as it absorbs the amino acids from foods, the intestine is able to influence

* Notice that this is the proportion of *protein* in these foods, not of the quantities of the foods themselves. The recommendations in our Four Food Groups for the vegan, page 322, show how to apply this proportion to everyday foods for good balance.

the pattern of amino acids entering the bloodstream throughout the day, largely independent of what has been eaten and when.

Under normal circumstances, that is, the body easily makes the fine adjustments in amino acid balance for us if we just give it an adequate amount of protein and calories in a roughly balanced diet. Actually, for an adult, perhaps only one fifth of the total protein requirement needs to supply the essential amino acids in a balanced pattern. This is a very small amount, easy to get from ordinary foods. Our total nutritional needs, however, are best served by a rough protein food-group balance among *all* the foods meeting our protein requirement. The basic nutritional issue is not whether an amino acid is in limited supply but whether the whole diet is balanced. Even when there is enough of a food to meet the requirement for a particular limiting amino acid, the diet can be very one-sided: all corn, for example, or all rice.* But a diet wholly designed to balance protein by food groups falls naturally into a pattern which is well balanced for meeting our other nutritional needs, too. This is because many of the scarcer nutrients, like B vitamins and trace minerals, follow the distribution of protein in whole foods. So a good, mixed diet whose protein can be efficiently used by the body will go a long way toward meeting an individual's requirements for *all* the nutrients, giving a wide margin of good nourishment. Real protein deficiency, brought on by a diet unusually low in protein and lacking in variety, usually only accompanies a general state of malnourishment.

PROTEIN DEFICIENCY: HOW REAL A DANGER?

Buffering systems like the amino acid pool provide plenty of protection for the roughly balanced diet but only temporary protection against extremes. If a person suddenly shifts to a diet much too low in total protein, or severely deficient in a

---

*Corn is the one food in which amino acid imbalance may have deleterious effects, even when enough is eaten to supply the limiting amino acid. The relationship between its leucine (which is abundant) and its tryptophan (which is limited) may be part of the reason why it so readily brings on pellagra when it is not supplemented.[16] With the exception of a diet whose only protein source is corn, however, the amino acids found in natural foods are unlikely to have adverse effects.

limiting amino acid, or simply too low in total calories to meet the demands for energy *and* protein synthesis together, it takes only a short time for the intestinal amino acid pool to be depleted.[17] The body then draws on the amino acids released by the turnover of less critical protein tissues like the muscles to maintain vital organs like the heart and kidneys. During real starvation, the less essential protein tissues are progressively broken down to be burned as fuel for the brain and central nervous system, and the muscles waste away.

In a sense, then, protein deficiency may be said to begin as soon as the body's functioning is compromised by having to consume body protein to meet its needs. The human body can lose almost 5 percent of its protein and still adapt easily. As the loss increases, however, the deterioration of body functioning gets more and more severe. Final, irreversible damage to body tissues—the incontrovertible sign of real protein deficiency—occurs only after a large amount of body protein is lost.[18] Unfortunately, there is no simple way to measure the earlier stages of marginal deficiency, which would help to identify potential cases of full-blown malnutrition in time to reverse the damage.[19]

In any case, real protein deficiency is almost always the companion of caloric deficiency—not just too little protein but too little food, causing outright starvation. As long as enough calories are eaten to meet energy needs, almost any mixture of foods likely to be eaten anywhere in the world contains enough protein to fill the adult protein requirement; only diets exceedingly low in protein and high in starch do not.*[20] Americans having inadequate diets, especially women concerned about their figures, are among those who commonly eat too little food—they eat too few calories and too little protein to meet total protein-energy needs, even though they may be meeting the recommended levels for the essential amino acids.

If you are living where there is an abundant and varied food supply, protein deficiency is quite unlikely—unless, of course, you eat very little good-quality food. Still, you should include some protein food at each meal, since the body does have a

*Monotonous diets consisting of plantain or root foods like cassava or sweet potatoes are particularly notorious for causing malnutrition.

constant need for protein. Check your diet for protein adequacy by making sure that you are getting enough calories from a good mixture of foods, supplying the total RDA for protein.

THE SPECIAL PROTEIN NEEDS OF CHILDREN

Infants and young children have the greatest need for nourishment per unit of body weight: not just for protein, which is necessary as the basic material for growth, but also for calories and other nutrients. The person most vulnerable to malnutrition is the young child who has just been weaned, for his needs are great and he may not be adequately fed. If the available food lacks variety and consists mostly of a single starchy cereal or root like rice or potatoes, the child may not be able to eat enough of such bulky food to get the energy he needs, and the little protein the diet supplies will be burned for fuel. Some fat or oil, which is much more concentrated in energy than carbohydrate is, makes it easier for a child to eat the amount of calories he needs—which is why children under three should be given whole milk rather than skim. The child also needs *good-quality* protein, high in the essential amino acids, since his requirement for these nutrients is proportionately greater than the adult's: 35 to 40 percent of the total protein RDA, as opposed to about 20 percent for adults.[21] A diet largely made up of a staple plant food low in one or two of the essential amino acids should be supplemented by other foods which can provide these nutrients, such as beans or milk.

The risk of malnutrition is greatest where the food supply is meager and lacks variety, but even then diet is not the whole picture. A child will very likely get along on a basically inadequate post-weaning diet until repeated infections increase his nutritional needs enough to precipitate a full-blown case of malnutrition. The protein-calorie deficiency diseases like kwashiorkor are characteristically precipitated by measles, diarrhea, or parasitic infestation in the child who has been weaned to a diet of unsupplemented cereals or roots or to inadequate liquid concoctions.[22] These illnesses cut the appetite and interfere with food absorption while increasing the need for calories and protein.

Often governments or relief organizations have tried to deal with widespread malnourishment by providing supplementary protein foods. These have very little effect if a family cannot afford enough food for everyone to have their fill. If the parents don't understand the special needs of growing children, they may feed them inadequately even when there is enough food. But generally the underlying cause of malnutrition is simply poverty: people do not have the sanitation, medical care, and purchasing power they require to overcome malnutrition.

THE PROTEIN WORKSHEET

Page 390 shows our worksheet for learning about protein in food. The foods are listed in order of decreasing protein concentration and the columns show the quantity of protein in each food, the ratio of calories to protein supplied, and how the limited amino acids of each compare to the ideal pattern.

The second column is especially interesting if you are counting calories. You can see in several categories that as the protein becomes more "dilute," the calories per gram of protein increase—you're getting more calories for less protein. So if you're trying to lose weight, you will want to choose your protein sources from those foods which are more concentrated in protein. Nuts and seeds, though they often contain large quantities of protein, are high in calories per gram of protein because of their high fat content. But don't ignore them on that account. Even in small quantities they can be an important source of other nutrients—2 tablespoons of sunflower seeds, for example, makes a valuable contribution to your requirement for vitamin B-6. Cheese, too, is high in calories because of its fat, but it is a concentrated, high-quality protein and an ounce of it goes a long way (it has about 7.5 grams of protein).

Milk, as you will see from the chart, has no limiting amino acids. Its 3.5 grams of protein per 100 grams seems low until you realize that 100 grams is less than half a cup. Two cups of milk yields 17 grams of protein, or about one-third the adult daily requirement, for just 320 calories—176 calories for skim milk.

When comparing grains with legumes, remember that most

grains triple their volume with water when cooked, whereas legumes only double; the values given are for raw weight. Legumes are indeed concentrated protein. That is why roughly only one serving of them is required to complement the protein in six servings of grain. Vegetables, on the other hand, are not usually a major source of protein—you'd have to eat quite a large amount of them to get much protein at all. Nevertheless, in a diet like ours containing generous amounts of vegetables, the protein from high-quality vegetables adds up remarkably fast. The dark leafy greens—broccoli, spinach, and collards, for example—often have very good quality protein, so good that they fill in the last gap of missing amino acids for the all-plant vegan diet.*

To round out our picture of the protein personality of these foods, we have included their limiting amino acids, if any, and what percent these amino acids supply of the ideal pattern. If you have already studied amino acids compared to older standards such as the egg standard described in the note on page 379, you can see how much better these foods are for meeting our needs than was previously thought.

The more you learn about the protein and other nutrients in the foods you serve, the less effort it takes to plan nourishing meals. By getting familiar with this protein worksheet, your choice of high-quality protein sources from among the Four Food Groups will soon become second nature.

---

* A food should provide at least 2 grams of protein per 100-gram serving to make a protein contribution worth noting. Vegetables which do not give this minimum include eggplant, carrots, beets, turnips, tomatoes, pumpkin, cassava or manioc, sweet potatoes, cabbage, endive, and lettuce.

SOURCE REFERENCES

1. E. F. Phipard, Protein and amino acids in diets, in *Improvement of protein nutriture,* National Research Council, Committee on Amino Acids (Washington, National Academy of Sciences, 1974), p. 167.

2. A. E. Harper, Basic concepts, in *Improvement of protein nutriture,* p. 14.

3. Harper, Basic concepts, p. 2.

4. National Research Council, Food and Nutrition Board, *Recommended dietary allowances,* 8th rev. ed. (Washington, National Academy of Sciences, 1974), pp. 37–38.

5. NRC, *Recommended dietary allowances,* p. 38.

6. NRC, *Recommended dietary allowances,* p. 44.

7. NRC, *Recommended dietary allowances,* p. 46.

8. NRC, *Recommended dietary allowances,* p. 44.

9. Joint FAO/WHO Ad Hoc Committee on Energy and Protein Requirements, *Energy and protein requirements,* FAO Nutrition Meetings Report Series, no. 52, WHO Technical Report Series, no. 522 (Rome, Food and Agriculture Organization of the United Nations, 1973), p. 55.

10. Food and Agriculture Organization of the United Nations, Nutrition Division, *Protein requirements: Report of a joint FAO/WHO expert group,* FAO Nutrition Meetings Report Series, no. 37, WHO Technical Report Series, no. 301 (Geneva, World Health Organization, 1965).

11. FAO/WHO, *Energy and protein requirements,* p. 64.

12. California Nutrition Council, Statement regarding protein requirements, 9 November 1973 (duplicated typescript).

13. Conversation with Doris H. Calloway, Professor of Nutrition, Department of Nutritional Sciences, University of California, Berkeley, November 6, 1974.

14. E. S. Nasset, Amino acid homeostasis in the gut lumen and its nutritional significance, *World Review of Nutrition and Dietetics* 14: 134–153, 1972.

15. Nasset, Amino acid homeostasis, p. 135.

16. A. E. Harper, Effects of disproportionate amounts of amino acids, in *Improvement of protein nutriture,* p. 159.

17. Harper, Basic concepts, p. 12.

18. G. G. Graham, Effects of deficiency of protein and amino acids, in *Improvement of protein nutriture,* p. 186.

19. Graham, Effects, p. 110.

20. A. E. Harper and D. M. Hegsted, Improvement of protein nutriture, in *Improvement of protein nutriture,* p. 186.

21. H. H. Williams et al., Nitrogen and amino acid requirements, in *Improvement of protein nutriture,* p. 42.

22. Graham, Effects, pp. 113–114.

Protein & Calorie Content of Protein Source Foods

	% Protein in edible portion	Calories per gram of protein	Limiting amino acids (% of ideal pattern)‡
DAIRY PRODUCTS & EGGS			
Nonfat dry milk	35.9	10	*
Whole dry milk	26.4	19	*
Cheddar cheese, ripened	25.0	16	*
Cottage cheese, uncreamed	17.0	5	*
creamed	13.6	8	*
Egg, whole (hen's)	12.9	13	*
Egg white	10.9	5	*
Cream cheese	8.0	47	T 86
Skim milk or buttermilk	3.6	10	*
Whole milk (cow's)	3.5	19	*
Yogurt, low-fat	3.4	15	*
Goat's milk	3.2	21	M †
Whey, fluid	0.9	29	*
GRAINS (RAW)			
Oatmeal	14.2	27	L 73
Wheat: hard red spring	14.0	24	L 56
white bread flour (80% extraction)	12.0	30	L 41
gluten	88.9	4	L 28, T 95
germ	26.6	14	*
bran	16.0	13	L 85
Triticale	14.0	†	L 60, T †, M †
Rye, whole-meal	12.1	28	L 67, T 69
Buckwheat	11.7	29	L 75
Bulgur wheat (parboiled)	11.2	32	L 51
Sorghum	11.0	30	L 40, T 95
Millet	9.9	33	L 67
Barley, pot	9.6	36	L 68
Cornmeal, whole-ground	9.2	39	L 53, T 57
Rice, brown	7.5	48	L 75
parboiled, "converted"	7.4	50	L 69
polished (white)	6.7	54	L 71

*No limiting amino acids   †Values not available   ‡T=tryptophan, L=lysine, M=total methionine and cystine

	% Protein in edible portion	Calories per gram of protein	Limiting amino acids (% of ideal pattern)‡
LEGUMES (RAW)			
Soybeans	34.1	12	M 99
fermented (tempeh)	16.9	10	*
cake or curd (tofu)	7.8	9	*
Soy milk	3.4	10	*
Peanuts	26.0	22	L 70, M 92, T 96
Fava beans (broad beans)	25.1	13	M 58, T 81
Lentils	24.7	14	M 65, T 90
Mung beans	24.2	14	M 47, T 75
Peas	24.1	14	M 77, T 84
Black-eyed peas	22.8	15	M 86
Common (red, white, pinto, black)	22.5	15	M 73, T 95
Garbanzos (chickpeas)	20.5	18	T 81, M 85
Limas	20.4	17	T 75, M 86
NUTS & SEEDS			
Pumpkin seeds	29.0	19	L 76, M †
Sunflower seeds	24.0	23	L 71
Walnuts, black	20.5	31	*
Pistachios	19.3	31	T 95, L 96
Sesame seeds	18.6	30	L 54
Almonds	18.6	32	L 44, T 80
Cashews	17.2	33	L 91
Cocoa (high-fat)	16.8	18	L 97, M †
Walnuts (English or Persian)	14.8	44	L 30, T 95
Brazil nuts	14.3	46	L 55, T 90
Filberts (hazelnuts)	12.6	50	M 47, L 58
Pecans	9.2	75	L 89
Coconut (dried kernel)	7.2	92	L 69
Carob flour	4.5	40	T 57
VEGETABLES (RAW)			
Immature seeds			
Limas, green	8.4	15	M 83
Peas	6.3	13	M 72, T 95
Corn	3.5	27	T 59, L 73
Black-eyed peas (in pods)	3.3	13	T 95, M †

*No limiting amino acids   †Values not available   ‡T=tryptophan, L=lysine,   M=total methionine and cystine

	% Protein in edible portion	Calories per gram of protein	Limiting amino acids (% of ideal pattern)‡
Green leaves			
Kale (without stems)	6.0	9	L 61, M 69
Brussels sprouts	4.9	9	M 58
Collards (without stems)	4.8	9	*
Pigweed and lambsquarters	4.2	10	*
Parsley	3.6	12	M †
Spinach	3.2	8	*
Turnip greens	3.0	9	M 69
Mustard greens	3.0	10	L 95, M 96
Swiss chard	2.4	10	L 78, T 96, M †
Beet greens	2.2	11	L 56, M 67, T 95
Watercress	2.2	9	M †
Other vegetables			
Red pepper (hot)	3.7	25	T 93, M †
Broccoli	3.6	9	M 96
Mushrooms	2.7	10	M 38, L 88, T 96
Cauliflower	2.7	10	M †
Asparagus	2.5	10	M 84, L 89
Okra	2.4	15	T 54, L 65, M 87
Beans, snap	1.9	17	M 82
Roots			
Potato	2.1	36	M 72, L 94
Yam	2.1	48	L 81
Sweet potato	1.7	67	L 67
Cassava	1.1	†	M 66, L 82
YEAST			
Brewer's	38.8	7	M 95
Torula	38.6	7	T 42
Active dry	36.9	8	T 87

*No limiting amino acids   †Values not available   ‡T=tryptophan, L=lysine, M=total methionine and cystine
Adapted from Watt & Merrill 1964 (Ag. Handbook no. 8), FAO/WHO 1970, and Orr & Watt 1957

Vitamins

Vitamins perform such different tasks that they sometimes seem to differ in more than they have in common. We know that they are present in food only in exceedingly small quantities, that they are absolutely essential for life, and that though they are organic, they cannot be made by the body. Like the essential amino acids, they must be supplied by what we eat. Beyond that, however, their functions for most of us are shrouded in mystery.

THE WORK OF VITAMINS

Perhaps what draws vitamins together most as a group is the way they work. Without vitamins, the food we eat could not be put to use. One of their most important roles is to help the foodstuffs and their components move step by step along the long pathways of biochemical reactions by which food is utilized for energy, repair, and all the other processes essential to life.

There are hundreds of such pathways in the human body, many of them in every cell: pathways for utilizing carbohydrate and others for utilizing fat; pathways for energy production and still others for protein synthesis. The foodstuffs play a very passive role through all these processes. They provide the raw material for each step or reaction of the pathway, but the body would quickly starve if these reactions were left to chance. At every step of every pathway, therefore, the process is aided and speeded up by enzymes—large, keylike proteins shaped just right for interlocking with two or more substances to bring them together so that the reaction can occur. Through all these processes, though the substances they bring together are transformed, the enzymes themselves remain unchanged.

Most vitamins are either parts of enzymes or help bring enzymes together with the substances they transform. An enzyme is made by the body to interlock with certain specific substances and no others. Vitamins, however, may help all along a pathway, often along several pathways. They too have a keylike structure, but theirs is a skeleton key that can recognize and interlock with many different substances. Like enzymes, vitamins remain unchanged throughout these processes, which is why such small quantities are required for health. Their job is simply to help speed up the millions of reactions that life depends on by bringing the right things together at the right time.

Most vitamins are soluble in water, so that they can be carried by the blood throughout the body and absorbed by the cells where they are needed. However, since any excess of them in the diet is washed out in the urine, water-soluble vitamins cannot be stored by the body and must be kept in fairly constant supply. Other vitamins, to serve different purposes, are fat-soluble and resistant to water, so that they concentrate in the fatty tissues of the body like the adipose tissue and the cell membranes. Fat-soluble vitamins can be stored in these

---

FAT-SOLUBLE AND WATER-SOLUBLE VITAMINS

FAT-SOLUBLE	*Vitamins A, D, E, & K*	*Soluble in fat but not in water, requiring dietary fat for absorption into body*
		Stored in fatty tissues of body
		May build up to toxic levels (usually through use of vitamin supplements)
WATER-SOLUBLE	*Vitamin C*	*Soluble in water but not in fat*
	B vitamins (Thiamin, Riboflavin, Niacin, B-6, B-12, Folacin, Pantothenic acid, Biotin, Choline)	*Cannot be stored in body, so no danger of toxic buildup, but should be present in diet every day*

locations too, as well as in the liver, but they can also build up to toxic levels when taken in large amounts.

According to their function, therefore, vitamins are active in different tissues of the body. Those working in energy metabolism are present in every cell. Many involved in protein and DNA synthesis are also present in every cell, but are concentrated in the parts of the body where cell turnover is most rapid, such as in the lining of the digestive tract, the bone marrow that makes red blood cells, and the glands which produce hormones.

The B-complex vitamins, which are all essential in the utilization of food for energy, provide a good illustration of how most vitamins work. The burning of food for energy is not a single, simple process like the burning of wood for heat. In order for the energy to be usable, the "fire" must be controlled in a long sequence of chemical reactions which proceed rapidly but only one step at a time. Vitamins control many of these steps. In the simple burning of a single molecule of glucose, the B vitamins niacin, thiamin, riboflavin, and pantothenic acid are all required just to prepare the fuel for the fire. As the glucose gets closer to the steps which actually yield energy, it is broken down into the same carbon substances that amino acids and fat are eventually broken down to, joining a large, common stockpile of fuel in which each foodstuff has lost its separate identity. As these compounds enter the fire of oxidation, the same vitamins once again participate in the steps which release energy. At the same time, along other pathways, these same B vitamins may be working along with other vitamins in the opposite direction, in synthesizing sugars, amino acids, and fats.

When a vitamin is absent from the diet, the pathways it participates in are broken, and though all the required raw materials may be present, those biochemical processes cannot be completed. Cells may be unable to repair themselves with new proteins, or they may starve in the midst of adequate fuel for being unable to complete the burning. In any case, the result is tissue damage, which shows up first in the parts of the body where the vitamin is most active. This is a vitamin deficiency, and it makes itself known through a wide range of sometimes eerie malfunctions—rashes, sores, dizziness, anxiety—as disparate as the range of functions the vitamin serves. Loss of appetite, for example, is one symptom of damage to the digestive cells.

Because a vitamin often cooperates with many other vitamins to do a particular task, their deficiency symptoms often overlap. Fatigue, for example, will occur when any of the B vitamins is missing, for all are required together for energy metabolism. A deficiency of one vitamin manifests itself as a *syndrome*—a whole pattern of symptoms, any of which might easily be caused by other physical problems as well. For these reasons and because a diet deficient in one vitamin is often deficient in several others, the experience of a skilled physician is usually necessary to make an accurate diagnosis.

Research into vitamins is far from complete. The fourteen which we describe are those recognized today by the nutrition sciences. More may still be discovered; certainly, more will be learned of the ones we already know. Active areas of research today include how vitamins affect tissues, the requirements at different times during life, precise amounts in foods, the effects of deficiency, and the interaction of vitamins with other nutrients, drugs, and hormones. The following pages are just an introduction to the vitamins as nutrients—vitamin therapy is another world.

Vitamin A

CAROTENE; PROVITAMIN A; RETINOL

FAT-SOLUBLE

SOURCES
Adult RDA *is 4000–5000* IU

22000 sorrel, *1 cup cooked*
19000 lambsquarters, *1 c. ckd.*
15000 carrots, *1 cup cooked*
13000 butternut squash,
      1 cup baked
12000 dandelion greens,
      1 cup cooked

Vitamin A is a fat-soluble vitamin primarily active in the fatty membranes of the cells which cover the outer and inner surfaces of the body, like the skin and the mucous membranes that line the mouth, respiratory passages, and digestive and urinary tracts. It is essential for the health of these tissues and the organs they protect. Growing children also require vitamin A for many of the processes of growth, including the formation of bones and tooth enamel. Most commonly, however, vitamin A is associated with night vision, for it is a component of the pigment which enables the eye to readjust to darkness after exposure to bright light—as, for example, after the glare of headlights from a passing car while one is driving at night.

Like other fat-soluble vitamins, vitamin A can be stored, but if the diet is lacking in the vitamin for a few months the body's reserves will be depleted and the eyes will develop temporary "night blindness," which can be cured by adding the vitamin to the diet. This is the most common threat of vitamin A deficiency among Americans. In much of the rest of the world, however, where an adequate food supply is often absent, the much more critical signs of long-term deficiencies threaten large numbers of people. Under such circumstances the cells of the mucous membranes dry up and become scaly or horny, and since it is mucous that protects from debris and bacteria, the organs it protects become wide open to infection. The eye is the first to dry out; its structure disintegrates and it becomes infected. An estimated eighty thousand children around the world become permanently blind each year from prolonged absence of vitamin A. Perhaps half this number eventually die from other effects of deficiency, as the mucous membranes that line the respiratory, digestive, and urinary tracts become infected with diseases like tuberculosis or pneumonia. Children who survive these afflictions will often be stunted in growth because of the additional role vitamin A plays in bone formation.

Vitamin A can be synthesized by human beings and animals from its provitamin, the substance called carotene which gives plants like carrots and apricots their rich, deep yellow-orange color. Carotene is also abundant in dark green leafy vegetables, though its color is masked by the green chlorophyll. In general, whether orange or green, the deepness of the color is a good clue to how rich a vegetable is in provitamin A. "Active" vitamin A, however—the retinol family of compounds—may also be supplied directly, through foods of animal origin in which the vitamin has already been made and stored.

The recommended dietary allowance for vitamin A is based based on the assumption that one half of the vitamin will come from vegetable sources (carotene) in the diet and the other half from animal sources (retinol). Since almost all of the vegetarian's A comes from carotene, only about one sixth of

9800	Hubbard squash, *1 cup baked*
9200	sweet potato, ckd., *1 lg.*
9200	cantaloupe, *½ melon*
9100	turnip greens, *1 c. ckd.*
9100	kale, *1 cup cooked*
8100	mustard greens, *1 c. ckd.*
7400	beet greens, *1 c. cooked*
5300	bok choy, *1 cup cooked*
5300	papaya, *1 medium*
4600	persimmon, *1 medium*
4500	broccoli, ckd., *1 stalk*
4500	spinach, raw, *1 cup chopped*
3300	red pepper, sweet, raw
2900	apricots, *2 to 3 medium*
2300	nectarine, *1 medium*
2200	acorn squash, *½ baked*
1400	romaine lettuce, *4 leaves*
1300	peach, *1 medium*
1300	asparagus, *1 cup cooked*
1200	butter lettuce, *8 large leaves*
1100	tomato, raw, *1 medium*
750	prunes, with juice, *5 ckd.*
630	grapefruit, pink, *½*
590	egg, *1 large*
470	butter, *1 tablespoon*
470	margarine, fortified, *1 tablespoon*
370	cheddar cheese, *1 ounce*
350	milk, whole, *1 cup*

which can be actively used by the body, the RDA leaves little margin of safety and should be considered a minimum requirement. Vitamin A is easy to come by in the United States, however, for fresh vegetables and fruit give an abundance. Milk is an important source for children. But be careful if you are relying heavily on vitamin supplements, for retinol—often supplied in vitamins as retinyl palmitate—can be toxic in large doses. Like other fat-soluble vitamins, retinol cannot pass out of the body through the urine but is stored in the liver and fatty tissues of the body. In adults, the high doses of retinol found in vitamin pills can build up to a toxic level,* causing headache, nausea, diarrhea, loss of appetite, blurred vision, loss of hair, and cessation of menses. Toxic reactions in children may follow when the RDA is exceeded by a factor of ten,[4] and show up first as excessive irritability, swelling over the long bones of the body, and dry, itching skin. It is very difficult to get too much vitamin A from food sources, however—and, fortunately for vegetarians, carotene is not toxic in any quantity. So eat all the squash and melons and green leafy vegetables you want: the worst that can happen is a little yellowing of your soles and palms!

Vitamin D

Vitamin D's main responsibility is to regulate the metabolism of calcium and phosphorus, which combine as calcium phosphates in the bones to make them strong and rigid. Vitamin D increases the absorption of these essential minerals from the intestine, helps to keep them in the blood at the proper level for bone mineralization, and mobilizes them out from the bones again when necessary. It also regulates their excretion via the kidneys. When vitamin D stores are inadequate, even if there is plenty of calcium in the diet, not enough is absorbed to mineralize the bones. In an infant or child this deficiency results in the disease called rickets, in which the rapidly growing bones grow soft and eventually bend under the weight of

*In adults, among the lowest doses reported to cause toxicity are 100 times the RDA in a single dose, 20 times the RDA over many doses, and 6 times the RDA for regular daily doses.[1,2,3]

the body. In adults, the same disorder is called osteomalacia or adult rickets. Although technically a calcium deficiency, these conditions are almost always the result of inadequate stores of vitamin D.

Interestingly, food sources of vitamin D are limited, and a perfectly reasonable and well-balanced diet may not supply the amount required to prevent deficiency. Our most efficient source of the vitamin is not a food at all, but exposure to sunlight, which transforms a related provitamin substance in the skin into a substance which the kidney can change into active vitamin D. Like other fat-soluble vitamins, the sunlight-activated provitamin D can be stored away in the liver.

With this adaptive capacity to store and synthesize, adults seem to be able to make up for marginal deficiencies of vitamin D in the diet with even a little exposure to sunlight. Consequently, there is no *adult* RDA for vitamin D. However, during periods of growth—in infants, children, and adolescents, and women during pregnancy and lactation—400 International Units a day is recommended to provide optimum bone growth. (As little as 100 IU a day may be enough to prevent rickets and maintain normal body functions.) Human milk has only about 20 IU per liter (or quart), though the amount is affected by the mother's own vitamin D stores. Nursing mothers, therefore, should get ample vitamin D from fortified milk or sunshine, and would be wise to sunbathe their babies as well. Infants too should get their 400 IU per day, and a vitamin supplement in this range is often advised to make up any possible deficiency.

Even for adults, though—especially for older adults—food sources of vitamin D are becoming increasingly important in our artificial life style, for we are often cut off from sunlight for much of the year by window glass, clothing, smog, and indoor living. Pigmentation in the skin impedes vitamin D synthesis too, rendering dark-skinned children in northern latitudes particularly susceptible to rickets.* It has been estimated that exposure to the noonday sun for five minutes in a bathing suit in

*In tropical latitudes, skin pigmentation may provide protection against too *much* exposure to the sun.[5]

Washington, D.C., provides the equivalent of 200 to 300 units of vitamin D.[6] A little can go a long way, and the body seems to be able to store enough vitamin D during warm weather to last through the winter if necessary.

Fortifying milk with vitamin D has largely solved the problem for urban Americans. Milk is the ideal food to fortify, since it is already an excellent source of calcium and phosphorus too. However, excessive use of fortified foods or vitamin supplements creates the possibility of getting too *much* vitamin D, impossible from natural food sources and sunlight. Amounts above 2000 IU per day can produce dangerously high levels of calcium in the body, leading to the deposit of calcium in unwanted places like the blood vessels and the kidneys. Supplementation of your diet, either in food or in vitamin pills, should never exceed the recommended daily allowance of 400 IU.

Vitamin D is relatively stable in foods, and will survive storing, processing, and cooking.

Vitamin E

ALPHA-, BETA-, GAMMA-, DELTA-TOCOPHEROL

FAT-SOLUBLE

Vitamin E is found naturally in unsaturated oils, where it acts as an antioxidant—a kind of scavenger for destructive substances which would otherwise react with the oil's unsaturated bonds and cause rancid decomposition. All vitamin E in the diet, whether of animal or plant origin, comes ultimately from the unsaturated oils of plant foods, so a food's content of vitamin E generally goes hand in hand with its content of unsaturated fatty acids. Vegetable oils, consequently, are the richest sources of vitamin E, with wheat germ oil leading the others by far.

In the body, vitamin E also seems to work as an antioxidant, protecting the polyunsaturated fats in all the cell membranes of the body. These fatty components of the body may "go rancid"—undergo oxidative destruction—just like other fats and oils, and it has been suggested that this kind of destruction may be a significant part of the aging process.[7] (The trace mineral selenium can also perform as an antioxidant to protect cells, sparing vitamin E.) Early experiments with rats suggesting a connection between vitamin E and sexual fertility—*tocopherol* means "ability to bear young"—have not been paralleled by studies with humans.

The amount of vitamin E needed in the diet varies from person to person, and a minimum requirement has not yet been established. Deficiency in humans has only been demonstrated in low birth weight infants, where it shows up as an anemia caused by the rupture of red blood cell membranes (hemolysis). For adults it is known that the fatty acid makeup of our cell membranes reflects the proportions of saturated to unsaturated fats in our diet. The more unsaturated fats we eat, the greater the proportion of unsaturated fats in the cell membranes of our bodies, and consequently the greater the need for vitamin E. Fortunately, since vitamin E in food goes hand in hand with polyunsaturated fats, more of the latter means more of the former too. If your diet is low in polyunsaturated fat, you will be getting relatively little vitamin E—but your requirement will be lower as well. The RDA for vitamin E, consequently, has simply been set according to the vitamin E content of the average American diet, which maintains a ratio of vitamin E to polyunsaturated fatty acids of about 0.5. This ratio is apparently quite adequate for maintaining a satisfactory level of the vitamin in our tissues. Since grains are the richest whole-food source of vitamin E, most vegetarians get larger than average amounts.

Vitamin E is present in a wide series of varying chemical forms called tocopherols, each with different levels of potency or activity. Gamma-tocopherol, for example, has only about 10 percent the activity of alpha-tocopherol, the most active form of vitamin E.[8] The activity of alpha-tocopherol in the body has been made the basis for measuring the activity of the others—the so-called International Unit (IU) for vitamin E. Though the exact effectiveness of other tocopherols has not been established, it appears that alpha-tocopherol contributes about 80 percent of the vitamin E activity in our diet; the remaining 20 percent comes from the other, weaker forms of tocopherol together. A few oils, such as corn oil and soybean oil, are relatively high in gamma-tocopherol and therefore

VITAMIN E CONTENT OF FOODS

Values next to food names give vitamin E activity in International Units (IU).
Adult RDA *is 12–15* IU.

OILS
.1 coconut, *1 tablespoon*
3.6 corn, *1 tablespoon*
8.9 cottonseed, *1 tablespoon*
1.1 olive, *1 tablespoon*
6.0 palm, *1 tablespoon*
3.2 peanut, *1 tablespoon*
4.6 rapeseed, *1 tablespoon*
8.5 safflower, *1 tablespoon*
3.4 sesame, *1 tablespoon*
3.4 soybean, *1 tablespoon*
10.3 sunflower, *1 tablespoon*
13.1 walnut, *1 tablespoon*
28.3 wheat germ, *1 tablespoon*

NUTS & SEEDS
6.1 almonds, *15*
1.4 brazil nuts, *4 medium*
.1 chestnuts, *2 large*
.2 coconut, *¼ c. dry shredded*
4.7 filberts (hazelnuts), *10*
1.4 peanuts, *1 tablespoon*
.3 pecans, *12 halves*
3.5 sunflower seeds, *2 tbsp.*
4.6 walnuts, *8 to 15 halves*

GRAINS & GRAIN PRODUCTS
.7 barley, whole-grain, *¼ cup dry*
Tr bread: white, *1 slice*
.1 whole meal, *1 slice*
.3 whole meal, germ-enriched, *1 slice*
1.5 cornmeal, yellow, *1 cup*
.2 millet, *¼ cup dry*
.8 oatmeal, *½ cup dry*
1.1 rice: brown, *⅓ cup dry*
.1 white, *¼ cup dry*
1.7 rye, whole-grain, *⅓ c. dry*
.4 spaghetti, *¼ lb. dry*
.1 tortilla, corn, *1 dried*
1.5 wheat, whole-grain, *⅓ c. dry*

GRAINS *(cont.)*:
Tr wheat flour, bleached, *1 cup sifted*
.4 unbleached, *1 c. sifted*
Tr wheat bran, *¼ cup*
4.2 wheat germ, *¼ cup*

LEGUMES, MATURE
1.6 peas, *½ cup dry*

VEGETABLES
.2 artichoke, *1 medium*
3.7 asparagus, *5 to 6 spears*
Tr beans, snap, *1 cup cut*
6.6 beet greens, *½ pound*
2.2 broccoli, *5½" stalk*
2.3 brussels sprouts, *3 large*
.3 cabbage, *1 cup shredded*
.6 carrot, *1 medium*
.2 cauliflowerets, *1 cup*
.3 celery, *1 med. outer stalk*
1.5 corn, *1 medium ear*
.3 cucumber, *1 small*
4.5 leeks, *3 to 4*
.2 lettuce, *1 cup chopped*
.1 mushrooms, *3 large*
.2 okra, *1 cup slices*
.5 onions, *1 cup chopped*
.2 parsley, August, *¼ cup chopped*
.7 November, *¼ cup chopped*
1.5 parsnip, *½ large*
.2 peas, *1 cup*
10.9 spinach, *½ pound*
9.7 sweet potato, *1 medium*
.5 tomato, *1 medium*
7.5 turnip greens, *½ pound*
.2 watercress, *10 sprigs*

FRUITS
1.8 apple, *1 medium*
.7 banana, *1 medium*

FRUITS *(cont.)*:
8.6 blackberries, wild, *1 cup*
1.5 cultivated, *1 cup*
.2 cherries, *10*
.6 grapefruit, *½ medium*
.2 melon, *1 cup diced*
.4 orange, *1 medium*
1.2 pear, *1 medium*
.6 plum, *1 large*
.8 raspberries, *1 cup*
.5 strawberries, *1 cup*

DAIRY PRODUCTS & EGGS
.5 butter, *1 tablespoon*
0 egg white, *1 large*
.6 egg yolk, *1 large*
.3 milk (3.5% fat), *1 cup*

MISCELLANEOUS
2.2 chocolate, unsweetened, *1 ounce*
Tr molasses, *1 tablespoon*
0 yeast: brewer's, *1 tbsp.*
Tr torula, *1 tablespoon*

There are several different tocopherols in foods. Each tocopherol has a different level of biological activity, but only the activity of alpha- and gamma-tocopherol has been precisely determined. All values given here include alpha-tocopherol content; gamma-tocopherol content has been included also wherever data were available, as for all the oils. The resulting alpha-tocopherol equivalent, measured in milligrams, has been multiplied by 1.5 to give International Units (IU). *Values are adapted from Slover 1971 and Dicks 1965.*

proportionately lower than other oils in the vitamin E activity they contribute. A variety of oils and whole-food sources of vitamin E, however, easily brings the vitamin E activity of our diet up to the average level recommended by the RDA. Too refined a diet excludes the best whole-food sources of the vitamin, like the germ of the wheat berry and leafy greens.

Vitamin E is the only vitamin that is unstable in freezing. Its presence in foods is severely reduced by processing; refinement of grain, for example, removes much of its vitamin E content. Oils in particular may vary greatly in vitamin E content, according to their processing and handling. Rancidity destroys vitamin E, so proper storage is essential. In addition, crude vegetable oils, rich in vitamin E, undergo a great deal of processing to be made palatable, and this reduces their vitamin E content. The effects of refinement on an oil's nutrient content probably deserve more attention, in view of the central place such oils occupy in the American diet. But again, the closer the food is to its whole, natural state, the better for *all* its nutrients—not just vitamin E.

Vitamin K

Vitamin K, necessary for the normal clotting of blood, is partly synthesized by bacteria in the intestine. Deficiencies only occur with abnormal medical problems like poor absorption, treatment with anticoagulants, or a disturbance of the intestinal bacteria during antibiotic treatment. Occasionally, newborn infants have trouble before their intestinal bacteria are established. The body's small need, 50 micrograms per day, is easily supplied by a diet of whole foods.

FAT-SOLUBLE

GOOD FOOD SOURCES:

leafy green vegetables, egg yolk, soybean oil

POOR SOURCES:

most cereals, fruits, and carrots and peas

Vitamin C
ASCORBIC ACID

Vitamin C was the first food element to be associated with its deficiency disease, when sailors in the eighteenth century found that a little fresh fruit added to their food stores at each port could prevent scurvy. The vitamin was then called the "antiscorbutic (antiscurvy) factor," from which the name

WATER-SOLUBLE

FRESH FRUITS
240 guava, *medium*
170 papaya, *medium*
120 orange juice, *1 cup*
 90 cantaloupe, *½ melon*
 88 strawberries, *1 cup*
 81 mango, *medium*
 66 orange, *medium*
 54 grapefruit, *½ medium*
 39 lemon, *medium*
 31 red raspberries, *1 cup*
 30 blackberries, *1 cup*
 27 tangerine, *medium*
 26 pineapple, *1 cup diced*
 20 blueberries, *1 cup*
 12 banana, *medium*

RAW VEGETABLES
150 red pepper, sweet, *med.*
 94 green pepper, *medium*
 42 cabbage, *1 cup chopped*
 28 tomato, *medium*
 28 spinach, *1 cup chopped*
 20 mung bean sprouts, *1 cup*

COOKED VEGETABLES
160 broccoli, *1 stalk*
140 brussels sprouts, *8*
140 collard greens, *1 cup*
110 sorrel, *1 cup*
100 kale, *1 cup*
 74 lambsquarters, *1 cup*
 71 kohlrabi, *1 cup diced*
 70 green pepper, *medium*
 69 cauliflowerets, *1 cup*
 67 mustard greens, *1 cup*
 58 tomato, *1 cup*
 50 spinach, *1 cup*
 48 cabbage, *1 cup*
 44 rutabagas, *1 cup sliced*
 34 turnip, *1 cup diced*
 32 peas, *1 cup*
 32 okra, *1 cup slices*
 29 green lima beans, *1 cup*
 28 chard leaves, *1 cup*
 25 sweet potato, baked
 22 potato, boiled

ascorbic acid is derived. Most of the world is now aware of the importance of fresh food in the diet, especially fresh fruits and vegetables, so scurvy has largely disappeared.

Because vitamin C is one of the most reactive of vitamins, it is one of the most versatile in the body—and, as we shall see, one of the most unstable in food. In fact, scurvy results in such widespread and seemingly unrelated tissue damage in the body that vitamin C's action is thought to be much more general than a limited participation in enzyme systems alone. In the body it acts as a transporter of hydrogen, taking it on and giving it up in many metabolic reactions. Probably C plays a role in many other types of reactions as well. It is especially important in the formation of collagen, an essential constituent of the connective tissue which cements our body cells together. The bones and teeth continually need vitamin C to repair their connective tissue, and without well-formed collagen, cuts and burns cannot heal.

Infections decrease the amount of vitamin C in the tissues, so an adequate pool of C in the body apparently helps it combat infections. Whether or not the current studies indicate that the severity and duration of colds can be reduced by large amounts of vitamin C, larger than that found in food, is controversial and depends to some extent on which scientific standards are used to interpret the available data. Identifying the role which vitamin C plays in infectious illness continues to be the subject of active research.

In addition to bleeding gums, mild vitamin C deficiency causes listlessness, fleeting joint pains, and poor endurance. Prolonged deficiency leads to the rupture of the tiniest blood vessels in the body, which shows up as little red spots of blood under the skin called petechiae. Very little vitamin C, as little as 10 milligrams a day, is required to prevent these symptoms. The recommended dietary allowance, however, is higher. It used to be based on the amount required to saturate body tissues, but because saturation is no longer thought to provide any special benefit, the RDA is now set somewhere between saturation and the 10 milligrams required to replace what the body's metabolism uses in a day. This is about 45 milligrams, or the amount in one small orange.

The vitamin C in growing plants is stable, but when the plants are damaged by cutting or bruising, an enzyme is activated which destroys the vitamin. Vitamin C is also easily destroyed by heat, alkalis, and catalysts like the metals in iron and copper pans. It is better preserved in acids, such as in citrus fruits, so that even canned grapefruit juice is an excellent source of vitamin C. It is so reactive with oxygen that even the small amount of oxygen that is normally dissolved in water is enough to destroy substantial amounts of the vitamin. Boiling water for even one minute before it is used for cooking dissipates the oxygen and reduces the destruction. Of course, the other methods of preserving water-soluble vitamins in food storage and preparation need to be followed too.

Thiamin

VITAMIN B-I

Thiamin (formerly called vitamin B-1) is required at several stages for carbohydrate and protein to be utilized for energy. Ultimately, it is involved in the release of energy from fat as well. The daily requirement for thiamin, therefore, is determined according to energy needs or caloric intake: when the energy value and especially the carbohydrate content of your diet increases, so does your need for thiamin. However, even on low-calorie diets, the daily intake of this vitamin should never drop below 1 milligram. The energy requirements of the body continue to take first priority no matter what the caloric value of the diet, and like the other water-soluble vitamins, thiamin is not easily stored in the body and is quickly depleted if this minimum requirement of 1 milligram per day is not maintained.

When thiamin intake is inadequate, the metabolism of carbohydrate compounds (including the carbohydrate portion of protein that is burned for energy) cannot be completed, and the intermediate byproducts of oxidation build up to toxic levels in the body and create some of the problems of thiamin deficiency. Because the brain and central nervous system depend completely on glucose for energy, they are especially sensitive to lack of thiamin. Thiamin is sometimes called the

WATER-SOLUBLE

SOURCES
Adult RDA is 1.0–1.5 mg

1.2 brewer's yeast, *1 tbsp.*
1.1 torula yeast, *1 tbsp.*
.66 whole wheat flour, *1 cup*
.56 rice bran, *¼ cup*
.51 pinto beans, *1 cup cooked*
.48 rice polishings, *¼ cup*
.45 peas, fresh, *1 cup cooked*
.44 wheat germ, *¼ c. toasted*
.42 millet, *¼ cup dry*
.38 soybeans, *1 cup cooked*
.38 wheat berries, *⅓ cup dry*
.36 piñon nuts, *1 ounce*
.36 sunseeds, *2 tbsp.*
.35 black beans, *1 cup cooked*
.33 barley, *¼ cup dry*
.31 rye berries, *⅓ cup dry*
.31 lima beans, green, *1 c. ckd.*
.30 split peas, green, *1 c. ckd.*
.27 navy beans, *1 cup cooked*
.25 spinach, *1 cup cooked*
.24 orange, *1 large*
.23 avocado, *½ medium*

.23 asparagus, *1 cup cooked*
.20 kidney beans, *1 c. cooked*
.19 oatmeal, *1 cup cooked*
.18 rice, brown, *1 cup cooked*
.18 sesame seeds, *2 tbsp.*
.18 yam, *1 cup cooked*
.18 wheat bran, *¼ cup*
.16 broccoli, cooked, *1 stalk*
.16 bulgur wheat, *⅓ cup dry*
.15 whole wheat bread,
         2 slices

"morale vitamin"—mild deficiencies reduce stamina, causing depression, irritability, and inability to concentrate. If the deficiency goes uncorrected, fatigue, lack of appetite, muscle cramps, weight loss, and constipation set in. The end result of prolonged thiamin deficiency is beriberi, where the feet and legs grow stiff and painful and become numb and tingling. Ultimately the leg muscles atrophy and paralysis sets in.

Beriberi has been prevalent in the Orient since the nineteenth century, when polished white rice brought in by Western traders replaced the whole-grain rice with its thiamin-rich hull that was the staple in the traditional diet. In the West, too, thiamin deficiency is associated with refined carbohydrate foods, which increase the body's need for thiamin without contributing any of the vitamin themselves. In the United States, frank deficiencies have been greatly reduced by the enrichment of white flours and refined cereals, but the real problem is posed by the purest, most thoroughly refined carbohydrates in our national diet: alcohol and sugar. These "foods" not only do not supply any thiamin; they crowd out other sources of thiamin in the diet by satisfying the appetite with empty calories alone. Thiamin deficiency symptoms, in fact, are not uncommon in alcoholics, though they often go unrecognized in the midst of many other medical problems. A diet strong in whole-grain products and light on refined carbohydrates, however, should have no trouble in providing for daily thiamin needs.

Riboflavin
VITAMIN B-2

WATER-SOLUBLE

SOURCES
Adult RDA is 1.1–1.6 mg

.61 cottage cheese, *1 cup*
.51 low-fat milk, *1 cup*
.44 yogurt, low-fat, *1 cup*
.41 whole milk, *1 cup*

Riboflavin carries hydrogen through many steps in the metabolism of carbohydrate, fat, and protein as a component of several different enzymes, until the hydrogen finally unites with oxygen to form the byproduct of water. Thus riboflavin is necessary for energy release, protein synthesis, and many other reactions promoting the body's growth and repair. Deficiency usually goes along with other B-vitamin deficiencies, and shows a wide variety of symptoms because of riboflavin's wide distribution in the body. The most characteristic symptom is cracking and soreness at the corners of the mouth, a condition called cheilosis. Other symptoms include a purple color to the tongue, swollen membranes in the mouth and throat, and eyes that are irritable, watery, and bloodshot. A scaly, greasy rash appears on the face, and normal growth may be interrupted in children.

For most vegetarians, as for most Americans in general, milk is the primary source of riboflavin; so if you're a vegan, relying on plant foods alone, make sure you know where you're getting your riboflavin from. Leafy green vegetables, beans, and nutritional yeast are good sources of this vitamin.

Since riboflavin is easily destroyed by light, milk and milk products should not be stored in clear glass containers except in places that are usually dark, like the inside of a refrigerator. (Some states require milk to be sold in amber milk bottles.) Milk left in direct sunlight for two hours can lose 50 to 70 percent of its riboflavin.

.40 torula yeast, *1 tablespoon*
.38 collard greens, *1 c. cooked*
.36 broccoli, cooked, *1 stalk*
.34 brewer's yeast, *1 tbsp.*
.32 mushrooms, *1 cup cut*
.29 camembert cheese,
       1⅓ ounce wedge
.29 okra, *1 cup cooked*
.27 butternut squash, *1 c. baked*
.26 almond meal, *¼ cup*
.26 asparagus, *1 cup cooked*
.26 cheddar cheese, *2 ounces*
.26 sorrel, *1 cup cooked*
.25 spinach, *1 cup cooked*
.23 avocado, *½ medium*
.22 beet greens, *1 cup cooked*
.22 brussels sprouts, *1 c. ckd.*
.22 millet, *¼ cup dry*
.20 wheat germ, *¼ cup*
.19 chard, *1 cup cooked*
.18 split peas, green, *1 c. ckd.*
.18 pinto beans, *1 cup cooked*

Niacin

NICOTINIC ACID; NICOTINAMIDE; NIACINAMIDE

Niacin, a B vitamin, is essential to virtually every biochemical pathway in the metabolism of carbohydrate, fat, and protein for energy. If it is lacking, the cells' energy reactions are completely blocked, which may result in tissue damage throughout the body. The skin, digestive tract, and nervous tissues particularly suffer from lack of niacin. Outright deficiency results in pellagra, the "disease of the four Ds"—dermatitis, diarrhea, dementia, and death—characterized by a rough, red, symmetrical rash on the face and hands. Subclinical deficiencies, now more common in the United States than outright pellagra, are marked by nervous irritability, headaches, insomnia, digestive disorders, and a swollen, sore, red tongue. In children, weakness and failure to grow properly may be seen as well.

Pellagra has been uncommon in the United States now for some years, but at the turn of the century it was a serious problem in the South. At that time the diet of the poor depended heavily on cornmeal and salt pork, both very poor sources of

WATER-SOLUBLE

SOURCES
Niacin equivalent in milligrams (niacin content in mg plus 1 mg of niacin / 60 mg of tryptophan) Adult RDA *is 13–18 mg*

15.6 tofu, *4 ounce piece*
11.5 soybeans, *½ cup dry*
 8.5 rice polishings, *¼ cup*
 8.0 cottage cheese, *1 cup*
 7.3 bulgur wheat, *¾ cup dry*
 7.2 peas, *½ cup dry*
 6.0 collard greens, *½ lb. raw*
 5.8 navy beans, *½ cup dry*
 5.6 mung beans, *½ cup dry*
 5.6 peas, fresh, *1 cup*
 5.5 pinto beans, *½ cup dry*
 5.5 kidney beans, *½ cup dry*
 5.3 lentils, *½ cup dry*
 4.9 black-eyed peas, *½ c. dry*

4.8 garbanzos, *½ cup dry*
4.8 lima beans, *½ cup dry*
4.8 wheat berries, *⅓ c. dry*
4.7 green limas, *1 cup raw*
4.5 buckwheat, *⅓ cup dry*
4.5 oatmeal, *¾ cup dry*
4.4 torula yeast, *1 tablespoon*
4.0 avocado, *½ medium*
4.0 peanuts, *2 tablespoons*
3.9 brewer's yeast, *1 tbsp.*
3.7 rice, brown, *⅓ cup dry*
3.4 peanut butter, *1 tbsp.*
3.2 wheat bran, *¼ cup*
3.2 kale, *¼ pound raw*
3.0 egg, *1 large*
3.0 mushrooms, raw, *3 large*
3.0 mango, *1 medium*
2.8 potato, raw, *1 cup diced*
2.8 spinach, *½ pound raw*
2.7 rye berries, *⅓ cup dry*
2.6 dates, *10 medium*
2.5 millet, *¼ cup dry*
2.5 brussels sprouts, *8 raw*
2.3 broccoli, raw, *1 stalk*
2.1 wheat germ, *¼ cup*
2.1 milk, *1 cup*
2.0 sesame seeds, *2 tbsp.*
2.0 sunflower seeds, *2 tbsp.*
1.9 asparagus, raw,
    5 to 6 spears
1.6 cantaloupe, *½ melon*
1.5 cheddar cheese, *1 ounce*
1.4 summer squash, raw,
    1 cup diced
1.4 banana, *large*
1.4 guava, *medium*
1.2 cornmeal, unbolted,
    ⅓ cup dry

niacin. The traditional corn-based diets of many parts of Latin America, too, are notorious for causing pellagra even today. Corn-based diets like these are characteristically deficient not only in niacin but in riboflavin, thiamin, and other B vitamins. They are also severely imbalanced in their amino acid pattern and, in particular, extremely low in the limiting amino acid tryptophan, which the body normally converts into niacin. Since corn is so readily pellagra-producing, it is a poor food to base a limited diet on unless other foods like legumes can be included to make up its deficiencies.

Because tryptophan is converted into niacin in the body, the amount of tryptophan in the diet greatly influences its "niacin equivalent" value. For every 60 milligrams of tryptophan eaten, 1 milligram of niacin will be formed. One quart of milk, for example, contains only 1 milligram of niacin but 480 milligrams of tryptophan, enough to make 8 milligrams of niacin; so its total niacin equivalent is 9 milligrams. You can figure the niacin equivalent of your diet by dividing the milligrams of tryptophan by 60. Where figures for tryptophan are lacking, since most protein in a mixed diet (including milk and eggs) averages about 1.2 percent tryptophan, you may count on about 1 milligram of niacin for every 5 grams of protein in your diet—1 milligram for every 6 grams of protein if you're a vegan.

The amount of niacin we need daily is difficult to determine for a number of reasons. First is the variation in the amount of niacin that a person may be getting from tryptophan. Second, some of the niacin that is found in grains is bound up chemically so as to be unavailable to the body. (In Mexico and some parts of Latin America, the traditional way of grinding corn with lime water releases much of its niacin again, and in these areas pellagra is usually absent.) Third, some intestinal bacteria are able to synthesize niacin to a greater or lesser degree according to variations in the individual diet. (A vegetarian diet is more favorable for such synthesis than some meat diets.[9]) To allow for such wide variations, the RDA is set generously above the minimum.

Vitamin B-6

PYRIDOXINE

Vitamin B-6 plays many important roles in the body, but it particularly stars in protein metabolism. It is required for the synthesis of nonessential amino acids and for converting certain amino acids to hormones or other protein-containing regulators—including the synthesis of niacin from tryptophan. B-6 is also essential for burning protein for energy and for converting glycogen to glucose to provide energy for muscle tissues. It is required for the production of red blood cells and the proper functioning of nervous tissue, and may help in the metabolism of polyunsaturated fatty acids.

Anemia and nervous disorders are characteristic of too little B-6, and some of the symptoms—a greasy rash around the eyes, cheilosis at the corners of the mouth, and a sore mouth with a red, sore tongue—are similar to those of niacin and riboflavin deficiency. Dizziness, nausea, vomiting, weight loss, irritability, confusion, anemia, kidney stones, and convulsions may follow, but are rarely seen isolated from other vitamin deficiencies.

Because B-6 is essential in so many ways to protein metabolism, the requirement for it has been set according to protein intake. The precise amount required is still uncertain—adequate data are simply not yet available—but the B-6 content of many normal American diets may be marginal or even lower than what is necessary for human well-being. One reason for this is that food processing—specifically, milling and heat—can drastically reduce a food's B-6 content. About 75 percent of the vitamin B-6 in wheat is lost during the milling of white flour and is not replaced by enrichment. Other processed or refined foods often contain less than half of the B-6 that was present in their natural state. Vitamin B-6, in fact, was proved essential (as recently as 1951) by the discovery that babies fed entirely on a particular formula, which had been sterilized at a heat high enough to destroy most of its vitamin B-6, became irritable and convulsive.

The second reason for the present concern over B-6 in the

WATER-SOLUBLE

SOURCES
Adult RDA is 2.0 mg

.8 rice bran, ¼ *cup*
.8 rice polishings, ¼ *cup*
.85 soybeans, ½ *cup dry*
.68 kale, ½ *pound raw*
.64 spinach, ½ *pound raw*
.61 banana, *medium*
.57 buckwheat flour, *1 cup*
.57 navy beans, ½ *cup dry*
.57 lentils, ½ *cup dry*
.54 garbanzo beans, ½ *cup dry*
.52 lima beans, ½ *cup dry*
.50 pinto beans, ½ *cup dry*
.48 black-eyed peas, ½ *c. dry*
.46 avocado, ½ *medium*
.41 whole wheat flour, *1 cup*
.38 potato, raw, *1 cup diced*
.38 rye flour, dark, *1 cup*
.35 raisins, *1 cup*
.34 rice, brown, ⅓ *cup dry*
.30 broccoli, raw, *1 stalk*
.30 asparagus, raw,
    12 to 14 spears
.30 wheat germ, ¼ *cup*
.26 brussels sprouts, *8 raw*
.24 torula yeast, *1 tablespoon*
.24 lima beans, green, frozen,
    1 cup
.24 beet greens, ½ *pound raw*
.23 cantaloupe, ½ *melon*
.23 green peas, *1 cup raw*
.22 sunflower seeds, *2 tbsp.*
.22 sweet potato, raw, *1 small*
.21 cauliflowerets, *1 cup raw*
.20 brewer's yeast, *1 tbsp.*
.20 leeks, *3 to 4 raw*

American diet is that certain conditions may elevate the normal need for this vitamin. Steroid contraceptive pills, a dramatically important instance, increase the need for vitamin B-6 well beyond what could possibly be supplied by diet alone. Alcoholism also increases the requirement, as may old age and certain drugs. A mixed diet strong in whole grains, however, should be able to meet all normal requirements for vitamin B-6 easily.

Vitamin B-12

COBALAMIN

WATER-SOLUBLE

SOURCES
Adult RDA is 3.0 µg

1.2	cottage cheese, *½ cup packed*
1.0	milk, whole or skim, *1 cup*
1.0	egg, *large*
.95	dried skim milk, regular, *¼ cup*
.54	buttermilk, *1 cup*
.50	Swiss cheese, *1 ounce*
.50	edam cheese, *1 ounce*
.49	camembert cheese, *1⅓ ounce wedge*
.39	bleu cheese, *1 ounce*
.28	cheddar cheese, *1 ounce*
.28	brick cheese, *1 ounce*
.28	mozzarella cheese, *1 ounce*
.28	whey, fluid, *7 tbsp.*
.27	yogurt, *1 cup*
.06	cream cheese, *1 ounce*
.04	cream, light, *1 tablespoon*

Vitamin B-12 deserves special attention in a book like this, for it is the one nutrient which an all-plant or vegan diet does not naturally include. Such a diet will eventually pose a serious threat if it is not supplemented with vitamin B-12, because all the B-12 available to man comes from nonplant sources—ultimately bacteria and fungi. Plants have no need for vitamin B-12—it is the one vitamin they cannot synthesize—so their root nodules absorb only minute quantities from bacteria in the soil. Animals, however, take in B-12 directly from the soil as well as from animal feeds, and all except man have microorganisms in their intestines which can synthesize the B-12 they need. Animal products, consequently, are the only natural foods capable of filling human needs. Even yeast, which is an excellent source of the other B vitamins, contains no B-12 unless it is grown on media rich in that vitamin. In a world which will be relying increasingly on plant foods, vitamin B-12 may well prove to be a critical nutrient.

The metabolic functions of B-12 are not entirely understood, but it is essential for the functioning of most body cells. Like folacin, it is most important for its role in the synthesis of nucleic acids like DNA and RNA, the materials in the nucleus of every cell which enable the cell to divide. When cells are deficient in B-12, certain compounds along the pathway leading to DNA and RNA cannot be synthesized, making it impossible for cells to divide properly. This shows up first in tissues which multiply rapidly, especially the bone marrow, which produces red blood cells. In B-12 deficiency, as in folacin deficiency, the marrow begins to produce *megaloblasts*, immature red blood cells that are abnormally large, too few in number, and incompletely developed, resulting in the severe physical weakness of megaloblastic anemia. Disturbances of the alimentary canal, another tissue where cell turnover is high, include a sore, glossy tongue, indigestion, abdominal pain, and constipation or diarrhea. These symptoms, which are the first to show, are characteristic of folacin deficiency as well, or may even be due to other causes. They are important, however, as first warning signals of the most severe damage that prolonged lack of B-12 can inflict—damage to the central nervous system. Nervous tissue, myelin specifically, deteriorates with lack of B-12. Ultimately deterioration affects the spinal cord itself. The first signs of damage are a characteristic sore back, numbness and tingling in the feet, and diminished vibration and position sense. Then follow unsteadiness, poor memory, confusion, moodiness, delusions, overt psychosis, and eventually death.

B-12 deficiency can arise in two ways: either from lack of enough B-12 in the diet (unlikely except for vegans) or from malabsorption of dietary B-12. The latter case, a disorder which develops in later life and is probably genetic in origin, results in a serious illness called pernicious anemia, which can only be treated by injection of B-12 for the rest of one's life. Dietary deficiency, on the other hand, is cured simply by adding B-12 to the diet. The anemia of either type of disorder clears up immediately with added B-12, but the nervous system takes considerable time to repair itself.

One of the long-term puzzles in the study of B-12 was the fact that dietary deficiencies of this vitamin do not show up even in pure vegans for five to ten years. It appears now that the body conserves B-12 and can store enough of it to last two or three years or even longer. When the vitamin passes out of the body in bile salts, it can be reabsorbed in the intestine and recycled, so that very little actually leaves the body.

Another puzzle was the fact that vegans with an otherwise nourishing, varied diet show only the neurological signs of B-12 deficiency, not the anemia. The reason seems to be the close relationship between B-12 and folacin: abundant folacin in the diet can retard the damage to blood cells which would normally occur with lack of B-12. The average vegetarian diet has enough folacin for this "sparing" effect to take place. Unfortunately, the neurological deterioration of B-12 deficiency continues even without anemia, and often goes undetected until it has grown fairly severe.

The joint recommendation for vitamin B-12 given by the Food and Agriculture Organization and the World Health Organization of the United Nations is 2 micrograms a day, an amount that is supplied by two glasses of milk or a glass of milk and an egg. This amount leaves a generous margin of safety, since the minimum daily requirement is quite small—a daily consumption in food of 0.1 microgram will keep a *normal, healthy* person from developing deficiency symptoms.[10] People with digestive or other physiological problems may not get by on so little, and pregnant women have a special, additional need which brings their daily recommended allowance to 3 micrograms.

Please don't court a B-12 deficiency. Vegan friends have asked us to point out that commercial B-12 supplements are not taken from liver, as is often believed; bacterial cultures can provide B-12 quite inexpensively without cost to life. Some vegans prefer to seek out the specially grown nutritional yeasts, but these can be expensive. We have given suggestions for the vegan's dietary supplementation in the chapter on the Four Food Groups.

As you can see from the list in the margin (p. 410), most milk products, except butter, are good sources of B-12. Yogurt is fair. B-12 is destroyed by heat and light, which can reduce its presence in milk. Up to 10 percent is lost during pasteurization, and as much as 30 percent if milk is boiled for two to five minutes—more, of course, if it is boiled longer.[11]

Folacin

FOLIC ACID (PGA); TETRAHYDROFOLIC ACID

Folacin, one of the most commonly marginal vitamins in the average American diet, is not a single substance, but an important group of compounds in the B complex family. The name is derived from the Latin word for foliage or leaf (*fo-lium*) because folacin is widely found in green, leafy plants. However, like other micronutrients involved in protein utilization or synthesis—for example, vitamin B-6, vitamin B-12, and zinc—it generally accompanies protein in whole foods.

Like vitamin B-12, folacin is essential for the formation of nucleic acids like DNA and RNA in the cell nuclei, so the cell cannot divide properly to make new cells without it. Synthesis and breakdown of amino acids, also necessary for cell replication, require folacin as well. So folacin deficiency shows up first in parts of the body where cell turnover is greatest, especially the bone marrow which produces red blood cells. The primary deficiency symptom is an anemia called megaloblastic or macrocytic anemia, also found in B-12 deficiency, in which the immature red blood cells or megaloblasts fail to develop properly: they are fewer, larger, and carry less oxygen than normal red blood cells. The digestive tract, whose cells are also rapidly replaced by new cells, is also affected, resulting in a smooth, red tongue and diarrhea.

Folacin deficiency is particularly likely to show up during pregnancy, for the baby in the womb requires folacin to grow and a mother on an average diet may well be getting only marginal amounts. As many as one in three pregnant women in the world may have folacin deficiencies. Anemia in pregnancy, though, may have other causes. Only anemias due to folacin deficiency will benefit from treatment with extra folacin in pills—so if you suspect you're anemic, see your doctor; he can examine the oxygen-carrying cells in your blood to see what may be wrong with them.

A deficiency of vitamin B-12 also results in an anemia which will respond to folacin supplementation,[12] but this only masks the first warning signals of a B-12 deficiency. For this reason, the amount of folacin that can be legally added to a single vitamin pill has been restricted to 0.1 milligram. In synthetic form, this amount has about four times the activity of folacin in food, making it equivalent to the adult RDA.

There are many different compounds found in food with different degrees of folacin activity, so it has been difficult for scientists to measure the folacin activity of foods. Research on

FOLACIN CONTENT OF FOODS

Values next to food names give total folate in micrograms (μg).
Adult RDA is 400 μg.

LEGUMES, MATURE
125 garbanzos, *½ cup dry*
122 kidney beans, *½ cup dry*
102 lima beans, *½ cup dry*
33 peas, *½ cup dry*
132 white beans, *½ cup dry*
236 soybeans, *½ cup dry*
298 soy flour, *1 cup stirred*

VEGETABLES
64 asparagus, *5 to 6 spears*
40 beans: wax, *1 cup pieces*
44   green, *1 cup pieces*
93 beets, *2 medium*
72 broccoli, *1 medium stalk*
97 brussels sprouts, *3 large*
69 cabbage, *1 cup shredded*
15 carrot, *1 medium*
31 cauliflowerets, *1 cup*
5 celery, *1 med. outer stalk*
18 corn, *1 medium ear*
27 cucumber, *1 small*
13 eggplant, *2 slices*
20 endive, *1 cup cut*
102 lettuce, romaine, *1 cup cut*
16 mushrooms, *3 lrg. or 7 sm.*
27 onion: Spanish,
     1 cup chopped
2   green, bulb,
     1 tablespoon chopped
14 pepper: green, *1 med. pod*
38   red, *1 medium pod*
21 potato, fresh, *1 medium*
20   after storage, *1 medium*
11 radishes, *10 medium*
463 spinach, *½ pound*
31 squash, winter, *3½ oz.*
84 sweet potato, *1 medium*
7 tomato, *1 medium*
26 turnip, *1 cup diced*

FRUITS
10 apple, *1 medium*
4 apricots, *¼ c. dried halves*
41 avocado, *½ medium*
36 banana, *1 medium*
9 blueberries, *1 cup*
49 cantaloupe, *1 cup diced*
6 cherries, *10*
17 dates, *10 medium*
3 figs, *2 small dried*
10 grapes: blue, *1 cup*
4   red, *1 cup*
6 grape juice, *1 cup*
15 grapefruit, white, *½ med.*
13   pink, *½ medium*
52   juice, *1 cup*
5 lemon, *1 medium*
3 lime, *1 medium*
7 nectarine, *1 medium*
60 orange, *1 medium*
164 orange juice, fresh, *1 cup*
3 peach, *1 medium*
19 pear, *1 medium*
16 pineapple, *1 cup diced*
1 plum, *1 yellow*
2 prunes, *5 large*
1 raisins, *¼ cup*
24 strawberries, *1 cup*
18 tangerine, *1 medium*
5 watermelon, *1 cup diced*

GRAINS & GRAIN PRODUCTS
10 barley, pot, *¼ cup dry*
11 bread: white, *1 slice*
15   whole wheat, *1 slice*
26   whole wheat, homemade,
     1 slice
7   rye, dark, *1 slice*
30 cornmeal, *1 cup dry*
31 flour: all-purpose, *1 c. sifted*

GRAINS *(cont.)*:
80   whole wheat, *1 c. stirred*
99   rye, dark, *1 cup*
12 macaroni, *¼ pound dry*
34 oatmeal, quick, *¾ cup dry*
37 rice, long-grain, *¼ c. dry*
15 spaghetti, *¼ pound dry*
28 wheat, cracked, *⅓ c. dry*
17 wheat bran, *¼ cup*
52 wheat germ, *¼ cup*

NUTS
14 almonds, *15*
19 cashews, *14 large*
8 coconut, fresh, shredded,
     ¼ cup
10 filberts (hazelnuts), *10*
13 peanut butter, *1 tbsp.*
10 peanuts, *1 tbsp. chopped*
4 pecans, *12 halves*
9 pistachios, *30*
10 walnuts, *8 large halves*

DAIRY PRODUCTS & EGGS
6 cheddar cheese, mild, *1 oz.*
3 egg white, *1 large*
50 egg yolk, hard-cooked, *1 lrg*
37 milk, whole, *1 cup*
27 yogurt, *1 cup*

MISCELLANEOUS
3 molasses, light, *1 tbsp.*
286 yeast: active dry, *1 tbsp.*
308   brewer's, *1 tablespoon*
240   torula, *1 tablespoon*

Adapted from Butterfield &
Calloway 1972, Hoppner et al.
1972, and Dong & Oace 1973.

this subject is still active. To check your diet, make sure that it includes the richest sources of this vitamin, dark green leaves. Beans, green vegetables, nuts, fresh oranges, and whole wheat products are good too. Poor sources are meat (except liver), eggs, root vegetables, most fruits, milled cereal products, dried milks, sugar, and fat. So it is fairly easy for a diet to be deficient in folacin, especially when it includes processed foods.

Keep in mind that normal cooking temperatures can destroy up to 65 percent of the folacin in vegetables, and three days' storage at room temperature can destroy 70 percent. Your best source is a dark green like romaine lettuce picked right out of the garden.

Pantothenic Acid

Pantothenic acid is a part of Coenzyme A, one of the most important substances in human metabolism, since it sits at the "crossroads of metabolism" where food can either be broken down further to release energy or built up again into more complicated compounds.

Panto signifies "everywhere," for pantothenic acid is found in every cell of living tissues. It is, therefore, found in all whole, natural foods, though it is more concentrated in the foods rich in the other B vitamins, like whole grains and legumes. Even otherwise inadequate diets are likely to contain just enough pantothenic acid, and its deficiency is probably seen only in multiple nutritional deficiencies like those which accompany alcoholism. Milling and freezing foods both destroy a substantial portion of their pantothenic acid content, lowering the overall content of many people's diets.

Biotin

Biotin is a lesser-known B vitamin which mostly works in connection with the amino acid lysine in transporting carbon dioxide to other organic compounds—reactions which are closely involved with those of pantothenic acid. It is also required for releasing energy from glucose and for the synthesis of

WATER-SOLUBLE

SOURCES
5–10 mg/day is probably adequate for most people.

1.8	broccoli, raw, *1 stalk*
1.8	soybeans, *½ cup dry*
1.6	rice polishings, *¼ cup*
1.3	lentils, *½ cup dry*
1.2	brewer's yeast, *1 tbsp.*
1.2	peas, fresh, *1 cup*
1.1	brussels sprouts, *8 raw*
1.0	wheat berries, *⅓ cup dry*
.90	oatmeal, *¾ cup dry*
.83	whole milk, *1 cup*
.82	sweet potato, raw, *1 small*
.75	egg yolk, *large*
.68	cantaloupe, *½ melon*
.62	dates, *10 medium*
.51	strawberries, *1 cup*

WATER-SOLUBLE

glycogen, fatty acids, certain amino acids, and nucleic acids like DNA. It is synthesized by intestinal bacteria in amounts close to what we require, so food easily makes up the difference. The only threat of deficiency comes from a protein substance called avidin, found in raw egg whites, which binds up biotin in the intestine. Even brief cooking, however, destroys avidin. A diet would have to consist mostly of raw egg whites, eight to ten a day, to produce deficiency in this way—so an occasional eggnog poses no threat.

Choline

Choline is a B vitamin found in phospholipids, phosphorus-containing fatlike substances like lecithin which are essential to the transport and metabolism of fats in the body. Though it is essential in the body, choline has not yet been shown to be essential in the human diet. However, since it *is* essential for young animals, especially when they are on a low protein diet, it may prove to be a dietary essential for human beings as well. It is widely found in food and can be synthesized in the body with the help of vitamin B-12, folacin, and the amino acid methionine, so deficiency seems unlikely, except perhaps in young children on extremely low protein, highly refined diets.

SOURCE REFERENCES

1. National Research Council, Food and Nutrition Board, *Recommended dietary allowances,* 8th rev. ed. (Washington, National Academy of Sciences, 1974), p. 54.

2. H. Jeghers and H. Marraro, Hypervitaminosis A: Its broadening spectrum, *American Journal of Clinical Nutrition* 6:335–339, 1958.

3. M. S. Rodriguez and M. I. Irwin, A conspectus of research on vitamin A requirements of man, *Journal of Nutrition* 102:909–968, 1972.

4. Lloyd J. Filer, Jr., Excessive intakes and imbalance of vitamins and minerals, in *Nutrients in processed foods, vol. 1: Vitamins, minerals* (Acton, Mass., Publishing Sciences Group, 1974), p. 25.

5. W. A. Krehl, Nutrition and diseases of the skin, in *Modern nutrition in health and disease: Dietotherapy,* 5th ed., ed. Robert S. Goodhart and Maurice E. Shils (Philadelphia, Lea & Febiger, 1973), p. 949.

6. R. E. Scully, J. J. Galdabini, and B. U. McNeely, Case records of the Massachusetts General Hospital, Case 43-1975, *New England Journal of Medicine* 293:980, 1975.

7. M. K. Horwitt, Vitamin E, in *Modern nutrition in health and disease,* p. 184.

8. J. G. Bieri and R. P. Evarts, Gamma-tocopherol metabolism, biological activity and significance in human vitamin E nutrition, *American Journal of Clinical Nutrition* 27:980–986, 1974.

9. L. Jean Bogert, George M. Briggs, and Doris H. Calloway, *Nutrition and physical fitness,* 9th ed. (Philadelphia, Saunders, 1973), p. 138.

10. Victor Herbert, Folic acid and vitamin B-12, in *Modern nutrition in health and disease,* p. 232.

11. Joint FAO/WHO Expert Group on Requirements of Ascorbic Acid, Vitamin D, Vitamin B-12, Folate, and Iron, *Requirements of ascorbic acid, vitamin D, vitamin B-12, folate, and iron,* FAO Nutrition Meetings Report Series, no. 47, WHO Technical Report Series, no. 452 (Rome, Food and Agriculture Organization of the United Nations, 1970), p. 41.

12. Victor Herbert, Drugs effective in megaloblastic anemias: Vitamin B-12 and folic acid, in *The pharmacological basis of therapeutics,* 5th ed., ed. Louis S. Goodman and Alfred Gilman (New York, Macmillan, 1975), p. 1327.

Minerals

Of the more than one hundred elements found in nature, four make up a full 96 percent of the body's weight: oxygen, carbon, hydrogen, and nitrogen. The elements composing the remaining 4 percent are collectively referred to as minerals.

Like vitamins, minerals play much more important roles in the body than the quantities of each might indicate. In combination with organic compounds, they are found as constituents of vitamins, enzymes, and hormones, as well as of cells and especially of the hard tissues of the body like bones and teeth. Vitamin B-12, for example, contains the mineral cobalt, which is why it is also called cobalamin. But minerals are also found in the body in inorganic forms, either in combination with each other or as free atoms. In combination with each other, they form neutral salts; but when these salts are dissolved, as in the water of the body's fluids, they break up into ions, the uncombined atoms of their elements. Depending on the element, ions carry positive or negative electrical charges of different strengths: sodium and potassium ions, for example, are positively charged, while chloride and fluoride ions are negative. When ions are dissolved in water their solutions will conduct electricity, giving them the name "electrolytes." Further, because similarly charged particles repel each other and oppositely charged particles attract, mineral ions can interact with each other in several fascinating ways, making possible functions like the contraction and relaxation of muscles and the transmission of impulses through the nerves.

In addition to its charge, positive or negative, the uniqueness of a mineral is determined by its atomic weight and the arrangement of its electrons. Some minerals having similar characteristics, such as in the arrangement of their electrons, can take the place of each other in metabolic processes. Fluoride, for example, is similar to an ion which normally enters tooth enamel to make it hard, and can take the place of that ion to make the enamel even harder. Almost as familiar, unfortunately, is the example of strontium 90, a radioactive by-product of atomic explosions which can double for calcium in calcium-rich foods like milk. Eventually, like calcium, it is deposited in the bones, where it becomes a reservoir of destructive radiation.

Minerals are so closely integrated into the body that their turnover is much slower than that of other nutrients like protein and vitamins. Mineral deficiencies therefore take longer to show up. Six minerals are required in larger quantities than the others, so they are sometimes called "macrominerals": sodium, potassium, chloride, calcium, phosphorus, and magnesium, all of which are required in the diet in amounts of 100 milligrams per day or more. The others are called "trace minerals," and include the fourteen minerals which we know to be required by the body in amounts from 100 milligrams per day down to just a few micrograms. To get an idea of these quantities, remember that 100 *grams* is the approximate weight of one small serving of food like rice or vegetables. The total amount of vitamins needed in a day is about 200 milligrams, which might be the size of a pea or a small pill. A nutrient needed in the microgram range—one thousand times less than a milligram—could be as tiny as a grain of sand.

Other minerals, too, are present in the body—minerals like lead, gold, and mercury, which enter the body in the same way as essential trace minerals, from the soil through the plants we eat. These, however, have not been shown to have any necessary function in the body, and some may be dangerous even in minute quantities. As environmental pollution adds more and more of these elements to the food chain, they may well pose a serious public health hazard. Lead and mercury are all-too-familiar examples.

Sodium, Potassium, and Chloride

The cells of the body, tiny self-contained units which comprise all tissues, are constantly bathed in fluids inside and outside the cell membranes. These membranes are continuously monitoring two-way traffic as the blood circulating outside the cells brings nutrients, oxygen, and water to pass into each cell and picks up the waste products which pass out. The movement of these fluids in and out of the cells is largely determined by the relative concentration of salts in the fluids on either side of the membranes. Outside the cell, the positive ion sodium and the negative ion chloride play the critical roles, balanced inside the cell primarily by the positive ion potassium. These ions also are essential for maintaining body fluids at a very slightly alkaline level—a function known as acid-base balance.

Fluid balance and acid-base balance involve highly complicated mechanisms, wonderfully precise but too involved to enter into here in any detail. Both, however, deserve some general discussion in relation to specific questions about diet.

FLUID BALANCE AND SALT

Sodium is the key element in regulating fluid balance. The amount of this mineral circulating in the blood is kept closely monitored by the kidney, which senses the concentration of sodium in the blood and retains or excretes water in the body to maintain the blood at the proper concentration as necessary. This mechanism is extremely responsive and flexible, enabling the body to conserve sodium efficiently when sodium in the diet is low and to get rid of excess quantities through the urine when it is high. However, sodium balance is not maintained without some cost, and this cost may be significant if sodium intake is excessive over a long period of time. Adding water to the bloodstream to dilute high concentrations of sodium increases both the volume of blood in the blood vessels and the amount of fluid flowing into body tissues. The tiny arteries carrying blood to the tissues then constrict in an attempt to keep the cells from being oversupplied. This peripheral constriction causes increased pressure in the larger vascular system, which is why excessive sodium intake over a long period

SODIUM IN COMMON FOODS
(in milligrams)

2000 salt, *1 teaspoon*
1300 soy sauce, *1 tablespoon*
 560 cottage cheese, *1 cup*
 520 oatmeal, cooked and
   salted, *1 cup*
 500 corn, *1 cup canned*
 500 miso, *1 tablespoon*
 500 pizza, *12" dm., ⅙*
 500 homemade soup,
   salted, *1 cup*
 490 tomato juice, *1 c. canned*
 350 dry beans, cooked &
   salted, *½ cup*
 320 buttermilk, *1 cup*
 320 American cheese, *1 oz.*
 240 sweet roll, *4" diameter*
 200 potato chips, *10*
 200 cheddar cheese, *1 ounce*
 200 salad dressing, *1 tbsp.*

of time can lead to or aggravate hypertension (high blood pressure).

Table salt, of course—sodium chloride—is the primary villain in this process. The body *can* maintain sodium balance over a wide range of salt intake, but it seems clear that very little if any needs to be *added* to foods for any nutritional reason. A diet of basic foods with no salt added will contain 2 to 3 grams of sodium, about the equivalent of a teaspoonful of table salt. (A teaspoon of salt contains approximately 2 grams of sodium and 3 grams of chloride, and weighs altogether 5 grams.) This is about five times the amount of sodium the body needs per day to replace what it excretes under normal circumstances. For Americans, however, the average daily intake of sodium is equivalent to what is found in 2 to 3 teaspoonfuls of table salt, or 10 to 15 grams. Some of this sodium comes from milk, eggs, certain vegetables, and meat, all of which are naturally more salty than other foods. Much more significant, however, is the salt which has been added commercially to bread, butter, cheese, margarine, and thousands of processed "convenience" food products. In addition is the salt we shake on foods ourselves, either in cooking or at the table.

Sodium, in fact, deserves to be considered a potentially dangerous food additive because of the high levels of it we consume today in commercial food products, especially salty snack foods like pretzels and potato chips. Sodium chloride is not even the sole offender: other sodium salts like monosodium glutamate (MSG) and sodium bicarbonate (baking soda) contribute to high sodium intake too. So when you are reading labels, be aware that *any* of the words *sodium, Na, soda,* or *salt* means a potential increase in your body's sodium load.

The possible relationship between salt and blood pressure deserves the attention of most Americans, even though some individuals are undoubtedly more susceptible to salt's effects than others. In general, populations in which salt is eaten in large quantities have higher blood pressures than those in which it is not. In one community in northern Japan where the average salt consumption exceeds 25 grams a day, there is an extremely high incidence of hypertension, and the number one

190 green olives, *2*
180 popcorn, salted, *1 cup*
150 peanuts, roasted & salted, *¼ cup*
140 butter or margarine, *1 tablespoon*
130 bread, *1 slice*
120 milk or yogurt, *1 cup*
100 peanut butter, salted, *1 tablespoon*

FOODS LOW IN SODIUM:

whole grains and legumes prepared without salt, nuts (unless commercially salted), most fresh vegetables & fruits

SOURCES OF POTASSIUM

(in milligrams)

1200 butternut squash, *1 cup baked*
1200 lima beans, dry, *1 c. ckd.*
1160 spinach, *1 cup cooked*
1000 black beans, *1 cup cooked*
 970 soybeans, *1 cup cooked*
 940 pinto beans, *1 cup cooked*
 790 navy beans, *1 cup cooked*
 750 acorn squash, *½ baked*
 720 green lima beans, *1 c. ckd.*
 710 papaya, *medium*
 680 cantaloupe, *½ melon*
 650 avocado, *½ medium*
 650 raisins, *½ cup*
 630 kidney beans, *1 c. ckd.*
 600 chard, *1 cup cooked*
 600 prune juice, *1 cup*
 590 parsnips, *1 cup cooked*
 590 split peas, *1 cup cooked*
 580 blackstrap molasses, *1 tablespoon*
 520 dates, *10 medium*
 500 potato, cooked
 500 orange juice, *1 cup*
 490 skim milk powder, *¼ c.*
 480 beet greens, *1 cup*
 440 banana, *medium*
 430 low-fat milk, *1 cup*
 430 kohlrabi, *1 cup cooked*
 420 peas, fresh, *1 cup*
 420 brussels sprouts, *1 c. ckd.*
 410 nectarine, *medium*

cause of death is stroke. Inland Japanese, who eat much less salt, are much less severely affected. Many primitive ethnic groups with very low sodium intakes have very little hypertension.[1] Since low salt diets can reduce the blood pressure of hypertensive people, doctors usually restrict the *sodium* content of such patients' diets anywhere from 0.5 grams to 2 grams a day, amounts which preclude any added salt or any very salty foods. For people with normal blood pressure, salting lightly in cooking and not at all at the table is the best policy.

Of course, there *are* times when our needs for sodium and chloride are increased. Fever and heavy sweating, for example, both cause sodium loss through the skin. Excessive sweat losses (for most people, more than 4 liters a day) can lead to serious shifts of body fluids away from vital places. The first sign of this is muscle cramping, often referred to as "heat cramps"—not to be confused with heat exhaustion or prostration and heat stroke, which have different causes and treatments. Losses from sweating are properly replaced by drinking fluids until thirst is quenched and by adding additional salt to food—up to 7 grams extra a day for heavy work in a hot climate.

Abnormal loss of electrolytes may also occur from the use of medicinal diuretics, which increase water loss from the body by sending sodium and potassium out in the urine so that a lot of body fluid will accompany them. Too much potassium is easily lost in this way, dangerously upsetting the body's electrolyte balance. People taking certain diuretics, therefore, may be given potassium supplementation or encouraged to eat potassium-rich foods.

ACID-BASE BALANCE

Some approaches to diet place a lot of emphasis on acid-base balance within the body. Body cells are unable to function in an excessively acid or alkaline environment. The processes of life, therefore, depend on various buffering systems which absorb excess acid or alkali to keep the body's fluids at the proper balance, just slightly on the alkaline side of neutral. Minerals are an integral part of these processes.

The metabolism of many foods, especially high-protein ones like meat, produces acidic byproducts because of the acidic chloride, phosphorus, and sulfur ions in their protein complexes. Since the end products of energy metabolism are predominately acid wastes, the body's usual problem is to dispose of excess acid. Fruits and vegetables, on the other hand, though sometimes acid to the taste, liberate alkaline byproducts when metabolized, because of the sodium and potassium they contain. Once released from food, alkaline minerals like sodium and potassium commonly react with acids in the body to form neutral salts. So it is easier for the body to maintain a state close to neutrality when acid-producing and alkaline-producing foods approximately balance each other in the diet.

In general, because of its high protein intake, the American diet is predominately acid producing, where a meatless diet is usually alkaline producing or close to neutral. In either case, there is no cause for worry. Since acid-base balance is far too critical a matter to leave to our individual choice of foods, the body has many well-developed buffering systems for absorbing excess acid or alkali. Combining acid and alkaline minerals to form neutral salts is one of these; the salts are then excreted through the kidney. Another mechanism is the excretion of metabolic wastes by carbon dioxide, which is carried from the body via the lungs every time we exhale. The main threat to acid-base balance comes not from the mineral content of the diet but from diseases which upset the body's regulatory mechanisms: respiratory disorders, uncontrolled diabetes, or prolonged vomiting or diarrhea, to name just a few.

Calcium and Phosphorus

Read also the paragraphs on vitamin D, page 398.

Calcium and phosphorus are the most abundant minerals in the body. A full 99 percent of the body's calcium and about 80 percent of its phosphorus are locked up together in the complex compounds which make the bones and teeth hard and strong. These deposits, however, are not static, but are

Spinach, chard, sorrel, beet greens, lambsquarters, parsley, chocolate, rhubarb, and wheat bran are not included since their calcium is poorly utilized, due to their oxalic acid content.

400 skim milk powder, *¼ cup*
360 collard leaves, *1 c. ckd.*
350 low-fat milk, *1 cup*
300 buttermilk, *1 cup*
290 whole milk, *1 cup*
280 blackstrap molasses,
      2 tablespoons
270 sesame seed meal, *¼ cup*
270 yogurt, *1 cup*
270 Parmesan cheese,
      ¼ cup grated
260 Swiss cheese, *1 ounce*
250 bok choy, *1 cup cooked*
230 cottage cheese, *1 cup*
220 edam cheese, *1 ounce*
210 cheddar cheese, *1 ounce*
200 kale, *1 cup cooked*
180 mustard greens, *1 c. ckd.*
160 broccoli, cooked, *1 stalk*
150 okra, cooked, *1 cup slices*
150 tofu, *4 ounce piece*
150 dandelion greens, *1 c. ckd.*
140 Masa Harina, *1 cup dry*
130 soybeans, *1 cup cooked*
120 tortillas, *2*
120 carob flour, *¼ cup*
100 rutabagas, *1 cup cooked*

Other sources of calcium which can be utilized by the body include chalk, limestone, granite, eggshell, sea shells, and hard water.

constantly being mobilized out of the bones into the bloodstream and mineralized back into the bones again in response to the body's needs, for both these minerals play vital roles throughout the rest of the body too. The remaining 1 percent of the calcium is found mostly in the body's fluids, making possible the transmission of nerve impulses and the coagulation of blood. Calcium is also required in the proper balance for muscles like the heart muscle to relax and contract. The remaining 20 percent of the body's phosphorus is distributed throughout the body, a little in every cell, for phosphorus is highly reactive and is involved in all energy-yielding reactions in the body.

The amount of calcium we require is a subject of great interest, for it varies in relation to a number of other factors. Ordinarily, the body maintains a state of balance between the calcium it takes in and the calcium it excretes, by accustoming itself to the amount of calcium it usually gets and then adjusting the amount that it will absorb to meet its daily needs. In parts of the world where diets are usually low in calcium, the body maintains calcium balance by absorbing and conserving the little it gets with a high degree of efficiency. People on such diets are usually shorter than those who get more liberal amounts of calcium in their food, but their bones are equally well formed and just as strong as those of their Western counterparts. On the other hand, in countries like the United States where great quantities of calcium are recommended and consumed, mostly in milk, the body maintains calcium balance by operating at much lower efficiency. In the American diet, only 20 to 40 percent of the calcium eaten is absorbed.

When the body is used to getting such large amounts of calcium daily, it grows accustomed to passing on most of the calcium it takes in. If for any reason it begins to receive a dramatically smaller amount, there will be a period of several weeks or even months before it can readjust its accustomed rate of low absorption to a higher level of efficiency. During this period the body will be in negative calcium balance, drawing on the reserve stores of calcium in the bones to make up its needs even though the amount of calcium in the diet might be quite adequate at a higher rate of absorption.

Other factors than the body's need for calcium and the accustomed level of calcium in the diet affect the absorption and utilization of this mineral. Probably the most important such factor is the amount of vitamin D in the body, which regulates calcium absorption and utilization. Calcium-phosphorus deficiency, which results in soft or brittle bones (rickets in children, osteomalacia in adults) may therefore be due not only to shortages of calcium or phosphorus but also to inadequate vitamin D, even when these minerals are adequate in the diet.

Calcium absorption is also affected by the level of phosphorus in the diet, and is enhanced when these two minerals are supplied in approximately equal amounts. In the absence of other evidence, the recommended dietary allowance for phosphorus has been tentatively set equal to that for calcium for this reason. Commonly, phosphorus is more plentiful in the diet—milk is the one food in which both minerals occur in equal proportions—but wide variations in the ratio can be easily tolerated when there is ample vitamin D.

Equally interesting to vegetarians is the fact that excessive amounts of protein in the diet decrease the efficiency of calcium utilization, especially when calcium intake is low. This is probably a factor in osteoporosis, the brittle-bone condition so prevalent in the aged. Though formerly thought to be attributable to calcium deficiency alone, osteoporosis is now associated not only with inadequate calcium intake but with excessive protein intake also.[2] Calcium absorption is decreased also by excess fat in the diet, which locks up calcium in the intestine into unabsorbable soaps; by foods high in oxalic acid (see page 424), which binds up calcium into insoluble salts; and by large amounts of dietary fiber. Phytic acid, a phosphorus compound which also binds up calcium and other minerals in the intestine, is of enough interest to vegetarians to warrant its own discussion below.

In meeting your need for calcium, then, the entire dietary pattern must be considered. Vitamin D in particular is of critical importance—especially when calcium intake is low or when the need for bone mineralization is greatest, as for growing children, especially adolescents, and pregnant and nursing

SOURCES OF PHOSPHORUS
Adult RDA *is 800 mg*

430 pinto beans, *1 cup cooked*
420 black beans, *1 cup cooked*
370 cottage cheese, *1 cup*
350 rice bran, *¼ cup*
330 garbanzo beans, *1 c. ckd.*
320 soybeans, *1 cup cooked*
320 Masa Harina, *1 cup dry*
300 rice polishings, *¼ cup*
300 skim milk powder, *¼ cup*
290 lima beans, *1 cup cooked*
280 wheat bran, *¼ cup*
280 navy beans, *1 cup cooked*
270 rye berries, *⅓ cup dry*
260 wheat berries, *⅓ cup dry*
260 kidney beans, *1 cup cooked*
230 milk, *1 cup*
230 wheat germ, *¼ cup*
220 yogurt, *1 cup*
210 green lima beans, *1 c. ckd.*
200 pumpkin seeds, *2 tbsp.*
180 buckwheat, *⅓ cup dry*
160 Swiss cheese, *1 ounce*
160 peas, fresh, *1 cup cooked*
150 tofu, *4 ounce piece*
150 corn, *1 cup cooked*
140 sesame seed meal, *¼ cup*
140 almond meal, *¼ cup*
140 nutritional yeast, *1 tbsp.*
140 cheddar cheese, *1 ounce*
110 broccoli, cooked, *1 stalk*
100 collard greens, *1 c. ckd.*
 60 kale, *1 cup cooked*
 60 bok choy, *1 cup cooked*

mothers.* Vegans in particular need to be careful about both calcium and vitamin D, because they do not use milk or other dairy products. For older people, including dairy products in the diet every day is important for keeping their bones well mineralized. The recommended dietary allowance (RDA) is set quite high—800 milligrams for adults—to provide the maximum retainable amount of calcium for bone growth and storage with the low efficiency of absorption associated with high calcium, high protein American diets. Adults who don't eat excessive amounts of protein, however, will probably be able to maintain calcium balance on considerably less calcium than the American-oriented RDA recommendation. Vegans especially will find it more realistic to follow the United Nations agencies' recommendation of 400 to 500 milligrams a day, which has been found to be quite safe in populations whose diets supply considerably less calcium than ours.

PHYTIC ACID

Phosphorus is supplied in abundance by almost any diet, since the distribution of this mineral in food roughly parallels that of protein. To the vegetarian, it is of special concern only in one particular form. A great deal of the phosphorus in the outer portion of whole grains and legumes occurs in phytic acid or "phytate," a highly reactive substance that has the capacity to lock up minerals in the intestine like calcium, zinc, and iron that are needed in the body, forming the insoluble salts which it cannot absorb. Unfortunately, the duodenum, where most of these minerals are normally absorbed, provides a perfect environment for this process. Yet whole populations live on diets which would theoretically produce rickets, osteomalacia, iron deficiency anemia, and zinc deficiencies, but in fact do not. Clearly some compensating processes are at work.

One such mechanism is an enzyme called phy*tase* in the intestine. This enzyme breaks up phytic acid compounds and

*It comes as a surprise to many pregnant women that *adult* teeth begin to form in the womb, and are almost complete by the third year of life even though they have not yet broken through the skin. The strength of adult teeth, therefore, is determined by the availability of calcium very early in life.

thereby gives the body the ability to handle a certain amount of phytate in the diet.[3] Also, the body has an amazing ability to metabolize a nutrient when its supply is limited. This is particularly well documented for calcium. Experiments have shown that adding foods rich in phytic acid to an otherwise normal diet will produce an initial disruption in calcium absorption, but that normal absorption resumes after a short time if the overall calcium intake is adequate.[4] Vitamin D is thought to be crucial to this adaptive capacity, which may explain why people in parts of the world where exposure to sunlight is great can get by on low calcium, high phytate diets.

In cases where mineral deficiencies *have* been induced by phytic acid, other circumstances have contributed as well. Rickets and osteomalacia, for example, were seen in Britain during the Second World War, when the country suddenly switched to whole wheat flour without milk to supply calcium and with very little sunlight for vitamin D. More recently, in the Middle East, mineral deficiencies have been associated with parasitic diseases and diets whose staple is unleavened bread. All these diets contained only marginal amounts of the minerals which became deficient. So phytic acid alone is not likely to bring on mineral deficiencies.

Vegetarians, and especially vegans or anyone seeking to minimize his or her dependence on dairy products, should be aware that their diet is rich in phytic acid and take a simple step to compensate for it. Phytase, the enzyme which splits phytic acid in the intestine, is also present in whole-grain wheat and rye, to a lesser extent in whole-grain barley and buckwheat,[5] and in yeast.[6] During breadmaking, the conditions required for leavening—a medium moisture range and a warm but not hot temperature—activate this enzyme and enable it to break down much of the phytic acid in the grain. So for the vegetarian, leavened bread should be a staple item in a good, mixed diet.

If you like, you can increase the contribution of phytase in your bread by favoring the conditions which activate it. The first step is to let the dough rise two or even three times to allow a longer leavening period. Since phytase favors a slightly acidic environment, you may also include acidic ingredients like molasses, yogurt, sour milk, or fruit juice in the dough. In foggy Denmark, where calcium deficiency has been aggravated by low stores of vitamin D because of inadequate sunlight, these techniques have greatly reduced the phytic acid in the traditional Danish rye bread, and now there's an official government-issued starter for this staple of the Danish diet.

Magnesium

Magnesium has played a central role in the evolution of life. It is abundant in the sea water from which living organisms evolved, and is an essential ingredient of chlorophyll, the compound which enables plants to transform carbon dioxide and water into life-giving oxygen and carbohydrate. Magnesium is found throughout the body, for it is an important activator of enzymes, especially those involved in the transfer of energy. It is required for protein synthesis, the contraction of muscles, and the conduction of nerve impulses. Over half the magnesium in the body is deposited in the bones. Most of the rest is in the soft tissues, but an extremely important fraction is found as ions in the body's fluids.

Magnesium salts are similar in many ways to calcium salts; both are rather insoluble and compete with each other for absorption. Magnesium is lost during refinement, but deficiency is not usually seen in anyone eating basic foods. When it *is* found, it accompanies other deficiencies, as in alcoholism, protein-calorie deficiency, diabetes, or diuretic therapy.

Magnesium follows the distribution of protein and phosphorus in the plant kingdom, with whole grains, nuts, beans, and green leaves being very good sources. The RDA is roughly 50 percent higher than the minimum requirement, giving a wide margin of safety.

Trace Minerals

The story of trace minerals is unfolding in investigative laboratories today just as the mysteries of vitamins were unraveled in the 1930s. Using highly sophisticated equipment and environmental controls, researchers have been able to identify

MAGNESIUM CONTENT OF FOODS

Values next to food names give magnesium content in milligrams.
Adult RDA is 300–350 mg.

LEGUMES, MATURE
173 beans: white, *½ cup dry*
150   red, *½ cup dry*
196 black-eyed peas, *½ cup dry*
76 lentils, *½ cup dry*
162 limas, *½ cup dry*
278 soybeans, *½ cup dry*
173 soybean flour, full-fat, *1 c.*
133 tofu, *2½" × 2¾" × 1"*

GRAINS & GRAIN PRODUCTS
21 barley, pearl, *¼ cup dry*
72   whole-grain, *¼ cup dry*
8 breads: french, *1 slice*
10   rye, light, *1 slice*
23   pumpernickel, dark, *1 sl.*
6   white, *1 slice*
22   whole wheat, *1 slice*
149 buckwheat, whole, *⅓ c. dry*
47   flour, light, *1 cup*
129 cornmeal, bolted, *1 c. dry*
65   degermed, *1 cup dry*
25 macaroni, ckd. tender, *1 c.*
94 millet, *¼ cup dry*
50 oatmeal, *1 cup cooked*
57 rice, brown, *1 cup cooked*
16 rice, white, *1 cup cooked*
64 rye flour, light, *1 cup*
107 wheat berries, *⅓ cup dry*
64 wheat bran, *¼ cup*
69 wheat germ, *¼ cup*
136 whole wheat flour, *1 cup*
29   all-purpose, *1 cup*

NUTS & SEEDS
41 almonds, *15*
34 brazil nuts, *4 medium*
75 cashews, *14 large*
14 coconut, dried, *¼ cup*
28 filberts (hazelnuts), *10*
19 peanuts, *1 tbsp. chopped*
28 peanut butter, *1 tablespoon*
21 pecans, *12 halves*
24 pistachios, *30*
33 sesame seeds, whole, *2 tbsp.*

NUTS & SEEDS *(cont.)*:
7 sunflower seeds, *2 tbsp.*
15 walnuts: black, *4 to 5 halves*
10   English, *4 to 7 halves*

VEGETABLES
20 asparagus, *5 to 6 spears*
35 beans, snap, *1 cup pieces*
27 beets, *2 medium*
241 beet greens, *½ pound*
24 broccoli, *1 medium stalk*
44 brussels sprouts, *3 large*
9 cabbage, *1 cup shredded*
17 carrot, *1 medium*
24 cauliflowerets, *1 cup*
9 celery, *1 outer stalk*
148 chard, Swiss, *½ pound*
129 collards, *½ pound*
26 corn, *1 medium ear*
82 dandelion greens, *½ lb.*
16 eggplant, *½ cup diced*
42 kale, *¼ pound*
6 lettuce, head, *1 c. chopped*
13 mushrooms, *4 large*
61 mustard greens, *½ lb.*
20 onion, *1 cup chopped*
32 parsnip, *½ large*
51 peas, *1 cup*
13 pepper, green, *1 medium*
51 potato, *1 medium*
200 spinach, *½ pound*
21 squash, summer, *1 c. diced*
50 sweet potato, *1 medium*
17 tomato, *1 medium*
26 turnips, *1 cup diced*
132 turnip greens, *½ pound*

FRUITS
13 apple, *1 medium*
10 apple juice, bottled, *1 cup*
13 apricots, *2 to 3 medium*
51 avocado, *½ medium*
39 banana, *1 medium*
43 blackberries, *1 cup*
26 cantaloupe, *1 cup diced*
46 dates, *10 medium*

FRUITS *(cont.)*:
10 figs, fresh, *2 large*
21   dried, *2 small*
17 grapefruit, *½ medium*
30 grape juice, bottled, *1 cup*
5 lemon juice, *¼ cup*
36 mango, *1 medium*
18 nectarine, *1 medium*
14 orange, *1 medium*
27 orange juice, fresh, *1 cup*
10 peach, *1 medium*
20 pineapple, *1 cup diced*
6 plum, *1 large*
20 prunes, *5 cooked*
26 prune juice, bottled, *1 cup*
13 raisins, *¼ cup*
18 strawberries, *1 cup*

DAIRY PRODUCTS & EGGS
13 cheese: cheddar, *1-oz. slice*
2   Parmesan, *1 tbsp. grated*
2 cream, light, *1 tbsp.*
5 egg, whole, *1 large*
3   white of large egg
3   yolk of large egg
19 ice cream, *1 cup*
32 milk, cow's: whole, *1 cup*
34   skim, *1 cup*
34   buttermilk, *1 cup*
43   dry skim, regular, *¼ c.*
24   dry skim, instant, *¼ c.*

MISCELLANEOUS
30 chocolate, sweet, *1 oz.*
21 cocoa, dry, *1 tablespoon*
5 coffee, instant dry, *1 tsp.*
Tr mayonnaise, *1 tbsp.*
2 salad dressing, french,
     1 tablespoon
6 salt, *1 teaspoon*
11 yeast: active, *1 cake*
18   brewer's, *1 tablespoon*
13   torula, *1 tablespoon*

Adapted from Watt & Merrill
1964 (Ag. Handbook no. 8)

Iron
Iodine
Copper
Zinc
Manganese
Cobalt
Molybdenum
Selenium
Chromium
Nickel
Tin
Silicon
Fluorine
Vanadium

more and more roles played by the microscopic quantities of these elements in laboratory animals, usually as parts of enzymes or activators of enzyme systems in body cells. Frequently, an element's function is no sooner demonstrated in animals than suspected deficiency states are uncovered in human populations. Chromium, for example, was found to be necessary for proper insulin function in laboratory animals, leading investigators to look for and identify low levels of chromium in middle-aged diabetics. The fourteen trace elements listed on this page are now known to be essential for mammals, and most of them are probably essential for human beings as well.

In a sense, however, it is misleading to think of any one trace mineral as being essential or nonessential apart from the others. First of all, they interact widely with each other and with other nutrients, and the requirements for any one may vary extensively depending on the presence of the others. Some elements are able to take the place of others in reactions, so that enough of one reduces the need for another; in other cases, however, increased amounts of one trace mineral only increase the need for certain others. Secondly, the amount of these micronutrients that is beneficial is sometimes only slightly less than the amount which is toxic or poisonous. Safe amounts, therefore, depend on the amounts of *all* of these elements together in the diet, as well as on the other environmental elements with which they may interact.

A deficiency of any one trace mineral is not likely to be a matter of life and death; the interdependence of these elements contributes instead to a kind of twilight zone of marginal metabolic disorders. Toxic levels of such minerals, on the other hand, are a real threat in today's polluted environment. A recent WHO expert committee on trace minerals sums up the situation by saying, "There is no single minimum dietary requirement or single maximum safe intake of a trace element: there is a series of such minimum requirements and maximum safe intakes depending upon the nature of the whole diet and the whole environment."[7]

Deficiency problems, then, may best be understood as *imbalances* in the whole pattern of trace mineral needs. Cadmium, for example, a heavy metal used in industry for plating iron and steel, is now finding its way into our water supplies through the recycling of metals. In the body, cadmium is toxic, and low levels of copper (which we get from meat and green vegetables) may lower the body's tolerance of this pollutant even further. Zinc, found in animal foods, whole grains, and legumes, may actually reverse some of cadmium's adverse effects. But zinc and copper interact not only with cadmium, but also with each other: when zinc concentration is high in relation to copper, it may contribute to elevated blood cholesterol, and copper concentration high in relation to zinc has been shown to create zinc deficiency in animals.[8] Interactions like these are many and complex, and none of them are completely explored. A few are better established than others: deficiencies of iron and iodine, for example, are known to exist; zinc and chromium levels are believed to be marginal in many people's diets.[9] But supplementation with the more recently discovered essential trace elements must be discouraged until we know more about their interrelationships and effects.

As the puzzle of information about trace elements begins to come together, the picture that emerges shows some clear implications for our modern way of life. Lack of variety in food selection may imbalance an individual diet, but more commonly trace mineral imbalances are found on a much broader scale, as the methods of modern industry and agriculture alter the proportions of these minerals in the whole environment. Deficiencies, for example, may arise from refining grain, which removes some needed iron, manganese, chromium, zinc, and other essential minerals from the food supply of whole populations. Toxicity in other trace minerals is closely connected with environmental pollution, as the use of fossil fuels and modern industrial methods increases the contamination of the environment with heavy metals like cadmium, mercury, arsenic, and lead. Mercury poisoning from seafood is an all too familiar example. Mothers, too, may have heard of the danger of lead poisoning in children from lead-based paints on houses, toys, pencils, toothpaste tubes, and other easily accessible items. But lead poisoning is being identified as an environmental issue as well. Recent studies have shown not only heavy concentrations of lead from car fumes and industrial waste in the dust and dirt of city streets, but also a high correlation between lead poisoning and the hand-to-mouth activity of small children, which brings dirt contaminated with lead into their mouths countless times in a normal day.[10] Water supplies, too, often show serious trace mineral imbalances not just from water pollution but also from water treatment. Studies of large populations have shown a greater incidence of cardiovascular disease among those who drink soft water—water with a low mineral content. Specific elements have not yet been implicated, however, and the metabolic disturbances from mineral imbalance which contribute to cardiovascular disease are likely to be many and subtle, so the only possible recommendation for the present is that it is unwise to soften water artificially at its source.

Equally subtle is the impact of modern agricultural methods on the trace mineral content of our natural food supply. The soil in which plant foods and fodders are grown is the ultimate source of almost all our minerals, for plants absorb minerals from the soil through their roots. The supply of iodine, copper, zinc, chromium, and selenium in foods is particularly influenced by the mineral content of soils,[11] which naturally varies widely from one region to another. Even from the same soil, different plants absorb different minerals, so a variety of foods is essential if one is to get the full range of these micronutrients. But if the soil itself has an unbalanced mineral content, the foods grown in that soil cannot make up the balance. Iodine, for example, has always been deficient in the Great Lakes and Pacific Northwest, and since iodine is essential for the formation of thyroid hormones, the thyroid disease of goiter was prevalent in those areas until iodine was added to salt. In general, Americans are protected from such deficiencies by the fact that our food supply comes from so many different places and has such variety, though food refining weakens this safeguard greatly. Also, plants do not grow well in trace mineral–deficient soil, making the yield of such crops low. Animal products, too, are usually considered a safeguard for trace mineral balance in the diet, for by and large animals need the same minerals we do in order to live. Ultimately, however, animals too are dependent on the trace mineral balance of soils—a balance that may be altered wherever foods are grown by the methods of modern American agriculture. Elements like nitrogen and phosphorus in fertilizers are now added in great quantity to our soils to speed up plant growth, while other minerals depleted from the soil by plants are not replenished. Often these imbalances cannot be accurately measured for an individual crop; the quantities of each element are too small, their dietary functions too closely interrelated, the variations from crop to crop and from sample to sample too wide. With the microminerals, it simply is not clear what effects any given manipulation of the environment may have. It is clear only that the impact of technology on our food supply is far-reaching and complex—and a potential danger. The WHO committee on trace elements concludes: "The monitoring of changes in the trace element content of the diet due to agricultural practices and to changing dietary practices is essential to ensure that a safe and adequate trace element composition in foods is maintained."[12]

With most other aspects of nutrition, nourishment is a matter of making wise choices in our individual food selection: choosing to eat foods that provide particular nutrients, choosing not to eat foods with no nutrient value at all. With trace minerals, the choices we make take in a much larger picture. Though there is still room for wise choices at the level of the individual diet, the most important choices are made not for ourselves alone but for our whole society, and encompass not just food selection but the basic decisions about how we use resources every day. The cost of our highly industrialized way of life is not immediately visible, but it is extremely high, and trace element nutrition is only part of the cost we pay. We can lower that cost, not only to ourselves but to the rest of the world and its children, by making intelligent choices in countless little places throughout the day: driving less and walking more, repairing things instead of throwing them away, not buying what we do not need, growing our food in our own backyard. Such choices do make our own lives healthier, but much more important is the satisfaction of knowing that our whole life style is adding to the health and welfare of all, in which our own health and welfare are included.

IRON

More people are deficient in iron than in any other nutrient—not only in the United States but in many other countries, both rich and poor. Iron deficiency anemia has become increasingly common as foods have become more refined, and especially as we have abandoned old-fashioned cast iron cooking pots, which add large quantities of iron to the food cooked in them.

In the body, iron is essential to the enzyme systems which carry oxygen, for it has the capacity to take on and give up oxygen. For example, it is indispensible in every cell for the enzymes which carry oxygen so that food can be burned for fuel. The symptoms of iron deficiency are pale skin, weakness, shortness of breath, lack of appetite, and a slowing down of all the body's vital processes. Severe iron deficiency over a long period of time can lead to death.

By far the greatest concentration of iron is in hemoglobin, a protein in red blood cells which incorporates iron in its molecular structure to transport oxygen from the lungs to all body tissues. Iron is also a constituent of myoglobin, a protein in muscles which provides a reservoir of oxygen for muscle metabolism. The second largest concentration of iron in the body is in the places where iron is stored—the liver, spleen, and bone marrow. These stores must be depleted before anemia can develop.

What iron the body has is carefully recycled, as from old blood cells to new. Unlike most other nutrients, the body has no mechanism by which it can excrete iron excesses, so substantial amounts usually do not leave the body except through bleeding, as from hemorrhage or menstruation. A minute amount of iron—an average of 1 milligram per day—is also lost regularly in cells which are cast off from the body by the intestinal tract, urinary tract, and skin.

This loss is the basis of our minimum requirement for iron. Some groups of people, however, have an increased requirement for this mineral, and are particularly vulnerable to iron

SOURCES
Adult RDA is 10–18 mg

10.5 prune juice, *1 cup*
 7.9 black beans, *1 cup cooked*
 6.9 garbanzo beans, *1 c. ckd.*
 6.1 pinto beans, *1 c. ckd.*
 5.1 navy beans, *1 c. cooked*
 5.1 lima beans, dry, *1 c. ckd.*
 4.9 soybeans, *1 cup cooked*
 4.8 rice bran, *¼ cup*
 4.4 rice polishings, *¼ cup*
 4.3 lima beans, green, *1 c. ckd.*
 4.2 lentils, *1 cup cooked*
 4.0 spinach, *1 cup cooked*
 3.9 peach halves, dried, *5*
 3.9 millet, *¼ cup dry*
 3.4 sunchokes, *4 small*
 3.4 split peas, green, *1 c. ckd.*
 3.2 blackstrap molasses,
     1 tablespoon
 2.9 peas, fresh, *1 cup*
 2.8 beet greens, *1 c. cooked*
 2.6 raisins, *½ cup*
 2.6 chard, *1 cup cooked*
 2.4 dates, *10 medium*
 2.4 sesame meal, *¼ cup*
 2.3 tofu, *4 ounce piece*
 2.2 tomato juice, *1 cup*
 2.1 wheat berries, *⅓ cup dry*
 2.1 butternut squash,
     1 cup baked
 2.0 pumpkin seeds, *2 tbsp.*
 1.9 wheat bran, *¼ cup*
 1.9 wheat germ, *¼ cup*
 1.8 soybean milk, *1 cup*
 1.8 kale, *1 cup cooked*
 1.8 prunes, *5 cooked*
 1.7 acorn squash, *½ baked*
 1.7 brussels sprouts, *8 cooked*
 1.5 torula yeast, *1 tbsp.*
 1.5 strawberries, *1 cup*
 1.4 potato, cooked, *large*
 1.4 oatmeal, *1 cup cooked*

deficiency anemia. Teenagers of both sexes need to build up reserves of iron during the years of maximum growth: teenage boys have an additional requirement for building up large quantities of red blood cells, and teenage girls require more iron because of the onset of menstruation. Women, in fact, often have marginal stores of iron because of losses in menstruation. When such women become pregnant, outright deficiency is quite common, because the baby has first claim on all the mother's nutrients. Old people sometimes suffer from slow internal bleeding (as from the intestine) which causes them to become anemic. The one group which does not have to worry about iron is adult men in good health—in fact, they may even build up too much iron in their bodies by eating too much iron-rich food.

Because the body cannot vary its iron excretion, its only control over the amount of iron it has is through the amount it absorbs. Like many other nutrients, iron is best absorbed when the body needs it most. When the diet is customarily supplying enough of this mineral, only an average of 10 percent of what is eaten may be absorbed; but when iron stores are low, efficiency of absorption may double or even triple. Unfortunately, even extra absorption cannot compensate when the diet continues to be deficient.

Factors affecting iron absorption are various and complex and of crucial interest to vegetarians, especially to those who come from one of the population groups with increased iron requirements just mentioned, such as women or adolescents. Since the iron in meat is absorbed by a different mechanism than is iron from other sources, the vegetarian diet must be considered in a different light from the standard recommendations.

The main factor governing absorption is always the body's need for iron, but there are other factors too. One of these is the form of iron in the diet. Iron exists in two states of ionization, ferrous (carrying two positive charges) and ferric (carrying three positive charges), and ferrous iron is much more easily absorbed. In its metallic state, iron is more easily absorbed in smaller particles than in large. Iron also reacts with other nutrients in the intestine, and these may increase or decrease its absorption. Phytic acid in the hulls of grain binds up iron just as it does calcium and therefore hinders absorption of both, as do large amounts of fiber in the diet. On the other hand, the sulfur-containing amino acids,[13] citric acid, calcium, and vitamin C all enhance absorption. High-quality protein from meat or soybeans has also been shown to enhance the absorption of iron from plant sources—enough for United Nations agencies to recommend an extremely high allowance of iron for countries where meat and soybeans form less than 10 percent of the calories of a diet.[14] Vitamin C, too, is of great importance to vegetarians, since it specifically enhances the absorption of iron from plant sources, partly by reducing ferric iron to the more absorbable ferrous form. Once again, in evaluating your iron status it is the whole dietary picture that must be taken into account.

Women in the United States whose caloric intake is between 1800 and 2000 calories average about 9 to 12 milligrams of iron in their daily diet. Since the U.S. recommended allowance is 18 milligrams a day, they must either carefully include iron-rich sources or use supplements to meet the RDA. Iron pots can go a long way in meeting the need: longer cooking times and acid ingredients will both increase the amount of iron that passes into food cooked in them, as you can see from the table below.

IRON CONTENT & IRON COOKWARE

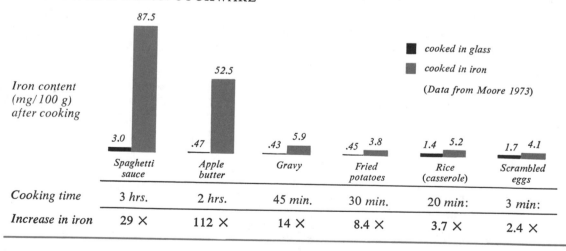

Iron content (mg/100 g) after cooking

cooked in glass
cooked in iron

(Data from Moore 1973)

	Spaghetti sauce	Apple butter	Gravy	Fried potatoes	Rice (casserole)	Scrambled eggs
Glass	3.0	.47	.43	.45	1.4	1.7
Iron	87.5	52.5	5.9	3.8	5.2	4.1
Cooking time	3 hrs.	2 hrs.	45 min.	30 min.	20 min.	3 min.
Increase in iron	29 ×	112 ×	14 ×	8.4 ×	3.7 ×	2.4 ×

Other food sources of iron are listed in the margin on page 434. Food composition charts may be misleading when it comes to iron because of wide variations in mineral content (up to 500 percent for iron[15]) depending on where the food was grown. Milk, incidentally, is iron-poor, something for women to keep in mind if they are tempted to meet their protein requirements primarily with skim milk products. Protein needs may be met with fewer calories by such foods, but iron and B vitamin needs are not.

Unfortunately, people suffering from iron deficiency anemia are often not aware of it. Since storage iron can be depleted completely before the hemoglobin in the blood is affected, you may be without iron reserves for an emergency even if you are not anemic. Restoration of these reserves is a long, slow process, taking up to six months even with the help of large doses of iron in pills. A yearly blood test can detect anemia and indicate its cause—there are other causes of anemia than iron deficiency. However, people vulnerable to iron deficiency who are not anemic must also be vigilant about this nutrient because it is very important to maintain adequate iron stores.

Variety and a well-balanced diet will go a long way toward supplying the iron you need. Little amounts from many places add up significantly, and other nutrients from a mixed diet like the copper in green leaves, the protein in your soybeans, and the vitamin C and citric acid in citrus fruit all help to absorb the iron you consume. In addition, the iron-deficient vegetarian should make a point of using cast iron pots for cooking and be sure to include foods rich in vitamin C, such as citrus fruits, along with iron-rich foods at every meal.

ZINC

Zinc is involved in the enzyme reactions of most of the major biochemical pathways of the body, and is essential for the growth and repair of tissues, perhaps because of its role in the synthesis of proteins and nucleic acids like DNA and RNA. Almost all the zinc in the body is bound up chemically where it is, so there is no reserve pool of zinc available which the body can draw on when it is needed for the synthesis of new cells.

ZINC CONTENT OF FOODS

*Values next to food names give zinc content in milligrams (mg).
Adult RDA is 15 mg.*

LEGUMES, MATURE
1.8 beans, common, *1 c. ckd.*
3.0 black-eyed peas, *1 c. ckd.*
2.0 garbanzos, *1 cup ckd.*
2.0 lentils, *1 cup cooked*
1.7 limas, *1 cup cooked*
0.3 peanuts, roasted, *1 tbsp.*
0.5 peanut butter, *1 tbsp.*
2.1 peas, green, *1 cup ckd.*

GRAINS & GRAIN PRODUCTS
0.1 barley, whole, *¼ cup dry*
0.4 bread: rye, *1 slice*
0.2   white, *1 slice*
0.5   whole wheat, *1 slice*
1.3 buckwheat, whole,
       ⅓ cup dry
0.7 corn grits, *1 cup dry*
2.1 cornmeal, bolted,
       1 cup dry
0.2 crackers, graham, *2*
0.1   saltines, *10*
0.6 granola, *1 ounce*
0.7 macaroni, *1 cup cooked*
0.9 millet, whole, *¼ cup dry*
1.2 oatmeal, *1 cup cooked*
3.1 rice bran, *1 cup*
1.2 rice, brown, *1 cup ckd.*
0.6 rice, white parboiled,
       1 cup cooked
1.4 soy flour, *1 cup stirred*
5.9 soy meal, *3½ ounces*
1.0 soy protein, *¼ cup*
     wheat berries:
2.3   hard, *⅓ cup dry*
1.8   soft, *⅓ cup dry*
1.5   white, *⅓ cup dry*
1.8   durum, *⅓ cup dry*
5.7 wheat bran, *1 cup*
3.2 wheat germ, toasted,
       ¼ cup

GRAINS *(cont.)*:
     wheat flours:
2.9   whole, *1 cup stirred*
0.8   all-purpose, *1 cup sftd.*
0.9   bread flour, *1 cup sftd.*
0.3   cake flour, *1 cup sftd.*
1.2 wheat cereal, whole-meal,
       1 cup cooked

DAIRY PRODUCTS & EGGS
0.2 butter, *1 cup*
0.01   *1 tablespoon*
0.5 cheese, cheddar, *1 slice*
0.5 egg, whole, *1 large*
0.5   yolk, *1 large*
0.01   white, *1 large*
0.6 ice cream, *1 cup*
0.9 milk, fluid, *1 cup*
1.9   canned, evaporated,
       1 cup
3.1   dry, nonfat, *1 cup*

VEGETABLES
0.4 beans, snap green,
       French-cut, *1 cup ckd.*
0.3 cabbage, common,
       shredded, *1 cup raw*
0.6   *1 cup boiled, drained*
0.3 carrot, raw, *1 medium*
0.5   *1 cup cooked, drained*
0.7 corn, sweet yellow,
       1 cup boiled, drained
0.4 lettuce, *⅙ head*
0.2   loose-leaf, *1 cup chpd.*
0.6 onions, mature,
       1 cup chopped
0.3   young green,
       1 cup chopped
1.2 peas, green immature,
       1 cup boiled, drained
0.3 potato, *1 medium pared,
       boiled, drained*

VEGETABLES *(cont.)*:
0.4   *1 medium boiled in
       skin, drained, pared*
0.5 spinach, raw,
       1 cup chopped
1.3   *1 cup boiled, drained*
0.2 tomato, raw, *1 medium*
0.5   *1 cup boiled*
0.5   *1 cup canned, w. liq.*

FRUITS
0.08 apple, *1 medium*
0.3 applesauce,
       unsweetened, *1 cup*
0.3 banana, *1 medium*
0.2 orange, *1 medium*
0.2 orange juice, canned,
       1 cup
0.05   fresh or frozen, *1 cup*
0.2 peach, raw peeled,
       1 medium
0.3   canned, *1 cup slices*

MISCELLANEOUS
0.01 beverages, carbonated,
       12-ounce bottle
0.3   *12-ounce can*
1.6 cocoa, powder, *1 ounce*
0.3   *1 tablespoon*
0.05 coffee, *6 fluid ounces*
0.5 margarine, *1 cup*
0.03   *1 tablespoon*
0.4 oil, salad or cooking,
       1 cup
0.1 sugar, white granulated,
       1 cup
0.04 tea, *6 fluid ounces*
0.8 yeast, active dry, *1 tbsp.*
0.4   brewer's, *1 tablespoon*
0.8   torula, *1 tablespoon*

*Sources: Murphy et al. 1975,
Prasad 1966*

Therefore, zinc in the diet is required for growth and tissue repair and to replace losses in sweat. In growing people, deficiencies result in loss of appetite, failure to grow, and immaturely developed sexual organs. Taste and smell become less acute and wounds heal slowly when zinc in the diet is inadequate.

Zinc is an important nutrient for the vegetarian to watch out for, because it may easily be marginal in a meatless diet. Cereals, as we have seen, are high in phytic acid, which binds up zinc and other minerals in the intestine and thus greatly reduces their absorption. As with many other trace minerals, animal food sources are the most concentrated and the most easily absorbed. For a meatless diet, the best sources are legumes, whole grains, and milk products. Vegetables (including leafy greens) and fruits are poor sources, and most city water supplies supply virtually no zinc at all.

As with other nutrients, the recommended dietary allowance for zinc is set high: high enough, in fact, that it is hard to meet it with the standard American diet. Though gross zinc deficiencies have not been found in the United States, the soil in many parts of the country is extremely low in this mineral, and marginal deficiencies have been known to occur. In other countries, however, full-blown zinc deficiencies have been seen. In areas of Iran and Egypt, for example, the average diet depends largely for its zinc on unleavened bread, in which the phytate-destroying enzyme, phytase, is inactive. Such a diet is inadequate for replacing the exceptionally large zinc losses caused by problems like intestinal bleeding due to parasites or large sweat losses in a hot climate.

SOURCE REFERENCES

1. Robert M. Kark and Joseph H. Oyama, Nutrition and cardiovascular–renal diseases, in *Modern nutrition in health and disease: Dietotherapy,* 5th ed., ed. Robert S. Goodhart and Maurice E. Shils (Philadelphia, Lea & Febiger, 1973), p. 865.

2. S. Margen et al., Studies in calcium metabolism. I. The calciuretic effect of dietary protein, *American Journal of Clinical Nutrition* 27: 584–589, 1974.

3. K. Bitar and J. G. Reinhold, Phytase and alkaline phosphatase activities in intestinal mucosae of rat, chicken, calf, and man, *Biochimica et Biophysica Acta* 268:442–452, 1972.

4. Food and Agriculture Organization of the United Nations, Nutrition Division, *Calcium requirements: Report of a joint FAO/WHO expert committee,* FAO Nutrition Meetings Report Series, no. 30, WHO Technical Report Series, no. 230 (Rome, 1962), p. 15.

5. H. Mollgaard et al., On phytic acid: Its importance in metabolism and its enzymic cleavage in bread supplemented with calcium, *Biochemical Journal* 40:589–603, 1946.

6. J. G. Reinhold et al., Availability of zinc in leavened and unleavened wholemeal wheaten bread as measured by solubility and uptake by rat intestine in vitro, *Journal of Nutrition* 104:976–982, 1974.

7. Joint FAO/WHO Expert Committee on Trace Elements in Human Nutrition, *Trace elements in human nutrition,* WHO Technical Report Series, no. 532 (Geneva, World Health Organization, 1973), p. 7.

8. FAO/WHO, *Trace elements,* p. 12.

9. National Research Council, Food and Nutrition Board, *Recommended dietary allowances,* 8th rev. ed. (Washington, National Academy of Sciences, 1974), p. 91.

10. J. S. Lin-Fu, Vulnerability of children to lead exposure and toxicity. I, *New England Journal of Medicine* 289:1229–1232, 1973.

11. L. Jean Bogert, George M. Briggs, and Doris H. Calloway, *Nutrition and physical fitness,* 9th ed. (Philadelphia, Saunders, 1973), p. 261.

12. FAO/WHO, *Trace elements,* p. 64.

13. Carl V. Moore, Iron, in *Modern nutrition in health and disease,* ed. Goodhart and Shils, pp. 300–301.

14. Joint FAO/WHO Expert Group on Requirements of Ascorbic Acid, Vitamin B-12, Folate, and Iron, *Requirements of ascorbic acid, vitamin B-12, folate, and iron,* FAO Nutrition Meetings Report Series, no. 47, WHO Technical Report Series, no. 452 (Rome, Food and Agriculture Organization of the United Nations, 1970), pp. 49, 55, 59.

15. E. M. Wien, D. R. Van Campen, and J. M. Rivers, Factors affecting the concentration and bioavailability of iron in turnip greens to rats, *Journal of Nutrition* 105:459–465, 1975.

Preserving Nutrients in the Kitchen

Throughout our recipe section there are references to cooking and storage methods which reduce the destruction of nutrients. Fats, for example, will turn rancid if not stored carefully; protein under certain circumstances is bound up by heat; and vitamins can easily be lost from food during cooking. A summary of the conditions which adversely affect these important nutrients is presented here.

Although cooking is generally destructive to nutrients, we should not forget that it also has advantages. It softens and breaks down the cellulose or fibrous coverings which enclose many plant nutrients, making their starch, protein, and vitamins available to us. Some nutrients which are in a bound form in raw food, such as the niacin and tryptophan in cornmeal, are released when the food is heated. Finally, cooking destroys toxic substances in some foods (like soybeans) and makes palatable other foods which we would otherwise not even eat.

If you are using whole, basic foods, the time that kitchen practices become most critical to your nourishment is when a variety of fresh foods is difficult to come by. If potatoes are the only fresh food in your diet, for example, and the only source of vitamin C, then how you care for them and cook them becomes most important. People on restricted diets, too, need to be especially careful about nutrient losses.

The greatest danger to water-soluble nutrients, and the only real threat to minerals, is that they may leach into cooking water. Consequently, the water in which vegetables are cooked will contain most of the starch, vitamins, minerals, and amino

acids they have lost, so the water should never be wasted. It is a vitamin-rich broth that can often be used in place of water— as, for example, a base for soups and sauces. Cooking with small amounts of water or steam will reduce the loss of water-soluble vitamins. Pressure cooking reduces cooking time and thus reduces losses even more.

The water-soluble vitamins are generally less stable in food than the fat-soluble ones. The unstable nutrients are more easily destroyed by cooking and are slowly lost during storage, even in the refrigerator. Unsaturated fats, including linoleic acid, and the fat-soluble vitamins associated with them are both unstable, so they can also be destroyed during storage and cooking.

Nutrient losses during cooking are difficult to pin down exactly. Different samples of the same food will contain different amounts of nutrients to start with, and their nutrient content will vary widely depending on the cooking practices used.

THE DECOMPOSITION OF FATS (RANCIDITY)

Fats spoil by becoming rancid. In this process oxygen from the air reacts with the unsaturated double bonds in the fat, using the energy from heat or light. Because even predominately saturated fats usually contain some unsaturated fatty acid chains, they too can go rancid, though usually not as quickly as unsaturated fats. This decomposition produces substances called peroxides or free radicals, highly reactive substances which destroy vitamins and are physiologically destructive when ingested. It has been suggested that peroxides may even play a role in the aging process. As fat decomposition in food continues, other compounds form, producing the disagreeable odors and flavors of rancidity.

The vitamins E and C naturally present in food act as antioxidants, combining with peroxides to halt decomposition. Once they are used up in this way, however, they are no longer available to the body as vitamins. In food processing, vitamin E or C is frequently added to food to delay rancidity—as are BHA and BHT, synthetic antioxidants whose safety has not been proven.[1]

In the kitchen, oils should be stored in the refrigerator in airtight containers with a minimum of air space at the top, and protected from light. Foods containing large amounts of these oils, such as whole-grain flours and nut meats, also need cool, dark, airtight storage. Nuts in the shell and whole grains are well protected from air by their natural covering, so storage is not as critical for them. Since rancid oils and foods containing rancid oils have a distinctly bitter taste, they can be identified by taste and discarded rather than eaten.

There are two important clues which warn you of chemical changes in oils and fats when cooking. The first is that the fat will darken in color; the second is that it will begin to smoke. By and large, a fat will get hot enough for either of these changes only when it is heated by itself for some time (as in frying) instead of being added to watery liquid or baked in bread. The smoke point of commonly used polyunsaturated oils is around 400°F (200°C), a common temperature for home frying. About 20 percent of an oil's polyunsaturated fatty acids is destroyed at this temperature.[2] Light sautéing (as of an onion), however, is harmless as long as the temperature is carefully controlled.

THE DESTRUCTION OF PROTEIN BY HEAT (THE BROWNING REACTION)

Heating foods, whether in processing or in cooking, can considerably damage their protein content, for with heat, amino acids become bound up with sugars present in the food and are then unavailable to the body. Lysine is especially liable to this transformation. The reaction is colorless at first, but soon produces the brown color which gives it the name "browning reaction."

Several conditions are necessary for the browning reaction to occur. First, the food must contain some sugar. Second, it should contain moisture in a middle-moisture range, neither too wet nor too dry. Third, it must be heated. Mild heating is generally harmless, but at higher temperatures, protein damage is proportional to the time of heating—the longer the food is heated, the greater the damage. The temperature at which protein destruction starts varies from food to food. Wet ingredients that are baked (like bread) or moist food that is heat-dried both pass through a middle-moisture range that favors browning. Very dry food that is toasted, or food cooked in a lot of water like oatmeal, loses less by browning.

In bread, browning occurs mostly on the crust of a loaf during baking, binding up 10 to 15 percent of the bread's lysine. Adding milk powder to the bread increases the lysine loss because it reacts with the milk's sugar. Milk powder itself undergoes browning during storage even though it doesn't actually turn brown, and it may have undergone browning during processing too. Browning renders many processed breakfast cereals low in protein, and often protein concentrates are made under conditions that favor browning. Because the protein is bound only so far as to be unavailable to the body but is released by the strong chemicals which test for protein in food, the protein listing on a label may not accurately reflect what is available to nourish us.

Most of us have enough protein in our diet to spare some to the browning of our food. However, we should keep in mind that grain's limiting amino acid, lysine, is the one which is affected. Some processed foods, such as very thin, thoroughly browned breakfast cereals, touted as "high protein" foods, may not be very good protein sources.

SOURCE REFERENCES

1. Michael F. Jacobson, *Eater's digest: The consumer's fact-book of food additives* (Garden City, N. Y., Doubleday, Anchor Books, 1972), pp. 88–89.
    2. A. E. Bender, The fate of vitamins in food processing operations, in University of Nottingham Residential Seminar on Vitamins, 1970, *Proceedings of the University of Nottingham Residential Seminar on Vitamins* (Edinburgh, Churchill Livingstone, 1971), p. 73.

Vitamin Losses

Outside column gives range of cooking losses in percent

Vitamin A is stable during mild cooking but destroyed at high temperatures in the presence of oxygen, such as when oils are kept at high temperatures for frying. It is also destroyed when a stored fat turns rancid. It is unstable to acid but stable to alkali.

VITAMIN A
0–40%[1]

Vitamin D is stable for practical purposes during cooking and storage. Some may be lost in dried milk during storage.

VITAMIN D
0–25%[2]

Vitamin E losses occur in fats primarily when they go rancid or are used for deep fat frying. The free fatty acid derivatives (peroxides) that form under these circumstances react with the vitamin E and destroy it (see p. 400). Air, light, and alkalies enhance the destruction. Uniquely, vitamin E is also destroyed by freezing.

VITAMIN E
0–55%[1]

Vitamin C (ascorbic acid) is more readily destroyed than the other vitamins, so it is often used as an index of nutrient preservation in fruits and vegetables: if it is preserved, the other nutrients will be preserved too. It decomposes quickly in the presence of air, heat, alkali, and certain metals like the iron and copper in pots, and leaches readily into cooking water. Vitamin C destruction begins as soon as a plant is harvested, because the tissue damage activates an enzyme which destroys vitamin C. Blanching the vegetable inactivates this enzyme, and should therefore always be done before a food is frozen so that vitamin C is retained during storage. Fortunately, this enzyme is not present in citrus fruits. Vitamin C is most stable in acid fruits because of the acid and several other constituents they contain, and citrus fruit juices which are stored in the refrigerator in sealed containers having only a small airspace will retain most of their vitamin C content for several days.

VITAMIN C
0–100%[1]

Thiamin, along with vitamin C, is one of the most easily destroyed vitamins. It is unstable to heat in neutral or alkaline conditions and is destroyed by the oxygen in air. Losses can be great when grains are boiled in naturally alkaline water or baked with alkaline baking powders. Baking bread results in a 15 to 30 percent thiamin loss, mostly

THIAMIN
0–80%[1]

in the crust; toasting a slice for 30 to 70 seconds destroys an additional 10 to 30 percent. Thiamin is also readily destroyed by sulfur dioxide, which is sometimes used to preserve vitamin C.

RIBOFLAVIN
0–75 % [1]

Riboflavin is most sensitive to light, especially as temperature and alkalinity increase. If it is dry or in an acid medium, it is stable to heat. The riboflavin in our best source, milk, is jeopardized when milk is exposed to direct sunlight in clear glass containers, and about 50 percent is destroyed in two hours—20 percent on an overcast day.

NIACIN
0–75 % [1]

Niacin is one of the most stable B vitamins, primarily lost from food only by leaching into cooking water.

VITAMIN B-6
0–40 % [1]

Vitamin B-6 is sensitive to heat in some foods. It is also sensitive to light, especially in alkaline conditions. Much is lost from our national diet by food refinement and processing.

VITAMIN B-12
0–30 % [3]

Vitamin B-12 is stable to heat in neutral solutions but not in most foods, which are either acid or alkaline. Up to 30 percent is destroyed in milk which has been boiled for several minutes.

FOLACIN
0–100 % [1]

Folacin is stable to heat in acid media but readily destroyed in neutral or alkaline conditions.[2] An average of half is said to be lost during cooking[2] and even more during reheating, since ascorbic acid is usually no longer present to protect it. Destruction is accelerated by air and light, so green vegetables should be stored in dark, airtight places in the refrigerator. When vegetables are stored at room temperature, up to 70 percent of their folacin is lost in three days.

Sources: 1. Harris & von Loesecke 1960 2. Bender 1971 3. FAO/WHO 1970

Suggestions for Further Reading

Ahrens, Richard A. Sucrose, hypertension, and heart disease: An historical perspective. *American Journal of Clinical Nutrition* 27:403–422, 1974.

A review of the literature from the nineteenth century to the present about the possible role that sucrose plays in the etiology of arteriosclerotic and degenerative heart disease.

Altschul, Arron M. *Proteins: Their chemistry and politics.* New York, Basic Books, 1965.

A basic presentation of the chemistry of proteins and their role in national diets. Although this book is now ten years old, we found Chapter 11, "The effects of heat on food protein," especially useful.

Altschule, Mark D., ed. Symposium on atherosclerosis. *Medical Clinics of North America* 58(2), 1974.

Evaluates the research on the prevention of atherosclerosis, including a critical challenge of cholesterol and saturated fat as dominating causative factors. Discussions cover other possible causative factors like neurogenic factors, smoking, and trace mineral imbalances, and what is known of the biological processes resulting in atherosclerosis.

Bogert, Lotta Jean, George M. Briggs, and Doris Howes Calloway. *Nutrition and physical fitness.* 9th ed. Philadelphia, Saunders, 1973.

A basic text which we found to be the most detailed and practical in its approach of the many we looked at. It is an excellent reference text for the lay reader. Our discussion of vitamins and minerals is based essentially on this book.

Bourne, Malcolm C. Recent advances in soybean milk processing technology. *PAG Bulletin* 10, 1970 (FAO/WHO/UNICEF Protein Advisory Group, New York).

Describes the chemistry, processing methods, and nutrition of the hot water–grind process for making soybean milk without a bitter, beany flavor.

Briggs, George M. Sugar, nutrition and disease; addendum to testimony at hearing on alternative sources of funding for nutrition education programs before the California Senate Subcommittee on Agriculture, Food and Nutrition, 8 October 1974, San Francisco.

Summary of the current status of research about sugar and disease, with a bibliography.

Burkitt, D. P., A. R. P. Walker, and N. S. Painter. Dietary fiber and disease. *Journal of the American Medical Association* 229: 1068–1074, 1974.

A review of the research about the ill effects of diets low in fiber. One of the contributors, D. P. Burkitt, is the physician who has made the medical community aware of this issue.

Christensen, Clyde M., and Henry H. Kaufmann. *Grain storage: The role of fungi in quality loss.* Minneapolis, University of Minnesota Press, 1969.

Discusses all the factors which might affect the quality of grains from the time they leave the field until they reach the miller or are otherwise used.

Goodhart, Robert S., and Maurice E. Shils, eds. *Modern nutrition in health and disease: Dietotherapy.* 5th ed. Philadelphia, Lea and Febiger, 1973.

A comprehensive presentation, essentially for health professionals, of nutrients and diet in the prevention and treatment of disease, written by experts in the field.

Hardinge, M. G., and F. J. Stare. Nutritional studies of vegetarians. II. Dietary and serum levels of cholesterol. *American Journal of Clinical Nutrition* 2:83, 1954.

An early study of the effects of a vegetarian diet on blood cholesterol levels.

Harris, Robert S., and Endel Karmas, eds. *Nutritional evaluation of food processing.* 2nd ed. Westport, Connecticut, Avi Publishing Co., 1975.

A recently updated edition of a classic text which deals with the effects of commercial handling and processing on the nutritive value of basic foods. The authors describe many of the processes, like the preparation of fruits and vegetables for canning and freezing, the milling of grains, and the processing of oils, and include a section on nutrient losses during the preparation of foods. There are many charts showing the nutrient content of foods after particular processes.

Joint FAO/WHO Ad Hoc Committee on Energy and Protein Requirements. *Energy and protein requirements.* FAO Nutrition Meetings Series, no. 52; WHO Technical Report Series, no. 522. Rome, Food and Agriculture Organization of the United Nations, 1973.

> An assessment of requirements for energy and protein by an international committee of experts. Includes the most recent FAO amino acid scoring pattern.

Joint FAO/WHO Expert Committee on Trace Elements in Human Nutrition. *Trace elements in human nutrition.*WHO Technical Report Series, no. 532. Geneva, World Health Organization, 1973.

> Describes the current knowledge of each trace element, including important discussions of trace element imbalance in human disease.

Joint FAO/WHO Expert Group on Requirements of Ascorbic Acid, Vitamin B-12, Folate, and Iron. *Requirements of ascorbic acid, vitamin B-12, folate, and iron.* FAO Nutrition Meetings Report Series, no. 47; WHO Technical Report Series, no. 452. Rome, Food and Agriculture Organization of the United Nations, 1970.

Kon, Stanis K. *Milk and milk products in human nutrition.* 2nd ed. FAO Nutritional Studies, no. 27. Rome, Food and Agriculture Organization of the United Nations, 1972.

> A manual of dairy products which compares the milk of different animals, describes how various milk products are made, and tells what happens to their nutrient content. Includes dried milks, cultured milks, and different types of cheeses.

Lauler, David P., ed. *Infant nutrition: feeding the infant . . . building the man.* New York, MEDCOM, 1972.

> A booklet accompanying an educational film released by Wyeth Laboratories, which makes a strong case for mother's milk and the desirability of duplicating it as closely as possible in the production of commercial formulas. Includes contributions by Dr. Jeremiah Stamler.

Mayer, Jean. *Human nutrition: Its physiological, medical, and social aspects.* Springfield, Illinois; Thomas, 1972.

> A collection of 82 of Dr. Mayer's essays which have appeared mostly in medical literature from 1959 to 1971. Covers a wide range of basic and topical subjects on nutrition, including excellent essays on obesity and world nutrition.

Nasset, E. S. Amino acid homeostasis in the gut lumen and its nutritional significance. *World Review of Nutrition and Dietetics* 14:134–153, 1972.

> A review article about the role of the intestine in protein metabolism. Describes the process whereby the body balances dietary amino acids from its own intestinal pool.

National Research Council. Committee on Amino Acids [Food and Nutrition Board]. *Improvement of protein nutriture.* Washington, National Academy of Sciences, 1974.

A comprehensive presentation of current knowledge about protein. Includes basic concepts and a discussion of the practical implications of our current knowledge about protein for improving diets.

National Research Council. Food and Nutrition Board. *Recommended dietary allowances.* 8th rev. ed. Washington, National Academy of Sciences, 1974.

Standards of intake for each nutrient as determined by U.S. experts, including detailed discussions of the need for each nutrient in the diet and how the RDA was determined.

Newer concepts of coronary heart disease. *Dairy Council Digest* 45(6), 1974.

Although their viewpoint is influenced by special interests, the National Dairy Council here brings out some of the less well publicized theories relating to diet and heart disease—issues involving margarine, the homogenation of milk, dietary fiber, and trace elements.

Passmore, Reginald, et al. *Handbook on human nutritional requirements.* FAO Nutritional Studies, no. 61. Geneva, World Health Organization, 1974.

Summarizes the FAO/WHO recommended intakes of nutrients.

Sacks, Frank M., William P. Castelli, Allen Donner, and Edward H. Kass. Plasma lipids and lipoproteins in vegetarians and controls. *New England Journal of Medicine* 292(22): 1148–1151, 1975.

One of the latest studies on the blood lipids of vegetarians. This group was following a diet quite similar to the one recommended in this book.

Shulman, Alex G. High bulk diet for diverticular disease of the colon. *Western Journal of Medicine* 120:278–281, 1974.

Describes the treatment of diverticular disease with cereal fiber.

University of Nottingham Residential Seminar on Vitamins, 1970. *Proceedings of the University of Nottingham Residential Seminar on Vitamins.* Edinburgh, Churchill Livingstone, 1971.

Includes an interesting but highly technical article on the use of vitamins like C and E in food processing, and an excellent essay by A. E. Bender entitled "The fate of vitamins in food processing operations," similar to his earlier article in the *Journal of Food Technology* (1:261–289, 1966) but excluding the material from that article on the Maillard or browning reaction.

U.S. Department of Health, Education, and Welfare. National Institute on Alcohol Abuse and Alcoholism. *First special report to the U. S. Congress on alcohol and health*. DHEW publication no. (HSM) 72–9099. Washington, Govt. Printing Office, 1971 [i.e., 1972].

A comprehensive report on the medical, social, and other important aspects of alcoholism.

U.S. Department of Health, Education, and Welfare. National Institute on Alcohol Abuse and Alcoholism. *Second special report to the U.S. Congress on alcohol and health: New knowledge*. DHEW publication no. (ADM) 75–212. Rockville, Md., Department of Health, Education, and Welfare, 1974 [i.e., 1975].

Published not to replace the first report (above), whose findings remain valid, but to complement it with new knowledge.

Weininger, J., and George M. Briggs. Nutrition update. *Journal of Nutrition Education* 6:139–143, 1974; 7:141–144, 1975.

Annual appraisals of developments in many of the most active and sometimes controversial areas of nutrition research today, including the roles of several specific nutrients and nutritional aspects of conditions like obesity and cancer.

Weiss, Theodore J. *Food oils and their uses*. Westport, Conn., Avi Publishing Co., 1970.

The basic chemistry of oils and fats, followed by a technical summary of how oils and fats are treated and made into various food products. Describes the special properties and uses of various individual oils.

West, R. O., and O. B. Hayes. Diet and serum cholesterol levels: A comparison between vegetarians and nonvegetarians in a Seventh Day Adventist group. *American Journal of Clinical Nutrition* 21:835–862, 1968.

BASIC REFERENCES ON FOOD COMPOSITION

Adams, Catherine F. *Nutritive value of American foods in common units*. Agriculture Handbook no. 456, U.S. Department of Agriculture. Washington, Govt. Printing Office, 1975.

Converts the values in Agriculture Handbook no. 8 (Watt and Merrill, below) to values corresponding to commonly used measures and common foods. Represents the USDA's careful research into what constitutes an average portion for some 1500 food items.

Bowes, Anna, and Charles F. Church, comps. *Food values of portions commonly used.* 11th ed. Philadelphia, Lippincott, 1970.

Contains values for a broad range of foods in common portions, giving most of the important nutrients. Includes many commercial and processed foods.

Food and Agriculture Organization of the United Nations. Food Policy and Food Science Service. *Amino-acid content of foods and biological data on proteins.* FAO Nutritional Studies, no. 24. Rome, Food and Agriculture Organization of the United Nations, 1970.

Latest compilation of the amino acid content of foods and biological data on single foods and mixtures of foods.

Orr, Martha L. *Pantothenic acid, vitamin B-6 and vitamin B-12 in foods.* Home Economics Research Report no. 36, U.S. Department of Agriculture. Washington, Govt. Printing Office, 1969.

Gives values for these nutrients per 100 grams of food—nutrients which don't appear in the USDA Agriculture Handbook no. 8 (Watt and Merrill, below).

Watt, Bernice K., and Annabel L. Merrill. *Composition of foods: Raw, processed, prepared.* Agriculture Handbook no. 8, U.S. Department of Agriculture. Washington, Govt. Printing Office, 1964 [revised Dec. 1963].

Values for many nutrients per 100 grams of food. This is the authoritative work on which other food composition tables are based.

BOOKS WRITTEN FOR THE LAY READER

Friedman, Mayer, and Ray H. Rosenman. *Type A behavior and your heart.* New York, Knopf, 1974.

Discusses the risk factors for heart disease, including diet, as background for presentation of the Type A or "hurry sickness" theory of compulsive, time-driven behavior. This book was written to help people overcome their vulnerability to the epidemic of heart disease.

Jacobson, Michael F. *Eater's digest: The consumer's fact-book of food additives.* Garden City, N.Y.; Doubleday, Anchor Books, 1972.

A usable, readable, and pointed reference, which examines more than 50 common food additives in detail.

Lappé, Frances Moore. *Diet for a small planet.* 2nd ed. New York, Ballantine, 1975.

An especially important presentation of the ecological importance of vegetarianism, updated in 1975. Although the presentation of protein nutrition could be safely simplified—see our chapter on protein—*Diet for a small planet* made a significant and lasting contribution to vegetarian nutrition. The recipes are delicious.

Lerza, Catherine, and Michael F. Jacobson, eds. *Food for people, not for profit: A source book on the food crisis.* New York, Ballantine, 1975.

The official Food Day handbook, a collection of essays that have appeared over the past ten years on a wide range of subjects pertinent to the current food crisis. Fascinating and informative reading from the food activists.

Mayer, Jean. *A diet for living.* New York, McKay, 1975.

Answers to Americans' most common questions about nutrition, from basic nutrition and health to overweight problems and kitchen matters, mostly drawn from the newspaper and magazine columns of one of the most prominent American nutritionists.

U.S. Department of Agriculture. *Food.* Yearbook of Agriculture, 1959. Washington, Govt. Printing Office, 1959.

Although much of this book is dated, two of its essays are still useful: "Storing perishable foods at home" and "Conserving nutritive values."

Wickstrom, Lois. *Food Conspiracy cookbook.* San Francisco, 101 Productions, 1974.

Tells how people can get together to avoid the supermarket by buying food wholesale, based on the author's personal experience.

Yudkin, John. *Sweet and dangerous.* New York, Bantam, 1973.

Everyone should be alerted to the possible dangers of sugar-eating. Here Dr. Yudkin, a pioneering researcher in the field, presents his views in popular language.

Recommended Daily Dietary Allowances (RDA)

Food and Nutrition Board, National Research Council (Revised 1974)*

	Age years	Weight kg	Weight lbs	Height cm	Height in	Energy kcal	Protein g	Vit. A[a] RE[b]	Vit. A[a] IU	Vit. D IU	Vit. E[c] IU
Infants	0 – ½	6	14	60	24	kg×117	kg×2.2	420	1400	400	4
	½ – 1	9	20	71	28	kg×108	kg×2.0	400	2000	400	5
Children	1 – 3	13	28	86	34	1300	23	400	2000	400	7
	4 – 6	20	44	110	44	1800	30	500	2500	400	9
	7 – 10	30	66	135	54	2400	36	700	3300	400	10
Men	11 – 14	44	97	158	63	2800	44	1000	5000	400	12
	15 – 18	61	134	172	69	3000	54	1000	5000	400	15
	19 – 22	67	147	172	69	3000	54	1000	5000	400	15
	23 – 50	70	154	172	69	2700	56	1000	5000		15
	51+	70	154	172	69	2400	56	1000	5000		15
Women	11 – 14	44	97	155	62	2400	44	800	4000	400	12
	15 – 18	54	119	162	65	2100	48	800	4000	400	12
	19 – 22	58	128	162	65	2100	46	800	4000	400	12
	23 – 50	58	128	162	65	2000	46	800	4000		12
	51+	58	128	162	65	1800	46	800	4000		12
Pregnant[g]						+300	+30	1000	5000	400	15
Lactating[h]						+500	+20	1200	6000	400	15

RECOMMENDED INTAKES OF NUTRIENTS, FAO/WHO†

	Age years	Weight kg	Weight lbs	Energy kcal	Protein g	Vit. A RE	Vit. E IU
Children	under 1	7.3	16	820	[i]14	[j]300 μg	[k]10.0 μg
	1 – 3	13.4	29	1360	[i]16	[j]250	[k]10.0
	4 – 6	20.2	44	1830	[i]20	[j]300	[k]10.0
	7 – 9	28.1	62	2190	[i]25	[j]400	[k]2.5
Men	10 – 12	36.9	81	2600	[i]30	[j]575	[k]2.5
	13 – 15	51.3	113	2900	[i]37	[j]725	[k]2.5
	16 – 19	62.9	138	3070	[i]38	[j]750	[k]2.5
	adult	65.0	143	3000	[i]37	[j]750	[k]2.5
Women	10 – 12	38.0	83	2350	[i]29	[j]575	[k]2.5
	13 – 15	49.9	110	2490	[i]31	[j]725	[k]2.5
	16 – 19	54.4	119	2310	[i]30	[j]750	[k]2.5
	adult	55.0	121	2200	[i]29	[j]750	[k]2.5
Pregnant[g]				+350	[i]38	[j]750	[k]10.0
Lactating[h]				+550	[i]46	[j]1200	[k]10.0

*Allowances are intended to provide for individual variations among most normal persons as they live in the U.S. under usual environmental stresses. If the RDA are met from a variety of common foods, the diet will also provide other nutrients for which human requirements are not so well defined. (See text.)

†U.N. recommendations, 1961–1972.

[a]Assumed to be as retinol in milk during first 6 months of life. All later intakes are assumed to be half as retinol and half as beta-carotene when calculated from international units; as retinol equivalents, three fourths are as retinol and one fourth as beta-carotene.

[b]Retinol equivalents. One retinol equivalent = 1 μg of retinol or 6 μg of beta-carotene.

[c]Total vitamin E activity, estimated to be 80% as alpha-tocopherol and 20% other tocopherols.

[d]Allowances refer to dietary sources; pure folacin may be effective in doses less than one-fourth the RDA.

[e]Although allowances are expressed as niacin, an average of 1 mg of niacin will also be contributed by every 60 mg of dietary tryptophan. (See p. 408)

Vit. C mg	Folacin d µg	Niacin e mg	Riboflavin mg	Thiamin mg	Vit. B-6 mg	Vit. B-12 µg	Calcium mg	Phosphorus mg	Iodine µg	Iron mg	Magnesium mg	Zinc mg
35	50	5	0.4	0.3	0.3	0.3	360	240	35	10	60	3
35	50	8	0.6	0.5	0.4	0.3	540	400	45	15	70	5
40	100	9	0.8	0.7	0.6	1.0	800	800	60	15	150	10
40	200	12	1.1	0.9	0.9	1.5	800	800	80	10	200	10
40	300	16	1.2	1.2	1.2	2.0	800	800	110	10	250	10
45	400	18	1.5	1.4	1.6	3.0	1200	1200	130	18	350	15
45	400	20	1.8	1.5	2.0	3.0	1200	1200	150	18	400	15
45	400	20	1.8	1.5	2.0	3.0	800	800	140	10	350	15
45	400	18	1.6	1.4	2.0	3.0	800	800	130	10	350	15
45	400	16	1.5	1.2	2.0	3.0	800	800	110	10	350	15
45	400	16	1.3	1.2	1.6	3.0	1200	1200	115	18	300	15
45	400	14	1.4	1.1	2.0	3.0	1200	1200	115	18	300	15
45	400	14	1.4	1.1	2.0	3.0	800	800	100	18	300	15
45	400	13	1.2	1.0	2.0	3.0	800	800	100	18	300	15
45	400	12	1.1	1.0	2.0	3.0	800	800	80	10	300	15
60	800	+2	+0.3	+0.3	2.5	4.0	1200	1200	125	f18+	450	20
80	600	+4	+0.5	+0.3	2.5	4.0	1200	1200	150	18	450	25

Vit. C mg	Folacin d µg	Niacin e mg	Riboflavin mg	Thiamin mg	Vit. B-12 µg	Calcium mg	Iron mg
20	60	5.4	0.5	0.3	0.3	500–600	l5–10
20	100	9.0	0.8	0.5	0.9	400–500	l5–10
20	100	12.1	1.1	0.7	1.5	400–500	l5–10
20	100	14.5	1.3	0.9	1.5	400–500	l5–10
20	100	17.2	1.6	1.0	2.0	600–700	l5–10
30	200	19.1	1.7	1.2	2.0	600–700	l9–18
30	200	20.3	1.8	1.2	2.0	500–600	l5–9
30	200	19.8	1.8	1.2	2.0	400–500	l5–9
20	100	15.5	1.4	0.9	2.0	600–700	l5–10
30	200	16.4	1.5	1.0	2.0	600–700	l12–24
30	200	15.2	1.4	0.9	2.0	500–600	l14–28
30	200	14.5	1.3	0.9	2.0	400–500	l14–28
30	400	+2.3	+0.2	+0.1	3.0	1000–1200	m
30	300	+3.7	+0.4	+0.2	2.5	1000–1200	m

f This increased requirement cannot be met by ordinary diets; the Food and Nutrition Board recommends a supplementary source of iron.
g Latter half of pregnancy.
h First six months.
i As egg or milk protein ("balanced" or highly utilizable protein; see text).
j As micrograms of retinol (1965 recommendation); 0.3 µg of retinol≅1 IU.
k As micrograms of cholecalciferol; 10 µg of calciferol≅400 IU.
l Lower value should be used when more than 25% of the diet's calories come from animal foods; the higher value applies when animal foods supply less than 10% of the calories.
m Supplementation is recommended when iron stores are depleted at the beginning of pregnancy; if iron status is satisfactory, the regular recommended intake applies.

THE U.S. RDA

"U. S. Recommended Daily Allowances"—Food and Drug Administration standards for nutrition labeling of foods,* based on the 1968 RDA.

	Adults and children over 4	Infants and children under 4
Protein	65 grams	28 grams
Vitamin A	5000 IU	2500 IU
Vitamin C	60 milligrams	40 milligrams
Thiamin	1.5 milligrams	0.7 milligrams
Riboflavin	1.7 milligrams	0.8 milligrams
Niacin	20 milligrams	9 milligrams
Calcium	1 gram	0.8 grams
Iron	18 milligrams	10 milligrams
Vitamin D	400 IU	400 IU
Vitamin E	30 IU	10 IU
Vitamin B-6	2 milligrams	0.7 milligrams
Folacin	0.4 milligrams	0.2 milligrams
Vitamin B-12	6 micrograms	3 micrograms
Phosphorus	1 gram	0.8 grams
Iodine	150 micrograms	70 micrograms
Magnesium	400 milligrams	200 milligrams
Zinc	15 milligrams	8 milligrams
Copper	2 milligrams	1 milligrams
Biotin	0.3 milligrams	0.15 milligrams
Pantothenic acid	10 milligrams	5 milligrams

*Including foods that are also vitamin–mineral supplements. (Labels for nonfood vitamin–mineral supplements follow a slightly different format.) No dietary supplements will give you more than 150 percent of the U.S. RDA for any nutrient; larger quantities will be sold as drugs.

Nutrient Composition of Foods

While you are studying nutrition and trying to apply it to meal planning and food preparation, you will want to refer to the following food composition tables to learn what nutrients each food contains. If you add up the values given for all the foods you eat over several days and then figure an average for each nutrient, you can compare the results to the Recommended Daily Dietary Allowances (RDA) on pages 454–455. This will give you an idea of the adequacy of your diet and identify any nutrients that might be low. For comparison, a table listing the nutrient intakes recommended by United Nations agencies follows the RDA table. These recommendations take into consideration the different conditions and problems of less affluent nations, whose diets are often much simpler than those in the United States. In evaluating your diet, however, you should always keep in mind that there is considerable variation in the nutrient composition of different samples of the same food. Research values like those in the tables which follow are averages rather than absolutely accurate figures, and the variation from sample to sample can be as much as 30 percent for some nutrients. RDA figures, too, are averages, and are intended to stay on the safe side of a wide range of individual needs.

In learning about the nutrients in different foods, you will also want to make use of the Nutrition Information listed on product labels. For a given serving size, the amount of calories, protein, carbohydrate, and fat is listed first; then the protein, vitamins, and minerals in the serving are listed as percentages of the U.S. RDA—the "Recommended Daily Allowances" established for labeling standards by the Food and Drug Administration, shown on page 456.

CONTENTS OF THE FOOD TABLES

28 grams = 1 ounce
100 grams = 3½ ounces
454 grams = 1 pound
1 teaspoon = 5 milliliters
1 quart = about 1 liter

1000 micrograms = 1 milligram
1000 milligrams = 1 gram
1000 grams = 1 kilogram
.001 gram = 1 milligram
.001 milligram = 1 microgram

3 teaspoons = 1 tablespoon
4 tablespoons = ¼ cup
5⅓ tablespoons = ⅓ cup
16 tablespoons = 1 cup
1 cup = 8 fluid ounces
1 cup = ½ pint
2 cups = 1 pint
4 cups = 1 quart
4 quarts = 1 gallon

100° F = 38° C *warm water*
180° F = 82° C *very hot water*
250° F = 121° C *very slow oven*
300° F = 149° C *slow oven*
325° F = 163° C *slow oven*
350° F = 177° C *moderate oven*
375° F = 191° C *moderate oven*
400° F = 204° C *hot oven*
425° F = 218° C *hot oven*
450° F = 232° C *very hot oven*
To convert °F to °C, subtract 32°, multiply by 5, and divide by 9 [(°F − 32) × 5 ÷ 9 = °C].

Foods are listed in our tables in common measures. Values, including the weight of the food in grams, are for the edible portion (EP) of the food only; for example, values for an artichoke are for the soft leaf ends and heart only, though we have indicated the number of whole artichokes that the figures may represent. The tables are organized around the Four Food Groups for a Meatless Diet, emphasizing whole foods and staples. The section entitled Our Recipes & Commercial Foods lists selected recipes from this book and, for comparison, many commercial food products. The table for Other Items lists many fractioned food staples like fats and sweeteners along with other, miscellaneous items. From the foods listed in these tables you should be able to approximate values for any recipe or combination dish you want, being sure to keep in mind the nutrient losses in the kitchen discussed on pages 441 and following.

Most of our figures are from USDA Agriculture Handbook no. 456 (Adams in the bibliography beginning on page 447). Others are from Agriculture Handbook no. 8 (Watt and Merrill) and USDA Home Economics Research Report no. 36, *Pantothenic Acid, Vitamin B-6, and Vitamin B-12 in Foods* (Orr). Some of the figures are from Bowes and Church, *Food Values of Portions Commonly Used.* Other sources are listed on page 485. Important nutrients not included in these tables, such as folacin, vitamin E, and zinc, may be found in tables accompanying the discussions of these nutrients in the text.

ABBREVIATIONS AND SYMBOLS USED IN THE TABLES

sl. *slice*
c. *cup*
tbsp. *tablespoon*
tsp. *teaspoon*
lb. *pound*
oz. *ounce(s)*
2″ × 2″ *2 inches by 2 inches*
dm. *diameter*
lg. *large*
med. *medium*
sm. *small*
ckd. *cooked*

g *grams*
mg *milligrams*
µg *micrograms*
IU *International Units*
wt. *weight*
EP *edible portion*
Tr *trace amounts only*
− *lack of reliable data; believed to be present in a measurable amount*
* *our recipe*

Grains and Flours

Item / Measure	Uncooked wt.(EP) g / Cooked wt.(EP) g	Calories Kcal / Protein g	Carbohydrate g / Fiber g	Fat (total) g / Linoleic Acid g	Vitamin A IU / Vitamin C mg	Thiamin mg / Riboflavin mg	Niacin mg / Vitamin B-6 mg	Iron mg / Vitamin B-12 µg	Calcium mg / Phosphorus mg	Sodium mg / Potassium mg
Barley, whole-grain, hulled,a raw	204	936	170	5.7	—	1.2	13	1.2	180	41
1 cup		27	12	2.3	0	.45	.7	0	960	1280
¼ cup rounded	58	266	47	1.6	—	.33	3.7	.4	52	12
(makes 1 cup cooked)		7.6	3.5	.7	0	.13	.2	0	270	360
pot or Scotch,b dry	200	696	150	2.2	0	.42	7.4	5.4	68	—
1 cup		19	1.8	—	0	.14	—	0	580	590
¼ cup rounded	57	198	44	.6	0	.12	2.1	1.5	19	—
(makes 1 cup cooked)		5.5	.5	—	0	.04	—	0	170	170
pearl, light,b dry	200	698	160	2.0	0	.24	6.2	4.0	32	6
1 cup		16	1.0	—	0	.10	.45	0	380	320
¼ cup rounded	57	199	45	.6	0	.07	1.8	1.1	9	2
(makes 1 cup cooked)		4.7	.3	—	0	.03	.13	0	110	91
Buckwheat, whole-grain, raw	163	546	120	3.9	0	.98	7.2	5.0	190	—
1 cup		19	16	1.2	0	c.3	—	0	460	730
⅓ cup rounded	65	218	47	1.6	0	.39	2.9	2.0	74	—
(makes 1 cup cooked)		7.6	6.4	.5	0	c.1	—	0	180	290
Buckwheat flour, dark	98	326	71	2.4	0	.57	2.8	2.7	32	—
1 cup sifted		12	1.6	.8	0	.15	.57	0	340	—
light	98	340	78	1.2	0	.08	.4	1.0	11	—
1 cup sifted		6.3	.5	.4	0	.04	—	0	86	310
Cornmeal, unbolted,d dry	122	433	90	4.8	e620	.46	2.4	2.9	24	1
1 cup		11	2.0	2.4	0	.13	.30	0	310	350
⅓ cup (makes 1 cup	41	144	30	1.6	e210	.15	.8	1.0	8	—
cooked polenta)		3.7	.7	.8	0	.04	.10	0	100	120
bolted d	122	442	91	4.1	e590	.37	2.3	2.2	21	1
1 cup		11	1.2	2.1	0	.10	.31	0	270	300
degermed, unenriched d	138	502	110	1.7	e610	.19	1.4	1.5	8	1
1 cup		11	.8	.9	0	.07	—	0	140	170
Masa Harina, enriched f	110	404	84	4.4	—	.48	5.3	4.8	140	15
(Quaker Oats Co.), 1 cup		10	2.6	—	0	.34	—	0	320	—
Corn flour	117	431	90	3.0	e400	.23	1.6	2.1	7	1
1 cup sifted		9.1	.8	1.6	0	.07	—	0	92	—
Corn grits (hominy grits)	160	579	120	1.3	700	.70	5.6	4.6	6	2
degermed, enriched, dry, 1 cup		14	.6	.7	0	.42	.24	0	120	130
cooked		125	27	.2	150	.10	1.0	.7	2	500
1 cup	245	2.9	.2	.1	0	.07	—	0	25	27
Grain mixes: *All in One (p.116)	116	403	74	6.9	e110	.81	4.1	6.5	83	3
dry, 1 cup		18	3.5	—	0	.24	—	0	640	530
¼ cup scant	28	97	18	1.7	e30	.19	1.0	1.6	20	1
(makes 1 cup cooked)		4.2	.8	—	0	.06	—	0	150	130

aValues from Source 9.

bPearling removes the hulls and outer portions of the kernel by abrasive action. What remains after the first 3 pearlings is sold as Scotch or pot barley; pearl barley is what remains after 6 pearlings, having lost about 74% of the grain's protein, 85% of the fat, 97% of the fiber, and 88% of the mineral constituents of the original barley. (Source 14)

cValues from Source 9.

dBolted cornmeal retains 95% of the original kernel—the hull is removed by crude sifting but the germ and endosperm remain. Degermed meal and grits are highly refined; both bran and germ are completely removed. Enrichment may then be added.

eValues based on yellow varieties. White varieties have only trace amounts of vitamin A.

fThe Mexican method of preparing cornmeal is to grind it with lime water, which adds calcium. The product shown here is also enriched with niacin, iron, thiamin, and riboflavin.

[459]

	Uncooked wt. (EP) g / Cooked wt. (EP) g	Calories Kcal / Protein g	Carbohydrate g / Fiber g	Fat (total) g / Linoleic Acid g	Vitamin A IU / Vitamin C mg	Thiamin mg / Riboflavin mg	Niacin mg / Vitamin B-6 mg	Iron mg / Vitamin B-12 µg	Calcium mg / Phosphorus mg	Sodium mg / Potassium mg
*Stuart's Choice (p. 116), dry, 1 cup	144	484	100	3.8	210	.59	4.5	4.6	51	2
		14	3.3	—	0	.16	—	0	500	120
3 tablespoons (makes 1 cup cooked)	28	90	20	.7	40	.11	.9	.9	10	Tr
		2.8	.6	—	0	.03	—	0	98	8
Millet, whole-grain, raw, 1 cup	202	660	150	5.9	0	1.5	4.6	14	40	—
		20	6.5	2.0	0	.77	—	0	630	870
¼ cup rounded (makes 1 cup cooked)	58	190	42	1.7	0	.42	1.3	3.9	12	—
		5.7	1.9	.6	0	.22	—	0	180	250
Oats, rolled, dry, 1 cup	80	312	55	5.9	0	.48	.8	3.6	42	2
		11	1.0	2.3	0	.11	.11	0	320	280
cooked, 1 cup	240	132	23	2.4	0	.19	.2	1.4	22	520
		4.8	.5	.9	0	.05	—	0	140	150
Potato flour, whole, 1 cup stirred	184	646	150	1.5	Tr	.77	6.3	32	61	63
		15	2.9	—	35	.26	.01	0	330	2900
Rice, brown, long-grain, raw, 1 cup	185	666	140	4.3	0	.63	8.7	3.0	59	17
		14	1.7	1.4	0	.09	1.0	0	410	400
cooked, 1 cup	195	232	50	1.6	0	.18	2.7	1.0	23	550
		4.9	.6	.5	0	.04	—	0	140	140
short-grain, raw, 1 cup	200	720	150	3.8	0	.68	9.4	3.2	64	18
		15	1.8	—	0	.10	1.1	0	440	430
Rice, parboiled ('converted'), dry, 1 cup	185	683	150	.6	0	.81	6.5	5.4	110	17
		14	.4	—	0	.07	.79	0	370	280
cooked, 1 cup	175	186	41	.2	0	.19	2.1	1.4	33	630
		3.7	.2	—	0	.02	—	0	100	75
Rice flour, brown[g], 1 cup stirred	120	432	93	2.8	0	.41	5.6	1.9	38	11
		9.0	1.1	—	0	.06	.66	0	260	260
Rice bran, 1 cup	102	282	52	20	0	2.3	30	20	78	Tr
		14	12	6.7	0	.26	[h]3.0	0	1400	1500
1 tablespoon	6	18	3	1.2	0	.14	1.9	1.2	5	Tr
		.8	.7	.4	0	.02	[h].2	0	89	96
Rice polishings, 1 cup stirred	105	278	61	13	0	1.9	30	17	72	Tr
		13	2.5	4.6	0	.19	[h]2.9	0	1200	750
1 tablespoon	7	17	4	.9	0	.12	1.8	1.1	4	Tr
		.8	.2	.3	0	.01	[h].2	0	73	47
Rye berries, raw, 1 cup	177	591	130	3.9	0	.76	2.8	6.5	67	2
		21	3.5	1.7	0	.39	—	0	670	830
⅓ cup rounded (makes 1 cup cooked)	71	237	52	1.6	0	.31	1.1	2.6	27	1
		8.6	1.4	.7	0	.16	—	0	270	330
Rye flour, dark, 1 cup	128	419	87	3.3	0	.78	3.5	5.8	69	1
		21	3.1	—	0	.28	.38	0	690	1100
light, 1 cup sifted	88	319	69	.9	0	.13	.5	1.0	19	1
		8.3	.4	—	0	.06	.08	0	160	140
Soybean flour, full-fat, 1 cup stirred	70	295	21	14	80	.60	1.5	5.9	140	1
		26	1.7	7.4	0	.22	.40	0	390	1200
low-fat, 1 cup stirred	88	313	32	5.9	70	.73	2.3	8.0	230	1
		38	2.2	3.1	0	.32	.60	0	560	1600
defatted, 1 cup stirred	100	326	38	.9	40	1.1	2.6	11	270	1
		47	2.3	—	0	.34	.72	0	660	1800
Triticale,[i] whole-grain, raw, 1 cup	155	—	—	—	0	—	—	8.0	51	7
		25	—	—	0	—	—	0	760	680

[g]Values adapted from those of brown rice.   [h]Values adapted from Source 10.   [i]Values from Sources 11 and 12.

	Uncooked wt.(EP) g / Cooked wt.(EP) g	Calories Kcal / Protein g	Carbohydrate g / Fiber g	Fat (total) g / Linoleic Acid g	Vitamin A IU / Vitamin C mg	Thiamin mg / Riboflavin mg	Niacin mg / Vitamin B-6 mg	Iron mg / Vitamin B-12 µg	Calcium mg / Phosphorus mg	Sodium mg / Potassium mg
flour, refined	116	—	—	1.9	0	—	—	1.5	26	4
1 cup	14	—	—	.8	0	—	—	0	220	190
Wheat berries, raw: hard red spring, 1 cup	175	578	120	4.7	0	1.0	7.5	5.4	63	5
	24	4.0	2.1	0	.21	[j].8	0	670	650	
⅓ cup rounded (makes 1 cup cooked)	67	221	46	1.8	0	[k].38	[l]2.9	2.1	24	2
	9.4	1.5	.8	0	.08	[l].3	0	260	250	
hard red winter, 1 cup	175	578	120	4.4	0	.91	7.5	6.0	81	5
	22	4.0	1.9	0	.21	[j].8	0	620	650	
soft red winter, 1 cup	175	571	130	4.2	0	.75	6.3	6.1	74	5
	18	4.0	1.9	0	.19	[j].9	0	700	660	
white, 1 cup	175	586	130	3.5	0	.93	9.3	5.3	63	5
	16	3.3	1.5	0	.21	[j].9	0	690	680	
durum, 1 cup	175	581	120	5.8	0	1.2	7.7	7.5	65	5
	22	3.2	2.4	0	.21	—	0	680	760	
Wheat, cracked, dry 1 cup	155	509	110	3.3	0	.67	5.5	5.5	66	2
	16	3.9	—	0	.17		0	620	—	
⅓ cup rounded (makes 1 cup cooked)	66	217	48	1.4	0	.29	2.4	2.4	28	1
	6.8	1.4	—	0	.07		0	270	—	
Wheat, rolled, dry 1 cup	85	289	65	1.7	0	.31	3.5	2.7	31	2
	8.4	1.9	—	0	.10	—	0	290	320	
cooked 1 cup	240	180	41	1.0	0	.17	2.2	1.7	19	710
	5.3	1.2	—	0	.07	—	0	180	200	
Wheat, bulgur (parboiled red wheat), dry, 1 cup	170	602	130	2.6	0	.48	7.7	6.3	49	—
	19	2.9	1.1	0	.24	.38	0	580	390	
¾ cup (makes 1 cup cooked)	128	452	97	1.9	0	.36	5.8	4.7	37	—
	14	2.2	.8	0	.18	.29	0	430	290	
Wheat flour: whole wheat[m] 1 cup stirred	120	400	85	1.8	0	.66	5.2	4.0	49	4
	16	2.8	.8	0	.14	.41	0	450	440	
80% extraction 1 cup sifted	110	402	82	1.4	0	.28	2.2	1.4	26	2
	13	.6	—	0	.08	.07	0	210	100	
whole wheat pastry[n] 1 cup stirred	148	496	110	3.0	0	.78	7.8	4.4	53	4
	14	2.8	—	0	.18	—	0	580	580	
gluten (45% gluten, 55% patent flour), 1 cup	140	529	66	2.7	0	—	—	—	56	3
	58	.6	—	0			0	200	84	
all-purpose (white), enriched[o] 1 cup sifted	115	419	88	1.6	0	.74	6.0	10	18	2
	12	.3	.7	0	.45	.07	0	100	110	
Wheat bran, crude 1 cup	52	111	32	2.4	0	.37	11	7.7	62	5
	8.3	4.7	1.1	0	.18	.43	0	660	580	
1 tablespoon	3	7	2	.1	0	.02	.7	.5	4	Tr
	.5	.3	Tr	0	.01	.03	0	41	36	
Wheat germ, crude 1 cup	82	298	38	8.9	0	1.6	3.4	7.7	59	2
	22	2.0	4.8	0	.56	[h].6.	0	920	680	
1 tablespoon	5	19	2	.5	0	.10	.2	.5	4	Tr
	1.4	.1	.3	0	.03	[h]Tr	0	57	42	
toasted 1 tablespoon	6	23	3	.7	10	.11	.3	.5	3	Tr
	1.8	.1	.3	1	.05	.07	0	70	57	
Wheat gluten[p] 3½ ounces	100	—	—	5.4	0	—	2.4	.6	—	—
	89	—	2.4	0	—	—	0	—	—	

[j]Values adapted from Source 9.
[k]0.34 mg when wheat is cooked.
[l]2.6 mg when wheat is cooked.
[m]Milled from hard (high gluten content) wheats.

[n]Values adapted from those of whole-grain white wheat, a soft (low gluten content) wheat.

[o]A combination of hard and soft wheat flours whose bran and germ have been removed. The flour is then enriched.
[p]Values from Source 10.

	Uncooked wt. (EP) g	Calories Kcal	Carbohydrate g	Fat (total) g	Vitamin A IU	Thiamin mg	Niacin mg	Iron mg	Calcium mg	Sodium mg
	Cooked wt. (EP) g	Protein g	Fiber g	Linoleic Acid g	Vitamin C mg	Riboflavin mg	Vitamin B-6 mg	Vitamin B-12 µg	Phosphorus mg	Potassium mg
Wild rice, raw	160	565	120	1.1	0	.72	9.9	6.7	30	11
1 cup		23	1.6	—	0	1.0	—	0	540	350
¼ cup	40	141	30	.3	0	.18	2.5	1.7	8	3
(makes 1 cup cooked)		5.6	.4	—	0	.25	—	0	140	88

Dry Legumes

	Uncooked wt. (EP) g	Calories Kcal	Carbohydrate g	Fat (total) g	Vitamin A IU	Thiamin mg	Niacin mg	Iron mg	Calcium mg	Sodium mg
	Cooked wt. (EP) g	Protein g	Fiber g	Linoleic Acid g	Vitamin C mg	Riboflavin mg	Vitamin B-6 mg	Vitamin B-12 µg	Phosphorus mg	Potassium mg
Bean mixes: *Breakfast Beans (p. 122)		265	48	1.7	50	.26	1.7	4.9	68	820
cooked, 1 cup		17	2.2	—	—	.15	—	0	240	800
***Red Bean Mix** (p. 257)		303	55	1.2	20	.36	1.5	6.2	110	550
cooked, 1 cup		20	2.8	—	—	.17	—	0	370	890
***White Bean Mix** (p. 257)		240	44	1.1	10	.26	.8	5.2	74	520
cooked, 1 cup		16	2.7	—	—	.13	—	0	270	940
Black beans, raw	200	678	120	3.0	60	1.1	4.4	16	270	50
1 cup		45	8.8	—	—	.40	—	0	840	2100
cooked[a]	100	337	61	1.4	30	.35	1.9	7.9	140	25
1 cup		22	4.4	—	—	.18	—	0	420	1000
Black-eyed peas (cowpeas), raw	170	583	100	2.6	50	1.8	3.7	9.9	130	60
1 cup		39	7.5	—	—	.36	.96	0	720	1700
cooked	250	190	34	.8	30	.40	1.0	3.3	43	20
1 cup		13	2.5	—	—	.10	—	0	240	570
Fava beans (broad beans), raw	454	1533	260	7.7	320	2.3	11	32	460	—
1 pound		110	30	—	—	1.4	—	0	1800	—
Garbanzo beans (chickpeas), raw	200	720	120	9.6	100	.62	4.0	14	300	52
1 cup		41	10	3.5	—	.30	1.1	0	660	1600
cooked[a]	100	338	61	4.6	50	.20	1.8	6.9	150	26
1 cup		20	5.0	—	—	.13	—	0	330	800
Great northern beans, raw	180	612	110	2.9	0	1.2	4.3	14	260	34
1 cup		40	7.7	—	—	.40	1.0	0	760	2200
cooked	180	212	38	1.1	0	.25	1.3	4.9	90	13
1 cup		14	2.7	—	0	.13	—	0	270	750
Lentils, raw	190	646	110	2.1	110	.70	3.8	13	150	57
1 cup		47	7.4	—	—	.42	1.1	0	720	1500
cooked	200	212	39	Tr	40	.14	1.2	4.2	50	
1 cup		16	2.4	—	0	.12	—	0	240	500
Lima beans, large, raw	180	621	120	2.9	Tr	.86	3.4	14	130	7
1 cup		37	7.7	—	—	.31	1.0	0	690	2800
small (baby limas), raw	190	656	120	3.0	Tr	.91	3.6	15	140	8
1 cup		39	8.2	—	—	.32	1.1	0	730	2900
cooked (large or small)		262	49	1.1		.25	1.3	5.9	55	4
1 cup	190	16	3.2	—	—	.11	—	0	290	1200
Mung beans, raw	210	714	130	2.7	170	.80	5.5	16	250	13
1 cup		51	9.2	—	—	.44	—	0	710	2200
cooked[a]	105	355	63	1.3	80	.25	2.4	8.1	120	6
1 cup		25	4.6	—	—	.20	—	0	360	1100
Mung bean sprouts, raw	105	37	7	.2	20	.14	.8	1.4	20	5
1 cup		4.0	.7	—	20	.14	—	0	67	230
cooked		35	6	.3	30	.11	.9	1.1	21	5
1 cup	125	4.0	.9	—	8	.13	—	0	60	200

[a]Nutrient losses calculated from averages for the legumes listed in Agriculture Handbook no. 8 (Source 3). Percentages of nutrients retained less than 100% are: calories 99%, fat 96%, thiamin 64%, riboflavin 89%, and niacin 89%.

	Uncooked wt.(EP) g / Cooked wt.(EP) g	Calories Kcal / Protein g	Carbohydrate g / Fiber g	Fat (total) g / Linoleic Acid g	Vitamin A IU / Vitamin C mg	Thiamin mg / Riboflavin mg	Niacin mg / Vitamin B-6 mg	Iron mg / Vitamin B-12 µg	Calcium mg / Phosphorus mg	Sodium mg / Potassium mg
Navy beans (small white), raw	205	697	130	3.3	0	1.3	4.9	16	300	39
1 cup		46	8.8	—	—	.45	1.1	0	870	2500
cooked		224	40	1.1	0	.27	1.3	5.1	95	13
1 cup	190	15	2.8	—	0	.13	—	0	280	790
Peanuts (see Nuts and Seeds, page 464)										
Peas, whole, raw	200	680	120	2.6	240	1.5	6.0	10	130	70
1 cup		48	9.8	—	—	.58	.26	0	680	2000
cooked[a]	100	338	60	1.2	120	.47	2.7	5.1	64	35
1 cup		24	4.9	—	—	.26	—	0	340	1000
split, raw	200	696	120	2.0	240	1.5	6.0	10	66	80
1 cup		48	2.4	—	—	.58	—	0	540	1800
cooked		230	42	.6	80	.30	1.8	3.4	22	26
1 cup	200	16	.8	—	—	.18	—	0	180	590
Pinto or **Calico beans,** raw	190	663	120	2.3	—	1.6	4.2	12	260	19
1 cup		44	8.2	—	—	.40	1.0	0	870	1900
cooked[a]	95	330	61	1.1	—	.51	1.9	6.1	130	10
1 cup		22	4.1	—	—	.18	—	0	430	940
Red or **Kidney beans,** raw	185	635	110	2.8	40	.94	4.3	13	200	19
1 cup		42	7.8	—	—	.37	.82	0	750	1800
cooked		218	40	.9	10	.20	1.3	4.4	70	6
1 cup	185	14	2.8	—	—	.11	—	0	260	630
Soybeans, raw, whole	210	846	70	37	170	2.3	4.6	18	480	11
1 cup		72	10	19	—	.65	1.7	0	1200	3500
cooked		234	19	10	50	.38	1.1	4.9	130	4
1 cup	180	20	2.9	5.3	0	.16	—	0	320	970
cooked, ground		416	34	18	100	.67	1.9	8.6	230	6
1 cup	225	35	5.1	9.6	0	.29	—	0	570	1700
Soy grits,[b] dry	153	617	51	27	120	1.6	3.4	13	350	8
1 cup		52	7.5	13	—	.47	1.2	0	850	2600
cooked		303	25	13	70	.49	1.4	6.3	170	5
1 cup	193	26	3.7	7.0	—	.21	—	0	420	1300
Soybean sprouts, raw	105	48	6	1.5	80	.24	.8	1.1	50	—
1 cup		6.5	.8	—	14	.21	—	0	70	—
cooked		48	5	1.8	100	.20	.9	.9	54	—
1 cup	125	6.6	1.0	—	5	.19	—	0	63	—
Soybeans, fermented, with cereal (miso), 1 tablespoon	17	29	4	.8	10	.01	.1	.3	12	500
		1.8	.4	.3	0	.02	—	0	53	57
Soybean curd (tofu), piece 2½″×2¾″×1″	120	86	3	5.0	0	.07	.1	2.3	150	8
		9.4	.1	2.6	0	.04	—	0	150	50
Soybean flour, full-fat	70	295	21	14	80	.60	1.5	5.9	140	1
1 cup stirred		26	1.7	7.4	0	.22	.40	0	390	1200
low-fat	88	313	32	5.9	70	.73	2.3	8.0	230	1
1 cup stirred		38	2.2	3.1	0	.32	.60	0	560	1600
defatted	100	326	38	.9	40	1.1	2.6	11	260	1
1 cup stirred		47	2.3	—	0	.34	.72	0	660	1800
Soybean milk, unfortified	220	73	5	3.3	90	.18	.4	1.8	46	—
1 cup fluid		7.5	0	—	0	.07	—	0	110	—
*Soy Milk (p. 134), fully fortified[c]		155	17	8.3	90	.18	.5	1.9	350	—
1 cup fluid	240	7.6	0	1.5	—	.07	—	4.0	110	—

[b] Values adapted from whole raw and cooked soybeans.

[c] Approximates energy content of whole milk for use as a milk substitute for small children. For other purposes it can be made lower in calories, carbohydrate, and fat by decreasing the oil and honey in the recipe (p. 134).

	Uncooked wt.(EP) g / Cooked wt.(EP) g	Calories Kcal / Protein g	Carbohydrate g / Fiber g	Fat (total) g / Linoleic Acid g	Vitamin A IU / Vitamin C mg	Thiamin mg / Riboflavin mg	Niacin mg / Vitamin B-6 mg	Iron mg / Vitamin B-12 μg	Calcium mg / Phosphorus mg	Sodium mg / Potassium mg
Soyagen,[d] dry ¼ cup (1 cup fluid)	28	163	13	6.3	—	—	—	—	190	—
		6.3	—	—	—	—	—	2.4	120	—
Soyamel,[d] 5 tbsp. dry to 7 oz. water (1 cup fluid)	28	140	16	6.0	1000	.45	3.0	4.5	150	—
		5.0	—	—	18	.60	.40	.48	150	—
Soya powder, Fearn (natural),[d] dry ¼ cup	28	98	6	7.4	—	.22	1.2	2.6	51	1
		12	—	—	—	.08	—	0	27	—
Soybean protein, dry 1 ounce	28	90	4	Tr	—	—	—	—	34	59
		21	.1	—	0	—	—	0	190	50

Nuts and Seeds

	Uncooked wt.(EP) g / Cooked wt.(EP) g	Calories Kcal / Protein g	Carbohydrate g / Fiber g	Fat (total) g / Linoleic Acid g	Vitamin A IU / Vitamin C mg	Thiamin mg / Riboflavin mg	Niacin mg / Vitamin B-6 mg	Iron mg / Vitamin B-12 μg	Calcium mg / Phosphorus mg	Sodium mg / Potassium mg
Almonds, whole, shelled 1 cup	142	849	28	76	0	[a].34	5.0	6.7	330	6
		26	3.7	14	Tr	1.3	.14	0	720	1100
10 nuts	10	60	2	5.4	0	.02	.4	.5	23	Tr
		1.9	.3	1.0	Tr	.09	.01	0	50	77
Almond meal, home-ground[b] ½ cup	57	341	11	31	0	.14	2.0	2.7	130	2
		11	1.5	5.6	Tr	.52	.06	0	290	440
Brazil nuts 3 large nuts	28	89	2	19	Tr	.13	.2	.5	25	Tr
		1.9	.9	7.1	—	.02	.05	0	94	97
Cashew nuts, roasted 1 cup	140	785	41	64	140	.60	2.5	5.3	53	21
		24	2.0	10	—	.35	—	0	520	650
14 large, 18 medium, or 26 small	28	159	8	13	30	.12	.5	1.1	11	4
		4.9	.4	2.0	—	.07	—	0	110	130
Chestnuts, fresh 10 nuts	73	141	31	2.0	—	.16	.4	1.2	20	4
		2.1	.8	.7	—	.16	.24	0	64	330
Coconut, fresh meat piece, 2″ × 2″ × ½″	45	156	4	16	0	.02	.2	.8	6	10
		1.6	1.8	.3	1	.01	.02	0	43	120
shredded 1 cup packed	130	450	12	46	0	.07	.7	2.2	17	30
		4.6	5.2	.9	4	.03	.06	0	120	330
dried, shredded 1 cup	62	344	33	24	0	.02	.4	2.2	27	11
		2.2	2.4	Tr	2	.02	—	0	120	500
Coconut water (liquid in coconut) 1 cup	240	53	11	.5	0	Tr	.2	.7	48	60
		.7	Tr	—	5	Tr	.08	0	31	350
Coconut milk (expressed from meat and water), 1 cup	240	605	12	60	0	.07	1.9	3.8	38	—
		7.7	—	Tr	5	Tr	—	0	240	—
Filberts (hazelnuts) 10 nuts	14	87	2	9.1	—	.06	.1	.5	29	Tr
		1.7	.4	.9	Tr	—	.08	0	47	97
Litchi nuts, dried 6 nuts	15	45	10	.1	—	—	—	.3	4	Tr
		.5	—	—	5	—	—	0	—	160
Macadamia nuts, roasted 6 whole nuts	15	109	2	11	0	.03	.2	.3	8	—
		1.4	.4	.2	0	.02	—	0	36	40
Peanuts, roasted with skin 1 cup chopped	144	838	30	72	—	.46	25	3.2	100	7
		38	3.9	21	0	.19	.58	0	590	1000
1 tablespoon chopped	9	52	2	4.5	—	.03	1.5	.2	6	Tr
		2.4	.2	1.3	0	.01	.04	0	37	63
roasted, salted, 10 Virginia or 20 Spanish	9	53	2	4.5	—	.03	1.5	.2	7	38
		2.3	.2	1.3	0	.01	.04	0	36	61
Peanut butter, small amount fat and salt added, 1 cup	258	1499	44	130	—	.34	40	5.2	160	1600
		72	4.9	36	0	.34	.85	0	1000	1700
1 tablespoon	16	93	3	7.9	—	.02	2.5	.3	10	97
		4.4	.3	2.2	0	.02	.05	0	65	110

[d]Values taken from label.   [b]Values adapted from whole-seed kernels.
[a]When roasted, decreases to .07 mg.

Uncooked wt.(EP) g	Calories Kcal	Carbohydrate g	Fat (total) g	Vitamin A IU	Thiamin mg	Niacin mg	Iron mg	Calcium mg	Sodium mg
Cooked wt.(EP) g	Protein g	Fiber g	Linoleic Acid g	Vitamin C mg	Riboflavin mg	Vitamin B-6 mg	Vitamin B-12 µg	Phosphorus mg	Potassium mg
moderate amount sugar, fat, and salt added, 1 tablespoon	94	3	8.1	—	.02	2.4	.3	9	97
16	4.0	.3	2.3	0	.02	.05	0	61	100
Pecans — 108	742	16	77	140	.93	1.0	2.6	79	Tr
1 cup halves	9.9	2.5	18	2	.14	.20	0	310	650
12 halves or — 15	104	2	11	20	.12	.2	.4	10	Tr
2 tablespoons chopped	1.4	.3	2.6	Tr	.02	.03	0	44	90
Pine nuts: pignolias — 28	156	3	13	—	.18	—	—	—	—
1 ounce	8.8	.3	6.2	—	—	—	0	—	—
piñon nuts — 28	180	6	17	10	.36	1.3	1.5	3	—
1 ounce	3.7	.3	—	Tr	.07	—	0	170	—
Pistachio nuts — 15	88	3	8.0	30	.10	.2	1.1	20	—
30 nuts	2.9	.3	1.0	0	—	—	0	75	150
Pumpkin or **Squash seed kernels** dried, 1 cup — 140	774	21	65	100	.34	3.4	16	71	—
	41	2.7	28	—	.27	c.13	0	1600	—
2 tablespoons — 18	97	3	8.2	10	.04	.4	2.0	9	—
	5.1	.3	3.4	—	.03	c.02	0	200	—
Sesame seeds, whole — 145	816	31	71	40	1.4	7.8	15	1700	87
1 cup	27	9.1	30	0	.35	—	0	890	1100
2 tablespoons — 18	101	4	8.8	Tr	.18	1.0	1.9	210	11
	3.3	1.1	3.8	0	.04	—	0	110	130
hulled — 16	94	3	8.6	—	.02	.8	.4	18	—
2 tablespoons	3.0	.4	3.6	0	.02	—	0	94	—
Sesame meal, home-ground[b] — 46	259	10	23	10	.45	2.5	4.8	530	28
½ cup	8.6	2.9	9.7	0	.11	—	0	280	330
1 tablespoon — 6	32	1	2.8	Tr	.06	.3	.6	67	3
	1.1	.4	1.3	0	.01	—	0	35	42
Sunflower seed kernels — 145	812	29	69	70	2.8	7.8	10	170	44
1 cup	35	5.5	43	—	.33	1.8	0	1200	1300
2 tablespoons — 18	102	4	8.6	10	.36	1.0	1.2	22	6
	4.4	.7	5.4	—	.04	.22	0	150	160
Sunflower meal, home-ground[b] — 45	252	9	21	20	.88	2.4	3.2	54	14
½ cup	11	1.7	14	—	.10	.56	0	380	410
1 tablespoon — 6	32	1	2.7	Tr	.11	.3	.4	7	2
	1.4	.2	1.7	—	.01	.08	0	47	52
Walnuts, black — 125	785	18	74	380	.28	.9	7.5	Tr	4
1 cup chopped	26	2.1	46	—	.14	—	0	710	580
4 to 5 halves or — 8	50	1	4.8	20	.02	.1	.5	Tr	Tr
1 tablespoon chopped	1.6	.1	2.9	—	.01	—	0	46	37
English or Persian — 120	781	19	76	40	.40	1.1	3.7	120	2
1 cup chopped	18	2.5	42	2	.16	.88	0	460	540
4 to 7 halves or — 8	52	1	5.1	Tr	.03	.1	.2	8	Tr
1 tablespoon chopped	1.2	.2	2.8	Tr	.01	.06	0	30	36

Vegetables

Artichoke, cooked	a	a12	.2	180	.08	.8	1.3	61	36
1 medium (3 per 2 pounds) — 120	3.4	2.9	—	10	.05	—	0	83	360

[c]Values for roasted seeds.
[b]Values adapted from whole-seed kernels.

[a]A large portion of the carbohydrate in fresh artichokes is inulin, which is of doubtful availability. During storage, inulin is converted to sugars.

Calories for 1 cooked medium artichoke, therefore, may range from 10 when the vegetable is fresh to as high as 53 when the vegetable has been stored.

Food	Uncooked wt.(EP) g / Cooked wt.(EP) g	Calories Kcal / Protein g	Carbohydrate g / Fiber g	Fat (total) g / Linoleic Acid g	Vitamin A IU / Vitamin C mg	Thiamin mg / Riboflavin mg	Niacin mg / Vitamin B-6 mg	Iron mg / Vitamin B-12 µg	Calcium mg / Phosphorus mg	Sodium mg / Potassium mg
Asparagus, cooked		12	2	.1	540	.10	.8	.4	13	1
4 spears, ½″ dm. at base	60	1.3	.4	—	16	.11	—	0	30	110
1 cup, 1½″ to 2″ pieces		29	5	.3	1300	.23	2.0	.9	30	1
	145	3.2	1.0	—	38	.26	—	0	73	260
Bamboo shoots, raw	151	41	8	.5	30	.23	.9	.8	20	—
1 cup, 1″ lengths		3.9	1.1	—	6	.11	—	0	89	810
Beans, green lima, cooked		189	34	.9	480	.31	2.2	4.3	80	2
1 cup	170	13	3.1	—	29	.17	—	0	210	720
Beans, snap: Green, raw	110	35	8	.2	660	.09	.6	.9	62	8
1 cup, 1″ to 2″ lengths		2.1	1.1	—	21	.12	.09	0	48	270
cooked		31	7	.3	680	.09	.6	.8	63	5
1 cup, 1″ lengths	125	2.0	1.2	—	15	.11	—	0	46	190
Wax or Yellow, cooked		28	6	.3	290	.09	.6	.8	63	4
1 cup, 1″ lengths	125	1.8	1.2	—	16	.11	—	0	46	190
Beets, cooked, peeled		32	7	.1	20	.03	.3	.5	14	43
2 beets, 2″ diameter	100	1.1	.8	—	6	.04	—	0	23	210
1 cup diced or sliced		54	12	.2	30	.05	.5	.9	24	73
	170	1.9	1.4	—	10	.07	—	0	39	350
Beet greens, cooked		26	5	.3	7400	.10	.4	2.8	140	110
1 cup leaves and stems	145	2.5	1.6	—	22	.22	—	0	36	480
Broccoli, raw	454	145	27	1.4	11000	.45	4.1	5.0	470	68
1 pound or 3 medium stalks		16	6.8	—	510	1.0	.89	0	350	1700
cooked		47	8	.5	4500	.16	1.4	1.4	160	18
1 medium stalk	180	5.6	2.7	—	160	.36	—	0	110	480
1 cup, ½″ pieces		40	7	.5	3900	.14	1.2	1.2	140	16
	155	4.8	2.3	—	140	.31	—	0	96	410
Brussels sprouts, 1 cup cooked		56	10	.6	810	.12	1.2	1.7	50	16
7–8 whole, 1¼″–1½″ dm.	155	6.5	2.5	—	140	.22	—	0	110	420
Cabbage: Common,[b] raw, coarsely shredded or sliced, 1 cup	70	17	4	.1	90	.04	.2	.3	34	14
		.9	.6	—	33	.04	.11	0	20	160
raw, finely shredded or chopped, 1 cup	90	22	5	.2	120	.05	.3	.4	44	18
		1.2	.7	—	42	.05	.14	0	26	210
cooked, shredded 1 cup		29	6	.3	190	.06	.4	.4	64	20
	145	1.6	1.2	—	48	.06	—	0	29	240
Red, raw, coarsely shredded or sliced, 1 cup	70	22	5	.1	30	.06	.3	.6	29	18
		1.4	.7	—	43	.04	.14	0	25	190
raw, finely shredded or chopped, 1 cup	90	28	6	.2	40	.08	.4	.7	38	23
		1.8	.9	—	55	.05	.18	0	32	240
Savoy, raw, coarsely shredded or sliced, 1 cup	70	17	3	.1	140	.04	.2	.6	47	15
		1.7	.6	—	39	.06	.13	0	38	190
Cabbage, Chinese,[c] raw	75	11	2	.1	110	.04	.5	.5	32	17
1 cup, 1″ pieces		.9	.4	—	19	.03	—	0	30	190
cooked		16	3	0	80	.14	1.6	.4	52	—
1 cup	164	2.4	—	0	52	.14	—	0	64	—
Cabbage, spoon,[d] raw	70	11	2	.1	2200	.04	.6	.6	120	18
1 cup, 1″ pieces		1.1	.4	—	18	.07	—	0	31	210
cooked		24	4	.3	5300	.07	1.2	1.0	250	31
1 cup, 1″ pieces	170	2.4	1.0	—	26	.14	—	0	60	360
Carrot, raw, 1 medium	72	30	7	.1	7900	.04	.4	.5	27	34
7½″ long, 1⅛″ diameter		.8	.7	—	6	.04	.11	0	26	250

[b]*Danish, domestic, and pointed types.*
[c]*Compact heading variety, also called celery cabbage or peh tsai.*
[d]*Nonheading green leaf variety, also called white mustard cabbage or pak choy.*

	Uncooked wt. (EP) g / Cooked wt. (EP) g	Calories Kcal / Protein g	Carbohydrate g / Fiber g	Fat (total) g / Linoleic Acid g	Vitamin A IU / Vitamin C mg	Thiamin mg / Riboflavin mg	Niacin mg / Vitamin B-6 mg	Iron mg / Vitamin B-12 µg	Calcium mg / Phosphorus mg	Sodium mg / Potassium mg
6 to 8 strips, approx.	28	12	3	.1	3100	.02	.2	.2	10	13
2½"×¼"		.3	.3	—	2	.01	.04	0	10	97
1 cup grated	110	46	11	.2	12000	.07	.7	.8	41	52
		1.2	1.1	—	9	.06	.16	0	40	380
cooked		45	10	.3	15000	.07	.7	.9	48	48
1 cup diced (¼"–½" cubes)	145	1.3	1.4	—	9	.07	—	0	45	320
Cauliflower, raw	100	27	5	.2	60	.11	.7	1.1	25	13
1 cup flowerets		2.7	1.0	—	78	.10	.21	0	56	300
cooked		28	5	.3	80	.11	.8	.9	26	11
1 cup flowerets	125	2.9	1.2	—	69	.10	—	0	53	260
Celery, raw, 1 large stalk	40	7	2	Tr	110	.01	.1	.1	16	50
8"×1½" (at root end)		.4	.2	—	4	.01	.02	0	11	140
3 small inner stalks	50	9	2	.1	140	.02	.2	.2	20	63
5"×¾"		.5	.3	—	5	.02	.03	0	14	170
1 cup diced	120	20	5	.1	320	.04	.4	.4	47	150
		1.1	.7	—	11	.04	.07	0	34	410
cooked		21	5	.2	390	.03	.5	.3	47	130
1 cup diced	150	1.2	.9	—	9	.05	—	0	33	360
Chard, Swiss, cooked		26	5	.3	7800	.06	.6	2.6	110	120
1 cup leaves and stalks	145	2.6	1.0	—	23	.16	—	0	35	460
1 cup leaves		32	6	.4	9400	.07	.7	3.2	130	150
	175	3.2	1.2	—	28	.19	—	0	42	560
Chicory or **Witloof,**[e] raw	53	8	2	.1	Tr	—	—	.3	10	4
head, 5" to 7" long		.5	—	—	—	—	.02	0	11	97
Chives, raw	3	1	Tr	Tr	170	Tr	Tr	.1	2	—
1 tablespoon chopped		.1	Tr	—	2	Tr	.01	0	1	8
Collard greens, cooked		42	7	.9	7800	.20	1.7	.9	220	36
1 cup leaves and stems	145	3.9	1.2	—	67	.29	—	0	57	340
1 cup leaves, cooked in		63	10	1.3	15000	.21	2.3	1.5	360	—
small amount of water	190	6.8	1.9	—	140	.38	—	0	99	500
1 cup leaves, cooked in		59	9	1.3	15000	.13	2.1	1.5	340	—
large amount of water	190	6.5	1.9	—	97	.27	—	0	91	460
Coriander (Chinese parsley)[f]	12	6	1	.1	1400	.01	.1	2.2	22	7
¼ cup leaves		.4	.1	—	16	.01	—	0	10	31
Corn, sweet, cooked whole ear,[g]	63	70	16	.8	[h]310	.09	1.1	.5	2	Tr
5"×1¾" diameter		2.5	.4	—	7	.08	—	0	69	150
kernels (cooked off cob,		137	31	1.7	660	.18	2.1	1.0	5	Tr
drained), 1 cup	165	5.3	1.2	—	12	.17		0	150	270
frozen, cooked, drained kernels		130	31	.8	580	.15	2.5	1.3	5	2
1 cup	165	5.0	.8	—	8	.10	—	0	120	300
canned kernels with liquid		174	43	1.1	740	.06	2.3	1.1	6	500
1 cup	210	5.3	1.7	—	11	.13	.42	0	150	200
Cucumber, raw, unpared	301	45	10	.3	750	.09	.6	3.3	75	18
1 large, 2⅛"×8¼" (11 oz.)		2.7	1.8	—	33	.12	.13	0	81	480
1 small, 1¾"×6⅜"	170	25	6	.2	420	.05	.3	1.9	42	10
		1.5	1.0	—	19	.07	.07	0	46	270
6 slices, ⅛" thick, from large	28	4	1	Tr	70	.01	.1	.3	7	2
cucumber, or 8 from small		.3	.2	—	3	.01	.01	0	8	45
pared	280	39	9	.3	Tr	.08	.6	.8	48	17
1 large, 2⅛"×8¼" (11 oz.)		1.7	.8	—	31	.11	—	0	50	450

[e] *Also called French or Belgian endive.*

[f] *Values from Source 13.*

[g] *Weight of entire ear is 140 g.*

[h] *Value is for yellow varieties; white varieties have very little vitamin A.*

	Uncooked wt.(EP) g / Cooked wt.(EP) g	Calories Kcal / Protein g	Carbohydrate g / Fiber g	Fat (total) g / Linoleic Acid g	Vitamin A IU / Vitamin C mg	Thiamin mg / Riboflavin mg	Niacin mg / Vitamin B-6 mg	Iron mg / Vitamin B-12 µg	Calcium mg / Phosphorus mg	Sodium mg / Potassium mg
6½ large slices or 9 small, ⅛" thick	28	4	1	Tr	Tr	.01	.1	.1	5	2
		.2	.1	—	3	.01	—	0	5	45
Dandelion greens, cooked, 1 cup not packed (½ cup packed)	105	35	7	.6	12000	.14	—	1.9	150	46
		2.1	1.4	—	19	.17	—	0	44	240
Eggplant, cooked 1 cup diced	200	38	8	.4	20	.10	1.0	1.2	22	2
		2.0	1.8	—	6	.08	—	0	42	300
Endive, curly, and **Escarole,** raw 1 cup small pieces	50	10	2	.1	1600	.04	.3	.9	41	7
		.9	.4	—	5	.07	—	0	27	150
Ginger root, fresh, 1 nub 2" long × 1¼" diameter	25	12	2	.3	Tr	Tr	.2	.5	6	2
		.4	.3	—	1	.01	—	0	9	66
Jerusalem artichoke or **Sunchoke** raw, 4 small, 1½" diameter	100	[i]	[i]17	.1	20	.20	1.3	3.4	14	—
		2.3	.8	—	4	.06	.07	0	78	—
Kale, cooked 1 cup leaves without stems	110	43	7	.8	9100	.11	1.8	1.8	210	47
		5.0	—	—	100	.20	—	0	64	240
Kohlrabi, cooked 1 cup diced	165	40	9	.2	30	.10	.3	.5	54	10
		2.8	1.6	—	71	.05	—	0	68	430
Lambsquarters or **Pigweed,** cooked 1 cup	200	64	10	1.4	19000	.20	1.8	1.4	520	—
		6.4	3.6	—	74	.52	—	0	90	—
Leeks, bulb and lower leaf, raw 3 to 4 leeks, 5" long	100	52	11	.3	40	.11	.5	1.1	52	5
		2.2	1.3	—	17	.06	.20	0	50	350
Lettuce, butterhead, 1 large outer or 2 medium inner leaves	15	2	Tr	Tr	150	.01	Tr	.3	5	1
		.2	.1	—	1	.01	.01	0	4	40
1 cup chopped	55	8	1	.1	530	.03	.2	1.1	19	5
		.7	.3	—	4	.03	.03	0	14	140
romaine or cos 1 leaf, 8½"×5½"	19	3	1	.1	360	.01	.1	.3	13	2
		.2	.1	—	3	.02	.01	0	5	50
1 cup chopped	55	10	2	.2	1000	.03	.2	.8	37	5
		.7	.4	—	10	.04	.03	0	14	140
loose leaf and red 1 leaf	12	2	Tr	Tr	230	.01	Tr	.2	8	1
		.2	.1	—	2	.01	.01	0	3	32
1 cup chopped	55	10	2	.2	1000	.03	.2	.8	37	5
		.7	.4	—	10	.04	.03	0	14	140
iceberg piece of leaf, 5"×4½"	20	3	1	Tr	70	.01	.1	.1	4	2
		.2	.1	—	1	.01	.01	0	4	35
1 cup chopped	55	7	2	.1	180	.03	.2	.3	11	5
		.5	.3	—	3	.03	.03	0	12	96
Mushrooms (Agaricus), raw 1 cup cut (7 small or 3 large)	70	20	3	.2	Tr	.07	2.9	.6	4	11
		1.9	.6	—	2	.32	.09	0	81	290
Mustard greens, cooked 1 cup leaves without stems	140	32	6	.6	8100	.11	.8	2.5	190	25
		3.1	1.3	—	67	.20	—	0	45	310
New Zealand spinach, cooked 1 cup	180	23	4	.4	6500	.05	.9	2.7	86	170
		3.1	1.1	—	25	.18	—	0	50	830
Okra, cooked, 1 cup slices or 9 pods, 3" long	160	46	10	.5	780	.21	1.4	.8	150	3
		3.2	1.6	—	32	.29	—	0	66	280
Onions, raw 1 cup chopped	170	65	15	.2	[h]70	.05	.3	.9	46	17
		2.6	1.0	—	17	.07	.22	0	61	270
1 tablespoon minced	10	4	1	Tr	Tr	Tr	Tr	.1	3	1
		.2	.1	—	1	Tr	.01	0	4	16
cooked 1 cup whole or sliced	210	61	14	.2	[h]80	.06	.4	.8	50	15
		2.5	1.3	—	15	.06	—	0	61	230

[i] *A large portion of the carbohydrate in fresh Sunchokes may be inulin, which during storage is converted to sugars. Caloric values, therefore, range from 7 calories per 100 g when the vegetable is fresh to 75 calories per 100 g after long storage.*

[h] *Value is for yellow varieties; white varieties have very little vitamin A.*

| | Uncooked wt.(EP) g | Calories Kcal | Carbohydrate g | Fat (total) g | Vitamin A IU | Thiamin mg | Niacin mg | Iron mg | Calcium mg | Sodium mg |
	Cooked wt.(EP) g	Protein g	Fiber g	Linoleic Acid g	Vitamin C mg	Riboflavin mg	Vitamin B-6 mg	Vitamin B-12 μg	Phosphorus mg	Potassium mg
Onions, young green (scallions) bulb and top, 1 tbsp. chopped	6	2	1	Tr	120	Tr	Tr	.1	3	Tr
		.1	.1	—	2	Tr	—	0	2	14
without top 1 tablespoon chopped	6	3	1	Tr	Tr	Tr	.Tr	Tr	2	Tr
		.1	.1	—	2	Tr	—	0	2	14
Parsley, raw 1 cup chopped	60	26	5	.4	5100	.07	.7	3.7	120	27
		2.2	.9	—	100	.16	.10	—	38	440
1 tablespoon chopped	4	2	Tr	Tr	300	Tr	Tr	.2	7	2
		.1	.1	—	6	.01	.01	0	2	25
Parsnips, cooked 1 cup diced		102	23	.8	50	.11	.2	.9	70	12
	155	2.3	3.1	—	16	.12	.14	0	96	590
Peas, green immature, raw 1 cup	145	122	21	.6	930	.51	4.2	2.8	38	3
		9.1	2.9	—	39	.20	.23	0	170	460
cooked 1 cup		114	19	.6	860	.45	3.7	2.9	37	2
	160	8.6	3.2	—	32	.18	—	0	160	310
frozen, cooked, drained 1 cup		109	19	.5	960	.43	2.7	3.0	30	180
	160	8.2	3.0	—	21	.14	—	0	140	220
Peas, edible pods, raw about 1 cup (30 pods)	100	53	12	.2	680	.28	—	.7	62	—
		3.4	1.2	—	21	.12	—	0	90	170
cooked 1 cup		64	14	.3	920	.33	—	.8	84	—
	150	4.4	1.8	—	21	.16	—	0	110	180
Peppers, sweet: Green, raw 1 pod, 2¾"×2½" dm.	74	16	.4	.1	310	.06	.4	.5	7	10
		.9	1.0	—	94	.06	.19	0	16	160
cooked 1 pod, 2¾"×2½" dm.		13	3	.1	310	.05	.4	.4	7	7
	73	.7	1.0	—	70	.05	—	0	12	110
Red, raw 1 pod, 2¾"×2½" dm.	74	23	5	.2	3300	.06	.4	.4	10	—
		1.0	1.3	—	150	.06	—	0	22	—
Potato, raw, without skin 1 cup diced	150	114	26	.2	Tr	.15	2.3	.9	11	5
		3.2	.8	—	30	.06	.38	0	80	610
boiled in skin[j] 2⅓" dm. × 4¾" long		173	39	.2	Tr	.20	3.4	1.4	16	7
	228	4.8	1.1	—	36	.09	—	0	120	930
1 medium round-type[j] 2½" diameter		104	23	.1	Tr	.12	2.0	.8	10	4
	136	2.9	.8	—	22	.05	—	0	72	560
boiled, pared before cooking 1 medium, 2½" diameter		88	20	.1	Tr	.12	1.6	.7	8	3
	135	2.6	.7	—	22	.05	—	0	57	380
mashed, with milk and margarine, 1 cup		197	26	9.0	360	.17	2.1	.8	50	700
	210	4.4	.8	2.1	19	.11	—	0	100	520
french-fried 10 strips, 2" to 3½" long		137	18	6.6	Tr	.07	1.6	.7	8	3
	50	2.2	.5	3.3	11	.04	—	0	56	430
Pumpkin, canned[k] 1 cup		81	19	.7	16000	.07	1.5	1.0	61	5
	245	2.5	3.2	—	12	.12	.14	0	64	590
Radishes, raw 10 medium, ¾" to 1" dm.	45	8	2	Tr	Tr	.01	.1	.5	14	8
		.5	.3	—	12	.01	.03	0	14	140
Rhubarb, raw 1 cup diced	122	20	4	.1	120	.04	.4	1.0	120	2
		.7	.9	—	11	.09	.04	0	22	310
Rutabagas, cooked 1 cup cubed or sliced		60	14	.2	940	.10	1.4	.5	100	7
	170	1.5	1.9	—	44	.10	.17	0	53	280
Salsify, cooked 1 cup cubed		l	l20	.8	10	.04	.3	1.8	57	—
	135	3.5	2.4	—	9	.05	—	0	72	360

[j]Dimensions refer to an unpeeled, un-cooked potato. Weight and nutrient values are for a whole potato minus 9% in skin and eyes.

[k]May be a mixture of pumpkin and winter squash.

[l]A large portion of the carbohydrate in fresh salsify may be inulin, which is of doubtful availability. During storage, inulin is converted to sugars. Calories for 1 cup cooked salsify, therefore, range from 16 when fresh to 94 after storage.

	Uncooked wt.(EP) g / Cooked wt.(EP) g	Calories Kcal / Protein g	Carbohydrate g / Fiber g	Fat (total) g / Linoleic Acid g	Vitamin A IU / Vitamin C mg	Thiamin mg / Riboflavin mg	Niacin mg / Vitamin B-6 mg	Iron mg / Vitamin B-12 μg	Calcium mg / Phosphorus mg	Sodium mg / Potassium mg
Shallot bulb, raw	10	7	2	Tr	Tr	.01	Tr	.1	4	1
1 tablespoon chopped		.3	.1	—	1	Tr	—	0	6	33
Sorrel or **Dock,** cooked		38	8	.4	22000	.12	.8	1.8	110	6
1 cup	200	3.2	1.4	—	110	.26	—	0	52	400
Spinach, raw	55	14	2	.2	4500	.06	.3	1.7	51	39
1 cup chopped		1.8	.3	—	28	.11	.15	0	28	260
cooked leaves		41	6	.5	15000	.13	.9	4.0	170	90
1 cup	180	5.4	1.1	—	50	.25	—	0	68	580
Sprouts: Alfalfa,[m] raw	57	23	—	.3	—	.08	.9	.8	16	—
1 cup		2.9	1.0	—	9	.12	—	0	—	—
Mung bean, raw	105	37	7	.2	20	.14	.8	1.4	20	5
1 cup		4.0	.7	—	20	.14	—	0	67	230
cooked		35	6	.3	30	.11	.9	1.1	21	5
1 cup	125	4.0	.9	—	8	.13	—	0	60	200
Soybean, raw	105	48	6	1.5	80	.24	.8	1.1	50	—
1 cup		6.5	.8	—	14	.21	—	0	70	—
cooked		48	5	1.8	100	.20	.9	.9	54	—
1 cup	125	6.6	1.0	—	5	.19	—	0	63	—
Squash, summer: Yellow, raw	130	26	6	.3	600	.07	1.3	.5	36	1
1 cup sliced or diced		1.6	.8	—	33	.12	.11	0	38	260
cooked		27	6	.4	790	.09	1.4	.7	45	2
1 cup sliced	180	1.8	1.1	—	20	.14	—	0	45	250
Scalloped, raw	130	27	7	.1	250	.07	1.3	.5	36	1
1 cup sliced or diced		1.2	.8	—	23	.12	.11	0	38	260
cooked		29	7	.2	320	.09	1.4	.7	45	2
1 cup sliced	180	1.3	1.1	—	14	.14	—	0	45	250
Zucchini, raw	130	22	5	.1	[n]420	.07	1.3	.5	36	1
1 cup sliced or diced		1.6	.8	—	25	.12	.11	0	38	260
cooked		22	4	.2	[n]540	.09	1.4	.7	45	2
1 cup sliced	180	1.8	1.1	—	16	.14	—	0	45	250
cooked		25	5	.2	630	.11	1.7	.8	53	2
1 cup diced	210	2.1	1.3	—	19	.17	—	0	53	300
Squash, winter: Hubbard, baked		103	24	.8	9800	.10	1.4	1.6	49	2
1 cup mashed	205	3.7	3.7	—	21	.27	—	0	80	560
boiled		71	16	.7	9600	.09	.9	1.2	40	2
1 cup cubed	235	2.6	3.3	—	14	.24	—	0	61	360
Butternut, baked		139	36	.2	13000	.10	1.4	2.1	82	2
1 cup mashed	205	3.7	3.7	—	16	.27	—	0	150	1200
boiled		100	26	.2	13000	.10	1.0	1.7	71	2
1 cup mashed	245	2.7	3.4	—	12	.25	—	0	120	840
Acorn, baked		86	22	.2	2200	.08	1.1	1.7	61	2
½ squash	156	3.0	2.8	—	20	.20	—	0	45	750
boiled		83	21	.2	2700	.10	1.0	2.0	69	2
1 cup mashed	245	2.9	3.4	—	20	.25	—	0	49	660
Sweet potato, baked in skin[o]		161	37	.6	9200	.10	.8	1.0	46	14
5"×2" potato	114	2.4	1.0	—	25	.08	—	0	66	340
boiled in skin[o]		172	40	.6	12000	.14	.9	1.1	48	15
5"×2" potato	151	2.6	1.1	—	26	.09	—	0	71	370
mashed		291	67	1.0	20000	.23	1.5	1.8	82	26
1 cup	255	4.3	—	—	43	.15	—	0	120	620

[m] *Adapted from values in Source 15.*
[n] *Value includes skin, as flesh has no appreciable vitamin A.*
[o] *Dimensions are for uncooked, unpeeled sweet potato. Weight and nutrient values are for whole potato minus 22% in skin when baked or 16% in skin when boiled.*

Food	Uncooked / Cooked wt.(EP) g	Calories Kcal / Protein g	Carbohydrate g / Fiber g	Fat (total) g / Linoleic Acid g	Vitamin A IU / Vitamin C mg	Thiamin mg / Riboflavin mg	Niacin mg / Vitamin B-6 mg	Iron mg / Vitamin B-12 μg	Calcium mg / Phosphorus mg	Sodium mg / Potassium mg
Tomato, raw, whole	123	27	6	.2	1100	.07	.9	.6	16	4
2⅜″ dm. (4¾ ounces)		1.4	.6	—	28	.05	.12	0	33	300
cooked		63	13	.5	2400	.17	1.9	1.4	36	10
1 cup	241	3.1	1.4	—	58	.12	—	0	77	690
canned		51	10	.5	2200	.12	1.7	1.2	14	310
1 cup with liquid	241	2.4	1.0	—	41	.07	.22	0	46	520
paste		46	11	.2	1900	.11	1.8	2.0	15	22
2 ounces or ¼ cup	57	1.9	.5	—	28	.07	.22	0	40	500
puree, canned		97	22	.5	4000	.22	3.5	4.2	32	1000
1 cup	249	4.2	1.0	—	82	.12	.38	0	85	1100
juice, canned		46	10	.2	1900	.12	1.9	2.2	17	490
1 cup	243	2.2	.5	—	39	.07	.47	0	44	550
Turnip, raw	130	39	9	.3	Tr	.05	.8	.7	51	64
1 cup diced		1.3	1.2	—	47	.09	.12	0	39	350
cooked		36	8	.3	Tr	.06	.5	.6	54	53
1 cup diced	155	1.2	1.4	—	34	.08	—	0	37	290
Turnip greens, cooked		29	5	.3	9100	.22	.9	1.6	270	—
1 cup	145	3.2	1.0	—	100	.35	—	0	54	—
Water chestnuts, Chinese, raw	25	20	5	.1	0	.04	.2	.2	1	5
4 chestnuts		.4	.2	—	1	.05	—	0	16	120
Watercress, raw	10	2	Tr	Tr	490	.02	.1	.2	15	5
10 sprigs		.2	.1	—	8	.02	.01	0	5	28
Yam, cooked		210	48	.4	Tr	.18	1.2	1.2	8	—
1 cup	200	4.8	1.8	—	18	.08	—	0	100	—

Fruits

Food	Uncooked / Cooked wt.(EP) g	Calories Kcal / Protein g	Carbohydrate g / Fiber g	Fat (total) g / Linoleic Acid g	Vitamin A IU / Vitamin C mg	Thiamin mg / Riboflavin mg	Niacin mg / Vitamin B-6 mg	Iron mg / Vitamin B-12 μg	Calcium mg / Phosphorus mg	Sodium mg / Potassium mg
Apple, raw, whole	106	61	15	.6	100	.03	.1	.3	7	1
small, 2½″ dm. (4 per lb.)		.2	1.1	—	[a]4	.02	.03	0	11	120
medium, 3″ diameter	166	96	24	1.0	150	.05	.2	.5	12	2
(2½ per pound)		.3	1.7	—	[a]7	.03	.05	0	17	180
large, 3¼″ diameter	212	123	31	1.3	190	.06	.2	.6	15	2
(2 per pound)		.4	2.1	—	[a]8	.04	.06	0	21	230
dried sulfured, uncooked	85	234	61	1.4	—	.05	.4	1.4	26	4
1 cup (15 to 20 slices)		.9	3.2	—	9	.10	.11	0	44	480
cooked, unsweetened		199	52	1.3	—	.03	.3	1.3	23	3
1 cup	255	.8	.7	—	Tr	.08	—	0	38	410
Apple juice, unsweetened		117	30	Tr	—	.02	.2	1.5	15	2
1 cup bottled or canned	248	.2	.2	—	2	.05	.07	0	22	250
Applesauce, unsweetened		100	26	.5	100	.05	.1	1.2	10	5
1 cup canned	244	.5	1.5	—	2	.02	.07	0	12	190
Apricots, raw, whole	107	55	14	.2	2900	.03	.6	.5	18	1
3 medium (about 12 per lb.)		1.1	.6	—	11	.04	.07	0	25	300
dried sulfured, uncooked	130	338	86	.7	14000	.01	4.3	7.2	87	34
1 cup (281g, 37 sm halves)		6.5	3.9	—	16	.21	.22	0	140	1300

[a]Values are averages for freshly harvested apples of the commercially important varieties, eaten with the skin. These are winter apples: Delicious, Golden Delicious, McIntosh, and Rome. The values are also typical of important varieties of fall apples, such as Jonathan, Wealthy, and Grimes Golden. Summer varieties, such as Gravenstein, Early Harvest, and Yellow Transparent, have a higher ascorbic acid content, about 11 mg per 100 g. Values per 100 g of other freshly harvested winter varieties are Willow Twig, 19 mg; Northern Spy, 16 mg; Yellow Newton, 14 mg; and Winesap, 8 mg.

	Uncooked wt. (EP) g / Cooked wt. (EP) g	Calories Kcal / Protein g	Carbohydrate g / Fiber g	Fat (total) g / Linoleic Acid g	Vitamin A IU / Vitamin C mg	Thiamin mg / Riboflavin mg	Niacin mg / Vitamin B-6 mg	Iron mg / Vitamin B-12 µg	Calcium mg / Phosphorus mg	Sodium mg / Potassium mg
cooked, unsweetened	250	213 / 4.0	54 / 2.5	.5 / —	7500 / 8	.01 / .13	2.5 / —	4.5 / 0	55 / 88	20 / 800
1 cup fruit and liquid										
canned halves, water pack	246	93 / 1.7	24 / 1.0	.2 / —	4500 / 10	.05 / .05	1.0 / —	.7 / 0	30 / 39	2 / 610
1 cup fruit and liquid										
heavy syrup pack	258	222 / 1.5	57 / 1.0	.3 / —	4500 / 10	.05 / .05	1.0 / .14	.8 / 0	28 / 39	3 / 600
1 cup fruit and liquid										
Apricot nectar	251	143 / .8	37 / .5	.3 / —	2400 / 8	.03 / .03	.5 / —	.5 / 0	23 / 30	Tr / 380
1 cup canned or bottled										
Avocado, California[b]	216	369 / 4.7	13 / 3.2	37 / 4.8	630 / 30	.24 / .43	3.5 / .91	1.3 / 0	22 / 91	9 / 1300
3⅛″ diameter, 10 ounces										
Florida[b]	304	389 / 4.0	27 / 4.6	33 / 4.3	880 / 43	.33 / .61	4.9 / 1.3	1.8 / 0	30 / 130	12 / 1800
3⅝″ diameter, 16 ounces										
Banana, whole, raw	95	81 / 1.0	21 / .5	.2 / —	180 / 10	.05 / .06	.7 / .48	.7 / 0	8 / 25	1 / 350
small, 7¾″ long										
medium, 8¾″ long	119	101 / 1.3	26 / .6	.2 / —	230 / 12	.06 / .07	.8 / .61	.8 / 0	10 / 31	1 / 440
large, 9¾″ long	136	116 / 1.5	30 / .7	.3 / —	260 / 14	.07 / .08	1.0 / .69	1.0 / 0	11 / 35	1 / 500
sliced	150	128 / 1.7	33 / .8	.3 / —	290 / 15	.08 / .09	1.1 / .76	1.1 / 0	12 / 39	2 / 560
1 cup										
Blackberries, raw[c]	144	84 / 1.7	19 / 5.9	1.3 / —	290 / 30	.04 / .06	.6 / .07	1.3 / 0	46 / 27	1 / 240
1 cup										
Blueberries, raw	145	90 / 1.0	22 / 2.2	.7 / —	150 / 20	.04 / .09	.7 / .10	1.5 / 0	22 / 19	1 / 120
1 cup										
Cantaloupe, raw	272	82 / 1.9	20 / .8	.3 / —	9200 / 90	.11 / .08	1.6 / .23	1.1 / 0	38 / 44	33 / 680
½ of 2⅓ lb. melon, 5″ dm.										
1 cup diced	160	48 / 1.1	12 / .5	.2 / —	5400 / 53	.06 / .05	1.0 / .14	.6 / 0	22 / 26	19 / 400
Casaba, raw, 7¾″×2″ wedge	140	38 / 1.7	9 / .7	Tr / —	40 / 18	.06 / .04	.8 / —	.6 / 0	20 / 22	17 / 350
of 6 pound melon										
Cherries, sour, red, raw	155	90 / 1.9	22 / .3	.5 / —	1600 / 16	.08 / .09	.6 / .10	.6 / 0	34 / 29	3 / 300
1 cup pitted										
sweet, raw	75	47 / .9	12 / .3	.2 / —	70 / 7	.03 / .04	.3 / .02	.3 / 0	15 / 13	1 / 130
10 cherries										
Cranberries, raw, whole	95	44 / .4	10 / 1.3	.7 / —	40 / 10	.03 / .02	.1 / .03	.5 / 0	13 / 10	2 / 78
1 cup										
Cranberry sauce, homemade	277	493 / .6	130 / 1.9	.8 / —	60 / 6	.03 / .03	.3 / —	.6 / 0	19 / 14	3 / 100
sweetened, 1 cup										
Cranberry juice cocktail[d]	253	164 / .3	42 / Tr	.3 / —	Tr / [e]40	.03 / .03	.1 / —	.8 / 0	13 / 8	3 / 25
1 cup bottled										
Dates, pitted	178	488 / 3.9	130 / 4.1	.9 / —	90 / 0	.16 / .18	3.9 / .27	5.3 / 0	100 / 110	2 / 1200
1 cup chopped										
10 medium	80	219 / 1.8	58 / 1.8	.4 / —	40 / 0	.07 / .08	1.8 / .12	2.4 / 0	47 / 50	1 / 520
Figs, raw	40	32 / .5	8 / .5	.1 / —	30 / 1	.02 / .02	.2 / .05	.2 / 0	14 / 9	1 / 78
1 small, 1½″ diameter										
1 medium, 2¼″ diameter	50	40 / .6	10 / .6	.2 / —	40 / 1	.03 / .03	.2 / .06	.3 / 0	18 / 11	1 / 97
dried, uncooked	30	82 / 1.3	21 / 1.6	.4 / —	24 / 0	.03 / .03	.2 / .05	.9 / 0	38 / 23	10 / 190
2 small										

[b]California avocados are on the market in the winter, Florida avocados in late summer and fall.

[c]Includes boysenberries, dewberries, and youngberries.

[d]33% cranberry juice.
[e]Vitamin C enriched.

Uncooked wt.(EP) g / Cooked wt.(EP) g	Calories Kcal / Protein g	Carbohydrate g / Fiber g	Fat (total) g / Linoleic Acid g	Vitamin A IU / Vitamin C mg	Thiamin mg / Riboflavin mg	Niacin mg / Vitamin B-6 mg	Iron mg / Vitamin B-12 μg	Calcium mg / Phosphorus mg	Sodium mg / Potassium mg
Gooseberries, raw — 150	59	15	.3	440	—	—	.8	27	2
1 cup	1.2	2.8	—	50	—	.02	0	23	230
Grapefruit, raw, white — 136	56	15	.1	10	.05	.3	.5	22	1
½ medium, 4″ diameter	.7	.3	—	52	.03	.05	0	22	180
pink or red — 144	58	15	.1	630	.06	.3	.6	23	1
½ medium, 4″ diameter	.7	.3	—	56	.03	.05	0	23	190
Grapefruit juice, fresh — 246	96	23	.2	200	.10	.5	.5	22	2
1 cup	1.2	Tr	—	93	.05		0	37	400
canned, unsweetened	101	24	.2	20	.07	.5	1.0	20	2
1 cup — 247	1.2	Tr	—	84	.05	.03	0	35	400
frozen, reconstituted — 247	101	24	.2	20	.10	.5	.2	25	2
1 cup	1.2	Tr	—	96	.04	.03	0	42	420
Grapes, adherent skin,[f] raw — 152	102	26	.5	150	.08	.5	.6	18	5
seeded, whole, 1 cup	.9	.8	—	6	.05	.12	0	30	260
seedless, whole — 50	34	9	.2	50	.03	.2	.2	6	2
10 grapes, ⅝″ dm. × ⅞″	.3	.2	—	2	.02	.09	0	10	87
slip skin,[g] raw — 101	70	16	1.0	100	.05	.3	.4	16	3
1 cup (about 38 grapes)	1.3	.6	—	4	.03	.08	0	12	160
Grape juice	167	42	Tr	—	.10	.5	.8	28	5
1 cup bottled or canned — 253	.5	Tr	—	Tr	.05	—	0	30	290
Guava, common, raw — 100	62	15	.6	280	.05	1.2	.9	23	4
1 medium	.8	5.6	—	h240	.05	—	0	42	290
Honeydew melon, raw — 149	49	12	.4	60	.06	.9	.6	21	18
7″×2″ wedge of 5¼ lb.	1.2	.9	—	34	.04	.08	0	24	370
Kumquat, raw — 19	12	3	Tr	110	.01	—	.1	12	1
1 medium	.2	.7	—	7	.02	—	0	4	44
Lemon, raw — 74	20	6	.2	10	.03	.1	.4	19	1
1 medium, 2⅛″ diameter	.8	.3	—	39	.01	.06	0	12	100
Lemon juice, fresh — 244	61	20	.5	50	.07	.2	.5	17	2
1 cup	1.2	Tr	—	110	.02	.11	0	24	340
1 tablespoon — 15	4	1	Tr	Tr	Tr	Tr	Tr	1	Tr
	.1	Tr	—	7	Tr	.01	0	2	21
Lemon peel, medium grated — 6	i	1	Tr	Tr	Tr	Tr	Tr	8	Tr
1 tablespoon	.1	—	—	8	Tr	—	0	1	10
Lime juice, fresh — 246	64	22	.2	20	.05	.2	.5	22	2
1 cup	.7	Tr	—	79	.02	.11	0	27	260
1 tablespoon — 15	4	1	Tr	Tr	Tr	Tr	Tr	1	Tr
	Tr	Tr	—	5	Tr	.01	0	2	16
Loganberries, raw — 144	89	22	.9	290	.04	.6	1.7	50	1
1 cup	1.4	4.3	—	35	.06		0	24	240
Loquats, raw — 123	59	15	.2	830	—	—	.5	25	—
10 fruits	.5	.6	—	1	—		0	44	430
Mango, raw — 201	152	39	.9	11000	.12	2.5	.9	23	16
1 medium	1.6	1.8	—	81	.12	—	0	30	440
Nectarine, raw — 138	88	24	Tr	2300	—		.7	6	8
1 medium, 2½″ diameter	.8	.6	—	18	—	.02	0	33	410
Orange, raw, California Navel[j] — 89	45	11	.1	180	.09	.4	.4	36	1
small, 2⅜″ diameter	1.2	.4	—	54	.04	.05	0	20	170
medium, 2⅞″ diameter — 140	71	18	.1	280	.14	.6	.6	56	1
	1.8	.7	—	85	.06	.08	0	31	270

[f]*Thompson Seedless, Emperor, Flame Tokay, Ribier, Malaga, and Muscat.*
[g]*Concord, Delaware, Niagara, Catawba, and Scuppernong.*
[h]*Values may range from 23 to 1160.*
[i]*Values cannot be calculated because the digestibility of peel is not known.*
[j]*Navel oranges are winter oranges; Valencias are summer.*

	Uncooked wt.(EP) g / Cooked wt.(EP) g	Calories Kcal / Protein g	Carbohydrate g / Fiber g	Fat (total) g / Linoleic Acid g	Vitamin A IU / Vitamin C mg	Thiamin mg / Riboflavin mg	Niacin mg / Vitamin B-6 mg	Iron mg / Vitamin B-12 µg	Calcium mg / Phosphorus mg	Sodium mg / Potassium mg
large, 3¹⁄₁₆″ diameter	171	87	22	.2	340	.17	.7	.7	69	2
		2.2	.9	—	100	.07	.10	0	38	330
California Valencia^j small, 2⅜″ diameter	98	50	12	.3	200	.10	.4	.8	39	1
		1.2	.5	—	48	.04	.06	0	22	190
medium, 2⅝″ diameter	121	62	15	.4	240	.12	.5	1.0	48	1
		1.4	.6	—	59	.05	.07	0	27	230
large, 3¹⁄₁₆″ diameter	189	96	23	.6	380	.19	.8	1.5	76	2
		2.3	.9	—	93	.08	.11	0	42	360
Florida (all varieties) average size, 2⅝″ diameter	141	66	17	.3	280	.14	.6	.3	60	1
		1.0	.7	—	63	.06	.08	0	24	290
Orange juice, fresh 1 cup	248	112	26	.5	500	.22	1.0	.5	27	2
		1.7	.2	—	120	.07	.10	0	42	500
canned, unsweetened 1 cup	249	120	28	.5	500	.17	.7	1.0	25	2
		2.0	.2	—	100	.05	.09	0	45	500
frozen, reconstituted 1 cup	249	122	29	.2	540	.23	.9	.2	25	2
		1.7	Tr	—	120	.03	.07	0	42	500
Orange peel, medium grated 1 tablespoon	6	i	2	Tr	30	.01	.1	Tr	10	Tr
		.1	—	—	8	.01	—	0	1	13
Papaya, raw 1 medium, 3½″×5⅛″ dm.	304	119	30	.3	5300	.12	.9	.9	61	9
		1.8	2.7	—	170	.12	—	0	49	710
Peach, raw, peeled 1 medium, 2½″ diameter	100	38	10	.1	1300	.02	1.0	.5	9	1
		.6	.6	—	7	.05	.02	0	19	200
sliced 1 cup	170	65	16	.2	2300	.03	1.7	.9	15	2
		1.0	1.0	—	12	.09	.04	0	32	340
dried sulfured, uncooked 10 med. or 9 large halves	130	341	89	.9	5100	.01	6.9	7.8	62	21
		4.0	4.0	—	23	.25	.13	0	150	1200
cooked, unsweetened 1 cup fruit and juice	250	205	54	.5	3000	.01	3.8	4.8	38	13
		2.5	2.5	—	5	.15	—	0	93	740
canned, water pack 1 cup fruit and liquid	244	76	20	.2	1100	.02	1.5	.7	10	5
		1.0	1.0	—	7	.07	.05	0	32	330
heavy syrup pack 1 cup fruit and liquid	256	200	52	.3	1100	.03	1.5	.8	10	5
		1.0	1.0	—	8	.05	.05	0	31	330
Peach nectar (40% fruit) 1 cup canned	249	120	31	Tr	1100	.02	1.0	.5	10	2
		.5	.2	—	Tr	.05	—	0	27	190
Pear, raw 3½″×2½″ diameter	164	100	25	.7	30	.03	.2	.5	13	3
		1.1	2.3	—	7	.07	.03	0	18	210
dried sulfured, uncooked 10 halves	175	469	120	3.2	120	.02	1.1	2.3	61	12
		5.4	11	—	12	.32	—	0	84	1000
cooked, unsweetened 1 cup fruit and juice	255	321	81	2.0	80	.01	.8	1.5	41	8
		3.8	7.4	—	5	.20	—	0	59	690
canned, water pack, 1 half 2¼″ dm., 2 tbsp. liquid	91	29	8	.2	Tr	.01	.1	.2	5	1
		.2	.6	—	1	.02	.01	0	6	80
heavy syrup pack, 1 half 2¼″ dm., 2 tbsp. liquid	94	71	18	.2	Tr	.01	.1	.2	5	1
		.2	.6	—	1	.02	.01	0	7	79
Pear nectar (40% fruit) 1 cup canned	250	130	33	.5	Tr	Tr	Tr	.3	8	3
		.8	.8	—	Tr	.05	—	0	13	98
Persimmon, Japanese, raw 3″×2½″ diameter	168	129	33	.7	4600	.05	.2	.5	10	10
		1.2	2.7	—	18	.03	—	0	44	290
native, raw 1 fruit	25	31	8	.1	—	—	—	.6	7	Tr
		.2	.4	—	16	—	—	0	6	76
Pineapple, raw 1 cup diced	155	81	21	.3	110	.14	.3	.8	26	2
		.6	.6	—	26	.05	.14	0	12	230
Pineapple juice, unsweetened 1 cup canned	250	138	34	.3	130	.13	.5	.8	38	3
		1.0	.2	—	23	.05	.24	0	23	370

Uncooked wt.(EP) g / Cooked wt.(EP) g	Calories Kcal / Protein g	Carbohydrate g / Fiber g	Fat (total) g / Linoleic Acid g	Vitamin A IU / Vitamin C mg	Thiamin mg / Riboflavin mg	Niacin mg / Vitamin B-6 mg	Iron mg / Vitamin B-12 µg	Calcium mg / Phosphorus mg	Sodium mg / Potassium mg
Plums, Damson, raw	100	66	18	Tr	300	.08	.5	.5	18	2
10 whole, 1" diameter		.5	.4	—	—	.03	.05	0	17	300
Japanese and hybrid, raw	66	32	8	.1	160	.02	.3	.3	8	1
1 whole, 2⅛" diameter		.3	.4	—	4	.02	.03	0	12	110
prune-type, raw	28	21	6	.1	k80	.01	.1	.1	3	Tr
1 medium, 1½" diameter		.2	.1	—	1	.01	.01	0	5	48
Pomegranate, pulp only	154	97	25	.5	Tr	.05	.5	.5	5	5
2¾"×3⅜" dm. fruit		.8	.3	—	6	.05	—	0	12	400
Prunes, dried "softenized"	97	215	57	.5	1400	.08	1.4	3.3	43	7
uncooked, 10 large		1.8	1.6	—	3	.14	.23	0	67	590
cooked, unsweetened		119	31	.3	750	.03	.7	1.8	24	4
5 whole, 2 tbsp. juice	100	1.0	.8	—	1	.07	—	0	37	330
Prune juice		197	49	.3	—	.03	1.0	10	36	5
1 cup bottled or canned	256	1.0	Tr	—	5	.03	—	0	51	600
Raisins, seedless	145	419	110	.3	30	.16	.7	5.1	90	39
1 cup not packed		3.6	1.3	—	1	.12	.35	0	150	1100
1½ tablespoons	14	40	11	Tr	Tr	.02	.1	.5	9	4
or ½ ounce package		.4	.1	—	Tr	.01	.03	0	14	110
Raspberries, raw, black	134	98	21	1.9	Tr	.04	1.2	1.2	40	1
1 cup		2.0	6.8	—	24	.12	.08	0	29	270
red	123	70	17	.6	160	.04	1.1	1.1	27	1
1 cup		1.5	3.7	—	31	.11	.07	0	27	210
Strawberries, raw, whole	149	55	12	.7	90	.04	.9	1.5	31	1
1 cup		1.0	1.9	—	88	.10	.08	0	31	240
Tangerine, raw	86	39	10	.2	360	.05	.1	.3	34	2
1 medium, 2⅜" diameter		.7	.4	—	27	.02	.06	0	15	110
Watermelon, raw, 10" dm (32 lb)	426	111	27	.9	2500	.13	.9	2.1	30	4
1/16 melon or 1" slice		2.1	1.3	—	30	.13	.29	0	43	430
1 cup diced	160	42	10	.3	940	.05	.3	.8	11	2
		.8	.5	—	11	.05	.11	0	16	160

Dairy Products and Eggs

Butter (see also **Fats,** page 480)	14	102	Tr	11	470	—	—	0	3	140
1 tablespoon		.1	0	.3	0	—	Tr	Tr	2	3
Cheese: American (pasteurized	28	105	Tr	8.1	350	.01	Tr	.3	200	c320
process), 1 ounce slice		6.6	0	.2	0	.12	—	—	c220	23
1" cube	18	65	Tr	5.2	210	Tr	Tr	.2	120	c200
		4.1	0	.1	0	.07	—	—	c140	14
Bleu or **Roquefort**	28	104	1	a8.3	350	.01	.3	.1	89	—
1 ounce		6.0	0	a.2	0	.17	.05	.39	96	—
1" cube	17	64	Tr	a5.0	210	Tr	.2	.1	54	—
		3.7	0	a.1	0	.11	.03	.24	59	—
Brick	28	105	Tr	8.2	350	—	Tr	.3	210	—
1 ounce		6.3	0	.1	0	.13	.02	.28	130	—
slice, ¼"×2¾"×1⅜"	16	59	Tr	4.7	200	—	Tr	.1	120	—
(1/18 of 10 ounce piece)		3.6	0	.1	0	.07	.01	.16	73	—

kValue applies to all prune-type plums except Italian prunes and Imperial prunes, which average 380 IU of vitamin A for one fruit.

aValues given are for bleu cheese; one ounce of roquefort cheese has 9.5 g total fat and 0.2 g linoleic acid.

cValues are for cheese processed with disodium phosphate as an emulsifying agent. If cheese does not contain this chemical, values per 1-ounce slice are sodium, 182 mg; potassium, 124 mg.

Item	Uncooked/Cooked wt.(EP) g	Calories (Kcal) / Protein (g)	Carbohydrate / Fiber (g)	Fat total / Linoleic Acid (g)	Vitamin A (IU) / Vitamin C (mg)	Thiamin / Riboflavin (mg)	Niacin / Vitamin B-6 (mg)	Iron (mg) / Vitamin B-12 (μg)	Calcium / Phosphorus (mg)	Sodium / Potassium (mg)
Camembert, wedge (1⅓ oz.) from 4 ounce package	38	114	1	9.9	380	.02	.3	.2	40	—
		6.7	0	.2	0	.29	.08	.49	70	42
1″ cube	17	51	Tr	4.4	170	.01	.1	.1	18	—
		3.0	0	.1	0	.13	.04	.22	31	19
Cheddar, 1 ounce or ¼ c. shredded	28	113	1	9.2	370	.01	Tr	.3	210	200
		7.1	0	.1	0	.13	.02	.28	140	23
slice, ¼″×2⅝″ diameter (1/14 of 12 ounce piece)	24	96	Tr	7.9	310	.01	Tr	.2	180	170
		6.0	0	.1	0	.11	.02	.24	120	20
1″ cube	17	68	Tr	5.6	230	.01	Tr	.2	130	120
		4.3	0	.1	0	.08	.01	.17	82	14
1 cup shredded (from 4 ounces)	113	450	2	37	1500	.03	.1	1.1	850	790
		28	0	.6	0	.52	.09	1.1	540	93
Cottage cheese, creamed 1 cup packed	245	260	7	9.8	420	.07	.2	.7	230	560
		33	0	.2	0	.61	.10	2.4	370	210
uncreamed, dry curd 1 cup packed	200	172	5	.8	20	.06	.2	.8	180	580
		34	0	Tr	0	.56	.08	2.0	350	140
low fat (2% fat)b 1 cup	223	200	8	4.0	160	—	—	—	120	—
		28	0	Tr	0	.34	—	—	—	—
Cream cheese 1 ounce or 2 tbsp.	28	104	1	9.5	440	.01	Tr	.1	18	71
		2.3	0	.2	0	.07	.02	.06	27	21
1″ cube	16	60	Tr	5.4	250	Tr	Tr	Tr	10	40
		1.3	0	.1	0	.04	.01	.04	15	12
Edam 1 ounce	28	87	1	7.8	510	.01	.1	.2	220	—
		7.7	0	.1	0	.14	.02	.50	140	—
Limburger 1 ounce	28	98	1	7.5	320	.02	.1	.2	170	—
		6.0	0	.1	0	.14	.02	.29	110	—
Mozzarella, part skim 1 ounce	28	—	—	4.6	—	—	—	—	—	—
		7.7	0	.1	0	—	.02	.28	—	—
Parmesan, grated 1 tablespoon	5	23	Tr	1.3	60	Tr	Tr	Tr	68	44
		2.1	0	Tr	0	.04	Tr	—	46	9
Ricotta, part skim 1 cup	229	—	—	20	—	—	—	—	—	—
		25	0	.4	0	—	—	—	—	—
Swiss, domestic 1 ounce or ¼ cup grated	28	105	Tr	7.7	320	Tr	Tr	.3	260	200
		7.8	0	.1	0	.11	.02	.50	160	29
slice, ¼″×2″×2″ (1/24 of 12 ounce piece)	14	52	Tr	3.9	160	Tr	Tr	.1	130	99
		3.9	0	.1	0	.06	.01	.25	79	15
1″ cube	15	56	Tr	4.1	170	Tr	Tr	.1	140	110
		4.1	0	.1	0	.06	.01	.27	84	16
Cream: half and half (11.7% fat) 1 cup	242	324	11	28	1200	.07	.1	.1	260	110
		7.7	0	.6	2	.39	—	—	210	310
1 tablespoon	15	20	1	1.8	70	Tr	Tr	Tr	16	7
		.5	0	Tr	Tr	.02	—	—	13	19
light, coffee (20.6% fat) 1 cup	240	506.	10	49	2000	.07	.1	.1	240	100
		7.2	0	1.1	2	.36	.08	.60	190	290
1 tablespoon	15	32	1	3.1	130	Tr	Tr	Tr	15	6
		.5	0	.1	Tr	.02	Tr	.04	12	18
heavy whipping (37.6% fat) 1 cup or 2 cups whipped	238	838	7	90	3700	.05	.1	.1	180	76
		5.2	0	2.0	2	.26	—	.43	140	210
Egg, chicken's, raw, whole extra large (27 oz. per dozen)	58	94	Tr	6.6	680	.06	Tr	1.3	31	70
		7.4	0	.7	0	.17	.06	1.2	120	74

bValues from Lady Lee label.

[476]

	Uncooked wt.(EP) g	Calories K cal	Carbohydrate g	Fat (total) g	Vitamin A IU	Thiamin mg	Niacin mg	Iron mg	Calcium mg	Sodium mg
	Cooked wt.(EP) g	Protein g	Fiber g	Linoleic Acid g	Vitamin C mg	Ribo-flavin mg	Vitamin B-6 mg	Vitamin B-12 µg	Phosphorus mg	Potassium mg
large (24 ounces per dozen)	50	82	Tr	5.6	590	.05	Tr	1.2	27	61
		6.5	0	.6	0	.15	.06	1.0	100	65
medium (21 oz. per dozen)	44	72	Tr	5.0	520	.05	Tr	1.0	24	54
		5.7	0	.6	0	.13	.05	.88	90	57
white of large egg	33	17	Tr	Tr	0	Tr	Tr	Tr	3	48
		3.6	0	—	0	.09	Tr	.03	5	46
yolk of large egg	17	59	Tr	5.7	580	.04	Tr	.9	24	9
		2.7	0	.6	0	.07	.05	1.0	97	17
hard cooked		82	Tr	5.6	590	.04	Tr	1.2	27	61
1 large	50	6.5	0	.6	0	.14	—	—	100	65
Ice cream (10% fat)	133	257	28	14	590	.05	.1	.1	190	84
1 cup		6.0	0	.4	1	.28	—	—	150	240
Ice milk (5.1% fat)	131	199	29	6.7	280	.07	.1	.1	200	89
1 cup		6.3	0	.2	1	.29	—	—	160	260
Kefir (from whole milk),[d] plain		168	12	8.6	—	—	—	—	—	—
1 cup (8 ounces)		9.5	0	—	0	—	—	—	—	—
Milk, cow's: whole (3.5% fat)	244	159	12	8.5	350	.07	.2	.1	290	120
1 cup		8.5	0	.2	2	.41	.10	1.0	230	350
low fat (2% fat; 2% nonfat milk solids added), 1 cup	246	145	15	4.9	200	.10	.2	.1	350	150
		10	0	.1	2	.51	—	—	280	430
skim	245	88	12	.2	10	.09	.2	.1	300	130
1 cup		8.8	0	—	2	.44	.10	1.0	230	360
buttermilk, cultured skim	245	88	12	.2	10	.10	.2	.1	300	320
1 cup		8.8	0	—	2	.44	.09	.54	230	340
evaporated, unsweetened		345	24	20	810	.10	.5	.3	640	300
1 cup canned	252	18	0	.5	3	.86	.13	.40	520	760
condensed, sweetened		982	170	27	1100	.24	.6	.3	800	340
1 cup canned	306	25	0	.7	3	1.2	.18	1.2	630	960
whey, fluid	100	26	5	.3	10	.03	.1	.1	51	—
7 tablespoons		.9	0	—	—	.14	.04	.28	53	—
Milk, cow's, dried: whole, regular	128	643	49	34	1400	.37	.9	.6	1200	520
1 cup		34	0	.6	8	1.9	.35	2.9	910	1700
nonfat, regular[e]	120	436	63	1.0	40	.42	1.1	.7	1600	640
1 cup		43	0	Tr	8	2.2	.46	3.8	1200	2100
nonfat, instant	104	373	54	.8	30	.36	.9	.6	1300	550
1 cup high-density[f]		37	0	Tr	7	1.8	.40	3.3	1000	1800
1 cup low-density[g]	68	244	35	.5	20	.24	.6	.4	880	360
		24	0	Tr	5	1.2	.26	2.2	680	1200
Milk, goat's	244	163	11	9.8	390	.10	.7	.2	320	83
1 cup		7.8	0	.5	2	.27	.11	.20	260	440
Milk, human	31	24	3	1.2	70	Tr	.1	Tr	10	5
2 tablespoons or 1 fluid oz.		.3	0	.1	2	.01	Tr	.01	4	6
Sherbet, orange	193	259	60	2.3	120	.02	Tr	Tr	31	19
1 cup		1.7	0	—	4	.06	—	—	25	42
Sour cream	240	454	8	44	1800	.09	.2	—	240	96
1 cup		6.7	0	1.0	—	.36	—	—	180	130
2 tablespoons	30	57	1	5.6	230	.01	Tr	—	31	12
		.8	0	.1	—	.04	—	—	23	17

[d]Values from the label of Alta Dena Dairy kefir.

[e]Requires 1 cup powder to 4 cups water for reconstitution.

[f]Requires ⅞ cup powder to 3¾ cups water to reconstitute 1 quart.

[g]Requires 1⅓ cups powder to 3¾ cups water to reconstitute 1 quart. This product is not suitable as a dry ingredient in cooking.

	Uncooked wt.(EP) g / Cooked wt.(EP) g	Calories Kcal / Protein g	Carbohydrate g / Fiber g	Fat (total) g / Linoleic Acid g	Vitamin A IU / Vitamin C mg	Thiamin mg / Riboflavin mg	Niacin mg / Vitamin B-6 mg	Iron mg / Vitamin B-12 µg	Calcium mg / Phosphorus mg	Sodium mg / Potassium mg
Yogurt, from whole milk 1 cup	245 	152 7.4	12 0	8.3 .2	340 2	.07 .39	.2 .11	.1 .27	270 210	120 320
from partially skimmed milk 1 cup	245 	123 8.3	13 0	3.7 .1	170 2	.10 .44	.2 .11	.1 .27	290 230	120 350

Our Recipes and Commercial Foods

YEAST BREADS AND ROLLS

	Uncooked/Cooked wt. g	Cal. / Protein	Carb. / Fiber	Fat / Linoleic	Vit A / Vit C	Thiamin / Riboflavin	Niacin / Vit B-6	Iron / Vit B-12	Calcium / Phosphorus	Sodium / Potassium
*Basic Whole-Grain Bread, p. 88 1 slice (14 per loaf)	 42	88 3.5	19 .6	.5 —	Tr Tr	.15 .04	1.2 .09	.9 0	11 100	77 100
Whole wheat bread, firm crumbª 1 slice (18 per 1 lb. loaf)	 25	61 2.6	12 .4	.8 .2	Tr Tr	.06 .03	.7 .04	.8 0	25 57	130 68
toasted 1 slice	 21	61 2.6	12 .4	.8 .2	Tr Tr	.05 .03	.7 —	.8 0	25 57	130 68
soft crumbª 1 slice (16 per 1 lb. loaf)	 28	67 2.6	14 .4	.7 .2	Tr Tr	.09 .03	.8 .05	.8 0	24 71	150 72
toasted 1 slice	 24	67 2.6	14 .4	.7 .2	Tr Tr	.07 .03	.8 —	.8 0	24 71	150 72
White bread, enriched, firm crumbª 1 slice (20 per 1 lb. loaf)	 23	63 2.1	12 Tr	.9 .2	Tr Tr	.09 .06	.8 .01	1.3 Tr	22 23	110 28
soft crumbª 1 slice (18 per 1 lb. loaf)	 25	68 2.2	13 Tr	.8 .2	Tr Tr	.10 .06	.8 .01	1.3 Tr	21 24	130 26
*Whole Wheat French Bread, p. 90 1 slice (14 per loaf)	 42	92 3.7	19 .6	.8 —	10 Tr	.15 .06	1.2 .10	.9 .01	21 110	82 110
French bread, enriched 1 slice, 5″ × 2½″ × 1	 35	102 3.2	19 .1	1.1 .3	Tr Tr	.14 .09	1.2 .02	2.0 0	15 30	200 32
*High Protein Bread, p. 91 1 slice (14 per loaf)	 49	105 5.3	21 .6	.9 —	Tr Tr	.18 .07	1.5 .13	1.1 .03	29 130	85 140
*Soy Bread, p. 92 1 slice (14 per loaf)	 54	105 5.0	20 .8	1.2 —	Tr Tr	.18 .06	1.3 —	1.3 0	21 120	78 170
*Rye Bread, p. 94 1 slice (14 per loaf)	 47	121 5.5	23 .7	1.7 —	Tr 1	.18 .07	1.1 .09	1.3 0	19 140	150 200
Rye bread (American), light 1 slice, 4¾″ × 3¾″ × ½	 25	61 2.3	13 .1	.3 —	0 0	.05 .02	.4 .02	.4 0	19 37	140 36
Pumpernickel 1 slice, 5″ × 4″ × ⅜	 32	79 2.9	17 .4	.4 —	0 0	.07 .04	.4 .05	.8 0	27 73	180 140
*Wheat Berry Dinner Rolls, p. 100 1 roll (24 per recipe)	 	116 4.7	24 .8	1.3 —	Tr Tr	.19 .07	1.6 .13	1.2 .02	24 130	125 140

QUICK BREADS AND MUFFINS

	wt. g	Cal. / Protein	Carb. / Fiber	Fat / Linoleic	Vit A / Vit C	Thiamin / Riboflavin	Niacin / Vit B-6	Iron / Vit B-12	Calcium / Phosphorus	Sodium / Potassium
*Date Nut Muffins, p. 105 1 muffin (12 per recipe)	 	154 4.8	21 .7	6.5 —	80 Tr	.14 .08	1.8 .13	1.1 .16	3 120	140 200
*Stratford Hall Biscuits, p. 105 1 biscuit (12 per recipe)	 	123 2.9	19 .5	4.4 —	160 Tr	.14 .06	1.3 —	.7 .03	29 110	210 120
*Corn Bread, p. 107 2½″ square (9 per pan)	 	161 4.6	26 .6	3.8 1.8	210 Tr	.22 .17	.8 .13	1.3 .22	81 180	380 220

ªOf the two types of bread on the market, the soft-crumb type is the more common. Firm-crumb bread resembles homemade bread in texture.

	Uncooked wt.(EP) g / Cooked wt.(EP) g	Calories Kcal / Protein g	Carbohydrate g / Fiber g	Fat (total) g / Linoleic Acid g	Vitamin A IU / Vitamin C mg	Thiamin mg / Riboflavin mg	Niacin mg / Vitamin B-6 mg	Iron mg / Vitamin B-12 μg	Calcium mg / Phosphorus mg	Sodium mg / Potassium mg

CRACKERS AND TORTILLAS

Food	Wt (EP) g	Cal / Prot	Carb / Fiber	Fat / Lino	Vit A / Vit C	Thia / Ribo	Niacin / B-6	Iron / B-12	Ca / Phos	Na / Potas
Graham crackers, plain		55	10	1.3	0	.01	.2	.2	6	95
2 pieces, 2½″ square each	14	1.1	.2	.3	0	.03	—	0	21	55
Ry-Krisp		42	10	.2	—	.04	.2	.5	7	110
2 crackers (36 per pound)	13	1.6	.3	—	—	.03	—	0	49	—
Saltines		48	8	1.3	0	Tr	.1	.1	2	120
packet of 4 crackers	11	1.0	Tr	.3	0	Tr	.01	0	10	13
*Whole Wheat Crackers, p. 108		86	8	2.8	Tr	.11	.9	1.0	75	180
1 cracker (24 per recipe)		2.1	.6	—	Tr	.04	—	0	77	88
Tortilla, from Masa Harina		63	14	.6	6	.04	.3	.9	60	—
1 tortilla, 6″ diameter	30	1.5	.3	—	0	.02	.02	0	42	—

BREAKFAST: CEREALS AND PANCAKES

Food	Wt (EP) g	Cal / Prot	Carb / Fiber	Fat / Lino	Vit A / Vit C	Thia / Ribo	Niacin / B-6	Iron / B-12	Ca / Phos	Na / Potas
Cooked: *All in One, p. 116	28	97	18	1.7	30	.19	1.0	1.6	20	1
scant ¼ cup (makes 1 c. ckd.)		4.2	.8	—	0	.06	—	0	150	130
Oatmeal		132	23	2.4	0	.19	.2	1.4	22	520
1 cup cooked	240	4.8	.5	1.0	0	.05	—	0	140	150
*Stuart's Choice, p. 116	28	90	20	.8	40	.11	.9	.9	10	Tr
3 tbsp. (makes 1 cup cooked)		2.8	.6	—	0	.03	—	0	98	8
Cracked wheat	38	127	28	.8	0	.17	1.4	1.4	16	Tr
¼ cup (makes 1 cup cooked)		4.0	1.0	—	0	.04	—	0	160	—
Dry: *High Protein Granola, p.117	28	122	13	6.6	10	.30	.7	2.0	66	5
about ¼ cup		4.8	.7	—	Tr	.08	.10	0	180	200
Quaker Oats "100% Natural"b		130	15	6	—	.06	.4	.4	40	—
plain, about ¼ cup	28	3	—	—	—	.03	—	—	—	—
with raisins and dates		120	17	5	—	.03	.4	.4	20	—
about ¼ cup	28	2	—	—	—	—	—	—	—	—
*Old-Fashioned Pancakes, p. 119		104	13	15	120	.14	.7	2.6	60	170
1 pancake (18 per recipe)		4.4	.3	—	Tr	.11	.08	.26	120	150

LUNCH: SANDWICH SPREADS

Food	Wt (EP) g	Cal / Prot	Carb / Fiber	Fat / Lino	Vit A / Vit C	Thia / Ribo	Niacin / B-6	Iron / B-12	Ca / Phos	Na / Potas
*Soy Spread, p. 140		73	6	4.0	150	.10	.4	1.2	34	140
2 rounded tablespoons		5.4	.7	2.4	3	.05	.02	0	77	270
*Swissy Spread, p. 141		56	1	4.0	130	.01	Tr	.2	81	160
2 rounded tablespoons		4.1	.1	.8	6	.07	.12	.28	64	30
*Favorite Peanut Butter Spread, p. 141		152	9	11	Tr	.07	3.6	.8	22	28
2 rounded tablespoons		6.2	.5	3.2	Tr	.04	.11	0	100	240

SOUPS

Food	Wt (EP) g	Cal / Prot	Carb / Fiber	Fat / Lino	Vit A / Vit C	Thia / Ribo	Niacin / B-6	Iron / B-12	Ca / Phos	Na / Potas
*Favorite Green Soup, p. 171		132	19	4.0	5000	.25	1.9	3.2	99	600
1 cup (⅛ of recipe)		7.8	1.3	2.4	52	.26	.26	0	110	460
*Corn Chowder, p. 172		112	14	5.4	720	.08	.7	4.3	120	430
1 cup (⅙ of recipe)		4.5	.5	.9	15	.19	.07	.50	120	300
*Hearty Pea Soup, p. 174		217	35	4.2	1400	.32	1.8	2.7	50	570
1 cup (⅛ of recipe)		10	1.7	2.4	26	.13	.11	0	170	660
*Vegetable Barley Soup, p. 175		166	23	6.2	3300	.16	1.7	.8	61	470
1 cup (1/10 of recipe)		3.8	2.0	3.9	15	.11	.22	0	120	370

SAUCES

Food	Wt (EP) g	Cal / Prot	Carb / Fiber	Fat / Lino	Vit A / Vit C	Thia / Ribo	Niacin / B-6	Iron / B-12	Ca / Phos	Na / Potas
*Yeast Butter, p. 225		860	6	92	3800	2.2	7.2	3	91	1100
½ cup		6.7	0	25	Tr	.92	.48	0	300	350

bValues from package label.

Item	Uncooked / Cooked wt. (EP) g	Calories Kcal / Protein g	Carbohydrate g / Fiber g	Fat (total) g / Linoleic Acid g	Vitamin A IU / Vitamin C mg	Thiamin mg / Riboflavin mg	Niacin mg / Vitamin B-6 mg	Iron mg / Vitamin B-12 μg	Calcium mg / Phosphorus mg	Sodium mg / Potassium mg
1 tablespoon		108	1	12	480	.28	.9	.4	11	140
		.8	0	3.1	Tr	.12	.06	0	37	43
*Cream Sauce, p. 230		436	24	35	800	.15	.8	.5	320	1400
1 cup		11	.4	10	2	.44	.15	1.0	300	420
1 tablespoon		27	1	2.2	50	.01	Tr	Tr	20	87
		.7	Tr	.6	Tr	.03	.01	.06	19	27

HEARTIER DISHES, GRAIN AND BEAN DISHES, AND NOODLES

Item	Uncooked / Cooked wt. (EP) g	Calories Kcal / Protein g	Carbohydrate g / Fiber g	Fat (total) g / Linoleic Acid g	Vitamin A IU / Vitamin C mg	Thiamin mg / Riboflavin mg	Niacin mg / Vitamin B-6 mg	Iron mg / Vitamin B-12 μg	Calcium mg / Phosphorus mg	Sodium mg / Potassium mg
*Lasagna al Forno, p. 241		424	51	15	7200	.19	1.5	3.0	200	550
1 serving (6 per recipe)		25	1.9	6.8	65	.33	.28	.42	200	760
Pizza, cheese, baked		1179	180	33	1900	.29	4.8	4.0	690	3000
12″ diameter pizza	482	44	1.4	4.4	29	.77	—	—	710	530
*Zucchini Oat-flake Loaf, p. 245		334	28	20	520	.58	1.9	3.5	150	450
1 serving (6 per recipe)		14	1.4	9.8	14	.26	.32	.50	400	450
*Tennessee Corn Pone, p. 262		266	39	7.1	440	.22	1.1	2.6	160	580
1 serving (10 per recipe)		13	1.7	1.7	1	.28	.27	.40	280	470
*Soy Burgers, p. 266		242	17	16	290	.26	1.4	3.0	130	410
1 burger (8 per recipe)		11	1.6	6.2	Tr	.15	—	.32	190	370
*Spanish Rice, p. 268		258	49	4.7	1000	.26	3.3	1.7	61	600
1 cup (¼ of recipe)		6.1	1.7	2.4	53	.10	.50	0	160	600
Macaroni, enriched		155	32	.6	0	.20	1.5	1.3	11	1
cooked until tender, 1 cup	140	4.8	.1	—	0	.11	—	0	70	85
Noodles, egg, enriched		200	37	2.4	110	.22	1.9	1.4	16	3
cooked, 1 cup	160	6.6	.2	—	0	.13	—	Tr	94	70
*Homemade, whole wheat, p. 244		211	32	6.1	300	.28	2.0	2.1	36	560
cooked, 1 cup (½ of recipe)		9.2	1.0	1.8	0	.12	.18	.50	220	200
Spaghetti, enriched		155	32	.6	0	.20	1.5	1.3	11	1
cooked until tender, 1 cup	140	4.8	.1	—	0	.11	—	0	70	85
100% whole wheat (Healthway),[b] 1 lb. package	454	1600	310	13	0	—	—	—	—	230
		61	7.3	—	0	—	—	0	—	—
Wheat–soy (Healthway)[b]		1600	280	13	0	—	—	—	—	230
1 pound package	454	100	3.4	—	0	—	—	0	—	—

DESSERTS

Item	Uncooked / Cooked wt. (EP) g	Calories Kcal / Protein g	Carbohydrate g / Fiber g	Fat (total) g / Linoleic Acid g	Vitamin A IU / Vitamin C mg	Thiamin mg / Riboflavin mg	Niacin mg / Vitamin B-6 mg	Iron mg / Vitamin B-12 μg	Calcium mg / Phosphorus mg	Sodium mg / Potassium mg
*Banana Bread, p. 277		119	16	5.5	250	.11	.7	.8	12	150
1 slice (18 per loaf)		2.2	.3	1.5	3	.04	.15	Tr	70	150
*Rice Cream Pudding, p. 279		305	53	6.9	220	.18	1.6	1.6	210	340
1 cup (¼ of recipe)		8.4	.5	1.0	1	.30	.26	.62	240	460
*Peanut Butter Bars, p. 280[c]		80	6	5.1	Tr	.06	1.6	.6	53	31
1 bar, 1½″ square × ½″		3.8	.3	1.4	Tr	.07		.06	83	140
*Oatmeal School Cookies, p. 281		47	7	1.5	Tr	.13	.2	.7	8	35
1 cookie (36 per recipe)		1.8	.2	—	Tr	.03	.10	0	65	80

Other Items

OILS, FATS, AND SALAD DRESSINGS

Item	Uncooked / Cooked wt. (EP) g	Calories Kcal / Protein g	Carbohydrate g / Fiber g	Fat (total) g / Linoleic Acid g	Vitamin A IU / Vitamin C mg	Thiamin mg / Riboflavin mg	Niacin mg / Vitamin B-6 mg	Iron mg / Vitamin B-12 μg	Calcium mg / Phosphorus mg	Sodium mg / Potassium mg
*Better-Butter (with safflower oil; page 123), 1 cup	230	1770	4	202	3800	.02	Tr	Tr	130	1700
		3.4	0	80	Tr	.14	.03	.03	93	160
1 tablespoon	14	111	Tr	13	230	Tr	Tr	Tr	8	100
		.2	0	5	Tr	.01	Tr	.01	6	10

[b] Values from package label. [c] Recipe is the version with toasted wheat germ and ground sesame seeds.

	Uncooked wt.(EP) g — Cooked wt.(EP) g	Calories Kcal — Protein g	Carbohydrate g — Fiber g	Fat (total) g — Linoleic Acid g	Vitamin A IU — Vitamin C mg	Thiamin mg — Riboflavin mg	Niacin mg — Vitamin B-6 mg	Iron mg — Vitamin B-12 µg	Calcium mg — Phosphorus mg	Sodium mg — Potassium mg
Butter, regular type 1 stick or ½ cup (¼ lb.)	113	812	1	92	3800	—	—	0	23	1100
	.7	.7	0	2.8	0	—	Tr	Tr	18	26
1 tablespoon or ⅛ stick	14	102	Tr	12	470	—	—	0	3	140
		.1	0	.3	0	—	Tr	Tr	2	3
pat, 1″ square × ⅓″ (90 per pound)	5	36	Tr	4.1	170	—	—	0	1	49
		Tr	0	.1	0	—	Tr	Tr	1	1
whipped type 1 stick or ½ cup (2⅔ oz.)	76	541	Tr	61	2500	—	—	0	15	750
		.5	0	1.8	0	—	Tr	Tr	12	17
pat, 1¼″ square × ⅓″ (120 per pound)	4	27	Tr	3.1	130	—	—	0	1	38
		Tr	0	.1	0	—	Tr	Tr	1	1
Margarine, regular type pat, 1″ square × ⅓″	5	36	Tr	4.1	170	—	—	0	1	1
		Tr	0	1.1	0	—	—	—	1	1
regular or soft type 1 stick or ½ cup (¼ lb.)	113	816	1	92	3800	—	—	0	23	1100
		.7	0	ᵃ25	0	—	—	—	18	26
1 tablespoon	14	102	Tr	12	470	—	—	0	3	140
		.1	0	ᵃ3.1	0	—	—	—	2	3
whipped type 1 stick or ½ cup (2⅔ oz.)	76	544	Tr	61	2500	—	—	0	15	750
		.5	0	17	0	—	—	—	12	17
pat, 1¼″ square × ⅓″ (120 per pound)	4	27	Tr	3.1	130	—	—	0	1	38
		Tr	0	.8	0	—	—	—	1	1
Mayonnaise, commercial 1 cup	220	1580	5	180	620	.04	Tr	1.1	40	1300
		2.4	Tr	89	—	.09	—	—	62	75
1 tablespoon	14	101	Tr	11	40	Tr	Tr	.1	3	84
		.2	Tr	5.6	—	.01	—	—	4	5
Oils, salad or cooking olive or peanut, 1 cup	216	1909	0	220	—	0	0	0	0	0
		0	0	ᵇ	0	0	0	0	0	0
1 tablespoon	14	119	0	14	—	0	0	0	0	0
		0	0	ᵇ	0	0	0	0	0	0
cottonseed, safflower, sesame, or soybean, 1 cup	218	1927	0	220	—	0	0	0	0	0
		0	0	ᵇ	0	0	0	0	0	0
1 tablespoon	14	120	0	14	—	0	0	0	0	0
		0	0	ᵇ	0	0	0	0	0	0
Salad dressings, commercial bleu cheese, 1 tablespoon	15	76	1	7.8	30	Tr	Tr	Tr	12	160
		.7	Tr	3.8	Tr	.02	—	0	11	6
French 1 tablespoon	16	66	3	6.2	—	—	—	.1	2	220
		.1	Tr	3.2	—	—	—	0	2	13
Italian 1 tablespoon	15	83	1	9.0	Tr	Tr	Tr	Tr	2	310
		Tr	Tr	4.7	—	Tr	—	0	1	2
Russian 1 tablespoon	15	74	2	7.6	100	.01	.1	.1	3	130
		.2	Tr	3.8	1	.01	—	0	6	24
Thousand Island 1 tablespoon	16	80	2	8.0	50	Tr	Tr	.1	2	110
		.1	Tr	4.0	Tr	Tr	—	0	3	18
Shortening, vegetable 1 cup	200	1768	0	200	—	0	0	0	0	0
		0	0	44	0	0	0	0	0	0
1 tablespoon	12	111	0	12	—	0	0	0	0	0
		0	0	3.0	0	0	0	0	0	0

SWEETENERS

	Uncooked wt.(EP) g — Cooked wt.(EP) g	Calories Kcal — Protein g	Carbohydrate g — Fiber g	Fat (total) g — Linoleic Acid g	Vitamin A IU — Vitamin C mg	Thiamin mg — Riboflavin mg	Niacin mg — Vitamin B-6 mg	Iron mg — Vitamin B-12 µg	Calcium mg — Phosphorus mg	Sodium mg — Potassium mg
Corn syrup 1 cup	328	951	250	0	0	0	0	13	150	220
		0	0	0	0	0	0	0	52	13

ᵃValues are for regular margarine. One tablespoon of soft-type margarine contains 4.4 g linoleic acid.

ᵇSee table on p. 365 for linoleic acid content of various oils.

	Uncooked wt.(EP) g / Cooked wt.(EP) g	Calories Kcal / Protein g	Carbohydrate g / Fiber g	Fat (total) g / Linoleic Acid g	Vitamin A IU / Vitamin C mg	Thiamin mg / Riboflavin mg	Niacin mg / Vitamin B-6 mg	Iron mg / Vitamin B-12 µg	Calcium mg / Phosphorus mg	Sodium mg / Potassium mg
Honey, strained or extracted 1 cup	339	1031	280	0	0	.02	1.0	1.7	17	17
		1.0	—	0	3	.14	.07	0	20	170
1 tablespoon	21	64	17	0	0	Tr	.1	.1	1	1
		.1	—	0	Tr	.01	Tr	0	1	11
Malt, dried 1 ounce	28	104	22	.5	—	.14	2.6	1.1	—	—
		.4	1.6		—	.09	—	0	—	—
Malt extract, dried 1 ounce	28	104	25	Tr	—	.10	2.8	2.5	14	23
		1.7	Tr	—	—	.13	—	0	83	65
Maple syrup 1 cup	315	794	200	—	—	—	—	3.8	330	32
		—	—	—	0	—	—	0	25	550
1 tablespoon	20	50	13	—	—	—	—	.2	20	2
		—	—	—	0	—	—	0	2	35
Maple sugar, 1 ounce piece 1¾" × 1¼" × ½"	28	99	26	—	—	—	—	.4	41	4
		—	—	—	0	—	—	0	3	69
Molasses,[c] light 1 cup	328	827	210	—	—	.23	.7	14	540	49
		—	—	—	—	.20	.66	0	150	3000
1 tablespoon	20	50	13	—	—	.01	Tr	.9	33	3
		—	—	—	—	.01	.04	0	9	180
medium 1 cup	328	761	200	—	—	—	3.9	20	950	120
		—	—	—	—	.39	.67	0	230	3500
1 tablespoon	20	46	12	—	—	—	.2	1.2	58	7
		—	—	—	—	.02	.04	0	14	210
blackstrap 1 cup	328	699	180	—	—	.36	6.6	53	2200	320
		—	—	—	—	.62	.67	0	280	9600
1 tablespoon	20	43	11	—	—	.02	.4	3.2	140	19
		—	—	—	—	.04	.04	0	17	580
Sorghum syrup 1 cup	330	848	220	—	—	—	.3	41	570	—
		—	—	—	—	.33	—	0	83	—
Sugar, cane or beet, brown 1 cup not packed	145	541	140	0	0	.01	.3	4.9	120	44
		0	0	0	0	.04	—	0	28	500
1 cup packed	220	821	210	0	0	.02	.4	7.5	190	66
		0	0	0	0	.07	—	0	42	760
1 tablespoon (weight varies)	14	52	14	0	0	Tr	Tr	.4	11	4
		0	0	0	0	Tr	—	0	5	32
white, granulated 1 cup	200	770	200	0	0	0	0	.2	0	2
		0	0	0	0	0	0	0	0	6
1 tablespoon	12	46	12	0	0	0	0	Tr	0	Tr
		0	0	0	0	0	0	0	0	Tr
Sugar cane juice, dehydrated[d] (jaggery), 1 cup	200	766	190	.2	0	.04	2.0	23	160	—
		.8	—	—	0	—	—	0	80	—
1 tablespoon	14	54	13	Tr	0	Tr	.1	1.6	11	—
		.1	—	—	0	—	—	0	6	—

BEVERAGES (NONALCOHOLIC)

	Uncooked wt.(EP) g / Cooked wt.(EP) g	Calories Kcal / Protein g	Carbohydrate g / Fiber g	Fat (total) g / Linoleic Acid g	Vitamin A IU / Vitamin C mg	Thiamin mg / Riboflavin mg	Niacin mg / Vitamin B-6 mg	Iron mg / Vitamin B-12 µg	Calcium mg / Phosphorus mg	Sodium mg / Potassium mg
Carbonated drinks: colas 12 fluid ounce bottle or can	369	144	37	0	0	0	0	—	—	—
		0	0	0	0	0	0	—	—	—
fruit-flavored 12 fluid ounce bottle or can	372	171	45	0	0	0	0	—	—	—
		0	0	0	0	0	0	0	—	—
ginger ale 12 fluid ounce bottle or can	366	113	29	0	0	0	0	—	—	—
		0	0	0	0	0	0	—	—	—

[c]Molasses is a byproduct when cane sugar is refined. Light molasses is what remains after the first extraction, medium after the second, and blackstrap after the third.
[d]Values from Source 13.

Food	Uncooked wt.(EP) g / Cooked wt.(EP) g	Calories Kcal / Protein g	Carbohydrate g / Fiber g	Fat (total) / Linoleic Acid g	Vitamin A IU / Vitamin C mg	Thiamin mg / Riboflavin mg	Niacin mg / Vitamin B-6 mg	Iron mg / Vitamin B-12 µg	Calcium mg / Phosphorus mg	Sodium mg / Potassium mg
Chocolate drink (with low-fat milk) 1 cup fluid	250	190	27	5.8	210	.10	.3	.5	270	120
		8.3	Tr	.2	3	.40	—	—	230	360
Cocoa, dry powder high- or medium-fat, 5¼ tbsp.	28	75	15	5.4	5	.03	.7	3.0	35	e2
		4.9	1.2	.1	0	.13	—	0	180	e430
low- or medium-fat 5¼ tablespoons or 1 ounce	28	62	15	3.6	5	.03	.7	3.0	43	e2
		5.4	1.5	.1	0	.13	—	0	190	e430
Cocoa or **chocolate powder** with dry skim milk, 4 heaping tsp.	28	102	20	.8	10	.04	.2	.5	170	150
		5.3	.1	Tr	1	.21	—	0	160	230
beverage powder without milk solids, 4 heaping teaspoons	28	98	25	.6	—	.01	.1	.6	9	76
		1.1	.3	Tr	0	.03	—	0	48	140
Coffee, black 6 fluid ounce cup	180	2	Tr	Tr	0	0	.5	.2	4	2
		Tr	Tr	—	0	Tr	Tr	0	7	65
instant powder, regular 1 teaspoon	.8	1	Tr	Tr	0	0	.2	Tr	1	1
		Tr	Tr	—	0	Tr	Tr	0	3	26
freeze-dried 1 teaspoon	.9	1	Tr	Tr	0	0	.3	.1	2	1
		Tr	Tr	—	0	Tr	Tr	0	3	29
Fruit juices (see **Fruit,** page 471)										
Malted milk, dry powder 3 rounded teaspoons or 1 oz.	28	116	20	2.4	290	.09	.1	.6	82	120
		4.2	.1	—	0	.15	—	—	110	200
Milk shake, chocolate^f large (10 ounce) glass	345	421	58	18	690	.12	.5	.9	360	—
		11	.3	—	4	.55	—	—	320	—
Malted milk shake, chocolate^g large (10 ounce) glass	365	502	72	20	890	.19	.5	1.3	420	—
		13	.3	—	4	.66	—	—	400	—
Ovaltine, plain with 8 ounces whole milk	259	221	22	10	1100	.39	2.3	4.0	370	—
		11	—	—	10	.67	—	—	310	—
Postum, 1 cup with 2 rounded tbsp. powder	185	36	8	Tr	—	—	—	.3	10	4
		.6	0	—	—	—	—	0	87	130
Tea, clear 1 cup		2	Tr	0	0	0	.1	.2	5	—
		.1	—	0	1	.04	—	0	4	—

BEVERAGES (ALCOHOLIC)

Food	Uncooked wt.(EP) g / Cooked wt.(EP) g	Calories Kcal / Protein g	Carbohydrate g / Fiber g	Fat (total) / Linoleic Acid g	Vitamin A IU / Vitamin C mg	Thiamin mg / Riboflavin mg	Niacin mg / Vitamin B-6 mg	Iron mg / Vitamin B-12 µg	Calcium mg / Phosphorus mg	Sodium mg / Potassium mg
Beer (alcohol 4.5% by volume) large (8 ounce) glass	240	101	9	0	—	.01	1.4	Tr	12	17
		.7	—	0	—	.07	.14	0	72	60
Gin, rum, vodka, or **whiskey** 1 jigger or 1½ oz., 86 proof	42	105	Tr	—	—	—	—	—	—	Tr
		—	—	—	—	—	—	0	—	1
Wine, dessert (alcohol 18% by volume), 1 glass (3½ fl. oz.)	103	141	8	0	—	.01	.2	—	8	4
		.1	—	0	—	.02	.04	0	—	77
table (alcohol 12% by volume) 1 glass (3½ fluid ounces)	102	87	4	0	—	Tr	.1	.4	9	5
		.1	—	0	—	.01	.04	0	10	94

MISCELLANEOUS

Food	Uncooked wt.(EP) g / Cooked wt.(EP) g	Calories Kcal / Protein g	Carbohydrate g / Fiber g	Fat (total) / Linoleic Acid g	Vitamin A IU / Vitamin C mg	Thiamin mg / Riboflavin mg	Niacin mg / Vitamin B-6 mg	Iron mg / Vitamin B-12 µg	Calcium mg / Phosphorus mg	Sodium mg / Potassium mg
Arrowroot flour 1 tablespoon	8	29	7	0	0	0	0	0	0	Tr
		0	0	0	0	0	0	0	0	0
Baking powder: double-acting^h 1 teaspoon	3	4	1	Tr	0	0	0	—	58	330
		Tr	Tr	—	0	0	0	0	87	5
phosphate type 1 teaspoon	4	5	1	Tr	0	0	0	—	240	310
		Tr	Tr	—	0	0	0	0	360	6

^e When cocoa powder is processed with alkalis, the sodium content increases and the potassium content decreases from what is shown here.

^f Made with 8 oz. whole milk, 2 oz. vanilla ice cream, and 1½ oz. chocolate syrup, blended.
^g Same ingredients as above plus 2 tablespoons malted milk, blended.

^h Double-acting baking powders are made with sodium aluminum sulfate and a calcium acid phosphate—in this case, monocalcium phosphate monohydrate.

	Uncooked wt.(EP) g / Cooked wt.(EP) g	Calories Kcal / Protein g	Carbohydrate g / Fiber g	Fat (total) g / Linoleic Acid g	Vitamin A IU / Vitamin C mg	Thiamin mg / Riboflavin mg	Niacin mg / Vitamin B-6 mg	Iron mg / Vitamin B-12 µg	Calcium mg / Phosphorus mg	Sodium mg / Potassium mg
tartrate type	3	2	Tr	Tr	0	0	0	0	0	200
1 teaspoon		Tr	Tr	—	0	0	0	0	0	110
low-sodium type	4	7	2	Tr	0	0	0	—	210	Tr
1 teaspoon		Tr	Tr	—	0	0	0	0	310	470
low-sodium, homemade[i]	3	2	1	Tr	0	0	0	—	—	620
1 teaspoon		Tr	Tr	—	0	0	0	0	—	—
Carob flour	35	63	28	.5	—	—	—	—	120	—
4 tablespoons or ¼ cup		1.6	2.7	—	—	—	—	0	28	—
Chocolate, bitter or baking	28	143	8	15	20	.01	.4	1.9	22	1
1 ounce		3.0	.7	.3	0	.07	.01	0	110	240
sweet, plain	28	150	16	10	Tr	.01	.1	.4	27	9
1 ounce or 1 square		1.2	.1	.2	Tr	.04	—	0	40	76
milk chocolate	28	147	16	9.2	80	.02	.1	.3	65	27
1 ounce		2.2	.1	.2	Tr	.10	—	0	65	110
Cornstarch	8	29	7	Tr	0	0	0	0	0	Tr
1 tablespoon not packed		Tr	Tr	—	0	0	0	0	0	Tr
Olives, green, pickled	46	45	.5	4.9	120	—	—	.6	24	930
10 large, ¾″ dm. × 1″		.5	.6	.3	—	—	—	0	7	21
ripe, Mission	46	73	1	8.0	30	Tr	—	.7	42	300
10 large, ¾″ dm. × 1″		.5	.7	.6	—	Tr	.01	0	7	11
ripe, salt-cured, Greek	33	89	2	9.5	—	—	—	—	—	870
10 extra large (137 per lb.)		.6	1.2	.7	—	—	Tr	0	8	—
Pickle, cucumber, dill	65	7	1	.1	70	Tr	Tr	.7	17	930
1 medium, 1¼″ dm. × 3¾″		.5	.3	—	4	.01	Tr	0	14	130
2 slices, 1½″ dm. × ¼″	13	1	Tr	Tr	10	Tr	Tr	.1	3	190
		.1	.1	—	1	Tr	Tr	0	3	26
sweet, 1 small	15	22	6	.1	10	Tr	Tr	.2	2	—
¾″ dm. × 2½″		.1	—	—	1	Tr	Tr	0	2	—
Popcorn, large kernel,[j] popped		23	5	.3	—	—	.1	.2	1	Tr
plain, 1 cup	6	.8	.1	.2	0	.01	.01	0	17	—
butter and salt added		41	5	2.0	—	—	.2	.2	1	180
1 cup	9	.9	.2	.2	0	.01	—	0	19	—
Salt, table	5.5	0	0	0	0	0	0	Tr	14	2132
1 teaspoon		0	0	0	0	0	0	0	—	Tr
Soy sauce	18	12	2	.2	0	Tr	.1	.9	15	1300
1 tablespoon		1	0	0	0	.05	—	0	19	66
Tapioca, pearl and quick cooking	152	535	130	.3	0	0	0	6	15	5
1 cup dry		.9	.2	—	0	0	0	0	27	27
Vinegar, cider	15	2	1	0	—	—	—	.1	1	Tr
1 tablespoon		Tr	—	0	—	—	Tr	0	1	15
Yeast, baker's, active dry	7	20	3	.1	Tr	.16	2.6	1.1	3	4
1 scant tbsp. or ¼ oz. pkg.		2.6	—	—	Tr	.38	.14	0	90	140
baker's, compressed	18	15	2	.1	Tr	.13	2.0	.9	2	3
1 cake, 1¼″ square × ¾″		2.2	—	—	Tr	.30	.11	0	71	110
Yeast, nutritional: brewer's	8	23	3	.1	Tr	1.2	3.0	1.4	[k]17	10
1 tablespoon		3.1	.1	—	Tr	.34	.20	0	140	150
torula, calcium fortified	8	22	3	.1	Tr	1.1	3.6	1.5	34	1
1 tablespoon		3.1	.3	—	Tr	.40	.24	0	140	160

[i]*Ingredients are cream of tartar 42.7%, potassium bicarbonate 30.3%, cornstarch 21.3%, and tartaric acid 5.7%.*

[j]*Small kernels may weigh as much as 6 g more per cup.*

[k]*Values range from 6 mg to 60 mg.*

Sources for Tables and Charts

Full citations for abbreviated references not listed here will be found in the Suggestions for Further Reading, pp. 447–453.

J. Périssé, F. Sizaret, and P. Francois, *FAO Nutrition Newsletter* 7(3):1, 1969; in *Energy and protein requirements*, FAO/WHO, 1973.

National Diets (p. 350)

Adapted from Watt & Merrill, *Composition of foods*.

Linoleic Acid (p. 365)

R. M. Feeley, P. E. Criner, and B. K. Watt, Cholesterol content of foods, *Journal of the American Dietetic Association* 61:134–149, 1972.

Cholesterol (p. 368)

Adapted from L. P. Posati, J. E. Kinsella, and B. K. Watt, Comprehensive evaluation of fatty acids in foods. I. Dairy products, *J. Am. Diet. Assoc.* 66:482–488, 1975; Posati, Kinsella, and Watt, Comprehensive evaluation . . . III. Eggs and egg products, *J. Am. Diet. Assoc.* 67:111–115, 1975; G. A: Fristrom et al:, Comprehensive evaluation . . . IV. Nuts, peanuts, and soups, *J. Am. Diet. Assoc.* 67:351–355, 1975; and Watt and Merrill, *Composition of foods*.

Fat in Foods (p. 371)

National Research Council, *Rec. dietary allowances* (1974), p. 44.

Essential Amino Acids (p. 380)

Adapted from Watt & Merrill, *Composition of foods*; FAO, *Amino-acid content*; and Martha L. Orr and Bernice K. Watt, *Amino acid content of foods*, U.S. Dept. of Agriculture Home Economics Research Report no. 4 (Washington, Govt. Printing Office, 1957).

Protein & Calories (p. 390)

H. T. Slover, Tocopherols in foods and fats, *Lipids* 6:291–296, 1971; M. W. Dicks, *Vitamin E content of food and feeds for human and animal consumption*, Agricultural Experiment Station Bulletin no. 435 (Laramie, University of Wyoming, 1965).

Vitamin E (p. 402)

Most values adapted from S. Butterfield and D. H. Calloway, Folacin in wheat and selected foods, *J. Am. Diet. Assoc.* 60:310–316, 1972; K. Hoppner, B. Lampi, and D. E. Perrin, The free and total folate activity in foods available on the Canadian market, *Canadian Institute of Food Science and Technology Journal* 5(2):60–66, 1972; and F. M. Dong and S. M. Oace, Folate distribution in fruit juices, *J. Am. Diet. Assoc.* 62:162–166, 1973.

Folacin (p. 414)

Adapted from Watt & Merrill, *Composition of foods*.

Magnesium (p. 429)

Data from Carl V. Moore, Iron, Table 6C-2, in *Modern nutrition in health and disease*, ed. Goodhart and Shils.

Iron Cookware (p. 437)

E. W. Murphy, B. W. Willis, and B. K. Watt, Provisional tables on the zinc content of foods, *J. Am. Diet. Assoc.* 66:345–355, 1975, and Ananda Shiva Prasad, ed., *Zinc metabolism* (Springfield, Ill., Thomas, 1966), p. 436.

Zinc (p. 438)

Vitamin Losses
(pp. 445–446)

1. Robert S. Harris and Harry von Loesecke, eds., *Nutritional evalua-tion of food processing* (New York, Wiley, 1960), pp. 1–4.
2. A. E. Bender, The fate of vitamins in food processing operations, in University of Nottingham, *Proceedings . . . on Vitamins*, pp. 71–72.
3. FAO/WHO, *Ascorbic acid, vitamin B-12, folate, and iron*, p. 41.

RDA *(pp. 454–455)*

National Research Council, *Rec. dietary allowances* (1974), p. 44.

FAO/WHO *Rec. Intakes*
(pp. 454–455)

Passmore, *Handbook on human nutritional requirements*, Table 1.

U.S. RDA *(p. 456)*

Nutrition labels and U. S. RDA, *FDA Consumer Memo*, DHEW Pub-lication no. (FDA) 74–2042 (Rockville, Md., U. S. Dept. of Health, Education, and Welfare, 1974).

Nutrient Composition
(pp. 459–484)

1. Adams, *Nutritive value of American foods.*
2. Orr, *Pantothenic acid, vitamin B-6 and vitamin B-12.*
3. Watt and Merrill, *Composition of foods.*
4. Bowes & Church, *Food values of portions commonly used* (1970).
5. L. P. Posati et al., Comprehensive evaluation of fatty acids in foods. I. Dairy products, *J. Am. Diet. Assoc.* 66:482–488, 1975.
6. Posati et al., Comprehensive evaluation . . . III. Eggs and egg products, *J. Am. Diet. Assoc.* 67:111–115, 1975.
7. G. Fristrom et al., Comprehensive evaluation . . . IV. Nuts, pea-nuts, and soups, *J. Am. Diet. Assoc.* 67:351–355, 1975.
8. John L. Weihrauch, John E. Kinsella, and Bernice K. Watt, Comprehensive evaluation . . . VI. Cereal products, *J. Am. Diet. As-soc.* 68:335–340, 1976.
9. National Research Council, Committee on Feed Composition, *Composition of cereal grains and forages,* National Research Council Publication no. 585 (Washington, National Academy of Sciences, 1958).
10. National Research Council, Committee on Feed Composition, *Composition of concentrate by-product feeding stuffs,* National Re-search Council Publication no. 449 (Washington, National Academy of Sciences, 1956).
11. Cho C. Tsen, ed., *Triticale: First man-made cereal* (St. Paul, Minn., American Association of Cereal Chemists, 1974).
12. K. Lorenz, F. W. Reuter, and C. Sizer, The mineral composi-tion of triticales and triticale milling fractions by X-ray flourescence and atomic absorption, *Cereal chemistry* 51(4):534–542, 1974.
13. Wallace R. Aykroyd, The nutritive value of Indian foods and the planning of satisfactory diets, 6th rev. ed. by C. Gopalan and S. C. Balasubramanian, Indian Council of Medical Research Special Report series, no. 42 (New Delhi, 1963).
14. Harris & von Loesecke, *Nutritional evaluation of food process-ing.*
15. *Nutrition and the M.D.* 2(12):4, December 1975.
16. R. M. Feeley, P. E. Criner, and H. T. Slover, Major fatty acids and proximate composition of dairy products, *J. Am. Diet. Assoc.* 66:140–146, 1975.

Index

Brussels Sprouts with Chestnuts, 188
Buckwheat flour
  in whole wheat bread, 82
  nutrients in, *table,* 459
  RECIPES:
  Buckwheat Pancakes, 120
  Everyone's Muffins, 102
  Pumpernickel, 92
Buckwheat groats, 255
  cooking, 255; *table,* 260
  in bread, 82
  with winter squash, 212
  SERVING SUGGESTIONS: 256
Buckwheat noodles, 234
Buckwheat muffins, 102
Buckwheat Pancakes, 120
Bulgur wheat, 254
  cooking, 255; *table,* 260
  nutrients in, 254; *table,* 461
  RECIPES:
  Bulgur Wheat Pilaf, 269
  Green Rice Casserole (variation), 267
  Stuffed Peppers, 202
  Tabouli, 155
  Zucchini Spinach Casserole, (variation), 209
  OTHER RECIPES CONTAINING:
  loaves, patties, and savory balls, 185, 265, 266
  SERVING SUGGESTIONS: 256, 261
Bulgur Wheat Pilaf, 269
  in Stuffed Chard Leaves, 241
Butter
  and cholesterol, 123; *table,* 368
  and saturated fat, 123
  nutrients in, *table,* 481
  See also Butters
Butterfat, 69–70
Buttermilk, 70
  and baking soda, 77
  nutrients in, *table,* 477
  with fruit salad, 274–275
  RECIPES CONTAINING:
  Buttermilk Pancakes, 119
  breads, 90, 95, 106
  desserts, 277, 281
  grain and bean dish, 262
  noodle casserole, 244
  sauces, 232–233
  vegetable dishes, 199, 210
Buttermilk Pancakes, 119
Buttermilk Sauce, 232
Butters
  Better-Butter, 123
  Lemon Butter, 227
  Nut and Seed Butters, 118

Butters *(cont.)*
  Yeast Butter, 225
  See also Butter

Cabbage, 190–191
  nutrients in, *table,* 466
  RECIPES:
  Cabbage Bhaji, 223
  Cabbage Kuchen, 251
  Coleslaw, 156
  Cream of Celery Soup with Cabbage, 173
  Simple Vegetable Filling for Blintzes, 247
  Stuffed Cabbage Rolls, 240
  Sweet and Sour Cabbage, 190
  OTHER RECIPES CONTAINING: 215, 217
  SERVING SUGGESTIONS: 190–191
Cabbage Bhaji, 223
Cabbage Kuchen, 251
Cakes
  frosting for, 278
  Banana Bread, 277
  Carrot Fruitcake, 276
  Pound Cake, 277
Calcium, 423–426
  absorption and utilization of, 424–427, 398–399
  abundance of, in body, 423
  content of, in foods, *table,* 459–484
  deficiency of, 425, 427. *See also* vitamin D, deficiency of
  food sources of, *tables,* 322, 424
  in all-plant or vegan diet, 426
  in hard tissues, 352, 423
  in milk, 319
  in soy milk, 136, 323
  persons requiring additional, 425–426
  recommended allowances for, 426; *tables,* 455, 456
  roles of, 352, 424
California Tossed Salad, 152
Calories, 334, 341, 343, 387
  and protein, *table,* 390–392
  content of, in foods, *table,* 459–484
  estimating need for, in daily diet, *table,* 342
  recommended allowances for, *table,* 454
  See also Reducing diet; Weight control
Canneloni, 235
Caraway Puffs, 103
Carbohydrate, 348–349, 354–362
  and weight, 312, 354, 355

Carbohydrate *(cont.)*
  as source of energy, 348–349, 354
  chemical makeup of, 348; *table,* 355
  content of, in foods, *table,* 459–484
  food sources of, 354–355
  in breakfast, 111
  in refined foods, 354
  in whole foods, 312, 354–355
  proportion of, in national diets, 350
  refined, and thiamin deficiency, 406
  role of, in diet, 354–355
  See also Alcohol; Fiber; Starch; Sugar
Cardiovascular disease
  and atherosclerosis, 365
  and cholesterol, 366
  and sugar, 366
  and trace minerals, 432
  extent of, in U. S., 365
  prevention of, 366
  risk factors in, 360, 366. *See also* Cholesterol
Carotene, *see* Provitamin A
Carrot Fruitcake, 276
Carrot Raisin Salad, 192
Carrots, 191–192
  nutrients in, *table,* 466–467
  tops of, for stock, 191
  RECIPES:
  Baked Carrots, 192
  Carrot Fruitcake, 276
  Carrot Raisin Salad, 192
  OTHER RECIPES CONTAINING:
  dessert, 280
  hearty dishes and casseroles, 243, 245, 249, 250
  mixed vegetable dishes, 216, 218, 221
  SERVING SUGGESTIONS: 191–192
Cashew Gravy, 229
  with cauliflower, 193
Casseroles, *see* Hearty dishes and casseroles
Cauliflower, 193–194
  nutrients in, *table,* 467
  nutritional value of, 193
  RECIPES:
  Greek Cauliflower, 194
  Cauliflower Eggplant Curry, 222
  mixed vegetable dish using, 218
  SERVING SUGGESTIONS: 193
Cauliflower Eggplant Curry, 222
Celery, 194
  nutrients in, *table,* 467

LAUREL'S KITCHEN *was created entirely by Laurel and her friends at Nilgiri Press, Berkeley. Laurel did the woodcuts, Barbara executed the figures and graphs, and Ani and Bron designed the tables at the end of the book; Nick and Laurel did the page design, Bert set the type, Roberta made the index, and Terry coordinated the production and did a lot of almost everything. The first printing of 5000 copies was printed by Jim and bound under Sarah's supervision by more friends than we have space to name, using equipment designed and built by Laurel's husband, Ed. This copy has been printed and bound commercially so that Laurel could get back to her kitchen. To all who created it,* LAUREL'S KITCHEN *is a work of love, and we hope it will serve you well in your kitchens and in your lives.*

Library of Congress Cataloging in Publication Data:

Main entry under title:

Laurel's kitchen : a handbook for vegetarian cookery and nutrition
　　Bibliography: p.
　　Includes index.
　　1. Vegetarianism.　I. Robertson, Laurel.　II. Flinders, Carol.
III. Godfrey, Bronwen.
TX837.L29　　　641.5′636　　　76–27701
ISBN 0–915132–07–9